A
HARD AND BITTER PEACE

A Global History of the Cold War

Edward H. Judge

LeMoyne College

John W. Langdon

LeMoyne College

PRENTICE HALL, Upper Saddle River, New Jersey 07458

Library of Congress Cataloging-in-Publication Data

JUDGE, EDWARD H.

  A hard and bitter peace : a global history of the cold war /
EDWARD H. JUDGE, JOHN W. LANGDON.

    p. cm

  Includes bibliographical references and index.

  ISBN 0-13-234451-3

  1. Cold War. 2. World politics—1945   I. Langdon, John W.
II. Title

  D843.J74 1996

  909.82—dc20   95-35639

Acquisitions editor: Sally Constable
Project manager: Edie Riker
Interior design: Joanne Riker
Cover design: Wendy Alling Judy
Photo editor: Lori Morris-Nantz
Photo research: Page Poore Kidder
Buyer: Nick Sklitsis
Editorial assistant: Tamara Mann

© 1996 by Prentice-Hall, Inc.
Simon & Schuster / A Viacom Company
Upper Saddle River, New Jersey 07458

Printed in the United States of America

10 9 8 7 6 5 4 3

ISBN   0-13-234451-3

Prentice-Hall International (UK) Limited, *London*
Prentice-Hall of Australia Pty. Limited, *Sydney*
Prentice-Hall Canada Inc., *Toronto*
Prentice-Hall Hispanoamericana, S.A., *Mexico*
Prentice-Hall of India Private Limited, *New Delhi*
Prentice-Hall of Japan, Inc., *Tokyo*
Simon & Schuster Asia Pte. Ltd., *Singapore*
Editora Prentice-Hall do Brasil, Ltda., *Rio de Janeiro*

This book is dedicated to

Henry and Edna Judge

Lisa and Heather Langdon

Contents

Part I   Origins of the Cold War

Part II   The Global Confrontation

9   The Perpetuation of the Cold War, 1957–1961   *138*

10   Crisis and Coexistence, 1961–1964   *159*

11   Vietnam War and Cold War, 1964–1970   *181*

12   China, SALT, and the Superpowers, 1967–1972   *202*

Part III   The Search for a Solution

17 The End of the Cold War, 1988–1991   286

18 A Hard and Bitter Peace   309

For Further Reading   315

List of Maps

Preface

Let the word go forth, from this time and place, to friend and foe alike, that
the torch has been passed to a new generation of Americans—born in this
century, tempered by war, disciplined by a hard and bitter peace...

President Kennedy's Inaugural Address
January 20, 1961

In conceiving and preparing this book, the authors were convinced of two
things. First, a history of the Cold War that provides a *global* perspective is
much more useful and valid than one which concentrates mostly on U.S.
diplomatic history. Second, since many of today's readers will either have little personal recollection of the Cold War or fading memories of its main
events, they will appreciate a book that explains its development in clear and
understandable language, taking little or nothing for granted.

Our goal, then, has been to present a lively and comprehensible history
of world affairs between 1945 and 1991, which can be used either as general
reading for those interested in the Cold War, as a textbook for courses on the
Cold War, or as a supplementary reading in courses dealing with modern history. In doing so, we have kept the needs of our readers foremost in our
minds. Focusing on personalities as well as events, we have attempted to
explain not only *what* happened, but *why* things happened as they did, and
how they were related to each other. We have also provided a variety of maps
and photographs to guide the reader through the geographic and conceptual labyrinths of the Cold War period. For those interested in delving further
into the issues addressed, we have furnished lists of readings relating to each
chapter and a list of general works on the Cold War. These are not intended
to be comprehensive bibliographies of all the relevant works but rather lists of
selected materials that are useful and accessible to our readers.

In preparing this book, we have adopted several conventions concerning transliteration. For Russian names, we have used the most common spelling, even in cases (such as Yeltsin, Yakovlev, Vyshinsky, and Shcharansky) where it does not fully correspond to the Library of Congress system. For Chinese names, we have generally used the "Pinyin" system. However, for names like Chiang Kai-shek and Kuomintang, which became familiar prior to the introduction of Pinyin, we have used the older "Wade-Giles" system, with the Pinyin version given in parentheses following their initial appearance.

We are thankful for the insights and ideas we have received from many colleagues and students during the preparation of this work. We are particularly grateful to our friends and colleagues, Joseph Curran, Douglas Egerton, and Mark Kulikowski who read it in various stages and provided many helpful suggestions. And above all we are indebted to our wives, Susan Judge and Janice Langdon, who have provided us with patient and good-humored support and encouragement throughout our academic careers.

The Seeds of Conflict

For almost half a century, from the end of World War II until the early 1990s, the political, social, cultural, and economic life of much of the world was caught up in an intense international struggle known as the Cold War. This struggle was perceived largely as a conflict between "East" and "West." Although the forces of the East were dominated by the Union of Soviet Socialist Republics and those of the West by the United States of America, the Cold War was more than a gigantic power struggle between two assertive superpowers. It was also a global rivalry between conflicting perspectives and world views, deeply rooted in the different historical experiences and perceptions of those who made up the East and the West. These experiences and perceptions did not cause the Cold War, but they did serve as the context within which the antagonists operated, and they did provide an environment which exacerbated the fears and suspicions of both sides.

THE DOMINANCE OF THE WEST

By the twentieth century, the West, which included mainly the industrialized nations of Europe and North America, had come to dominate the globe. After centuries of expansion, the major powers of Western Europe had managed to bring the rest of the world under their cultural and economic influence and, in many cases, under their direct political control. In the sixteenth and seventeenth centuries, they conquered and colonized the Americas, displacing the native cultures that had hitherto populated these lands. In the eighteenth and nineteenth centuries, they experienced revolutions in agriculture and industry, providing them with unprecedented wealth and power and with a vast technological edge over the non-European world. This in turn helped to trigger a new wave of imperialist expansion which brought much of Asia, and almost all of Africa, under European control. Whatever doubts there may have been about the wisdom and morality of these ventures, their very success seemed to bolster the confidence of the West and confirm the superiority of its values and institutions.

The most cherished values and institutions of the West, by this time, were those associated with political liberalism, laissez-faire capitalism, and Christian religion. Parliamentary assemblies and guaranteed freedoms had become part and parcel of the political terrain in the major Western nations, most of which were moving steadily toward full democracy. Free market economies, although often restricted and regulated in various ways, had become the order of the day, and industrial capitalism seemed to be creating immense wealth and unlimited opportunities. And even though the Christian church had long since ceased to be the dominant institution of Western civilization, Judeo-Christian ideals still had a powerful hold on the majority of persons of European descent. It is hardly surprising, then, that Western officials, entrepreneurs, and missionaries sought in various ways to transplant these institutions and ideals to colonial soil and thus "uplift" the colonial peoples by converting them to Western ways.

But the predominance of the West and the presumed superiority of capitalism, democracy, and Christianity were by no means universally appreciated. Among the non-Western victims of imperialist oppression and exploitation, there was a deep and growing resentment toward the Europeans and their institutions. Even in Europe itself, the sufferings and dislocation occasioned by the growth of industry and empire had led to the emergence of a number of "socialist" movements which sought to alter or overthrow the capitalist system.

THE RISE OF REVOLUTIONARY MARXISM

Prominent among these were the Marxists, the intellectual disciples of the nineteenth century's most influential critic of Western institutions and values. Reacting in horror to the brutalities of industrialization and the sufferings of the industrial working class, Karl Marx and his supporters had developed an ideological system which served both to explain the success of industrial capitalism and to forecast its eventual destruction. In so doing, they launched a bitter and relentless attack on those cherished institutions that Westerners valued the most: political liberalism, laissez-faire capitalism, and Christian religion.

According to Marxist critique, the history of Western society—for that matter, the history of *any* society—was a story of class conflict. The social class which controlled the means of production, the primary source of economic power and wealth, was in a position to establish and maintain the sort of political, cultural, and religious institutions that were most beneficial to itself. For centuries, as a result of the agrarian economy of medieval and early modern Europe, the primary means of production had been the land itself, and those who controlled the land—the landowning aristocracy and landed gentry—had thus been able to dominate political, social, and religious affairs. With the shift to a commercial and industrial economy, however, economic power had passed to an influential new class, the "bourgeoisie," whose wealth was based on capital investment rather than on real estate. By the end of the nineteenth century, with the rapid growth and spread of an urban industrial economy, the bourgeoisie had become the dominant class in the West. Since it now controlled the means of production, the bourgeoisie had been able to establish its own institutions, based on free market economics and liberal politics, in most Western countries.

From a Marxist perspective, these "bourgeois" institutions were largely exploitative, designed to perpetuate the power of the bourgeoisie over the great mass of the people. At the same time, however, the Marxists concluded that such institutions were by no means permanent. The same industrial process that was helping to solidify bourgeois control was also creating a new class of people, the urban "proletariat," who owned no property, possessed few rights, and had nothing to sell but their work. Crowded together in squalid factory towns and subjected to numerous forms of exploitation and abuse, they would sooner or later become conscious of themselves as an exploited class and join together to rise up against their exploiters. In so doing, it was foreseen, they would forcibly sweep away the institutions that had been used to oppress them and establish their own control over the means of production. This would bring about a "dictatorship of the proletariat," which would eventually develop into a worldwide socialist order based on equality and cooperation. The class struggle would come to an end, social classes would cease to exist, and even the state would eventually "wither away."

This Marxist socialist vision had a powerful attraction for many people who were disillusioned with the values and realities of Western society. It opposed the ethic of individualism and competition with one of collectivism and cooperation. It offered a "scientific" explanation for existing inequities and oppression. It held out the prospect that, by organizing themselves for revolutionary action, the downtrodden would eventually be able to settle scores with their oppressors. And it provided a vision of a better society in which conflict and greed would give way to social harmony and economic equality.

By the beginning of the twentieth century, however, the prospects for socialist revolution seemed to be receding in the industrialized West. In country after country, as Marx had foreseen, workers had begun to join together to defend their interests. They soon discovered, however, that their united actions made it possible to wrestle concessions from the industrial capitalists and to gain some influence in parliamentary politics. Labor unions were organized, strikes were initiated, and political parties designed to represent the workers' interests were formed. Conflict and violence often accompanied these developments, but the typical result was reform, not revolution. Trade unions were legalized, laws protecting the rights of workers were passed, and the vote was extended to working-class males. Most importantly, perhaps, the standard of living of the typical worker tended to improve, rather than deteriorate, over time. Capitalists and Socialists alike discovered that, once living and working situations improved, the workers tended to lose interest in revolution.

These developments occasioned a split in the socialist movement. Some Socialists, accepting the new realities, concluded that violent revolution was no longer necessary. "Evolutionary" Socialists, like Jean Jaurès in France and Eduard Bernstein in Germany, argued that the workers and their leaders could bring about a gradual transition to socialism by working within the system, using democratic and parliamentary means. They thus sought to build strong "social democratic" parties and to advance the interests of the workers, even if it meant collaborating with liberal and bourgeois political groups. As it attracted large numbers of followers and achieved some important successes, socialism in the West began to lose its revolutionary edge.

Other Socialists, however, like France's Jules Guesde, were disturbed by what they saw as rank opportunism. To them, collaboration with the bourgeoisie was a sellout which would lead inevitably to the compromising of socialist goals. From their perspective, no true socialism was possible until the bourgeoisie had been overthrown and the workers (or their representatives) had seized control of the means of production and the levers of political power. True Socialists must do all in their power to radicalize the workers and lead them on to revolution, rather than acceding to their tendency to become deradicalized by economic gain.

THE TRIUMPH IN RUSSIA OF MARXISM-LENINISM

In the East, where democratic institutions did not exist, socialism remained a radical and revolutionary force. This was particularly true in Russia, the vast "empire of the tsars," which was just beginning to industrialize. In a pamphlet called "What Is To Be Done," published in 1902, the Russian Marxist V. I. Lenin argued that Socialists must form themselves into a tightly organized party of professional revolutionaries who would serve as the "vanguard of the proletariat," fighting against both the aging autocratic regime and the emerging capitalist order. To accomplish these goals, Lenin himself went on to create his own "Bolshevik" movement within the context of Russian socialism.

Fatefully, despite its internationalist pretensions, Russian Marxism came to incorporate certain nationalistic and imperialistic tendencies which were deeply rooted in Russian culture. It interacted with Slavophilism, the conviction that Slavic ways of thinking and acting were superior to those of the West, to create an intolerant variant of socialism contemptuous of Western ways and values. And it emulated the Russian Orthodox conception of Moscow as the "Third Rome," the foreordained successor to Rome and Constantinople as the center of civilization, to produce a crusading fatalism convinced that not merely Marxism, but *Russian* Marxism, was the wave of the future. The superimposition of Marx's philosophy upon the Russian tradition was, therefore, fraught with consequences for future relations between East and West.

Meanwhile, Western domination of the globe provided the Marxists with fertile new ground for their critique of Western capitalism. Some asserted that Western European expansion was a logical outcome of industrial growth: with their insatiable need for raw materials, markets, and outlets for capital investment, Western governments had asserted economic hegemony, and often political control, over vast areas of the non-Western world. This theme was picked up in 1916 by Lenin, who argued in *Imperialism: The Highest Stage of Capitalism* that empire building was merely an advanced phase of capitalism and that imperialism and capitalism were for all intents and purposes identical. This analysis, although not fully supported by the historical evidence, provided a plausible explanation for Western expansionism. More importantly, perhaps, it became an essential ingredient of "Marxism-Leninism," a revised ideology that appealed to the nationalist aspirations of the victims of imperialism by linking their struggle for "national liberation" with the revolutionary socialist movement. Thus, as time went on, Marxism would be transformed from an antinationalist movement in which the "workers have no nation" into a pronationalist movement urging colonial peoples to fight for national independence from imperialist control.

The crisis of Western capitalism, so staunchly predicted by the Marxists, arrived with a vengeance in 1914. The First World War, pitting the major European powers in a deadly struggle against one another, exposed the horrible dangers of militarism, expansionism, and unbridled nationalism. But it also laid to rest the vision of an "internationalized" proletariat: Marxists watched with dismay as socialist leaders on both sides supported their nations' war efforts and as workers by the millions marched off to engage in combat against their fellow proletarians from other lands.

In the Russian Empire, as elsewhere, the war at first dealt a setback to the hopes and dreams of the revolutionary Socialists. In the beginning, flushed with patriotic enthusiasm, Russian workers supported the war effort with courage and commitment. The prospect of revolution, which had seemed to be growing brighter in the years before the war, suddenly dimmed considerably. But as the war dragged on and the humiliation of defeat set in, the Russian people turned increasingly against both their rulers and the war. Early in 1917, a series of stunning events in Petrograd, the empire's capital, resulted in the fall of the Russian monarchy. But the provisional government that replaced it, failing to comprehend the depth of popular hostility toward the war, sought to continue the conflict. Lenin and his Bolsheviks, seizing the opportunity, called for an end to the provisional government, an end to the war, and the redistribution of the land among the Russian peasants. They managed to stage a well-organized coup in November, seizing power in the name of the "soviets," or workers' councils, that had been formed in the wake of the first revolution.

THE SOVIET CHALLENGE AND THE WESTERN RESPONSE

The seizure of power in Russia by revolutionary Marxists sent shock waves throughout the Western world. The immediate concern was military: Lenin's determination to pull Russia out of the war posed a grave threat to the survival of Russia's embattled allies. But, in the long run, another concern was even more troubling to the leaders of the Western nations: the avowed Marxist goal of a worldwide socialist revolution that would bring a violent end to free market capitalism and liberal democracy. From their perspective, Bolshevik Russia was an outlaw state, a renegade nation that threatened the very existence of Western civilization.

In 1918, after the new Soviet regime withdrew from the war by signing the Treaty of Brest-Litovsk with Germany, the British, French, Americans ,and Japanese sent military forces to Russia, allegedly to protect supplies they had previously shipped to the tsarist government. Before long these forces became embroiled in a bitter civil war which pitted various anti-Bolshevik forces against the new Soviet regime. This "Allied intervention" was halfhearted and ineffective, and the Bolshevik-led "Red" army eventually defeated all of its "White" opponents. But the very fact that the "imperialists" had intervened, and had kept their armies on Russian soil even after the German defeat, left a legacy of bitterness and suspicion between Russia and the West.

Meanwhile, the vicissitudes of war had thrust to the fore the United States of America as a leader of the capitalist world. The Americans, by remaining neutral for the first two-thirds of the war, had seen a vast improvement in their economic and financial standing, especially with respect to the belligerent nations of Western and Central Europe. Once the United States finally did enter the war, in 1917, its vast resources and fresh troops eventually checkmated the exhausted forces of the German Empire and its allies. Furthermore, its idealistic propaganda sought to transform the conflict from an imperialist power struggle into a battle for democracy. The United States suffered less, and gained more, than any of the other major powers: it emerged from the war not just as the architect of Allied victory but as the world's leading capitalist and democratic power.

The United States of America seemed, in many respects, to be an ideal candidate for leader of the Western world. A young, vibrant, self-confident nation which had been founded on ideals of popular sovereignty, the United States had more recently emerged as a giant of industrial capitalism. Although they had acquired a modest overseas empire of their own, the Americans had not been a major participant in either the wholesale scramble for colonies or the rampant militarist nationalism that had helped to discredit the major European powers. Blessed by abundant resources and fertile farmland, and insulated by broad oceans from serious foreign threats, they had developed an almost mystic faith in the soundness of their economic values and political institutions. Their self-righteous pride and sense of destiny had been epitomized by Woodrow Wilson, their wartime president, who had tried to make the World War into a democratic crusade.

In the wake of World War I, however, the Americans were not yet ready to assume the mantle of world leadership. Fearful of becoming embroiled in European affairs, the U. S. Senate failed to ratify the Treaty of Versailles which the Allies imposed upon the defeated Germans. In so doing, the Americans also refused to join the League of Nations, the international peace organization which had been envisioned and initiated by their own president. Instead, they retreated behind the Atlantic to a limited isolation, playing a role in international diplomacy but keeping some distance from the rough and tumble world of European politics and problems.

The leadership of the capitalist world thus reverted, by default, to the British and French, the primary victors in World War I and the paramount imperialist powers. Crippled by four years of brutal war, however, and beset by domestic problems, the French had neither the energy nor the confidence to play a dominant role. Even the British, the very symbols of capitalist imperialism, were bogged down by numerous difficulties at home and in their colonies during the postwar era. The new order that emerged in these years, therefore, did not benefit from strong Western leadership on either side of the Atlantic.

Meanwhile, the Bolshevik victors in Russia had set about creating a new order of their own. Industries were nationalized, landowners and capitalists were expropriated, and remnants of the prewar order were brutally expunged. Opposition parties and political factions were persecuted and banned, and the Bolshevik party—having changed its name to "Communist"—established itself as the sole political power. A government hierarchy of soviets was formed, and, within a few years, the Russian Empire had been transformed into the Union of Soviet Socialist Republics.

It was in the arena of international affairs, however, that the Soviet Communists posed their greatest challenge to the capitalist West. Eschewing traditional diplomacy, they embarked on a global campaign to undermine and subvert the capitalist powers and their parliamentary governments. In 1919 they founded the Communist International (or "Comintern"), a worldwide association of communist parties. It was designed to coordinate and control the activities of the international communist movement as it sought to organize and inspire a series of socialist revolutions. Communist parties acquired a notable following, not only among the industrial proletariat of Western Europe, but also among the colonial peoples who had been subjugated by Western imperialism. Throughout Asia, and eventually in Africa and Latin America, Communists sought to identify with the nationalist aspirations and liberationist struggles of the oppressed and subjugated masses.

As time went on, however, and as the worldwide socialist revolution failed to materialize, the Soviet Union began to resemble more closely a traditional large power pursuing a standard foreign policy. In 1921, as they embarked on a "New Economic Policy" which restored some features of a market economy, the Soviets signed a trade agreement with Great Britain. Before long, having temporarily postponed their push for world revolution, they had begun talking about "socialism in one country" and coexistence with the capitalist world. The West, for its part, had abandoned its early efforts to overthrow the communist regime and had come to accept the Soviet state as an unpleasant but unavoidable reality. Several crises in the mid-1920s served to heighten tensions between East and West, but they did not destroy the sense of resigned yet wary tolerance that each had developed toward the other.

This tolerance was tested in many ways by the dramatic events of the 1930s. The Great Depression, beginning in 1929, shook the capitalist world to its core. Western leaders turned inward, focusing on domestic problems and seeking to resolve their economic crises, not always with much success. In many Western societies, socialist groups on the left and ultranationalist groups on the right won numerous new adherents among the unemployed and disenchanted. In Britain, France, and the United States, democratic and capitalist institutions were strong enough to weather the storm, albeit with some alterations. But in Germany, such institutions were threatened by the rapid growth of the racist and militarist Nazi movement and the growing strength of the Communists.

The Soviet Union, meanwhile, was undergoing a massive internal crisis of its own. Beginning in 1929, under the direction of Communist party boss Joseph Stalin, a series of "five-year plans" were employed to bring about rapid industrialization and collectivization of agriculture. The explicit goal was to catch up with the West, in order to ensure the survival of the USSR. The Soviets did in fact make up most of the gap, but millions also perished along the way, especially in the vicious civil war and forced famine that accompanied the collectivization drive in Ukraine. In the capitalist world, even the staunchest admirers of the Soviet experiment had difficulty defending a regime that slaughtered and starved its own citizens.

"COLLECTIVE SECURITY" AND ITS FAILURE

Be that as it may, events in central Europe soon conspired to bring about a measure of accommodation between the USSR and the West. In January of

1933, Nazi leader Adolf Hitler was named chancellor of the German Republic. Within a matter of months, he and his supporters had declared a national emergency, suspended basic freedoms, and initiated a wholesale assault upon the German Communist party. The democratic West watched apprehensively as Hitler restructured his country along militarist and racist lines, creating a highly regimented society under a brutal authoritarian regime. The communist East was equally distressed as the "Führer" and his henchmen launched an international crusade against the "Jewish-Bolshevik menace." Before long, both sides were even more alarmed as Hitler repudiated previous international agreements and began a massive program to rearm and remilitarize his country. Stalin and the Soviets were particularly fearful, since Hitler made little attempt to hide his anticommunist antipathies and his dreams of expansion to the east.

At first, neither side took any effective steps to counter the Nazi threat. The Soviets, consumed by their industrialization drive and the internal turmoil that accompanied it, had actually facilitated Hitler's rise, and they continued to do business with the Germans well after the Nazis took power. For a time, they even tended to view Hitler's regime as a fortuitous sign of the impending demise of the capitalist order. The Western nations, bogged down by the Great Depression and distracted by their own domestic woes, offered nothing but feeble protests as Hitler destroyed Germany's democracy and rebuilt its war machine. Many in the West, in fact, were not entirely displeased with the emergence of the Nazi Reich, which they saw as a formidable bulwark in central Europe against the spread of communism.

As time passed, however, and as the nature of the German threat became all too real, leaders on both sides sought to build bridges between East and West. In November of 1933, diplomatic relations were finally established between the Soviet Union and the United States. The following year, as part of its new foreign policy based on "collective security," the USSR joined the League of Nations and pledged to work for peace and disarmament. In May 1935, the Soviets and the French concluded a mutual assistance treaty, agreeing to cooperate in the event that either country became a victim of German aggression. Later that month the USSR made a similar pact with Czechoslovakia, pledging to assist the Czechs as long as France (which had committed itself to Czechoslovakia's defense in 1925) did so first. In 1936, the Soviets began actively aiding the Spanish republicans in their civil war against the fascist forces backed by Italy and Germany.

But the rapprochement between East and West proved more apparent than real. The League of Nations' failure to stop Italian aggression in Ethiopia in 1935 was a severe setback for the notion of collective security, as was the weak response of the Western powers to German reoccupation of the Rhineland in the following year. The French, British, and American governments refused to intervene in the Spanish civil war and instead pursued a policy of diplomatic neutrality. It is hardly surprising, then, that the Soviet leadership soon began to lose confidence in the ability or willingness of the Western powers to counter the fascist threat.

Nor is it surprising that the Western powers were beginning to question the value of any security arrangements that included the USSR. From 1936 through 1938, the Soviet leadership was decimated by the bizarre and terrifying developments that came to be known as the "Great Purges." Dozens of loyal Communists, including some of the most prominent early Soviet leaders, were placed on trial, accused of collaborating with the Nazis, forced to make public confessions, and summarily executed. The majority of the Party's Central Committee was removed, and thousands of ordinary people were arrested and imprisoned. In 1937, the purge machinery turned against the military command with devastating force. Roughly half of the officer corps was purged, including about 400 of 700 generals, three of the five marshals, and most of the members of the Soviet War Council. Hundreds of these soldiers, many of whom were experienced veterans and decorated heroes, were imprisoned or shot. Western leaders began to wonder anew how they could possibly trust a government that would so savagely turn against its own partisans and heroes. And even if the Soviets proved willing to collaborate against the Nazis, how effective could their war machine be after its leadership had been destroyed?

As if this were not enough, the remaining hopes for collective security were dealt a deadly blow by the Czech crisis of 1938. After Germany annexed Austria in March of that year—again with scant resistance from the Western powers—Hitler began demanding territorial concessions from his Czechoslovak neighbors. The Sudetenland, a border region inhabited mostly by Germans, was his stated objective, but the Czechs had no reason to believe that he would stop there. So they called upon their French and Soviet allies, both of whom pledged aid under the terms of their existing pacts. The Germans, who were not fully prepared for war in spring of 1938, at first backed down, but Hitler simultaneously began to plan for a full scale autumn invasion. By summer, he was again making demands, and as fall approached a new war in Europe seemed imminent. The Soviets called for a firm stand, but the British and French, fearful of being swept into war by obstinate and uncompromising Czechs, took it upon themselves to mediate the dispute. They offered concessions, in reply to which Hitler simply raised his demands. Finally on September 29, in a hastily arranged conference at Munich, Britain, France, and Italy agreed to give the Germans virtually all they had asked for. The Czechs were not invited, and the Soviets not even consulted. War was averted, at least for a time, but hopes for East-West collaboration against Hitler had all but disappeared.

It is doubtful that Stalin, who had little capacity for trust, ever placed too much confidence in collective security arrangements with the Western "imperialist" powers. But he may well have hoped that a war in Europe would work to his advantage by pitting the fascists against the capitalists in a bloody, debilitating carnage, with the USSR remaining largely on the sidelines. Now he had to face the possibility that the opposite might occur, and the West would choose to sit back and watch as Hitler moved eastward toward the Soviet heartland. This specter became even more haunting in March of 1939, when the Germans marched unopposed into Prague and occupied the bulk of what was left of Czechoslovakia.

Meanwhile, the Americans had remained largely uninvolved in European affairs. Although they had watched with alarm as the Nazis led Germany on a course of militarist expansionism, they were too engrossed in their own internal affairs to make a serious effort to counter the Nazi threat. Besides, in many respects the threat of world communism seemed every bit as dangerous as the Nazi Reich, and Stalin's regime—with its brutal civil wars, forced famines, and bloody purges—appeared no more attractive than Hitler's. American leaders, like their Soviet counterparts, were well aware of the dangers posed by German militarism, not to mention that of Japan. But, deeply distrustful of the Communists and wary of international commitments, they saw little potential or value in collaboration with the USSR.

THE MOLOTOV–RIBBENTROP PACT

Stalin watched apprehensively as Nazi Germany devoured what was left of Czechoslovakia on 15 March 1939. Poland obviously was next on the list, to be followed by the USSR itself. Little help could be expected from the capitalist-imperialist West, which seemed only too willing to let Germany move eastward toward the Soviet homeland. Stalin needed peace, at least until the USSR could rebuild its armed forces from the devastating effects of his purges. His desperate hope was that Hitler was flexible enough to put ideology aside (as Stalin himself had done in the 1920s, when he decided to build socialism in Russia rather than pursuing a world revolution) and take advantage of alternative means of enhancing German power.

Germany's digestion of Czechoslovakia shocked British prime minister Neville Chamberlain into the realization that Hitler's word could not be trusted. The Nazi dictator, who had hitherto claimed that he was interested only in areas populated by ethnic Germans, now stood revealed as an expansionist hungry for land, irrespective of the national origins of its populations. Britain and France responded by issuing a guarantee of Polish independence on 31 March 1939.

Hitler was now entangled in the morass of probabilities and possibilities so characteristic of great power diplomacy. It was *probable* that the guarantee was a bluff: if the British and French would not fight to defend Czechoslovakia, a state whose military potential was considerable, why would they fight to defend a weak and virtually indefensible Poland? But it was *possible* that they would, and if they did, Germany would be embroiled in a war with the West several years in advance of Hitler's expectations (which envisioned such a war sometime between 1943 and 1945). In such circumstances, it would be necessary to dispose of Poland rapidly before wheeling about to deal with the West.

The attitude of Russia, of course, would be crucial. It was *probable* that Stalin would not intervene to prevent Germany's destruction of Poland, given Soviet military unpreparedness and the lack of love lost between Russians and Poles. But it was *possible* that he would, and Hitler could not fight Russia, Britain, and France with any hope of success. Soviet neutrality was well worth purchasing, particularly since it might convince the British and French to refrain from implementing their guarantee. After all, they had defeated Germany in 1918 only with American help and a four-year naval blockade that slowly strangled their foe. Now America was neutral and isolationist, and an agreement with the Soviet Union would render Germany blockade proof by assuring it unlimited supplies of oil and grain. Foolish indeed would be the British government that would, under such unfavorable conditions, go to war for the independence of a nation it could not hope to save.

We do not know how much of this reasoning Stalin deciphered, but he certainly realized that the Anglo-French guarantee placed him in a perfect bargaining position. He could play the West off against Germany and take the better of the two deals. On 17 April the USSR quietly extended feelers toward Berlin. Two weeks later, Soviet Commissar for Foreign Affairs Maxim Litvinov, a Jew and a symbol of rapprochement with the West, was relieved of his duties and replaced by Viacheslav Molotov. Humorless, dour, and inflexible, soon to be nicknamed "Old Stonebottom" for his ability to negotiate for hours on end without getting up from the table, Molotov would handle Soviet diplomacy for the next seventeen years. A clever, skillful debater with a habit of stuttering when excited and an unerring eye for the bottom line, he was absolutely devoted to Joseph Stalin, and his appointment signaled Berlin that Stalin was willing to talk.

That summer, the on-stage drama of Germany's increasingly threatening actions toward Poland was complemented by backstage courtship rituals as both Hitler and the West pursued alliance with Russia under conditions of controlled panic. If the Soviet dictator had actually wanted a Western alliance, he would probably have courted Hitler publicly in order to obtain the best deal from England and France. Instead, he dealt publicly with the West in order to turn the screws on Hitler. As the Nazi leader's self-imposed late August deadline drew nearer, German foreign minister Joachim Ribbentrop became more and more insistent on reaching an agreement—and Stalin grew more and more coy.

The Western powers could perhaps have negotiated more vigorously, but it is hard to see what difference this would have made. The Soviets wanted a westward adjustment of their boundary with Poland and a free hand in the Baltic States (Estonia, Latvia, and Lithuania), which had been part of the Russian Empire before 1918. By late July the West had explicitly rejected such terms, for several good reasons. For one thing, the British and French had just guaranteed the independence of Poland. For another thing, they hated and feared bolshevism and held Soviet military potential in very low esteem. Finally, and most importantly, the territorial adjustments which Stalin wanted could be conferred by the West only at the price of a settlement more demeaning than that of Munich—and by the summer of 1939, appeasement of *any* dictator had been discredited by Hitler's rapacity.

Hitler, of course, could concede everything Stalin wanted, and by 23 August he had done so. The Molotov-Ribbentrop Pact, which astonished the world at the beginning of that final week of peace, ensured Soviet neutrality at colossal cost. Moscow gained the right to occupy Polish territory up to and beyond the Curzon Line, the ethnic frontier suggested by British foreign secretary Lord Curzon in 1919 as the appropriate border between Poland and Russia, and secured German acknowledgment of its vital interests in the former tsarist possessions of Bessarabia, Latvia, Estonia, and Finland. In exchange for all this, the USSR would graciously permit the capitalists and fascists to tear each other to pieces. Hitler got the worst of the bargain, since Soviet neutrality did *not* deter the British and French from going to war for Poland. If he wanted to proceed from there to seek living space in Russia, he would have to start from a position much farther west than the original Russo-Polish frontier. Above all, since Soviet defense of Poland had been doubtful from the outset, he had purchased dearly what he could probably have had for nothing.

In retrospect, it appears that Stalin was much less a fool than historians have often made him out. The Molotov-Ribbentrop Pact obtained for Russia a breathtaking set of territorial acquisitions and an extensive buffer zone against future German invasion. Had Stalin come to terms with the West, a poorly prepared Russia would quickly have been involved in war with Germany; by concluding an agreement with Hitler, he ensured his country against attack (at least for a time) from the only nation which posed a credible threat to the existence of the Soviet Union. If Stalin was anxious to avoid a German invasion, it made much better sense for him to deal with Hitler than with the West. Of course, he might be mistaken: Hitler might turn on him sooner than he anticipated. Time alone would tell, and in 1939 time seemed to be on Russia's side.

The Molotov-Ribbentrop Pact, of course, horrified and angered the West and confirmed its worst fears about Soviet duplicity and treachery. As a result, on the eve of World War II, relations between the communist East and the capitalist West were no better than they had been twenty years earlier. The two sides had learned to coexist, and on occasion they had even managed to talk about cooperation in the face of a common threat. But these efforts had proven futile, since there existed no real basis for long-term accommodation. The Western powers, after all, had forcibly intervened in Soviet affairs during the civil war and had openly condemned the Stalinist regime on numerous occasions since. And the Soviets were still committed to an ideology which called for the forcible destruction of the political, economic, and religious institutions most valued in the West. When push came to shove, each side had been willing to betray the other's interests, the West by appeasing Adolf Hitler at Munich, the Soviets by signing the Molotov-Ribbentrop Pact. The Cold War did not actually begin until after World War II, but the seeds of conflict had already been planted by the time that war began.

2

Adversaries and Allies, 1939-1945

On 1 September 1939, having purchased Soviet neutrality with the Molotov-Ribbentrop Pact, Nazi Germany launched a brutal invasion of Poland. Two days later Britain and France declared war on the Third Reich, thus beginning what was to become history's bloodiest and most devastating war. For the first two years of this conflict, both the USSR and the United States would remain on the sidelines, but by the end of 1941, the actions of the Axis powers would bring them both into the fray and help to create the Grand Alliance that would eventually win the war. For the next four years, the Soviets, Americans, and British were destined to be allies, united in the collective goal of defeating their common foe, but separated still by a vast chasm in their outlooks, interests, and ideologies.

THE NAZI ONSLAUGHT, 1939–1941

Stalin's willingness to enter into an agreement with Nazi Germany, and his participation with Hitler in the dismemberment of Poland during September-October of 1939, confirmed the West in its assessment of Soviet perfidy. With communist parties throughout the world now cooperating with Nazi expansionism, relations between the Soviet Union and the West were atrocious. This became especially evident during the "Winter War" between the USSR and Finland (October 1939–March 1940). Building on the Molotov-Ribbentrop Pact's concession of primary influence in Finland to the USSR, Stalin moved

15

to protect the land and sea approaches to Leningrad by pressuring the Finns into ceding territory that would give Russia control of the Gulf of Finland. In return he offered less desirable land in Russian Karelia, which was nevertheless twice the size of the areas requested from Finland. Influenced by their longstanding enmity with the Russians, the Finns refused, and the result was a war in which all the advantages seemed to rest with the USSR.

At first, the Red Army fared poorly. Overconfidence, mismanagement, and inadequate winter clothing all contributed to a stalemate by December and an astounding Finnish victory in January in central Finland. Fervent sympathy for Finland flourished in the West. Britain and France even went so far as to concoct an incredible scheme by which French forces in Syria would invade the USSR through the Caucasus and link up with an Anglo-French expeditionary force which would land in Finland and strike directly into the heart of Russia. Fortunately for the British and French, the Soviets rallied and defeated the Finns by 12 March. Had this not occurred, the West would likely have found itself at war with Germany and the USSR at the same time, the results of which could only favor Hitler.

Stalin, victorious despite multiple difficulties, pressed on. The Germans' spectacular defeat of France in June 1940 shattered his hopes that Hitler would be unable to turn east for some time. In June and July 1940, the USSR further secured its borders by annexing the Baltic States and bringing pressure to bear on Romania for the cession of Bessarabia and Bukovina.

Alarmed by this manifestation of Soviet expansionism so close to the Romanian oilfields at Ploesti, from which Germany derived nearly all of its petroleum of non-Russian origin, Hitler now recalculated his options. With his western flank secured by the defeat and occupation of France, he decided in midsummer to pursue his yen for living space in the east by invading the USSR in 1941. Despite his failure to win the Battle of Britain in the fall of 1940, he proceeded inexorably with his eastward expansion plans.

An operation of such magnitude could not be effectively concealed, even in the days before the deployment of espionage satellites. The Soviet government received numerous warnings of Germany's actual intentions from its agents abroad, from the British and American governments (including, as time grew short, personal messages from Winston Churchill and Franklin Roosevelt), and from a variety of German deserters. Even Richard Sorge, a German Communist who had constructed a valuable spy network from his position as a German diplomatic official in Tokyo, weighed in with unequivocal descriptions of the impending attack.

But even the best intelligence is worth little if the consumer chooses to disregard it. Stalin suspected the British of attempting to draw him into war with Germany and may have been so convinced of the value of the Nazi-Soviet accord that he couldn't see any reason for Hitler to destroy it. Alternatively, he may have been whistling past the graveyard, fearful of doing anything to provoke Hitler. His willingness to sign a nonaggression pact with Japan on 13

April points in that direction. Whatever the explanation, on 22 June 1941, as German armored spearheads crashed through inadequate Soviet defense lines, they passed shipments of timber, grain, and oil en route to Germany in final fulfillment of the Molotov-Ribbentrop Pact. Stalin could no longer be neutral; the German invasion transformed his country into the central battleground of World War II.

Western statesmen, desperate for any form of assistance against Hitler, welcomed Soviet entry into the war. Winston Churchill, long a steadfast anti-Communist, refused to take back anything he had said against the bolshevik regime. Nonetheless, he promptly offered Moscow all possible assistance, tartly observing that "if Hitler invaded Hell, I would at least make a favorable reference to the Devil in the House of Commons."

Favorable references were one thing and implementation of commitments quite another. British foreign secretary Anthony Eden lost no time in reminding Soviet ambassador Ivan Maisky that the USSR had watched with bemusement as Britain fought Germany alone. Terrified that Britain would do the same to Russia, Maisky pressed unceasingly for every possible proof of London's willingness to fulfill Churchill's pledges. The ambassador need not have worried; whatever Britain could give, it would give. But it was pouring money and materials into air defense, and it could not possibly give the Red Army everything it needed.

The United States could do that, but in June 1941 America was still neutral, in fact if not in spirit. The junior senator from Missouri, Harry S Truman, underscored that neutrality on 23 June 1941 with this recommendation: "If we see that Germany is winning we ought to help Russia and if Russia is winning we ought to help Germany and that way let them kill as many as possible, although I don't want to see Hitler victorious in any circumstances." President Franklin D. Roosevelt was no more infatuated with communist behavior than Truman, but he saw Hitler as the foremost threat to world peace and security and was thus unwilling to see any of Germany's enemies defeated. American neutrality legislation made the provision of substantial aid difficult until November 1941, when Roosevelt qualified the USSR for lend-lease aid by certifying that its defense against German invasion was vital to the defense of the United States. Once Japan bombed Pearl Harbor on 7 December and Germany followed suit four days later with its own declaration of war, all need for circumspection had passed. What Churchill would call "the Grand Alliance" had now become a reality.

THE GRAND ALLIANCE: ISSUES AND OPERATIONS

As Japanese bombs fell on Hawaii, Anthony Eden was boarding a ship to take him to Russia for a meeting with Stalin. The rough and risky voyage did little to alleviate his stomach flu, and on his arrival on 12 December he was informed that Japan had sunk two of Britain's finest battleships off Malaya. The year 1940 may have been, as Churchill alleged, Britain's "finest hour," but late 1941 was arguably its darkest. Eden had brought with him a boilerplate statement pledging Anglo-Soviet mutual respect and cooperation. He was startled to find that Stalin, perhaps emboldened by Britain's plight, was proposing nothing less than British confirmation of all territorial gains made by the USSR under the Molotov-Ribbentrop Pact and subsequent understandings with Germany, including the Soviet annexation of eastern Poland up to the Curzon Line.

Eden was confounded. Acceptance of these Soviet claims would betray what Britain had gone to war to preserve: the independence and territorial integrity of Poland. Churchill complained that Stalin's demands contradicted the Atlantic Charter of August 1941, a British-American agreement calling for national self-determination and opposing territorial aggrandizement, which had been endorsed by the USSR. He told Eden to defer consideration of frontier questions to the end of the war. Stalin, however, angrily replied that it seemed that the Atlantic Charter was directed against the USSR rather than the fascist powers. Eden assured him that this was not so, both in person and indirectly into the microphone he assumed was concealed in his quarters. Grumbling that he preferred the "practical arithmetic" of detailed, precise settlements to the "algebra" of vague, sentimental declarations, the Soviet ruler suggested postponement of a treaty until these questions could be settled.

The failure of Eden's mission revealed two themes that would recur repeatedly in the prehistory of the Cold War. First, the West would continually attempt to mollify Stalin and to assuage his fears of hostility and encirclement. This was futile, both because it could not be done and because it was unnecessary. The Soviet Communists would always be wary of capitalist powers, simply because they were capitalist—and Stalin would always be wary of anyone who happened still to be breathing. But this distrust constituted no impediment to an agreement, provided that it was spelled out precisely and in detail. Second, Stalin would continue to combine coldblooded realism with diplomatic audacity. With Hitler at the gates and Soviet losses and needs mounting hourly, he spoke of dividing the spoils of victory as though that victory were assured. He tried to secure Western endorsement of the vast territorial gains he had obtained from Hitler, then magnanimously accepted extensive military and economic assistance while agreeing in return to defer discussion of his outrageous demands. It was possible to negotiate with Stalin, but it would never be easy, and much of the history of the Grand Alliance revolves around the West's failure to realize how difficult it would be.

Closely linked with the frontier issue was the question of opening a second front to relieve German pressure on the Red Army—which, as Stalin incessantly reminded his allies, was the only army fighting Hitler in Europe. By the spring of 1942, when Soviet foreign commissar Molotov traveled to London and concluded an Anglo-Soviet treaty which made no reference to territorial concerns, the military situation was desperate. During his subsequent visit to Washington, in fact, Molotov's opposite numbers quipped that he seemed to know only four words of English: "yes," "no," and "second front." His forceful presentation of the catastrophic implications the loss of Ukraine and the Caucasus would have for the Allied war effort inspired President Roosevelt to declare that he anticipated the opening of a second front in 1942. No explicit promises were made, but for the moment, the question seemed settled to Soviet satisfaction. Then, as Molotov returned to Moscow via London, Churchill gave him a memo which forecast a landing in Europe in August or September 1942 but made plain that no irrevocable promise was being given. Nonetheless, Westerners who saw Molotov on his return to Moscow described him as "jubilant" (surely one of the few occasions on which so gloomy a diplomat merited that adjective), and Soviet radio began to speak of the impending invasion as a *fait accompli*.

It was, of course, anything but that. The British and Americans differed profoundly on the possibility of launching such an undertaking in 1942, and the Americans differed among themselves. Operation SLEDGEHAMMER, an invasion of northern France across the English Channel, was postponed until the following year, because to succeed it would require crushing force of a size and scope that could not be assembled quickly. Instead, the Western Allies decided upon Operation TORCH, an invasion of French North Africa in 1942.

To explain matters to Stalin, Winston Churchill traveled to Moscow from 12 through 16 August. It was the first meeting between the two leaders, and it was tempestuous. In a technique Stalin would use time and again in the future, a satisfactory opening session was followed by a harsh and unpleasant second day. Molotov reminded Churchill of what he had been told in London and Washington, while Stalin rudely accused the British of being afraid to fight the Germans and pay the blood tax inevitably associated with war. Churchill fought back, at times politely, at times indignantly, pointing out that no promises had been issued and that cogent military reasons argued against a second front in Europe in 1942. At the end of a grueling interview, Stalin admitted that he had no choice: he must accept the Allied actions, although he disagreed with them. The atmosphere lightened, and a convivial all-night banquet ended Churchill's visit on the evening of 15 August.

Operation TORCH proved successful. French North Africa was liberated, and in 1943 German forces would be expelled from Libya and Italy would be knocked out of the war. It was not an inconsequential operation, although no compelling evidence suggests that it took any German pressure off the Soviet front. It enabled the British and Americans to avoid a cross-Channel invasion in 1942, which would almost certainly have ended in disaster and might have lengthened the war. But from the standpoint of Western-Soviet relations, the alliance had been strained and little had been settled. Washington and London still sought to ease Stalin's fears, while Stalin still sought cold, hard commitments in lieu of honeyed words. Nothing short of a cross-Channel invasion would satisfy him, and that was destined to be delayed once again.

In January 1943, Churchill met with Roosevelt at Casablanca in newly liberated Morocco. Stalin too was invited but declined on the grounds that the ongoing battle for Stalingrad, which would soon result in a catastrophic German defeat, demanded his full attention. In his absence, the two Western leaders decided to focus in 1943 on an invasion of Sicily and Italy from North Africa. They met again in Washington in May and further agreed to postpone the invasion of France until the following year.

In early June, then, they informed Stalin of their decision. He was predictably bitter, reviewing the various assurances that both he and Molotov had been given regarding the second front. He charged the West with intentionally proceeding in bad faith, an accusation that provoked Churchill into a blistering rebuttal. If it had been the intent of the Western Allies to lay to rest the suspicions Stalin entertained concerning their motivations and intentions, they had been remarkably unsuccessful. The Soviet ruler was interested in actions, not words, and all the Western actions had thus far been concentrated around the Mediterranean.

Throughout the first half of 1943, in fact, Stalin cast about for other options, including the possibility of a separate peace with Germany. German foreign minister Ribbentrop, anxious to duplicate his feat of August 1939, apparently met Molotov behind Soviet lines in March. Other contacts were carried out in Scandinavia and Switzerland. The attempts came to nothing, because the two sides had incompatible goals: the Germans wished to retain Ukraine and much of Belorussia, while the Soviets wanted all of that back as well as the Baltic States, Bessarabia, Bukovina, and eastern Poland. Ribbentrop finally concluded that the positions were irreconcilable and spent his time in the late summer of 1944 trying to arrange a meeting with Stalin so that he might shoot him with a fiendishly prepared fountain pen.

Farcical and foredoomed though such negotiations may appear, there is substantial evidence that they were taken very seriously in London and Washington. It may be that such attention, hopefully leading to a relaxation of the West's attitude toward Soviet territorial gains, was all Stalin sought in the first place. In that case, the failure of the feelers served him well, since the final Soviet victory over Germany brought him acquisitions and influence far more extensive than anything Hitler could have offered him. In any event, as the first full-fledged summit of the three Allied leaders drew near, the British and Americans were on their guard and predisposed to take nothing for granted concerning Soviet participation in the war.

TEHRAN: THE ALLIES PLAN FOR A POST-NAZI WORLD

The first "Big Three" meeting of Churchill, Roosevelt, and Stalin took place at Tehran, the capital of Iran, from 28 November through 1 December 1943.

The site was selected to accommodate Stalin, who insisted that, owing to the complex military situation, he could not stray far from Russia. The American delegation was housed in the Soviet embassy because more secure accommodations could not be obtained. No doubt the rooms were filled with bugs, of the electronic as well as the multilegged variety. Given Roosevelt's predilection for wide-ranging conversations with anyone willing to listen, this arrangement gravely compromised the secrecy of U.S. communications. It could have proven disastrous had the Americans come to Tehran with a clear negotiating position. But this was not the case.

Franklin Roosevelt, the most personable U.S. president of the century, finally got his long-sought opportunity to speak with Stalin face to face. In American politics, the president was viewed as an inspirational moral leader whose incorrigible optimism and can-do mentality had brought his nation through the Great Depression and whose "first-class temperament" had enabled him to adjust political differences and solve intractable problems with aplomb. He was also, however, an erratic administrator with a visceral dislike for briefing books and a tendency to speak loosely about matters which he understood instinctively rather than intellectually.

These characteristics, so well suited to his job in Washington, placed Roosevelt at a disadvantage in dealing with Stalin. The Soviet ruler was not immune to personal charm and good fellowship, but he was not terribly susceptible to appeals based on moral concerns. He was also far better organized than the president, and he preferred to structure Allied agreements on the bedrock of national interests rather than the shifting sands of leadership personalities. Roosevelt's conduct toward Stalin reflected neither a hopeless naïveté nor the delusive ramblings of a terminally ill man, as his critics would later charge, but rather his standard operating procedure in political matters.

The disadvantages of Roosevelt's style surfaced quickly. Stalin no doubt expected to confront an English-speaking consortium which would present a united front at Tehran. Instead, Roosevelt seemed intent on demonstrating his independence from Churchill and his ability to construct a friendship with Stalin. From the opening session, the Western disorganization was evident: Stalin asked for the Anglo-American plans concerning the upcoming invasion of Europe, only to find that there was still much disagreement as to when it should occur. The issue was fought out openly between the Western delegations as Stalin watched curiously. Indeed, by pointing out that large-scale Soviet attacks in Eastern Europe could be coordinated with an amphibious landing in France, he himself helped to tip the scales in favor of setting a specific timetable for a cross-Channel invasion.

Worse was to follow from the Anglo-American side on the question of Polish borders. Rather than pressing for Soviet concessions, as he had previously agreed, Churchill referred to the Poles in disparaging terms as people who could never be satisfied. He suggested to Stalin that Poland's boundaries be shifted westward, using as an illustration a line of three matches and moving the easternmost one to the westernmost side. Roosevelt, in a separate interview with Stalin, endorsed the westward shift but otherwise said little of substance, depicting the Polish question mainly in terms of his needs to accommodate his Polish-American constituency back home.

Tehran laid much of the groundwork for postwar conditions. Military plans were completed for Germany's final defeat. An embryonic international organization, which Roosevelt described as "The Four Policemen" (Britain, China, United States, and USSR), was agreed upon in principle. Finland, Poland, and the Baltic States were discussed at length, with final decisions deferred to a future conference. Stalin agreed to eventual Soviet participation in the war against Japan and in return put forth claims to the Kurile Islands, the southern half of Sakhalin Island, and to railway and seaport rights in Manchuria. Much of what would later be finalized at Yalta was either decided or foreshadowed at Tehran.

Everyone left in high spirits. Roosevelt pointed with pride to the many accomplishments of Tehran, and Churchill characterized the atmosphere as one of "friendship and unity of immediate purpose." For the Soviets, things could not have gone much better. An official of the U.S. State Department observed that the Soviet attitude "was that if it could get what it wanted, the United States and Great Britain could take what they wanted, provided it was not something that the Soviet Union wanted." Nothing had surfaced to indicate that this attitude would be unacceptable to the West. There had been disagreements, and some matters had been deferred, but that was to be expected. The world through Stalin's eyes was not a place of unalloyed bliss but a place in which great nations dickered, bartered, and fought over the fates of millions of people. It had been this way for centuries, and if changes were possible in the future, Joseph Stalin did not expect to make them.

Unfortunately, the euphoria of Tehran lasted but a short while. When the conference adjourned, on the evening of 1 December, Europe was still dominated by Adolf Hitler. Allied forces had landed in Italy, but they had found the going rough, and the cross-Channel invasion was still a future projection. In the east, the German army still stood in western Russia and Ukraine, and bitter fighting was taking place around Kiev. It was all well and good to discuss future territorial dispositions in the abstract at Tehran, but when the armies of the Grand Alliance began to evict the Germans from France, Poland, and elsewhere, military considerations and political horse-trading would combine to create an entirely new context for Allied diplomacy.

ALLIED COOPERATION AND CONFRONTATION, 1944

As 1944 began, a sizable source of irritation between the West and the Soviets began to disappear. The long-awaited opening of the second front in northern France at last drew near. To coincide with the western "D-Day" invasion of 6 June 1944, the Soviets planned a major offensive on the eastern front for 22

June, the 132nd anniversary of Napoleon's invasion and the third anniversary of Hitler's. By August, their efforts had combined to crack the German defenses and to present the Grand Alliance with the heady prospect of victory in the not-too-distant future.

One of the casualties of the combined offensives was the spirit of comradeship that had pervaded Tehran. As the Red Army drove west and captured the city of Lublin on 24 July, the USSR recognized as the official government of Poland the National Committee of Liberation, a group of Communists and Socialists subservient to Moscow. This "Lublin government" would contend for power with the "London government," the Polish government-in-exile which had resided in London since the start of the war. As the Red Army approached Warsaw, the London government authorized a revolt by the Polish Home Army, an underground organization of 20,000 soldiers who were hopelessly outnumbered by the Germans and thus dependent for victory on Soviet help. By 1 August, when the uprising began, the Red Army was about ten miles northeast and twelve miles southwest of Warsaw along the Vistula River.

At this point, the Soviets halted and made no further efforts to advance into Warsaw. The London government asked the British to intervene militarily, or at least to drop weapons and supplies from the air. But the closest British and American air bases were in Italy, and given the range of the B-17 bombers then in use in Europe, the planes would have to land on Soviet airfields at Poltava to refuel before returning. The Red Air Force refused to give permission for such landings, although the fields were already being used by the Americans for shuttle bombing.

Controversy over Stalin's decision to let the Nazis destroy the Polish Home Army has raged since 1944. Probably it was based on two factors. First, the Red Army had outrun its logistical support; its units were tired and were being opposed by fresh German troops. Second, the Home Army was composed of the wrong kind of Poles: anti-Communists backing the London government. Certainly, it would have been out of character for Stalin to support the action. He had little use for any Poles and was ruthless enough to see his opportunity and profit from it.

Ultimately, the Soviets did offer aid in the form of air drops, and they did let the Americans use Poltava for refueling in mid-September. The Red Air Force even bombed German airfields during the U.S operations, but few of the supplies reached their targets. In one sense, Stalin's belated support was even more vicious than his original inactivity, for it raised the hopes of the Home Army, encouraged it to break off surrender negotiations with the Germans, and thus assured its eventual extinction.

From a Western perspective, Soviet behavior during the Warsaw uprising was thoroughly reprehensible. It demonstrated clearly the sort of policies Stalin was likely to follow in Eastern Europe once his armies took control. The spirit of Tehran had been modified substantially by the events in Poland, and the survival of the Grand Alliance beyond the end of the war was now anything but assured.

Still, the Western Allies pressed forward with efforts to create a new world body to replace the League of Nations, which had failed so miserably to prevent World War II. The Dumbarton Oaks Conference, which opened in Washington in the midst of the Polish disaster on 21 August, brought together British, Soviet, and U.S. delegations in an effort to create a more effective world body. Together they drew up plans for a new organization (later called the United Nations) which would include a deliberative General Assembly of all member states and a smaller, more powerful Security Council with the great powers as permanent members. Disputes arose, however, over membership and voting procedures, with the Soviets insisting that all sixteen republics of the USSR should sit in the General Assembly and that each member of the Security Council should have unlimited veto power over any council resolution. The Western powers objected, and final action was postponed until 1945.

Churchill endorsed the harmonious statements emanating from Dumbarton Oaks, but he was deeply disturbed by the implications of Soviet actions in Poland. Specifically, he feared the eventual designation of Eastern Europe as a Soviet sphere of influence, and as the conference ended in early October, he and Eden flew to Moscow to meet with Stalin and Molotov. There, in the absence of Roosevelt, he attempted to cut a deal with Stalin to guarantee the retention of Anglo-American influence in at least some areas either occupied or slated for occupation by the Red Army.

Unlike Roosevelt, Winston Churchill had never attempted to build a political career on personal charm and unswerving optimism; on the contrary, he was pugnacious, abrasive, and difficult to work with, an inveterate loner who delighted in taking unpopular stands and who, had he died in 1939 at the age of 64, would have gone down in history as a political failure. But like FDR he could be an inspirational speaker and leader, and his tremendous reserves of moral courage shone through in times of crisis. He was at his best when working in an atmosphere of desperate hardship and mortal danger— like the one he had inherited when he became prime minister in May of 1940. He would approach Stalin without illusions but with the firmly held conviction that if Britain and Russia were to coexist after the war, total Soviet control of Eastern Europe must be avoided, both for practical and for moral reasons.

At his initial discussion with Stalin, in the presence of Eden and Molotov, Churchill proposed a division of the Balkan peninsula between Soviet and Anglo-American influence, writing down the following percentages:

Romania:	Russia	90%	UK/USA	10%
Greece:	Russia	10%	UK/USA	90%
Yugoslavia:	Russia	50%	UK/USA	50%
Hungary:	Russia	50%	UK/USA	50%
Bulgaria:	Russia	75%	UK/USA	25%

"I pushed this across to Stalin," Churchill wrote in 1948. "There was a slight pause. Then he took his blue pencil and made a large tick upon it, and passed it back to us. It was all settled in no more time than it takes to set down."

The agreement, an effort to prevent the consolidation of a purely Soviet sphere of influence in Eastern Europe, speaks volumes about the attitudes of Allied leaders late in 1944. Churchill obviously was worried about Soviet expansionism and dubious as to the potential influence of the United Nations. Roosevelt confined his reactions to platitudes about peace in the Balkans—a stance that may have led Stalin to conclude that the United States had little interest in the area. Stalin, it is clear, was still quite willing to haggle over the fate of Eastern Europe, and not yet firmly bent on excluding Western influence and imposing communist regimes throughout the region.

Concerning Poland, Churchill's mission was less productive. He and Stalin were joined by Stanislaw Mikolajczyk, head of the London Polish government. The London Poles insisted on a provisional government in which five parties, including the Communists, would have equivalent representation. Stalin demanded a majority of seats for the Lublin Poles, who like Stalin himself endorsed the Curzon Line (discussed in Chapter 1) as the frontier between Poland and Russia. To compensate Poland for the territory this would cost it, Lublin proposed the shifting of Poland's western boundary to a line roughly configured by the rivers Oder and Neisse (the "Oder-Neisse Line"). Mikolajczyk opposed this arrangement, which would give the USSR the lands it had seized during its collaboration with Nazi Germany in 1939.

Days of bickering followed. In the end, Mikolajczyk agreed to try to get his government to accept the Curzon Line and to try to form a government acceptable to the USSR. Churchill told Stalin that unless the London Poles had more than half the seats, the West would never believe that the government was democratic, but Stalin held out for a majority for Lublin. Final action on Poland was deferred for a future conference of the Big Three, to be held in the Crimean resort city of Yalta in February 1945.

THE YALTA CONFERENCE, 4–11 FEBRUARY 1945

Roosevelt had insisted on postponing the next Big Three meeting until after his 1944 reelection and his inauguration in January 1945, a stance which accounted in part for Churchill's impatient flight to Moscow in October 1944. Stalin had proven similarly intractable concerning the location of the conference, alleging that his physicians had forbidden him to travel outside the USSR. The choice finally fell on Yalta, a remote Crimean city so inaccessible and unsanitary that Churchill later remarked that a worse site could not have been selected had ten years been spent in search of one.

To make matters worse, Roosevelt was suffering from a severe sinus infection, malignant hypertension, and congestive heart failure, conditions made worse by the long plane trip and the jolting six-hour jeep ride from the airstrip to Yalta. It is little wonder that he looked frail and sick, although there is no evidence that his illness affected his performance. FDR was never at his best at such meetings, and Yalta would be no exception.

Yalta proved a more organized meeting than Tehran. Military matters were handled first, with Stalin agreeing to delay the Red Army's drive to Berlin in order to coordinate it with a planned Western offensive in March. Discussion then centered on postwar plans for Europe. Hoping to discourage Germany from seeking a separate peace with the West, the Soviet leader demanded that its eventual dismemberment be included in the terms of surrender, but the United States and Britain demurred. Stalin later tried to secure massive reparations payments from Germany, but his overall figure of $20 billion (half of which would go to the USSR) was hotly contested by Britain. Both items were deferred. Churchill made an eloquent case for giving France a zone of occupation in Germany and a seat on the Allied Control Council that would temporarily govern that nation. Stalin was reluctant, but when Roosevelt observed that U.S. troops would be out of Europe within two years of the end of the war, he changed his mind and agreed to these requests, provided that the new French zone be carved out of the British and American zones, leaving the Soviet zone intact. He apparently believed that French participation might prove helpful in the absence of a lengthy U.S. occupation. Postwar Germany would thus be divided into four occupation zones: British, American, and French sectors in the west and a Soviet zone in the east. Churchill, fearful of a weakened postwar Europe dominated by Moscow, breathed a bit more easily at the prospect of French resurgence.

On 6 February, as the meeting entered its third day, Roosevelt made his first request: that the conference adopt the U.S. proposal on voting procedures in the Security Council of the United Nations. The American version guaranteed the five permanent members' right to veto any motion except those in which they were parties at interest. This was similar to a proposal rejected by the Soviets at Dumbarton Oaks, but this time Stalin agreed, simultaneously signaling his willingness to accept two additional General Assembly seats (for Ukraine and Belorussia) in lieu of the sixteen requested earlier. Somewhat perplexed, the British and Americans concurred, and the conference moved on to the Polish question.

Roosevelt displayed a lack of concern for the matter, saying that while he hoped the Soviets would make concessions to let the Poles "save face," he would not demand any. Churchill, aware that Britain had gone to war explicitly to secure Polish independence, proved a more formidable champion. He noted that the Curzon Line had already been conceded as Poland's border with the USSR; in return, the West required free elections and a new provisional government more representative of democratic parties. In reply, the Soviets proposed the Oder-Neisse Line as Poland's frontier with Germany, for the first time specifying the *western* Neisse, which would give the Poles far more German territory than the *eastern* branch of that river. Stalin was willing to

MAP 1 Territorial Changes after World War II

enlarge rather than replace the Lublin government and favored general rather than free elections. Stalemate loomed.

Gradually, the conferees nibbled away at the problem. Churchill objected to the western Neisse on the dubious ground that "it would be a pity to stuff the Polish goose so full of German food that it got indigestion." Stalin, graciously declining to develop the goose analogy further, made the outlandish statement that all the Germans had fled the area anyway—at which Admiral William Leahy whispered to Roosevelt, "The Bolshies have killed them all." This astonishing interchange ended with the West rejecting the western Neisse but accepting the addition of an uncertain number of unidentified Poles to the provisional government. On 8 February, Churchill turned to the election issue but failed to commit Stalin to a precise date. Against his better judgment, not wanting to break with Russia on the eve of Germany's collapse, he accepted Stalin's assurances that the Polish people would have the opportunity to express their will. Roosevelt was only too happy to defer final settlement of these issues.

Later, many would claim that Poland had been sold out at Yalta, like Czechoslovakia had been betrayed at Munich. Their anger is justifiable, but the comparison lacks merit. Czechoslovakia was independent in 1938, while Poland in 1945 had been a conquered and occupied nation for more than five years. Hitler was not the ally of Britain and France in 1938, and the German army was not in possession of Czechoslovakia during the Munich Conference. At Yalta, the British and Americans were in the unenviable position of delicately attempting to wring concessions from Stalin, whose help against Japan they needed badly. Acutely cognizant of the fact that the USSR had borne the brunt of the fighting against Germany, and aware of Stalin's intense desire for a Polish government friendly to Moscow, they were loathe to press him too strongly. Poland was treated shabbily at Yalta, but given the Red Army's occupation of the country and the political and military concerns just mentioned, it is difficult to envision a radically different outcome.

Eventually, the conference moved on to the situation in East Asia. The United States wanted the USSR to enter the war against Japan as soon as possible after Germany's defeat, so the Red Army could tie down Japan's large Kwantung Army in Manchuria and prevent its use in repelling an Anglo-American invasion of Japan. Stalin needed no convincing: a successful war against Japan would avenge Russia's defeat in the Russo-Japanese War of 1904–1905, establish a powerful Soviet presence in Manchuria, and perhaps earn for Moscow a zone of occupation in Japan itself. Nevertheless, he was able to wheedle substantial territorial concessions out of the Western Allies, including the southern half of Sakhalin Island and all of the Kurile Islands, as well as essential control of Manchuria and Outer Mongolia. Since in East Asia, unlike Eastern Europe, the Red Army was not already in possession of these areas, these Western concessions are open to question. Roosevelt and Churchill, without challenging Stalin's absurd claims that these

Churchill, Roosevelt, and Stalin at the Yalta Conference. (Franklin D. Roosevelt Library)

areas were historically Russian, conceded them willingly in order to obtain Soviet assistance. Both men were resolved on the destruction of the Japanese Empire; their willingness to grant substantial chunks of it to the USSR had less to do with any eagerness to appease Stalin than with their admitted intention to cripple Japan for the foreseeable future.

The Yalta agreements were signed on 11 February. All three leaders appeared delighted, believing they had made concessions only over unimportant matters and had secured their principal objectives. Churchill had gained the acceptance of France as a great power, so that Britain would not stand alone against Soviet ambitions in Europe. Roosevelt had obtained agreement on the voting procedure in the UN Security Council and had received Stalin's commitment to aid in the defeat of Japan. Stalin, while failing to gain acceptance of his German agenda, had nonetheless defended his position in Poland—at least until the next meeting of the Big Three. Each of them had gotten what he wanted most.

Yalta was, at least emotionally, the final celebration of the solidarity of the Grand Alliance. Within a few weeks, as Hitler's empire disintegrated, the defeat of their common enemy and their inability to resolve fully the vexing issues of Soviet security and expansion would shatter the alliance and reveal on the horizon the hazy outlines of the Cold War.

THE IMPACT OF GERMANY'S DEFEAT

After Yalta, Allied military cooperation began to fray. The Red Army, having postponed its advance on Berlin, turned its guns instead on Hungary, Czechoslovakia, Austria, and Denmark. The Anglo-American offensive began on schedule and at first found the going slow. Then on 7 March a chance occurrence triggered Stalin's suspicions. At Remagen on the Rhine, the American forces poured across the Ludendorff Bridge, which inexplicably had not been dynamited by the retreating Germans. Suddenly, the western front began to move, and Stalin, who had explored the possibility of a separate peace with Germany in 1943, now suspected his allies of having secretly arranged the preservation of the bridge so that most of Germany would fall to the West. Simultaneously, SS general Karl Wolff approached American and British agents in Switzerland with an offer to surrender all German forces in Italy. When the Western Allies rejected a Soviet request to be included in these talks, Stalin fired off a series of insulting telegrams to Churchill and Roosevelt, charging bad faith.

During the same period, Soviet actions in Eastern Europe disturbed the British and Americans. Deputy Foreign Minister Andrei Vyshinsky, former chief prosecutor at the Moscow Purge Trials of the 1930s, bullied the king of Romania into appointing a cabinet dominated by Communists. Leaders of the Polish Home Army were enticed into coming to Moscow to participate in talks about broadening the provisional government; once there, they were arrested. Churchill and Roosevelt sent stiff notes to the Kremlin in early April, referring to the breakdown of the Yalta accords and its implications for Allied unity. Roosevelt, who had been deluged by messages about Soviet misdeeds from W. Averell Harriman, the U.S. ambassador in Moscow, pounded the arm of his chair and told an aide, "Averell is right. We can't do business with Stalin. He has broken every one of the promises he made at Yalta." Stalin, who believed with some justification that Yalta had given him a free hand in Poland, was likewise suspicious of Anglo-American perfidy. Now he was determined to push the Red Army as far to the west as possible while Germany collapsed.

Churchill, convinced that the Red Army was dropping an "iron curtain" across Europe to seal off the Soviet-occupied areas, decided to press Roosevelt to have the United States drive eastward and take Berlin and Prague before the Russians could arrive. But on 12 April, Franklin Roosevelt died in Warm Springs, Georgia, of a massive cerebral hemorrhage. The news reached Moscow in the middle of the night, and Molotov rushed to the American embassy to pay his respects to Harriman. Stalin, ever suspicious, wondered if FDR's sudden death might be in any way unnatural. Shaking off the shock, he prepared to deal with Harry Truman, a politician virtually unknown in Moscow.

Truman, faced with a set of momentous decisions, recognized his own unfamiliarity with the position he now filled. A voracious reader, he briefed himself thoroughly during the next several weeks but considered himself Roosevelt's heir and was determined to fulfill all of his predecessor's promises. He also relied heavily on his existing advisors. Both of these factors left Churchill out on a limb when he tried to convince the new president to have the U.S. Army beat the Red Army to Berlin and Prague. Truman's advisors counseled against mixing military and political considerations, and the U.S. commander, General Dwight Eisenhower, was dead set against spending American lives to take territory which had already been promised to the Soviets.

Cooperation in military areas, however, was not matched by political harmony, as Truman relied on his advisors' negative views of Soviet behavior since Yalta. On 23 April, on his way to a San Francisco meeting which would establish the United Nations, Soviet foreign commissar Molotov stopped at the White House to meet the new U.S. president. Truman, who had read all of Harriman's dispatches, told the Soviet diplomat that he was gravely disappointed in Stalin's failure to implement the Yalta agreements on Poland. He characterized Soviet-American relations as "a one-way street" favoring Moscow and curtly dismissed Molotov's diplomatic rejoinder. When Molotov protested that "I have never been talked to like that in my life," Truman (according to his memoirs, but not the interpreter's notes) responded, "Carry out your agreements and you won't get talked to like that." It was apparent that Truman would deal with Stalin more directly and bluntly than had Roosevelt.

Thanks to the Soviet concessions at Yalta on United Nations membership and voting, the San Francisco Conference went well, and it succeeded in drafting a charter for the new world body. Meanwhile, as the members convened on 25 April, Soviet and American soldiers shook hands at Torgau on the Elbe River, cutting Germany in two. With the Red Army fighting in the streets of Berlin, Hitler killed himself on 30 April. When the new German government surrendered, to the British and Americans on the 8th of May and the Soviets on the 9th, American troops stood on soil assigned to the USSR, while Soviet soldiers occupied all of Berlin. Despite Churchill's efforts to have Truman postpone U.S. withdrawal pending satisfactory Soviet conduct in Eastern Europe, the occupied territories were exchanged in July, on the eve of the final Big Three conference in the Berlin suburb of Potsdam.

THE POTSDAM CONFERENCE, 17 JULY–2 AUGUST 1945

Compared with Yalta, the conference at Potsdam exhibited a troubling face. Roosevelt was gone, and Truman had met neither Churchill nor Stalin. When he did, he was startled to find himself at 5'9" the tallest and most vigorous of the three. He was also in no mood to take any guff from Stalin. By mid-July Truman had settled into office and was becoming more self-confident. A machine politician from Kansas City, he had fought for everything he had achieved in life, and he had in the process become an excellent poker player. His blunt, earthy language made him appear more confrontational than compromising, but just as a poker face conceals the reality of one's hand, Truman's bluntness permitted him to stake out a negotiating position from which he was willing to move, as long as the price was right. He arrived at Potsdam convinced that he held most of the high cards and that Stalin had made big gains at Tehran and Yalta by using transparent bluffs. Harry Truman might make mistakes—but not by underplaying a winning hand.

Stalin was unable to arrive until two days after the conference was scheduled to begin; it was later disclosed that he had suffered a mild heart attack. He was increasingly concerned about the behavior of the new American administration. Truman's decision to cut off lend-lease aid to Russia before the ink was dry on the German surrender had disturbed him deeply, even though the Americans had rescinded this decision a few days later in response to an international outcry.

Churchill, at seventy-one, was exhausted, preoccupied, and tormented by the nagging fear his party might have lost the recent British elections. His fears were confirmed in late July when the final results came in. The Labour party was swept into office, and its prime minister and foreign minister, Clement Attlee and Ernest Bevin, replaced Churchill and Eden at Potsdam.

The meetings were tense from the outset. The euphoria of victory, which had bubbled like vintage champagne at Yalta, had long since gone flat. Hitler was dead, Germany was prostrate, and the absence of a common enemy now called into question the future of the Grand Alliance. Stalin pressed for a settlement of the German reparations question, Western confirmation of the Oder-Neisse Line, the dissolution of the London Poles, assignment of Italy's North African colonies as Soviet trustees under the United Nations Trusteeship Council, and Soviet roles in Tangier, Syria, and Lebanon. Truman hoped to settle the Polish question in America's favor, prevent the Soviets from taking reparations from western Germany without providing food for hungry Germans, oust the procommunist governments of Romania and Bulgaria, and admit Italy to the United Nations. The British, partly because of their leadership transition, played a secondary role throughout.

Some issues were disposed of easily. Stalin's request for influence in North Africa and the Middle East was never given serious consideration.

Similarly, Truman's condemnation of Moscow's heavy hand in Romania and Bulgaria was countered by Stalin's willingness to give the British a free hand in Greece and to concede to the West a fifty-fifty say in Yugoslavia.

The real bargaining started over Germany. Stalin's demand for $10 billion in reparations was finessed by a counterproposal from the newly appointed American secretary of state, James Byrnes, who suggested that each side should take reparations from its own zone. This proposal confounded the Soviets, who knew that extracting reparations from their largely agricultural eastern sector would provide little of industrial value. Molotov tried to link the reparations issue with the Polish border question, but Byrnes turned the ploy around by offering the Soviets 25 percent of all industrial equipment found in the Ruhr, Germany's bombed-out industrial heartland, provided that Moscow accept the *eastern* rather than the western Neisse as Poland's western frontier. The Soviets were taken aback; bargaining with Roosevelt had been much more pleasant than dealing with Truman and Byrnes.

Faced with this situation, Stalin showed a readiness to compromise—and so did Jimmy Byrnes. On 30 July, ignoring his British allies, Byrnes offered Molotov a take-it-or-leave-it deal. The Americans would accept the western Neisse after all, defer the question of Italian membership in the United Nations, consider recognizing the governments of Romania and Bulgaria, and grant the Soviets a percentage of usable capital equipment found in the western zones of Germany. In return, the USSR would take reparations from its own zone alone. The Soviets disliked this, but in the end they went along, and the conference concluded without an open split.

Stalin's balance sheet at Potsdam was mixed. Most of the items he had wanted proved unobtainable, and the Grand Alliance had clearly fallen apart. Still, the damage had been limited. At least the West had been willing to bargain, a mode of discourse which the Soviet dictator always found congenial. After all, why should any realistic statesman have expected that the wartime alliance would survive Hitler's demise? The USSR had not been friends with Britain and the United States prior to 1941, and the unraveling of the alliance was merely a return to the *status quo ante bellum.* It did not mean that unrelenting hostility between the Soviets and the West was inevitable or even likely.

President Truman had also not gotten everything he wanted, especially with regard to Eastern Europe, but he had obtained a number of Soviet concessions and final confirmation of Moscow's readiness to enter the war with Japan. The problem was that he was no longer certain that Soviet entry into the Pacific War would be convenient for the United States. For the Americans had developed a new weapon which could bring Japan to its knees.

DIPLOMACY, DUPLICITY, AND THE ATOMIC BOMB

Rapid advances in physics had earlier raised the possibility that splitting the nuclei of heavy atoms could liberate vast amounts of energy and create bombs

A view of Hiroshima after the atomic blast of 6 August 1945. (U.S. Army Photo)

of awesome destructive force. By 1942, programs to build such a weapon had been under way in Germany, Great Britain, Japan, the United States, and the USSR. But only the United States had sufficient wealth, industrial plant, and scientific expertise to carry on such a complex project without endangering its war effort.

By the summer of 1944, the technical problems had been worked out, but it took another year to perfect the components and enrich a sufficient quantity of uranium fuel. At the Yalta Conference, the Americans sought Russian entry into the Pacific War without any firm evidence that the bomb would work. Besides, their priority had been to develop it for use against Germany and not Japan. By the summer of 1945, however, Germany had been defeated and Japan was still at war.

The first atomic bomb was tested successfully at Alamogordo, New Mexico, in the early morning of 16 July 1945. Its explosive yield equated to 18,600 tons of dynamite, the equivalent to a raid of 3,100 B-29 bombers. Truman received the news just as the Potsdam Conference opened on 17 July. A week later, after confirming with Churchill an earlier decision to use the bomb, he informally advised Stalin that the United States now possessed "a new weapon of unusual destructive force." Stalin seemed pleased and expressed his hope that the weapon would be put to good use against Japan, but showed no unusual interest. He certainly knew the general details of the project from Soviet agents like Klaus Fuchs and Alan Nunn May who were involved in the U.S. project, but he probably had no idea of how destructive the bomb would be.

The United States wasted no time in using the new weapon. The Japanese city of Hiroshima was destroyed on 6 August, followed three days later by the city of Nagasaki. On 8 August, as promised, the Soviet Union declared war on Japan. The Japanese government surrendered on 14 August, ending the Second World War. Ironically, although many Americans believe that the atomic bombs were solely or primarily responsible for the Japanese surrender, most of the available evidence points to the Soviet declaration of war as the final blow that broke Japan's will to resist.

In his memoirs, Truman stated that he decided to drop the bomb in order to save between 500,000 and a million American lives which would have been lost in an invasion of Japan. But this is special pleading after the fact. In reality, Truman made the decision for three reasons. First, he was determined to win the war with as small a loss of U.S. lives as possible and knew he would be held accountable by the American people if he did otherwise. It also should be noted that both Truman and the bomb's creators saw it simply as a remarkably powerful conventional weapon; the idea that it was a hideous device that should never be used was born *after* the horrifying effects of radiation sickness and atomic fallout became apparent. Second, the government had spent $2.5 billion on the project (an immense sum in those days), and to decide not to use the product of that massive effort seemed to make no sense. Finally, Truman had become convinced that Soviet entry into the Pacific War would complicate the postwar occupation of Japan; if using the bomb could avoid such complications by forcing a rapid Japanese surrender, so much the better.

This is not to say that the United States used "atomic diplomacy" at Potsdam. Despite the claims of many "revisionist" historians that Truman bullied the Russians once he knew about Alamogordo, the record tells a different story. Truman behaved in a forceful, blunt manner at Potsdam, but that was fully in keeping with his personality and style; he had blustered at Molotov on 23 April, before he knew that the bomb would work. Indeed, the only direct mention of the atomic bomb at the conference came in his casual conversation with Stalin, and that can hardly be construed as intimidation.

After the cataclysmic blasts at Hiroshima and Nagasaki, Stalin embarked on a crash program to create a similar weapon for the USSR. The leader of that project, nuclear physicist Igor Kurchatov, later recalled that Stalin convened a meeting, banged his fist on the table, and ordered: "Comrades, build me a bomb. The Americans have destroyed the balance of power." But even this did not mean that Cold War was inevitable. Instead, the Cold War was destined to arise out of continuing confrontations in the region which had vexed the Grand Alliance since its inception: Central and Eastern Europe.

3

The Formation of the Communist Bloc, 1944–1948

Since 1945, the question of how and why the Cold War began has been the subject of widespread controversy. One aspect of this debate involves responsibility for the conflict's outbreak. In the West, historians of the "traditional" or "orthodox" schools place principal blame on the USSR, while "revisionist" scholars emphasize U.S. guilt. "Realist" and "postrevisionist" writers often attempt to strike a balance between the two.

Another dispute concerns the principal location in which the Cold War originated. Some scholars contend that it began in the so-called Northern Tier of Iran, Turkey, and Greece. Others think it started in East Asia. But most agree that it originated in Europe, either in Germany (where a temporary military occupation turned into a lasting political division) or in Eastern Europe (where Soviet efforts to establish a buffer zone of friendly nations offended and frightened the West). The German roots of the Cold War will be traced in Chapters 4 and 5, while this chapter will discuss its origins in Eastern Europe.

SOVIET AND AMERICAN OBJECTIVES IN EASTERN EUROPE

The Second World War ended with Soviet troops occupying much of Eastern Europe. During the latter half of 1944 and early 1945, in its successful campaigns on the eastern front, the Red Army systematically defeated the German armies which controlled this region and liberated it from Nazi control. The Soviets paid a terrible price in resources and blood to accomplish this prodigious feat. What they gained, along with the defeat of their mortal enemy, was the power to determine the destiny of much of Eastern Europe during the postwar era. And that destiny, it turned out, was communist. By 1948 Communist governments were in power in Poland, Czechoslovakia, Hungary, Romania, Bulgaria, Yugoslavia, and Albania, and most of Eastern Europe had become part of a Communist bloc.

The *outcome* of the Soviet liberation of Eastern Europe is well known. But ever since these events transpired, the *intentions* of the Soviet government have been debated. During the first two decades of the Cold War, Western historians usually maintained that Stalin was determined from the beginning to turn Eastern Europe communist and followed a carefully prepared sequence of steps designed to achieve this end. This analysis gave way in the 1970s to an explanation which emphasized Stalin's flexibility and willingness to permit the development of governments like that of Finland, friendly to Moscow and subservient to its foreign policy goals while free to maintain multiparty political systems and free enterprise economies. More recent commentaries, such as the one presented here, have tended to accent the interplay of diverse and often conflicting factors in the formulation of Soviet policy. All of these approaches, however, suffer from lack of information as to the real motives of Joseph Stalin, one of the most enigmatic figures of the twentieth century. Roosevelt, Churchill, and their associates found themselves guessing at what was really in Stalin's mind; half a century later, so do we.

U.S. ambassador to Moscow W. Averell Harriman believed in 1945 that Stalin was juggling three options for Soviet policy, which might or might not be mutually incompatible. According to Harriman, Stalin wanted to preserve the Grand Alliance after the end of the war, turn Eastern Europe into a buffer zone between the USSR and Germany, and utilize the communist parties of Western Europe (which had played significant roles in resistance movements against Hitler) to subvert Western governments and prevent a return to their prewar animosity toward Moscow. The creation of "people's democracies" (one-party, communist-dominated governments which came to power through more or less rigged elections) in Eastern Europe may be viewed as an effort to blend these options, ensuring Soviet security while maintaining a positive image for communism in Western Europe and preserving postwar cooperation within the Grand Alliance. Joseph Rothschild has pointed out that such an analysis may explain the differing rates of communization of Eastern European nations between 1945 and 1948. Whether or not the Soviet Union intended to pursue these three options simultaneously, it seems clear that only the buffer zone option proved attainable. This may be explained by a comparison of Soviet objectives in Eastern Europe between 1944 and 1948 with American objectives during the same period.

Stalin's government appears to have worked toward the attainment of three objectives in Eastern Europe:

1. To install governments friendly to the USSR and to communism. At first, it was not essential that they be completely controlled by Communists; sooner or later, however, other political parties were expelled or integrated into a "popular front" or "workers' party" entirely dominated by Communists.

2. To create a buffer zone between the USSR and Germany, so that in the next war a German invasion of the Soviet Union would begin from much further west than in 1941. Such an invasion would have to move through countries friendly to Moscow and in some cases occupied by Red Army soldiers.

3. To exploit Eastern European economies for the economic reconstruction of the USSR. The war had wrecked most of the European portions of the Soviet Union, and rebuilding would require a great deal of time, substantial reparations from Germany, and abundant economic assistance from friendly countries. In return for their liberation from German rule, Moscow's new friends would be expected to provide as much economic support as possible for their exhausted benefactor.

The objectives of the United States and Great Britain were very different:

1. To enable Eastern European countries to elect democratically any government they chose. In some nations, like Bulgaria and Czechoslovakia, this might result in the election of communist governments; in others, like Poland, such a result would be out of the question (as Stalin himself admitted).

2. To open Eastern European countries to free trade, thereby helping them to modernize and helping the United States to find markets for its manufactured goods. This had been a guiding principle of U.S. secretary of state Cordell Hull, who believed firmly that wars began because of economic deprivation and that free trade throughout the world would promote prosperity to such an extent that war would become obsolete.

The problem was that these two sets of objectives were irreconcilable. Washington and London were not unsympathetic to Stalin's insistence on a Soviet security zone; nor did they object to the formation in Eastern Europe of governments friendly to Moscow. But if such governments could not be elected democratically, the Western Allies would oppose their forcible imposition. Similarly, Soviet economic exploitation of Eastern Europe was incompatible with both the area's economic advancement through free trade and

America's desire to expand its foreign markets: destitute people purchase few consumer goods. Moscow, for its part, feared Western economic penetration of its security zone as greatly as Western European nations feared communist political penetration. As for democratic elections, the Communist Party of the Soviet Union lacked any commitment to Western-style democracy, preferring instead the Leninist principle of "democratic centralism" (the obligation of all party members to fall in line behind the position articulated by the party leadership majority). Clearly, the seeds of conflict, sown in the misunderstandings and quarrels of the war years, were sprouting in the soil of opposing objectives in Eastern Europe.

Although Soviet goals in Eastern Europe did not *necessarily* involve the creation of communist governments, *realistically*, given Western attitudes, the attainment of those goals would be impossible in the absence of such governments. Specifically, the creation of friendly but noncommunist governments such as the one in Finland (often referred to as "Finlandization") would not have allowed Moscow to exploit the economies of Eastern Europe to the extent envisaged. Congruently, neither of the Anglo-American objectives was *necessarily* anticommunist, but *realistically* both were. In retrospect, given such firmly held yet discordant goals, it is hard to see how the Cold War could have been avoided.

Why didn't Stalin support rapid takeovers of Eastern European countries by communist parties advancing in the wake of the Red Army? If Harriman's theory is correct, the gains implicit in such action (greater efficiency in economic exploitation and guaranteed friendship with the USSR) would be outweighed by the liabilities of strained relations with America and Britain and alienation of Western European populations which might otherwise prove susceptible to communist penetration. After all, there was much that the Soviets stood to gain from good relations with the West, including a $6 billion loan they had requested early in 1945 and a favorable reparations settlement which would let them extract substantial resources from Germany. Neither was possible without Western good will. In addition, the forcible communization of Eastern Europe would certainly provoke resistance, which would belie Stalin's contention that communist parties there enjoyed widespread public support and force the Red Army to become intimately involved in domestic police work and social control. It was even possible that heavy-handed Soviet tactics would provoke direct Western intervention in Eastern Europe, an eventuality which would imperil all of Stalin's objectives in the region and the security of the USSR itself. Faced with such gruesome ramifications, it was best to proceed cautiously.

Stalin's discretion, regardless of its origins, confused his contemporaries and led to the adoption of different sets of tactics in each of the Eastern European countries. In each case, a communist regime eventually triumphed, despite the wide variety of maneuvers and approaches used to achieve Soviet objectives.

POLAND: FROM ONE MASTER TO ANOTHER

It was in Poland that Soviet actions most seriously endangered good relations between Moscow and the West. Germany's invasion of that unfortunate nation had started the war in 1939, and under the terms of the Molotov-Ribbentrop Pact, the USSR was entitled to conquer and occupy the provinces of Poland east of the Curzon Line. That line had been designated by the Treaty of Versailles in 1919 as the boundary between Poland and the Soviet Union, but Warsaw had never recognized its validity and had appropriated lands to the east of it under the terms of the Treaty of Riga in 1921, ending the brief Russo-Polish War. To complicate matters further, most of the residents of the disputed lands were Ukrainians, who had little love for either Poles or Russians. Once Stalin had taken these territories in 1939, he meant to retain them, and he had informed the British and Americans of that fact as early as 1941. For London, which had gone to war with Hitler in order to preserve Polish independence, this was a touchy and troubling matter.

Subsequent Soviet actions offered little reassurance. In the spring of 1943, German military units operating in European Russia unearthed mass graves in the Katyn Forest. Buried in them were more than 10,000 Polish military officers, last seen alive when the Soviets took them into custody in October 1939. Stalin indignantly denied responsibility and severed relations with the Polish government-in-exile situated in London when that body requested an investigation by the International Red Cross. Lavrenti P. Beria, chief of the Soviet secret police, admitted privately to Soviet generals that "a grave mistake" had been made in 1940 concerning the disposition of these prisoners. Not until 1991 did Moscow finally admit publicly that the officers had been murdered while in Soviet custody, but the incident further poisoned relations between the USSR and the Poles, who were convinced from the outset of Soviet guilt.

We saw in Chapter 2 that the Red Army's entry into Poland in 1944 resulted in the creation of the Lublin government as a communist-dominated rival to the London Poles. Stalin was obviously reluctant to deal with non-communist Poles; as he would later observe, "Any freely elected government [in Poland] would be anti-Soviet, and that we cannot permit." His posture during the tragic Warsaw uprising enraged the Poles even more and worried the West. By the time the war ended, Polish hatred of Germany had been largely replaced by animosity toward Russia, a fact which made it difficult for the Polish Communist party to win widespread support from the Polish people.

Ironically, Stalin's oft-repeated contention that it was in Poland's best interest to cultivate good relations with Russia was not devoid of good sense. The decisions of the Big Three to fix Poland's borders at the Curzon and Oder-Neisse Lines could easily be viewed favorably by Warsaw. Before the war, nearly a third of the country consisted of ethnic and religious minorities; now the border adjustments, coupled with the Nazi slaughter of Polish Jewry, had turned Poland into an overwhelmingly Roman Catholic and ethnically Polish nation (save for several million Protestant Germans living in the areas just east of the Oder-Neisse Line). The country's borders had been shortened dramatically and were now far more readily defensible, while Poland's pre-1939 landlocked status had been transformed through the acquisition of a Baltic coastline in excess of 300 miles. All of these gains, of course, were viewed with horror by the Germans, who could be expected to exert every effort in future years to reverse the verdict of Potsdam. Against such actions Soviet friendship provided the surest defense.

Stanislaw Mikolajczyk, leader of the Polish Peasant party and since 1943 prime minister of the London government-in-exile, apparently hoped that the restraint shown by Stalin in his dealings with Finland could be duplicated in Poland. Given the centrality of Poland to Soviet concerns as contrasted with the lesser significance of Finland, it is difficult to explain such optimism. But there is no doubt that Mikolajczyk held two high cards. His Peasant Party had been extremely popular between the wars, since it spoke for the farmers of what was then a heavily agricultural country; and in early 1946 the Polish Workers' party (Communist) was losing members while the Peasant party, increasingly identified with opposition to communism, was increasing in size. Properly manipulated, these factors could have lent partial substance to Mikolajczyk's hopes of turning Poland into another Finland.

Unfortunately for Mikolajczyk, his high cards were offset by the presence of the Red Army in Poland, Stalin's willingness to use intimidation in pursuit of Soviet objectives, and his own political ineptitude. The Communists, having been embarrassed by free elections in Hungary in 1945, were reluctant to test the sentiments of the Polish people in an open vote; but their allies, the Polish Socialist Workers' party, proposed a referendum to obtain authorization of the new frontiers, the nationalization of heavy industry, the distribution of rural lands to landless peasants, and the abolition of the Polish Senate (which had served as a bastion of the Polish elite between the wars). Mikolajczyk, hoping to use the referendum to solidify his claim to leadership, urged his party to vote against the portion dealing with the Senate while supporting its other provisions. This unwise maneuver split the Peasant party, and when Washington suspended economic credits to Poland in the midst of the campaign owing to the government's failure to hold free elections, the referendum's passage was assured.

The results encouraged the Communists and Socialists to combine with two smaller parties in a "Democratic bloc" and to schedule elections for January 1947. Those elections were blatantly rigged: Peasant party supporters were disenfranchised, arrested, or beaten, while public voting and stuffing of ballot boxes were carried out with impunity. The Democratic bloc took more than 80 percent of the votes to the Peasant Party's 10 percent. Mikolajczyk was dropped from the Polish cabinet and fled the country in October 1947. By

December 1948, the Communists had absorbed the Socialists into the Polish United Workers' party, and Poland was in all respects a one-party dictatorship.

Events in Poland exerted a powerful effect on the emerging Cold War. The Labour government in Britain, reminded daily by the Tory opposition that Britain's ostensible reason for going to war with Germany had been the preservation of Polish liberty, was outraged. In 1945, keenly aware of the importance of the Polish-American vote for the Democratic party in the United States, President Roosevelt had impressed upon Stalin the need to avoid actions in Poland which would alienate that segment of the electorate. In reporting to the Congress after the Yalta Conference, he had misled the American people concerning the true nature of the Polish situation, portraying Moscow and Washington as being in fundamental agreement on the future of that nation. Now, with Harry Truman in the White House and Soviet-American relations deteriorating rapidly, Stalin looked to his own interests and solidified his control over the most important piece of his developing security zone. His actions confirmed British and American opinions of Russian perfidy and intensified the animosity between the former allies.

ROMANIA: EXIT THE MONARCHY

Romania, like Poland, was traditionally hostile to Russia and had fought on the German side after 22 June 1941. Its oil fields at Ploesti and its disciplined dedication to the Axis cause made it Hitler's most useful ally. But by late summer of 1944, with Germany losing the war, the Romanians decided to switch sides. On 23 August, with the Red Army preparing to enter the country, King Michael orchestrated a coup which ousted the pro-Axis government of Marshal Ion Antonescu and then handed Germany a declaration of war. Since the German army was too busy in Poland and France to do anything about it, the gamble paid off, and Michael enjoyed immense public esteem. Stalin, cognizant of Romania's strategic significance and hostility toward Moscow, proceeded cautiously, decorating the popular king and authorizing underground activities by Communists like Gheorghe Gheorghiu-Dej and Ana Pauker, who had either resisted Hitler from within or had spent the war in Moscow. Nonetheless, by late 1944 there were fewer than a thousand Communists active in Romania.

In terms of influence, however, the Communists were more important than they appeared. Most of the Romanian army spent the winter of 1944–1945 fighting the Germans in Hungary and Czechoslovakia, giving the Communists a chance to build their strength. The overwhelming power of the Red Army, which had moved into Romania in August 1944, likewise played into their hand. In October 1944, the Communists helped form the National Democratic Front, cooperating with the Social Democrats, the trade unions, and two parties friendly to communism, the Plowmen's Front (peasants) and the Union of Patriots (business and professional people). Prime Minister

Nicolae Radescu, irritated by communist sponsorship of strikes, demonstrations, and confiscations of land, angrily vilified Ana Pauker and other Moscow-trained Communists in a speech on 24 February 1945. Stalin reacted at once, dispatching Deputy Foreign Commissar Andrei Vyshinsky to Bucharest, where he bullied King Michael into firing Radescu and accepting a National Democratic Front government under the leadership of Petru Groza, the procommunist head of the Plowmen's Front. Upon leaving the king's office, Vyshinsky apparently slammed the door with sufficient force to crack the plaster surrounding the frame. This may have convinced Michael to give in, although it is likely that the simultaneous Red Army occupation of Romanian army headquarters and the foreign and defense ministries was even more persuasive.

Groza's government promptly confiscated and redistributed all landed estates in excess of 120 acres, gaining significant popular backing in the process. That fall, the British and Americans declined to recognize the Groza regime because of its refusal to hold free elections. Michael attempted to exploit this situation to force Groza from power, but his efforts were ignored, and he passed into internal exile at his country estate, eschewing any role in government. In his absence, the Democratic Front enjoyed free rein and readily accepted the decision of the Moscow Conference of Foreign Ministers (December 1945) that free elections must be held. After eleven months of street fighting, selective terrorism, and similar intimidations, the elections were held on 19 November 1946. A combination of bullying tactics and ballot-box fraud assured victory for the Democratic Front.

The Communists held only a small minority of parliamentary seats, but they enjoyed the support of the Red Army and used it skillfully against their coalition partners. In the spring of 1947, they openly accused opposition party leaders of complicity with American imperialism, convicting them and sentencing them to lengthy prison terms. After two years of irrelevance, King Michael abdicated in December 1947 and left the country. Romania thereupon abolished the monarchy and became a "people's democracy," and in March 1948 the Communists absorbed all of their partners from the Democratic Front. With Gheorghiu-Dej as prime minister and Pauker as foreign minister, the Romanian Communists initiated agricultural collectivization and the nationalization of heavy industry. Simultaneously, the headquarters of the Communist Information Bureau (or Cominform, a successor to the Comintern which had been dissolved in 1943) were transferred to Bucharest, the Romanian capital.

Britain and America played virtually no role in these events. Unwilling to challenge the 1944 Moscow formula which gave Britain preponderance in Greece in return for Soviet preponderance in Romania, London kept a discreet silence. Washington protested vigorously and consistently over the lack of free elections in Romania, characterizing communist behavior as a violation of the Yalta agreements; but the United States was no more willing than

Britain to take meaningful action. Military intervention was out of the question, and in its absence, the Red Army controlled the field. Romania, like Poland, passed into the communist camp.

BULGARIA: THE FRUITS OF FRIENDSHIP WITH RUSSIA

Despite its wartime alliance with Germany, Bulgaria had long looked up to the Russians. Tsarist Russia had liberated it from Turkish rule in the nineteenth century; the Bulgarians used the Cyrillic alphabet, called their rulers "tsars," and were heavily influenced by Russian culture. Unlike Romania, Bulgaria did not participate in the German invasion of the Soviet Union on 22 June 1941. When the Red Army poured across Bulgaria's frontier with Romania on 8 September 1944, the Bulgarian government at once sued for an armistice, which Moscow quickly accepted. The following day the Soviets installed a coalition government under the Fatherland Front, an anti-German resistance movement with a strong communist element. Bulgaria then joined in the final assault on Germany. In recognition of these actions, Stalin demanded no reparations from Bulgaria after the end of the war.

From the beginning, Communists controlled the Ministry of Interior (hence the police) and the local militia. They used this position to purge the government of "German collaborators," ruthlessly killing at least 50,000 officials ranging from cabinet ministers to village councilors. They also used various tactics to intimidate or control other parties, but they ran into serious opposition from Nikola Petkov, the leader of a noncommunist party called the Agrarian Union. A staunch friend of Russia, Petkov was nonetheless anticommunist and tenaciously resisted the political maneuverings of the Bulgarian Communists and their Soviet friends. His popularity grew rapidly in the fall of 1945, and in January 1946 Stalin's point man Vyshinsky traveled to Sofia to try to convince Petkov to cooperate with the Fatherland Front. Soviet blandishments failed, and Petkov remained a powerful anticommunist rallying point.

This tense state of affairs persisted throughout 1946. On 8 September, a nationwide plebiscite forced the abdication of seven-year-old Tsar Simeon (his father, Tsar Boris, had died unexpectedly in 1943) and proclaimed Bulgaria a republic. Nineteen days later, a constituent assembly was elected to draw up a republican constitution; the Fatherland Front won more than three-quarters of the seats, but nearly a quarter of its delegates soon defected to the Petkov-led opposition. It appeared that Moscow would be compelled to choose between permitting the emergence of a pro-Russian, anti-Soviet leadership in Sofia or the extinction of that leadership by military force.

Stalin was saved from this unpleasant choice by the United States, which signed a peace treaty with Bulgaria on 10 February 1947 and ratified it on 4 June. This terminated the activities of the Allied Control Commission, which had given London and Washington some say in Bulgarian affairs and had thus given Petkov some leverage. On 5 June, Petkov was arrested as he spoke in parliament; he was tried, convicted of conspiracy, and hanged on 23 September. Eight days later the United States granted diplomatic recognition to the Bulgarian government, which was now solidly controlled by the Communists. It is difficult to avoid the conclusion that the United States, at loggerheads with the Soviet Union over Greece and Turkey (see Chapter 4), had made a calculated decision to write off Bulgaria, just as Churchill had done at Moscow in 1944. Bulgaria, like its northern neighbors, became part of the Communist bloc.

HUNGARY: FROM FREE ELECTIONS TO ONE-PARTY RULE

In 1944, the Hungarian leader, admiral Miklós Horthy, attempted to cancel his alliance with Hitler and bring Hungary into the war against Germany. Unfortunately, he failed where Romania and Bulgaria succeeded. The plan never got untracked, and Germany ousted Horthy in favor of direct military occupation and installation of a puppet government. As a result, fighting in Hungary was intense and protracted; when the Red Army finally expelled the Germans early in 1945, Budapest lay in ruins and famine threatened the country.

Stalin's attitude toward Hungary was curiously ambivalent. His Moscow agreement with Churchill had granted the Soviet Union preponderant influence there, but Soviet representatives acted with remarkable restraint compared to their conduct in Romania and Bulgaria. There was no systematic purge of collaborationist bureaucrats; the provisional government contained only two Communists, in the ministries of trade and agriculture; the Communist platform read like an electoral manifesto from the British Conservative party; and in November 1945, open, free, and honest elections were held throughout the country. Perhaps Stalin was testing the appeal of communism in Eastern Europe, or perhaps he was proceeding slowly in Hungary in order to calm Western fears over Soviet conduct in Poland. It is certain that Soviet leaders considered Hungary less strategically significant than either Poland or Romania.

Whatever Stalin's motives may have been, the election results were devastating for Moscow. The Smallholders party, a rural organization which had dominated Hungary between the wars, swept into power with 57 percent of the vote, while the Communists earned 17 percent, ranking them just behind the Social Democrats. Communist leader Mátyás Rákosi conferred with Stalin in Moscow, then returned to Budapest with the mission of undermining the Smallholders. For the next two years, the battle for Hungary was waged behind the scenes. The Communists enjoyed two advantages. The policies of Minister of Agriculture Imre Nagy, a flexible, reform-minded Communist, led to wide-scale redistribution of land to poor farmers and notable increases in communist popularity. Then, in February 1947, the British and Americans signed a peace treaty with Hungary (as they had with Bulgaria and Romania), thereby ending the authority of the Allied Control Commission and leading to Western recognition of the Hungarian government.

At first, it appeared that the Smallholders would be able to keep the Communists at bay. But their position was gradually eroded through intimidation and internal political maneuvering. In August 1947, another round of elections gave them 15 percent of the vote, down from 57 percent two years earlier. The Communists became the largest party, despite a relatively unimpressive showing of 22 percent of the vote. Slowly they consolidated their hold on power, building on the presence of the Red Army, the apparent inability or unwillingness of the West to intervene, the deepening confrontation between the USSR and the United States over Germany, and the apparent moderation of their leadership. By 1949, they had driven all other political parties underground or out of existence altogether. Elections that year were contested with a single list of candidates, and in August 1949, Hungary implemented a new constitution and became a "people's democracy."

Soviet control over Hungary, however, was not complete. Nagy proved too liberal for Stalin and was purged in the early 1950s, only to reemerge in 1956 as leader of a popular uprising against Soviet domination. Later, in the 1970s and 1980s, Soviet leaders would tolerate considerable free market economic experimentation by the Hungarian regime of János Kádár. The Hungarian example illustrates the diversity of Soviet tactics in Eastern Europe, just as it underscores the similarity of eventual outcomes. Hungary, like most other countries in this region, joined the Soviet sphere of influence and was counted on Moscow's side in the Cold War.

CZECHOSLOVAKIA: A BRIDGE GOES DOWN

Czechoslovakia was the most industrialized country of Eastern Europe and the one with the firmest grievance against Britain and France. Czech president Edvard Benes, having seen his nation betrayed at Munich, was convinced of the uselessness of Western friendship and the importance of coming to terms with Moscow. Stalin, after all, had professed his willingness to fight at Czechoslovakia's side against Germany in 1938 and, unlike the Poles, neither Czechs nor Slovaks harbored long standing bitterness against Russians. Since postwar Soviet control of Eastern Europe was apparently unavoidable, prudence appeared to dictate building a close relationship with Moscow. For Benes, this would involve no sacrifice of Western values, to which he remained committed; rather, Czechoslovakia would serve as a bridge between East and West, a nation friendly to and willing to do business with both sides. In December 1943, he traveled to Moscow and signed a treaty of alliance with the USSR.

After the war, it seemed for a time that the treaty might work. Stalin, aware that the Communist party was likely to become the strongest in Czechoslovakia and fully cognizant of Benes's good will, realized that free elections might well lead to a communist-dominated government. This in turn might make it possible to bring Czechoslovakia into the Soviet camp without wrecking the Grand Alliance. In May 1946, free parliamentary elections gave 38 percent of the vote to the Communists, who thereby became the largest party and organized a coalition government, along with the Social Democratic and several other parties. For a while, the premier, communist leader Klement Gottwald, worked to maintain close economic ties with the West and avoided any intimidation or persecution of noncommunist parties.

This promising state of affairs ended abruptly in the summer of 1947. When the United States organized the European Recovery Program or "Marshall Plan" (described in Chapter 4), European nations hastened to apply for membership. One of them was Czechoslovakia. The coalition government voted unanimously to take part, only to be vilified in a meeting with Stalin in July. The Czechs were told to withdraw their acceptance of American aid and instead urged to join in the "Molotov Plan," open to all socialist nations of Eastern Europe. The U.S. objective of free trade with this region clashed openly with the Soviet desire to avoid its penetration by the overpowering American economy.

Events moved rapidly. Czechoslovak Communists began to practice the same sort of bullying evident since 1945 in other Eastern European nations. On 20 February 1948, a number of noncommunist cabinet ministers resigned, hoping that the Social Democrats would join them and cause the government to fall. But since the Social Democrats remained in office, the government stayed in power, replacing the departing ministers with more subservient types. Foreign Minister Jan Masaryk, son of the founder of the Czechoslovak state, either fell or (more likely) was pushed to his death from an open window during the crisis. Gottwald's government then swiftly turned Czechoslovakia into a one-party state. The bridge between East and West was closed.

Despite the pressure exerted by Moscow and the presence of the Red Army, the coup of February 1948 appears to have been mainly the work of the Czechoslovaks themselves. The disastrous miscalculation by the minority ministers opened the door for Gottwald to consolidate his power by legal means and to avoid an open confrontation. The coup in Czechoslovakia frightened the West and led to a brief war scare, which was quickly followed by the blockade of Berlin. At the time, many thought that the USSR was preparing for a third world war, but in retrospect it seems that Stalin was simply shoring up his perimeter for the long, twilight struggle of the Cold War.

YUGOSLAVIA: TITO TRIUMPHANT

Nowhere was the diversity of Soviet responses to Eastern Europe more evident than in Yugoslavia. It seems likely that Soviet leaders never understood the situation there, and it is certain that they mishandled it badly.

Yugoslavia was unpredictable from the moment a coup in Belgrade overthrew a pro-German government in March 1941. An enraged Hitler deferred his offensive against Russia to teach the Yugoslavs a lesson: the Wehrmacht defeated them in eight days and fragmented the multinational state. But Hitler's commitments elsewhere led him to withdraw the German forces before they had destroyed all elements of the Yugoslav army, and some surviving units went underground. For the remainder of the war, they fought not only the Germans but also a volunteer force of Partisans led by Josip Broz (alias Tito), the general secretary of the Yugoslav Communist party. In a struggle complicated further by British, American, and Soviet aid to conflicting sides, the Partisans eventually caught the country's imagination and played the leading role in defeating the German occupiers by October 1944. Red Army units marched in simultaneously and behaved atrociously, raping women and burning villages throughout northern Yugoslavia. They were quickly withdrawn to fight elsewhere, but Yugoslavs were left with little appreciation for Soviet-style liberation.

Tito emerged from the conflict with tremendous popularity, based not only upon his victory but also upon his program. A beefy, savvy Croat, he deplored ethnic fragmentation and rivalries, denouncing them as Nazi tools and standing instead for full reunification of the country. This stance was not popular in his native Croatia, where aspirations for independence ran high; but Tito's trump card was his willingness to *practice* national unity as well as to *preach* it. Scrupulously avoiding any hint of ethnic prejudice or preferential treatment, while swiftly constructing an efficient, centralized administration, he won the trust of all Yugoslavs to a degree matched by no one before or since. Indeed, Tito may well have been the only Yugoslav ever who both believed in multinational unity and was able to make it work. He had the touch required to balance a liberal attitude toward cultural variety with a resolute rejection of the divisive pressures such variety can produce.

From the beginning, Belgrade's relations with Moscow were strained. Tito was so insistent in his territorial demands upon Italy that he provoked a postwar crisis, one which could have led to war with Britain and America. The Soviets uneasily supported his claims, but resented his dangerous independence. Tito also sent aid to the communist side in the Greek civil war, an act which embarrassed Stalin, who had assured Churchill that the British would be predominant in Greece and who knew that British and U.S. naval power precluded any significant Soviet gains there. Finally, Tito's loudly trumpeted plan to build a federation of Balkan states was viewed skeptically by Stalin, who had no desire to see the emergence of a powerful communist rival.

Even more serious were Yugoslavia's political and economic divergences from Moscow. Tito's government was communist but not Soviet: it sought to balance the aspirations of ethnic subgroups and to construct a distinctively Yugoslav path to socialism. Moscow expected Yugoslavia, like other Eastern European nations, to increase its production of raw materials and crops so as to help subsidize the USSR's recovery. The horrified Yugoslavs contended that this would condemn them to neocolonial status. Instead, they wanted Moscow to underwrite *their* industrialization program, the success of which would validate their unique path to socialism.

This was a dagger pointed at Stalin's heart. It was not that Yugoslavia's course was non-Marxist; indeed, Tito explicitly adopted a Stalinist economic model, emphasizing heavy industry, centralized economic planning, and nationalization of most enterprises. The danger lay in the possibility that Yugoslavia would become more successful economically than the USSR, thereby luring other Eastern European nations along alternative paths to modernization. This would deprive Moscow of the subservience of Eastern European states and prevent it from using those countries as suppliers of raw materials and consumers of low-quality Soviet finished goods. Stalin's chief priority was to *control* Eastern Europe; implanting communism there was secondary. That control, achieved in part at the cost of the Grand Alliance, was now jeopardized. Clearly, Tito had to be stopped.

Stalin struck in the spring of 1948. He recalled all Soviet military and civilian advisors from Yugoslavia, orchestrated its expulsion from the Cominform, and organized a trade boycott by all communist nations. Simultaneously, he called on loyal elements within the Yugoslav Communist party to overthrow Tito and his henchmen. There is no doubt that he fully expected to be successful, observing at the time, "I will lift my little finger and there will be no more Tito!" But even all ten of his fingers, in the form of clenched fists, failed to displace the Yugoslav leader. The boycott was particularly dangerous for Yugoslavia, given its anti-Western activities in Greece; but the United States, sensing an unexpected opportunity to foster dissension within the Soviet bloc, took up much of the slack. By 1952, one-third of Yugoslavia's imports came from America. Meanwhile, Tito pressed ahead with the development of the "separate Yugoslav path to socialism." He introduced free market factors of supply and demand into Yugoslav industrial production, liberating factories from total dependence on quotas set by a central planning board.

The economic well-being made possible by these reforms and by American imports played a significant role in Tito's survival. His ruthlessness in dealing swiftly with Stalinists within his own party also helped his cause. But three reasons for the failure of Soviet actions against Yugoslavia stand out. First, the immense wartime popularity earned by Tito and the Partisans (coupled with the atrocious conduct of the Red Army) united the Yugoslavs against Soviet meddling. Second, Tito's solicitude for the aspirations of the country's diverse ethnic groups won him support from all regions and from all who believed in national unity. Finally, Stalin's own restraint doomed his efforts.

The fact that Yugoslavia was not occupied by the Red Army gave Stalin much less leverage there than in other Eastern European nations. But in 1948, with Britain retreating from empire and the United States, largely disarmed, engaged in efforts to break the Berlin Blockade and preoccupied by a four-way presidential election campaign, an invasion of Yugoslavia by Soviet forces would have stood a strong chance of success. It is true that the USSR had no border with Yugoslavia, that the terrain within that country was mountainous and treacherous, and that Yugoslav resistance could be protracted and ferocious; but none of these factors would have inhibited an army which had triumphed over Nazi Germany. The United States, of course, could always threaten to use nuclear weapons, over which it still enjoyed a monopoly, but there was no reason to believe that Washington considered Yugoslavia as vital to Western interests as Berlin.

Perhaps that consideration best explains Stalin's conduct. Berlin was crucial to both sides in the Cold War, but Yugoslavia was not. Once his blows against Belgrade had failed to bring Tito down, Stalin may have reasoned that further action would entail more risks than could be justified by the benefits of success. Indeed, Tito's survival, while it embarrassed the Soviet Union, in no way prevented Stalin from doing what he wanted in Europe. Germany was an altogether different story. And that is where the Cold War began.

4

The Cold War Begins, 1945–1948

The sun that rose over Tokyo Bay on 2 September 1945 illuminated a world order that had changed dramatically since 1939. As the Japanese Empire signed the Instrument of Surrender and followed the Third Reich and the New Roman Empire into history's dustbin, the victors were able to begin the daunting task of keeping the hard-won peace and reorganizing the world. Winning the war had been wrenchingly difficult, but events would soon prove that it had been considerably easier for the Grand Alliance to defeat its enemies than for its members to preserve good relations among themselves in the absence of common foes. It would not be long before the Cold War would take the place of the brutal struggles of World War II.

THE GERMAN QUESTION

In the first half of the twentieth century, Europe's history was in large measure Germany's work. As a unified and immensely powerful nation, it had proven too large and strong for a small continent used to the fragile security conferred by a balance of power. The German Empire's belligerent tactics had led Europe into war in 1914. The failure of the victorious nations either to deal leniently with Germany or to demolish it had perpetuated the German problem after 1919. Hitler's brutal expansionism had led to another war in 1939 and called into being an unlikely opposing coalition of communist and capitalist powers. When the leaders of the Grand Alliance met between 1942 and

1945, it was easy for them to pontificate about the need to defeat Germany and prevent any return of its power. But it was not easy for them to solve the German problem, and their inability to do so was the principal factor in the development of the Cold War.

It wasn't that they didn't try: the conferences at Yalta and Potsdam discussed the German problem at great length. Nor did they misunderstand each other; they simply had different objectives. The Americans and British agreed on the necessity for a stringent peace, one which would greatly reduce German industrial production, provide reparations for the countries victimized by Nazi aggression, and promote political democracy. In 1944, they had toyed with the concept of dismembering Germany, but the Morgenthau Plan for the pastoralization and fragmentation of the country, approved by both Roosevelt and Churchill, was rejected by their staffs as impractical and as prejudicial to postwar efforts to rebuild all European economies. Soviet objectives differed both in tone and in substance. Stalin was determined to destroy German war-making capacity, primarily by exacting $20 billion in reparations, half of which would go to the USSR. He favored fragmentation of the country, with the industrial heartlands of the Saar and the Ruhr passing under international control. If Germany was to remain a unified nation, it should be crippled and neutralized.

Both sides agreed that postwar Germany should be divided into zones of occupation, with British and U.S. zones in the west and a Soviet sector in the east. Interestingly, although Stalin at Yalta had opposed an occupation zone for France, Charles de Gaulle's French provisional government adopted positions on Germany similar to those of Moscow. The French wished to fragment and democratize Germany, to internationalize the Ruhr while annexing the Saar and the left bank of the Rhine, and to extract heavy reparations in coal, money, and machinery. For all his alleged shrewdness, Stalin seems to have missed a marvelous opportunity to embarrass the British and Americans by endorsing the French positions.

By the time of the Potsdam Conference, however, the differences had widened. The British and Americans had come to realize that their zones contained most of the Germans, while the Soviet zone contained most of the food. They had also decided against dismantling German industry, since destroying Europe's most productive economy would cripple the continent's recovery and make Germany a permanent dependency of the Allies. They would now speak of reparations only in terms of exchange of West German industrial goods for East German food. The Soviets objected, since a prostrate Europe was not inconsistent with their hopes for the spread of communism, and since they feared the resurrection of German military might that economic recovery would make possible. Under such circumstances, no agreement was possible at Potsdam.

After the end of the war, the United States, secure in its monopoly of atomic weapons, had nothing further to fear from German military power.

MAP 2 Divided Germany

American policy henceforth stressed the desirability of a Germany strong enough to resist Soviet expansion and economically healthy enough to anchor a rebuilt, peaceful, and stable Europe. Stalin saw nothing attractive in this scenario and was in no frame of mind to consent to German reunification. So, as time went on, there was no meeting of minds, and the German question continued to bedevil relations between East and West.

POSTWAR ATTEMPTS AT ACCOMMODATION

In September of 1945, following the Japanese surrender, the foreign ministers of the five permanent members of the UN Security Council (the United States, USSR, Britain, France, and China) convened at London for the first postwar Conference of Foreign Ministers. It had been agreed at Potsdam that such meetings would take place as necessary to facilitate the transition from war to peace. This session was charged with drafting peace treaties between the Grand Alliance and Germany's wartime allies (Bulgaria, Finland, Hungary, Italy, and Romania), but it made little progress. Secretary of State Byrnes arrived with the atomic bomb "in his hip pocket" (as he put it), but if the Americans thought that the Soviets would roll over and play dead, they were mistaken. Foreign commissar Molotov proved as tough a negotiator as ever, and British foreign secretary Bevin made no more headway than did Byrnes. Britain and America pressed for compliance with the Yalta accords as they understood them: free elections in all Eastern European countries as quickly as possible. Molotov's position was that the Americans had their spheres of influence in Italy and Japan, while the British had theirs in Greece; the Soviet Union would intervene in neither, so the West had no business interfering in Eastern Europe. The Soviets also proposed that they assume trusteeship over the former Italian colony of Libya, a move which the West interpreted as an effort to probe in the direction of the Belgian Congo, which contained the world's richest supply of uranium (vital to the construction of atomic bombs).

The conference bogged down and adjourned without agreement, although some steps had been taken in the direction of draft treaties. Byrnes returned to Washington shrouded in gloom and uncertain of Soviet intentions. The British were even less pleased: they believed that the Soviets were bent on expansion in the Middle East and Mediterranean and that both the USSR and United States were becoming increasingly contemptuous of British opinions and interests. From the Soviet perspective, Western interest in Eastern Europe was both hypocritical and premature, since the German problem (which Moscow feared most) had not yet been dealt with. Attempting to settle affairs in Eastern Europe before guaranteeing Russia's safety from Germany was bound to increase Stalin's defensiveness. It was not an auspicious beginning for postwar diplomacy.

During the next few months, the Americans tried to develop an intelligible policy toward the USSR. Byrnes sent publisher Mark Ethridge and historian Cyril Black to the Balkans on a fact-finding mission. The Ethridge Report, submitted in December, recognized legitimate Soviet concerns in the region but emphasized the imperialistic nature of Moscow's postwar actions there. Simultaneously, the United States Congress approved a $3.5 billion loan to Britain, while Soviet requests for $6 billion in credits remained shelved. Byrnes decided to break the stalemate by proposing a December meeting of the Conference of Foreign Ministers in Moscow. Molotov accepted quickly, while the British, incensed that Byrnes had not consulted them, objected strongly but attended anyway.

In contrast to London, the Moscow Conference went smoothly, largely because the Balkan question was resolved in favor of the USSR. Romania and Bulgaria would add two non-Communists to their governments, in line with the Soviet interpretation of the Yalta provision for "free elections." Treaties for the Soviet satellites would be drafted at a forthcoming peace conference in Paris. Issues affecting Korea, China, and Japan were also settled, and the Soviets agreed to a joint American-British-Canadian proposal to establish a UN commission to control atomic energy. The sole item on which no agreement was reached concerned the withdrawal of British and Russian troops from Iran—a failure which would have serious consequences. But, on balance, Byrnes was well satisfied, and even Bevin was mildly appeased.

"TWO WORLDS" AND AN IRON CURTAIN

In Washington, however, Byrnes's superior held a different view. Harry Truman had given his secretary of state more discretionary authority than any other in living memory. Byrnes had responded by conducting diplomacy in great secrecy and arranging to present a radio report to the American people on the Moscow Conference without first briefing the president. He had decided against publishing the Ethridge Report before going to Moscow and had not even sent it to the president. Most importantly, his willingness to compromise at Moscow cut against the grain of current thinking in his own State Department and in the Oval Office. Truman, growing increasingly accustomed to his presidential authority, was becoming less tolerant of Byrnes's peccadilloes and less interested in compromising with what he considered unacceptable Soviet conduct in Eastern Europe.

On 5 January 1946, Truman met with Byrnes and made his position clear. Moscow's actions in the Balkans had turned Romania and Bulgaria into police states, and its pressure on Greece, Turkey, and Iran foreshadowed a wave of expansionism in the so-called Northern Tier. Byrnes's appeasement of Stalin at Moscow was not consistent with Truman's view of the interests of the United States, and those interests dictated a firmer American policy toward Moscow; as Truman put it, "I'm tired of babying the Soviets." Although this interview imparted a dramatic coloring to Truman's change of course, the actual change was far less striking. Truman, for all his vaunted decisiveness, had been vacillating since April 1945 between conciliation and confrontation with Moscow. In January 1946, in disgust with Soviet conduct in Eastern Europe, he came down on the side of confrontation; but he was a pragmatic politician who knew that changes of course were to be expected and were seldom permanent. America had not yet declared Cold War against the USSR.

One month after the Truman-Byrnes interview, however, it appeared that Stalin had issued his own declaration. In an election speech on 9 February to an assembly of voters in Moscow, he reasserted the validity of Marxist-Leninist thought, painted the contrast between capitalism and communism in vivid colors not used in official Soviet pronouncements since 1941, and declared that the world remained divided into two hostile camps, between which war was inevitable sooner or later. The Soviet people must prepare for conflict by tightening their belts yet further and emphasizing the development of heavy industry, as they had in the years before the German invasion.

Stalin's "two worlds" speech may not have been intended as a declaration of Cold War, but it was certainly taken that way in Washington—except by Supreme Court justice William O. Douglas, who saw it as a "declaration of World War III." One week later the Canadian government disclosed its roundup of a Soviet-sponsored atomic spy ring headed by Canadian scientist Alan Nunn May. Simultaneously, the Soviet government announced that it would not participate in the International Monetary Fund and the World Bank—a position which made sense to Soviet leaders fearful of capitalist penetration but which baffled Western analysts who knew that immense sums were needed to rebuild the USSR. Perplexed, the U.S. State Department solicited analyses of recent Soviet behavior from its resident experts, including George Kennan, then attached to the U.S. embassy in Moscow.

George Frost Kennan was a moody, introspective Wisconsin Presbyterian with a Princeton degree and nearly two decades of experience as a student of Russian affairs. Highly sensitive, mildly neurotic, and profoundly insightful, his gold-plated analytical abilities would now stamp him as the most influential American foreign service officer of the twentieth century. In reply to Washington's request for reflections on Soviet conduct, Kennan rose from a sickbed to compose an 8,000-word telegram which reached the State Department on 22 February 1946.

The "Long Telegram," as it came to be known, situated current Soviet behavior in a Russian mentality dating back centuries. Traditionally suspicious of foreigners and insecure in the face of Western technological superiority, the Russians had long since developed a neurotic outlook on the world (a condition with which Kennan had some personal familiarity). Soviet leaders clothed this world view in Marxist garments, but these were merely "fig leaves" designed to justify their reprehensible conduct toward their own citizens and their expansionist policies abroad. Stalin's 9 February speech was simply one more attempt to conceal Russian expansionism in the trappings of Marxist theory. Because these attitudes were so deeply rooted in Russian history, the Soviet government could not be reasoned with or mollified; only firm resistance backed by a willingness to use force could convince the Kremlin to back down.

Kennan had been saying these things for years. The Long Telegram became important only because Washington was finally ready to listen to such analysis. It transformed Kennan from an obscure foreign service officer into one of the country's top Soviet experts, but its effects on Truman and his advisors were far more significant. It satisfied their need for a conceptual framework that both explained Soviet conduct and offered a prescription for dealing with it. Within days, all of Washington was talking about it. On 27 February Republican senator Arthur Vandenberg, one of his party's foremost foreign policy spokesmen, denounced the USSR in a powerful speech in the Senate. The next day Byrnes took up the call for a firmer line toward Moscow in a speech dubbed by wags "The Second Vandenberg Concerto." Derived more from his 5 January discussion with Truman than from Kennan's writing, it nonetheless reinforced the impression the Long Telegram was making throughout the U.S. government.

Just ahead lay the most dramatic event of that turbulent winter. As the international tension increased, Winston Churchill, since 1945 leader of the Tory opposition to Clement Attlee's Labour government, came to America for a visit. Truman had arranged for him to give an address at Westminster College in Fulton, Missouri (Truman's home state), on 5 March. Churchill used the podium to deliver a ringing endorsement of joint Anglo-American action against the Soviet threat, depicting the situation in Eastern Europe in striking language:

> From Stettin in the Baltic to Trieste in the Adriatic, an iron curtain has descended across the Continent. Behind that line lie all the capitals of the ancient states of Central and Eastern Europe. Warsaw, Berlin, Prague, Vienna, Budapest, Belgrade, Bucharest, and Sofia, all these famous cities and the populations around them lie in what I must call the Soviet sphere. . . Whatever conclusions may be drawn from these facts—and facts they are—this is certainly not the Liberated Europe we fought to build up. Nor is it one which contains the essentials of permanent peace.

If Stalin's "two worlds" speech can be seen as a declaration of Cold War, it is difficult to view Churchill's "iron curtain" speech as anything less. As an opposition politician, he did not speak for the British government, but his stature as Britain's wartime leader lent an air of authority to anything he said. Stalin was shocked by the address, referring bitterly to the implicit racism of Churchill's call for an Anglo-American consortium against the Soviets and pointing out the British statesman's interwar endorsement of a *cordon sanitaire* around the USSR. The speech's impact was intensified by the fact that Truman sat on the platform behind Churchill, listening intently and nodding approvingly. The president later claimed that he had not read the address in advance, but this assertion may take its place in a long line of disingenuous remarks by a seasoned politico who knew exactly what he was doing.

Yet Truman himself had not denounced Soviet conduct. While Churchill and Stalin traded diatribes, he remained above the fray. When the American declaration of Cold War finally came, it would be couched not in terms of a confrontation between capitalism and communism, nor of the descent of an iron curtain, but of the need to forestall Soviet expansionist ambitions in the Northern Tier (Greece, Turkey, and Iran). Washington's conceptualization of Soviet intentions and actions was being influenced by the pragmatic, nonideological terminology of George Kennan's Long Telegram.

THE CONFRONTATION OVER IRAN

When British and Soviet troops ousted the pro-German Reza Shah Pahlavi and partitioned Iran between them in 1942, they signed a treaty pledging mutual withdrawal of their forces within six months after the end of the war (in the event, no later than 2 March 1946). London pulled out most of its troops by January, but Moscow stalled, demanding oil rights in northern Iran equivalent to those obtained by the British in the south. Simultaneously, the Soviets provoked an uprising by Azerbaijani separatists in the north. By 1 March, when the Soviet government announced that its soldiers would remain in Iran beyond the deadline, those forces were being augmented by additional tanks. Given Soviet behavior in Eastern Europe and recent Soviet pressure on Turkey, events in Iran appeared ominous. Churchill's iron curtain speech, delivered four days after the Soviet announcement, fell on eager ears.

Tehran responded by appealing to the Security Council of the United Nations in an effort to force the Soviets to comply with the treaty. Soviet ambassador Andrei Gromyko contended that the UN lacked jurisdiction over the matter and ostentatiously walked out of the deliberations. This gesture, conjuring up recollections of similar Japanese and German actions in the old League of Nations, sent a chill up Western spines and may have had a greater impact on public opinion in America and Britain than the crisis itself. On 6 March George Kennan delivered a stiff protest to Molotov, signaling that Washington would not remain indifferent to Soviet actions in Iran (Truman later claimed to have sent Stalin an ultimatum, but there is no evidence of this). The crisis deepened over the next fortnight, with widespread reports of Red Army troop movements within northern Iran in the directions of Tehran and Turkey. Washington kept the pressure on at the UN, refraining from bluster and threats, and making its position clear while leaving Stalin a face-saving way out if he wished to take it.

By 24 March he had decided to do just that. Moscow Radio announced troop withdrawals from Iran in accordance with what it termed an "agreement" between Moscow and Tehran. This was actually a unilateral Soviet decision to withdraw within six weeks while proposing a joint Soviet-Iranian oil company, which never came into being. The actual withdrawal was completed by 9 May, and the crisis ended with a significant diplomatic defeat for the Soviet Union. Stalin's decision appears to have been conditioned by an American response at once forceful and cautious. No threats concerning U.S. intervention in Iran were made, but Stalin was faced with the prospect of American action in areas of greater concern to him (such as Germany) if the crisis intensified. The Soviet withdrawal seemed to confirm the wisdom of the Long Telegram: If America stood up to the Russians, they would back down. But since Soviet hostility toward the West was rooted in centuries of Russian history, that hostility could not be expected to diminish, and the next crisis would not be long in coming.

THE GERMAN QUESTION REMAINS UNANSWERED

As the Iran confrontation was winding down, the Conference of Foreign Ministers was preparing to convene in Paris. Truman and Byrnes had decided to test Soviet intentions concerning Germany. In addition to the ongoing disputes over reparations and rehabilitation of the German economy, the lack of agreement as to the future status of Germany stiffened Soviet resolve to control Eastern Europe and intensified Western distrust of Moscow's ultimate intentions. Now Byrnes returned to an idea which he had floated informally at Potsdam and London: a four-power treaty guaranteeing the demilitarization of Germany for twenty-five years. While removing the greatest threat to Soviet security, such a pact would eliminate any justification for Soviet police-state tactics in Eastern Europe and would assure a long-term American military presence on the continent. It would, as Truman said, "call the Russians' bluff."

Molotov's reaction was noncommittal. Rather than demilitarization, he preferred to speak of immediate disarmament, a term by which he meant not only the liquidation of German military potential but reparations as well. The U.S. position was that reparations and recovery were incompatible. Byrnes concluded from this that Stalin was more interested in expansion than in security and began to think in terms of a permanent division of Germany. In June, he refused a Soviet offer to connect the opening of negotiations for a large American loan to discussions of the situation in Eastern Europe. One month later, the Americans and British began to combine their occupation zones into one economic unit, called by the slightly preposterous name of "Bizonia."

Finally, on 6 September, Byrnes delivered a major speech in Stuttgart to highlight the reversal of America's German policy. He assured the German people that U.S. occupation forces would remain in Germany as long as those of any other nation and explicitly posed the possibility that reunification might not occur. Roosevelt's wartime musings to the contrary, a permanent division of Germany had never become official U.S. policy. Now Truman, Byrnes, and the State Department factored Germany into their newly conceptualized view of Soviet expansionist tendencies and realized that a reunified Germany could fall under Russian domination, particularly since Moscow refused to consider zonal consolidation until its conditions were met. Washington deemed division of the country less objectionable than Soviet control, and "Bizonia" proved to be the first step down that road.

The Stuttgart speech was an important milestone in what was coming to be known as the Cold War. The term was first used in 1945 by the columnist Herbert Bayard Swope and later picked up by nationally syndicated columnist Walter Lippmann, who used it as the title of his 1947 book. Although the "war" was on, the United States, alone among the Big Three, had not yet declared it; and even after it was declared, there would still be time to draw back from committing to it irrevocably. But time was running out.

THE TRUMAN DOCTRINE

German issues dominated the headlines during the second half of 1946, but the Northern Tier, despite the solution of the Iranian crisis, continued to vex the allies-turned-adversaries. In August, Moscow had begun pressing Turkey for a Soviet military presence in the Dardanelles, the straits which controlled the access between the Mediterranean and the Black Sea. The United States, which in 1945 had been willing to consider increased Soviet influence in this area, now saw this as yet another Soviet expansionist threat and responded by sending a stern message to Moscow and warships to the region. In October, faced with American resolve, Stalin dropped his demands, lending further credence to the philosophy contained in the Long Telegram.

In Greece, however, the Communist insurgency which dated from 1944 intensified, backed surreptitiously by Marshal Tito of neighboring Yugoslavia. And, although it withdrew its Dardanelles claim, Moscow continued to suggest revisions in its borders with Turkey and to press for an agreement that would permit Soviet naval vessels unrestricted passage to and from the Black Sea.

All of this worried the British, who were increasingly preoccupied with brushfire insurgencies in their extensive empire on which the sun never set. They decided in early 1947 to cut their losses in areas they were unlikely to hold. India would be given its freedom and partitioned between Hindus and Muslims; the road to Mandalay would be turned over to an independent Burma; Palestine, after an excruciating moral and military struggle, would be partitioned between Jews and Palestinians. Most significantly for Washington, British economic and military assistance to Greece and Turkey could no longer be sustained in the face of a financial crisis so severe that portions of the British Empire were being liquidated. On 21 February, the first secretary

Harriman, Marshall, Truman, and Acheson, shown in a 1950
photo. (Abbie Rowe/Harry S Truman Library)

of the British embassy called upon Loy Henderson, director of the U.S. State
Department's Division of Near Eastern Affairs, and handed him two diplomatic notes.

The documents informed the United States that British aid to Greece
and Turkey would be terminated by 1 April 1947. Since it was a Friday afternoon and Secretary of State George Marshall (who had replaced Byrnes after
the 1946 congressional elections) was on his way to deliver an address at
Princeton University, Henderson took the notes to Undersecretary of State
Dean Acheson, who immediately began to work out the implications. With the
Dardanelles controversy still fresh in memory and with the Greek civil war
going badly for the anti-Communist forces, neither Acheson nor Henderson
were in any mood to temporize. By 24 February, they had worked out a

detailed plan for American assistance to Greece and Turkey and had submitted it for the consideration of Truman and Marshall.

Truman, Marshall, and Acheson made an unlikely trio. The president's lack of higher education never deterred him from surrounding himself with advisors who had enjoyed the intellectual stimulations he had lacked; his self-confidence shone through and enabled him to work with men of great ability without succumbing to either insecurity or defensiveness. He had named George Marshall secretary of state because he had lost confidence in Jimmy Byrnes and because his administration, slipping badly in public esteem after a crushing defeat in the 1946 congressional elections, needed an infusion of highly respected talent. Marshall was neither a genius nor a sage, but he had been America's leading soldier during the past war and had a reputation for unimpeachable integrity (a trait that Garibaldi would have deemed unacceptable in a diplomat). At State, he was fortunate enough to command the services of Dean Acheson, a tall, aristocratic Yalie with a bristling mustache, a caustic tongue, and a magnificently pragmatic and analytic mind. Acheson, who was intolerant of lesser minds (most of the human race) and who had an extremely low boring point, managed to irritate nearly everyone who knew him at one time or another. But he was unswervably loyal to Harry Truman, and that devotion, coupled with his considerable abilities, made his arrogance less insufferable—at least to the president. Together these three statesmen would declare Cold War on the Soviet Union and develop a plan for fighting it.

On 27 February, they met with congressional leaders to obtain an informal reading on their plan's prospects. Marshall presented the program in a straightforward, dry manner that left the legislators cold. In desperation, Acheson launched into a passionate declamation that compared the United States and USSR to Rome and Carthage. The choice, he said, was between freedom and bondage, between watching the Soviet tide roll over most of the world or taking prudent measures to stop it at once. America's security was at stake. Arthur Vandenberg broke the lengthy silence that followed Acheson's oration: if Truman articulated the problem in those terms, the Congress and the country would support him. Loy Henderson later recalled that Vandenberg was more direct: "Mr. President, the only way you are ever going to get this is to make a speech and scare the hell out of the country."

Truman did precisely that on 12 March. His style was uninspiring, but his message was forceful and provocative: the United States, which in the last war had become "the great arsenal of democracy," must now assume the financial burden of defending democracy throughout the world. Aid to Greece and Turkey cleared Congress in April by margins of two to one, and by the spring of 1949, the U.S.-backed Greek government had defeated the communist insurgency. Kennan was apprehensive about the universal scope of what became known as the Truman Doctrine, but neither Truman, Acheson, nor Marshall ever intended to commit the United States as cosmically as the speech implied. They knew that America had finite resources and that some requests for aid might be insincere efforts to milk Uncle Sam. In the next few years, they refused to dispute the communist coup in Czechoslovakia and limited the aid provided to Nationalist China. The Truman Doctrine was a response to a perceived threat of Soviet expansion in Europe and the Middle East; as such, it was more limited in scope than Truman seemed to indicate on 12 March 1947.

It was also, of course, the American declaration of Cold War. Truman had bided his time while Stalin and Churchill traded jibes in 1946, but now he would wait no longer. The German question still defied solution; the Eastern European nations were clearly within the Soviet orbit; the Northern Tier, despite Anglo-American diplomatic victories in Iran and the Dardanelles, remained threatened. It was time to pick up the gauntlet that Stalin had thrown down, to block the Communists and defend the West. Those kinds of decisions came easily to Harry Truman.

THE MARSHALL PLAN AND EUROPEAN RECOVERY

Truman's speech recognized no limits on American aid, but George Marshall focused the president's attention on Europe following his return from the Moscow Conference of Foreign Ministers (10 March–24 April). There he had spoken extensively with Stalin and learned that the Soviet leader believed that the final collapse of the European capitalist economies was at hand. Stalin had been predicting this ever since the war's end, but the terrible winter of 1946–1947 and the failure of Britain, France, and Italy to rebound from the war's devastation lent new authority to his words. American diplomats openly predicted that Communists were likely to win free elections in France and Italy in 1948 if economic conditions did not improve. Back in Washington, Marshall formed a Policy Planning Staff at the State Department and charged it with developing policies to counter Soviet expansion. At its head he placed George Kennan, author of the Long Telegram.

On 28 April Defense Secretary Forrestal, who had recommended Kennan for the job, came up with something for him to do. At lunch with Marshall, Forrestal observed that the Soviets were counting on economic despair to turn Europeans toward communism. The United States, the richest nation on earth, had the wherewithal in goods, food, and money to forestall this looming tragedy. All that was lacking was the will to act and a plan to act on. Marshall turned the matter over to the Policy Planning Staff and requested a solution within ten days—a tall order for a pensive intellectual with a new job, no office, and no staff. Kennan, awed by Marshall's command yet instinctively aware of his chance to make history, assembled the most talented Europeanists available and worked them round-the-clock. A week later the solution was ready.

No one person created the Marshall Plan; the idea, a logical outcome of the Truman Doctrine, had been bandied about within a select circle for weeks.

Kennan "simply" put it into appropriate form. He and his staff concluded that its emphasis should be pro-European rather than anti-Communist: the money would come from Washington, but the blueprints for its use would come from the countries themselves. Combining altruistic humanitarianism with enlightened self-interest, it would preserve in Western Europe both political freedom and the "open door" for U.S. commerce. Truman bought the concept, and Acheson disclosed it in a speech at Delta State Teachers College in Cleveland, Mississippi, on 8 May. Officially named the "European Recovery Program," it would, at Truman's insistence, be known popularly as the "Marshall Plan" (since Truman was disliked in the Republican-controlled Congress which would have to pass the requisite legislation, whereas Marshall's prestige transcended party loyalty).

Accordingly, the secretary of state announced the program formally in a commencement address at Harvard University on 5 June. Marshall's oratorical abilities compared unfavorably to those of a man reading a telephone directory line by line, and since commencement speeches are generally tolerated rather than listened to, his announcement received indifferent coverage in the press. Intriguingly, it was an open-ended invitation to all European countries, including the USSR and the nations in its sphere. Kennan advised Marshall to gamble on Soviet rejection, contending that communist nations who opened their doors to U.S. trade (and their books to American auditors, as the plan implied) would effectively be relinquishing control over their economies and thus paving the way for political freedom and the dissolution of the Soviet bloc. Luckily for Kennan the advice proved correct, since Soviet acceptance would have wrecked any chance that Congress would approve the plan. Washington did, however, hold out the hope that some Eastern European nations would enter the program and thereby loosen their ties with Moscow.

On 26 June 1947, representatives of seventeen European nations gathered at Paris for a series of meetings designed to lay the groundwork for the Marshall Plan. Molotov participated but soon withdrew following the rejection of his proposal that each nation should determine its own recovery needs and notify the United States accordingly. Washington insisted on its right to require extensive economic information in return for receipt of aid, and this Moscow would not accept. Molotov left the discussions on 2 July; shortly thereafter, the Soviets announced the creation of the "Molotov Plan" for the economic recovery of Eastern Europe and the USSR. Czechoslovakia and Poland, which had indicated strong interest in American aid, then announced that they would join the Molotov Plan instead. The remaining Western European nations went on to request $17 billion in American aid over a period of four years.

For the Soviets, the Marshall Plan was very dangerous. Not only did it threaten their grip on Eastern Europe, but also it fostered German economic recovery as the basis for a strong Europe, thus raising the specter of a renewed German threat to Soviet security. Stalin responded in September by creating the Communist Information Bureau (Cominform), a mechanism by which he could keep foreign communist parties in line with Moscow's directives. The wave of strikes which swept over France and Italy that autumn was orchestrated by the Cominform and seriously damaged the appeal of Stalinism in the nations of Western Europe.

For those nations, of course, the Marshall Plan was, as Ernest Bevin put it, "a lifeline to a sinking man." The devastated economies of "war-torn Europe" could now begin to rebuild. Not everyone was happy about German participation: French premier Georges Bidault begged Marshall to make haste slowly with respect to German revitalization, or else the French government would lose a confidence vote in the Chamber of Deputies before it could implement the plan! Even the United States Congress approached this matter with trepidation. Marshall himself had to lay it on the line: "The restoration of Europe involves the restoration of Germany. Without a revival of German production there can be no revival of Europe's economy. But we must be very careful to see that a revived Germany cannot again threaten the European community."

For the United States, secure for the moment in its nuclear monopoly, German restoration posed no threat. For Western Europe, desperate for capital and facing the genuine prospect of communist victories at the polls in 1948, the risk had to be run. But in the context of the intensifying Cold War, the reactions of Stalin, Bidault, and many members of the United States Congress to the rebuilding of Germany illuminate starkly the fateful effects of the failure of the Big Three to come to grips with the German question. In future years, there would be freezes and thaws in the Cold War, but there would be no hope for real peace until that question was answered.

CONTAINMENT: THE X-ARTICLE

Neither the USSR nor its adversaries expected an answer to the German question in the near future. But for the moment, neither side was anxious to escalate the Cold War. Moscow used the rest of 1947 to shore up its own position, implementing the Molotov Plan, consolidating its hold on Eastern Europe through the Cominform, proceeding at top speed with its nuclear weapons program, and clamping down on domestic dissent through the activities of Andrei Zhdanov, one of Stalin's closest associates. Zhdanov's address at the Cominform meeting in Warsaw on 22 September reiterated many of the points made in Stalin's "two worlds" speech of February 1946. The "Zhdanovshchina," which swept over Russia between September 1947 and Zhdanov's sudden death in July 1948, was characterized by suppression of any deviation from the Party's world view. One of its most prominent victims was the eminent Soviet economist Evgenii Varga, humbled and eclipsed because of his contention that the final crisis of capitalism was far away and that hopes for the quick collapse of Western economies were misplaced.

In Washington, a similar kind of "shoring up" had already begun, although America's own "Zhdanovshchina" of loyalty oaths, committee hearings, spectacular trials, and unsubstantiable McCarthyite accusations was still a few years away. What happened in the summer of 1947 was far more sedate and, in the long run, far more significant. Before becoming leader of the Policy Planning Staff, George Kennan had lectured at the National War College (a consequence of his authorship of the Long Telegram). In the fall of 1946, he had been one of several professors asked by Secretary of Defense Forrestal to comment on an internal working paper by Edward Willett linking Soviet objectives to Marxist-Leninist principles. Kennan, who felt that Willett overstated the degree of American military expenditure necessary to "contain" Russian expansion, disagreed with the working paper and was promptly asked to write one of his own. The result was a paper entitled "Psychological Background of Soviet Foreign Policy," which went through several drafts before its completion in January 1947.

Kennan had never intended the paper to be anything more than a sounding board for discussion within the Navy Department. But after he gave a well-received lecture to the Russian Study Group of the Council on Foreign Relations in January 1947, he was asked by the editor of the council's high-profile journal, *Foreign Affairs*, to submit for publication an article reflecting his views. Since his paper was already written and contained no classified information, he asked the State Department for authorization to publish it. He received permission but was forbidden to use his own name. He therefore signed the article with an "X" and sent it in. It appeared in *Foreign Affairs* in July 1947 under the title "The Sources of Soviet Conduct," just as Kennan arrived in Paris to attend the Marshall Plan meetings.

The X-Article, as it came to be known, turned out to be the most widely discussed publication of the century in the field of international relations. *Foreign Affairs* actually reprinted the article in July 1987 on the fortieth anniversary of its original publication. Its notoriety was not attributable to any mystery surrounding its author; columnist Arthur Krock had been given a copy of the original working paper by Forrestal and disclosed Kennan's identity in his column in the *New York Times*. Indeed, the views expressed in the article were so clearly Kennan's that the use of "X" was futile. The article's importance stemmed rather from the fact that it represented the first public use of the term "containment" as a recommendation for American policy toward the USSR.

Consistent with his presentation in the Long Telegram, Kennan argued that no variations in U.S. policy could convince the Soviets to trust Washington's intentions. Traditional Russian suspicion of the West, augmented by Marxist-Leninist dogma, was too strong for that. What could and should be done was to realize that Soviet expansion could be "contained by the adroit and vigilant application of counterforce at a series of constantly shifting geographical and political points." Once confronted, the Soviets would back off and apply pressure elsewhere. If they were opposed successfully at every turn, the inability of Marxism to defeat capitalism would place tremendous strains upon the Soviet system, leading either to its self-destruction from internal pressures or to its gradual transformation into a more benign force in international relations.

Kennan was not calling for military confrontation throughout the world, although columnist Walter Lippmann accused him of doing just that. Rather, he proposed a series of political, economic, and diplomatic confrontations, with the use of military force only as a last resort. Given his fears that the Truman Doctrine would lead to unwise American commitments to shaky and insincere regimes, beyond the scope of U.S. military power, he could hardly have argued otherwise. Yet the X-Article, coming so soon after the Truman Doctrine and appearing simultaneously with the Marshall Plan, was widely viewed as the logical blueprint for America's overall approach to the Cold War. The European Recovery Program, indeed, was immediately classified by nearly everyone as the first practical application of the containment theory—an interpretation which perplexed Marshall, who had never read the X-Article and was surprised to see it in print.

In 1946, Kennan's Long Telegram had arrived in Washington at precisely the moment when its arguments would fall on receptive ears. Now, in the summer of 1947, the X-Article's appearance provided a coherent rationale for actions which would have been taken by the Truman administration in any case. To maximize the article's impact yet further, events during the next several months intensified the Cold War and rendered Kennan's "blueprint" even more necessary to policymakers. On 29 October, Belgium, the Netherlands, and Luxembourg (the "Benelux" nations) built upon their Marshall Plan foundations by announcing plans to form a customs union—the embryonic stage of what would become the European Common Market. One month later, the London Conference of Foreign Ministers deadlocked over reparations and once again failed to resolve the German question.

Thus, as 1947 drew to a close, the battle lines had been drawn and the strategies set in place that would dominate Cold War policy for the next four decades. Hostility between the Soviet Union and the West, of course, was nothing new. What was unusual, and disturbing, was the increasingly confrontational tone adopted by both sides as they moved incrementally toward a showdown over Germany. By early 1948, no one doubted the Cold War's reality, but how long it would remain cold was by no means certain. Without a resolution of the German question, a third world war loomed as a real possibility.

5

The Battle for Germany, 1948–1952

Beginning in 1948, the Cold War took on a far more ominous character than it had hitherto acquired. Prior to this time, as relations between wartime allies had deteriorated, the international atmosphere had become charged with diplomatic declarations and denunciations, as each side maneuvered for power and position within its own sphere. Europe had been divided into Eastern and Western zones, separated by what Churchill had called the iron curtain. There had been threats and bluffs aplenty, but there had been no direct military confrontations between the superpowers and relatively little bloodshed.

All that was destined to change. The next few years would bring a Middle East war, the Berlin Blockade, the formation of NATO, the first Soviet A-bomb, the communist takeover of China, and the outbreak of a brutal conflict in Korea. Only a few years after the end of history's bloodiest war, the world had once again become a very dangerous place.

THE CRISES OF EARLY 1948

The first half of 1948 witnessed a series of confrontations and conflicts that served to heighten anxieties, exacerbate tensions, and intensify the crisis atmosphere that pervaded international affairs. In February, the communist coup in Prague consolidated Soviet control over Czechoslovakia, the last hope for neutrality and democracy in Eastern Europe, thus angering the West and causing fleeting fears of war. That same month an international conference discussing navigational rights on the Danube River established a governing commission limited to states bordering the river itself. This excluded Britain, France, and the United States, but since the USSR and its Eastern European clients were in the majority, their proposal was adopted. The West, which had consistently outvoted the Soviet Union in the United Nations and other international committees, now received a dose of its own medicine.

Ironically, the consolidation of Soviet control over Eastern Europe helped to expedite the formation of an anti-Soviet military alliance in the West. Influenced by February's developments, Britain and France, along with the Benelux nations (Belgium, Netherlands, and Luxembourg), completed their negotiations and signed the Treaty of Brussels on 17 March. An explicitly military convention, it created a fifty-year alliance providing for social, economic, and military cooperation in the event of armed attack on any of the signatories. It did not identify a likely enemy, since both Germany and the Soviet Union were considered potential threats. The five participants established a consultative council to oversee implementation of the treaty, and the council immediately instituted a standing military committee based in London. Contained therein were the seeds of the North Atlantic Treaty Organization that would be created the following year.

A few months later a war broke out in the Middle East, precipitated by the formation of a Jewish state in Palestine. This had been the main goal of the Zionist movement, a worldwide alliance of Jewish nationalists, founded in the 1890s, which had fostered Jewish settlement in the Arab lands that had once been Biblical Israel. During World War I, as the British had moved into the Middle East, they had issued the "Balfour Declaration," asserting their willingness to create in Palestine a "national home for the Jewish people." Once Britain had gained a League of Nations mandate over this area, however, its interest in Jewish settlement had waned, until Hitler's persecutions had brought the plight of the Jews back to center stage. In 1945, following full public disclosure of the Holocaust, Zionists had demanded permission for 100,000 European Jewish refugees to enter Palestine. In deference to the Arab population, however, the British had refused and had soon found themselves the targets of a Zionist guerrilla war. Frustrated, they had referred the matter to the UN, which in November 1947 had voted to partition Palestine into Jewish and Arab states. Arab irregulars continued the struggle, but by 14 May 1948, the Jews had emerged victorious and proclaimed the State of Israel.

Declarations of war soon followed from Egypt, Syria, Lebanon, Transjordan, and Iraq, but their poorly trained and shabbily equipped forces were no match for the Jews. Israel won handily and expanded its territories beyond those allocated by the United Nations. Nearly one million Palestinian Arabs became refugees, and a huge reservoir of resentment was created throughout the Arab world.

Ironically, the USSR and the United States found themselves on the same side of this question, and both quickly recognized the new Jewish state.

The Soviets supported Zionism, not out of affection for the Jews, but out of a desire to embarrass the British and expand their own influence in the region. In the United States, despite some sympathy for the anti-Soviet Arabs and some interest in Mideast oil, there was strong compassion for the Jewish people in light of the Nazi genocide. Still, the hatred and dislocation engendered among Arabs by the formation of Israel was destined to provide fertile soil for Cold War confrontations in the not-too-distant future.

To further complicate the international anxiety, in June of 1948 Stalin provoked his showdown with Tito. Yugoslavia was expelled from the Cominform, Soviet advisors were withdrawn, and Moscow initiated an economic boycott of the Balkan nation. By this time, however, the world's attention was focused, not on the war in the Middle East or the crisis in Yugoslavia, but on the momentous confrontation between the Soviet Union and the United States over the city of Berlin.

THE BLOCKADE OF BERLIN

The years between 1945 and 1948 had witnessed a gradual hardening of the Allied zones of occupation in Germany into what was coming to be viewed as a permanent division of that country. In 1946 the Communist and Socialist parties in the Soviet zone had merged to form the Socialist Unity party (SED), a development which helped to consolidate communist control in the eastern part of Germany. Britain and America had ended industrial shipments to the USSR, agreed to revive the economy of western Germany, and created "Bizonia" by merging their two zones of occupation in December 1946. The French, fearing the implications for German reunification, had at first refused to permit their zone to join, but as the Cold War intensified, their position weakened. In 1947, in order to receive Marshall Plan aid, France was forced to abandon most of its 1945 objectives. Integration of the French zone with Bizonia would not be far off.

By 1948, the West was ready to consolidate its portion of Germany without further consideration of Soviet views. The London Conference of Foreign Ministers in December 1947 had ended with harsh words and utter failure to make progress on the German problem. Moscow then initiated a final effort to prevent Western construction of a separate German state. On 20 March 1948, Soviet delegates walked out of the Allied Control Council for Germany, charging the West with undermining four-power administration of the country. Twelve days later the Red Army began obstructing traffic between Berlin and the Western occupation zones.

Berlin was an unlikely locale for the first major showdown of the Cold War. Like the country as a whole, the German capital had been divided into zones of occupation in 1945, even though it was located in the heart of Soviet-occupied eastern Germany (see Map 2, p. 53). The concept of a divided city enclosed totally within a single zone of occupation was nonsensical and was never intended as anything more than a temporary expedient. The United States Army, which might have captured it in 1945 before the Red Army arrived, declined the opportunity; since the city bore no military significance, and since it was scheduled to be divided anyway, the Americans were only too willing to let the Russians spend the lives necessary to take it. Because it was expected that U.S. troops would be withdrawn from Germany within a few years, and since the zonal divisions were temporary anyway, the question of Western access to the city did not arise until Secretary of State Byrnes made his 1946 Stuttgart speech promising that U.S. forces would stay in Germany as long as the Red Army did. By that time it was too late to rectify the situation, and West Berlin became a permanent hostage, ninety miles behind Soviet lines. Scene of hundreds of spy thrillers and countless real-life intrigues, it would gradually become the quintessential Cold War city, brooding, gray, and heartbreakingly divided—a depressing miniature of a divided Europe and a divided world. But in 1948, it became a major piece in a very dangerous chess game between the Soviet Union and the United States.

Certainly, Stalin viewed Western actions in early 1948 with alarm. Despite the fact that all three former members of the Grand Alliance had issued declarations of Cold War, no significant confrontation had yet occurred. But the Western decision to proceed independently toward the construction of a West German state threatened the Soviet objective of a permanently weakened Germany. Pressure on Berlin, obviously the most vulnerable spot in the Western position, might force the occupying forces to withdraw. In such circumstances, the West would be humiliated, and the creation of a West German state might be indefinitely postponed.

It was, of course, risky business. But Stalin had run risks throughout his life, and this must have seemed reasonably safe. He probably knew that most Western military analysts considered West Berlin untenable in the face of Soviet pressure, and that in the event of a conventional war in Central Europe, the Red Army held most of the logistical and numerical trump cards. America was largely demobilized and could not defend western Germany, let alone West Berlin, against a determined Soviet offensive. The Americans, of course, still monopolized the atomic bomb, but thirty months after Hiroshima and Nagasaki, they had made no move to use it against the Great Socialist Motherland. Would they use it to defend Berlin? Why? Which targets would they bomb, and how would they deliver the bombs? Could they be certain that B-29s would not be shot down by Soviet defenses? All in all, it didn't look like a particularly dangerous gamble.

So Stalin made his move, and the Cold War finally blossomed into outright confrontation. March, April, and May were filled with foreboding, as the Soviets demanded to examine freight and passengers on Western trains making the run to and from Berlin. On 1 June the United States, Britain, France, and the Benelux nations reached a six-power accord on Germany, involving a French decision to join their zone to Bizonia and the drafting of a federal constitution for the three combined sectors. On 18 June the West announced the abolition of all occupation currencies in West Germany and West Berlin, with a new currency called the deutsche mark replacing them. This removed a major obstacle to rapid German economic recovery. The Soviets responded by setting up their own East zone currency on 23 June, and on the following day, they cut off all road and rail access to West Berlin. The Berlin Blockade had begun.

The British and French, who were skeptical of both the value of West Berlin and the Western ability to run the Russian blockade, deferred to the United States. Counsels in Washington were divided. The American military commander in Germany, General Lucius Clay, suggested that a column of armor and infantry be sent toward Berlin with instructions to fight its way through. He was convinced that the Soviets would back down. But Truman, Marshall, Acheson, and most of official Washington were less sanguine about the prospects. Cutting bridges before and behind the column would strand it in hostile territory and make America look ridiculous. Truman on 29 June announced that the United States would remain in Berlin, and news was leaked that sixty B-29s were being hurriedly dispatched to England. It gave the Soviets pause, but it didn't invalidate Stalin's reasoning concerning the likelihood of atomic war. If he called Truman's bluff, the Americans would have to fold: the planes were not configured to carry atomic weapons, their fuel capacity was insufficient to make round trips over Soviet territory, and since the *entire* American atomic arsenal consisted of fewer than fifty bombs, the deployment of sixty bombers would have been laughable had not the stakes been so high.

After several days, it became apparent that the blockade was just that—a blockade, and not the prelude to a military strike. Now a solution presented itself. If West Berlin could be supplied by air, the Red Air Force would have to risk war by shooting down American planes in order to maintain the blockade. Since there were three airfields (Tempelhof, Tegel, and Gatow) in West Berlin, it was theoretically possible to fly in enough food and medicine to keep the city alive. Coal would be a more difficult challenge (early experiments with dropping coal by parachute resulted in substantial air pollution and large quantities of soot on the faces and uniforms of air force observers), but by the fall of 1948, even that was flown in, as C-47 transports landed in Berlin at a rate of one every three minutes. They flew in three carefully limited air corridors from Hamburg, Hanover, and Frankfurt, and Soviet air defenses let them through.

Stalin insisted that his price for calling off the blockade was a reasonable one: agreement by the West to abandon efforts to create a West German state. But he had little leverage. The Soviet effort to starve women and children made the Americans look like heroes. Russian conventional superiority could interdict American land forces, but Stalin was not prepared to go to war in the air. Leaving aside the issue of atomic weapons, he remembered the results achieved by American and British airpower just prior to the Normandy invasion, as well as the massive American conventional bombing of Japan in

The Berlin Airlift (Bettman)

1945. Unwilling to authorize the shooting down of American planes, he was forced to let the crisis drag on. As month followed month, it became obvious that his gamble had failed.

THE FORMATION OF NATO AND THE GERMAN FEDERAL REPUBLIC

Stalin's blockade did nothing to retard Western progress toward the creation of a West German state; if anything, it accelerated the process. It also provided the motivation necessary to encourage Western nations to put aside their differences and conclude a peacetime military alliance directed against the Soviet Union. This was the North Atlantic Treaty Organization (NATO), organized in Washington on 4 April 1949. The twelve nations of the alliance (Britain, France, Belgium, the Netherlands, Luxembourg, Italy, Portugal, Denmark, Iceland, Norway, the United States, and Canada) agreed to provide mutual assistance against any aggression occurring in the North Atlantic area and to collaborate closely in matters affecting strategic planning, arms

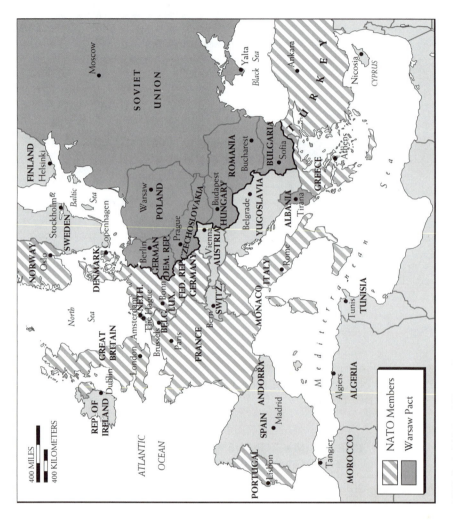

MAP 3 Cold War Alliance Systems

production, and military training. It was unprecedented for the American government to conclude alliances with European powers in peacetime, and its decision to do so here underscores the severity of the Soviet threat as seen from Washington.

Headquartered in Paris, NATO's first commander was U.S. general Dwight D. Eisenhower. On 20 December 1950, the signatories of the Brussels Treaty (the Western European Union) agreed to merge their military establishment with that of NATO. Moscow responded with categorical denials of any intention to invade Western Europe but with no comparable alliance until the formation of the Warsaw Pact in 1955.

By early 1949, Stalin was ready to acknowledge that the Berlin Blockade had failed. On 19 March, a constituent assembly in the Soviet occupation zone approved a draft constitution for a separate East German state. The following month saw the signing of an Occupation Statute for West Germany by all three Western occupying powers. The statute reserved considerable powers to the occupying authorities, but West Germans gained extensive autonomy. Dismantling of West German industries virtually ceased, and many restrictions on German industrial activities were removed. The Basic Law of the German Federal Republic was promulgated on 8 May, the fourth anniversary of Germany's surrender. It attempted to duplicate the democratic provisions of the old Weimar Constitution while avoiding repetition of that document's defects. The German Federal Republic, popularly known as West Germany, was officially proclaimed on 23 May, with its capital at Bonn.

Eleven days earlier, on 12 May 1949, the Berlin Blockade quietly ended. Like many subsequent Cold War confrontations, it proved to be counterproductive in that it helped to assure the completion of the very actions it was designed to prevent. In August, the Christian Democratic Union won the first West German elections; its leader, Konrad Adenauer (one of the few living anti-Nazi politicians who had served in a prominent position before Hitler's takeover), became federal chancellor on 15 September. On that same day, the last of the trials of former Nazi officials for war crimes ended in Nuremberg. Germany (at least the western portions) was clearly being transformed from an enemy into an ally of Washington. On 15 December the new state received its first allotment of Marshall Plan aid. The official establishment of the German Democratic Republic (East Germany) on 7 October completed the formal division of Germany into two separate states.

THE ADVENT OF THE ATOMIC ARMS RACE

In early September of 1949, as East and West Germany were consolidating their separate statehood, and as Communists were moving rapidly toward victory in the Chinese Civil War (Chapter 6), an American aircraft detected increased levels of radioactivity over the northern Pacific. Within the next week, further such evidence corroborated the fact that one of the West's worst

The mushroom cloud characteristic of atomic blasts became a familiar and ominous image during the nuclear arms race. (United States Air Force)

nightmares had been realized. Sometime in late August, years sooner than Western leaders had expected, the USSR had conducted a successful test of its first atomic weapon. Before long, both sides would be working on hydrogen bombs, thousands of times more powerful than the earliest atomic devices. The American monopoly had ended, and the nuclear arms race was on.

From the very dawn of the atomic age, it had been apparent that nuclear weapons posed a potential threat far greater than any weapon that had hitherto been invented. It seemed obvious that the United States, as possessor of such arms, would have an incalculable advantage in any military exchange with a potential adversary who was not so equipped. This, in turn, had made it all but inevitable that other nations would seek to obtain this same technology. Indeed, since 1945 a team of Soviet scientists led by Igor Kurchatov had been secretly working on just such a project.

From 1945 until 1949, as the sole possessor of atomic weapons, the United States had enjoyed a tremendous advantage in military potential and diplomatic leverage. But its options had by no means been unlimited. For one thing, while the United States and its allies demobilized, the Soviets had kept significant military forces under arms, leaving them with a substantial superiority in conventional forces. For another thing, there was little doubt that sooner or later they were bound to develop a nuclear capability of their own. Finally, the terrifying power of the atomic bomb, and the indiscriminate nature of devastation it caused, placed very real moral and political constraints upon its use by the United States.

Conscious of all these factors, then, and sensitive to world opinion, the Americans had sought to devise a policy which would simultaneously internationalize atomic energy, forestall Soviet acquisition of atomic weapons, and prevent a nuclear arms race. Their vehicle was the United Nations Atomic Energy Commission, an agency established in 1946 to monitor the development of nuclear technologies and ensure their peaceful use. In June of 1946, Bernard Baruch, the U.S. representative to this commission, had put forth a proposal to place all fissionable materials under international control, to set up an inspection system to make sure that all nations complied, and eventually to destroy all existing atomic weapons. This was, on its face, a very generous proposal, for the United States seemed to be offering to forgo possession of its most powerful and effective weapons.

The Baruch Plan, however, had been unacceptable to Moscow. It would have precluded the development of Soviet nuclear weapons, allowed foreign inspectors broad rights of investigation and intrusion into the closed Soviet society, and left the Americans with a permanent monopoly on the technological know-how of producing atomic weapons. It would not have required the United States to destroy its nuclear stockpile until after a system of strict controls and sanctions, enforced by an agency whose actions were not to be subject to any nation's veto, had been put into effect. Furthermore, as the Soviets knew through the work of a secret agent, Washington was secretly collaborating with London in efforts to gain control of the known sources of uranium and thorium and thus effectively monopolize atomic energy. Given all this, it is hardly surprising that the Soviets rejected the plan.

The following year, Soviet representative Andrei Gromyko had put forth his own proposal, based on Moscow's perception of how disarmament should proceed. The Gromyko Plan had called for the destruction of all existing nuclear stockpiles, followed by the implementation of a monitoring system based on periodic inspections of declared weapons facilities. It had no provisions for punishing violations or for unannounced visits to undeclared facilities. The United States, fearful that such a plan would allow the USSR to proceed secretly with its nuclear program, and unwilling to relinquish its nuclear advantage without an ironclad guarantee of Soviet compliance, would have none of this.

The positions staked out by the Baruch and Gromyko plans set the tone for the next several decades of arms control negotiations. To some extent, both the American and Soviet positions were designed as much for public consumption as they were for negotiation, with each side putting forth proposals it expected the other to reject. The United States, fearful that the Soviets would "cheat," was unwilling to enter any agreement that did not provide adequate safeguards to ensure that both sides complied or to cut back its weapons production until such safeguards were in place. And the USSR, with its penchant for secrecy and its fear of revealing its strengths and weaknesses to its enemies, was loath to let any outsiders inspect either its arms plants or its military installations.

The Soviet atomic blast in August 1949 destroyed any hope of preventing a nuclear arms race, at least for the time being. The Soviet nuclear program was obviously much further along than most Western experts expected, and Moscow clearly had no intention of abandoning its efforts to catch up with the West. And, as the Soviets began building their own atomic stockpile, the Americans abandoned any thought of agreeing to dismantle theirs. In matters of national security, each side preferred to rely on its own devices rather than international agreements, and neither side was anxious to grant the other access to its facilities. The nuclear arms race was fated to become the most frightening and ominous aspect of the Cold War, transmitting to that conflict an importance far beyond the policy goals of the leaders of East and West. At the same time, by making all-out war increasingly unthinkable, these horrific weapons would serve to place serious constraints upon the options and exploits of these leaders.

WEST GERMANY'S ROLE IN A STABLE EUROPE

Meanwhile, as the West tried to come to grips with the reality of an adversary armed with nuclear weapons, Moscow was confronted with the increasing consummation of one of its own most hellish nightmares. A strong German state, politically democratic and economically dynamic, was beginning to arise out of the ashes of war-torn western Germany.

West Germany became such a success story that it is difficult to remember how unlikely that success seemed in 1949. Democracy, after all, had never been the German way. The failure of the Weimar Republic, still fresh in the minds of most, argued against high expectations for the Federal Republic. Books like A. J. P. Taylor's *The Course of German History* (1945) asserted that Germans had a psychological predilection for authoritarian rule; less scholarly works claimed that they were genetically incapable of self-government. Brave indeed were the leaders who were prepared to stake their reputations on the survivability of German democracy.

Many factors combined to assure that, as a popular saying put it, "Bonn is not Weimar." Marshall Plan aid, managed skillfully by Finance Minister Ludwig

Erhard, rebuilt the German economy and made possible the *Wirtschaftswunder* (economic miracle), a fifteen-year period of full employment, geometric increases in the gross national product, and unprecedented prosperity. Soviet hostility from the Berlin Blockade through the building of the Berlin Wall in 1961 (Chapter 10) united West Germans behind their government.

Equally important was the role played by Adenauer, a crusty, cynical survivor of the concentration camp at Buchenwald who guided the Federal Republic through its first fourteen years. As early as 1919, he had advocated separating the Rhineland from Germany and had envisaged future Franco-German economic cooperation. Nicknamed "Der Alte" (the Old Man), he blended a passionate commitment to democracy with a paternalistic, authoritarian style which many Germans found reassuring. His personification of democratic virtues, combined with his systematic reiteration of the necessity of eventual German reunification (despite his personal misgivings on the subject), provided an indispensable transition between despotism and self-government. By the time he retired at the age of 87 in 1963, the survival of democracy in West Germany was no longer in doubt.

The new nation quickly involved itself with the flourishing movement toward greater unity in Western Europe. French foreign minister Robert Schuman and French Marshall Plan director Jean Monnet proposed in May 1950 the Schuman Plan, designed to integrate the coal and steel industries of the West. One year later it became the European Coal and Steel Community (ECSC), as six nations signed a treaty at Paris: France, Italy, the Benelux nations, and . . . West Germany! Schuman, Monnet, and Adenauer wanted to connect the German and French coal and steel industries so closely that war between the two nations would become not only unthinkable but economically impossible. France's reasons were obvious: with West Germany growing in strength and with Britain preparing to withdraw from the continent, Paris had no choice but to seek some sort of détente with Bonn. Adenauer was equally interested, seeing the French as a valuable counterweight to the USSR. His eagerness to cooperate with Paris, coupled with his assurances that West Germany would never seek to renew Germany's longstanding claims to Alsace and Lorraine, laid the foundations for the astonishing improvement in Franco-German relations that flourished in the 1960s.

German economic recovery, which the ECSC could only abet, was something with which the French could live and even prosper. German rearmament was a different story. Shortly after the outbreak of the Korean War (Chapter 7), Washington, fearing a Soviet plan to divert U.S. forces from Korea by causing trouble in Europe, pushed strongly for the creation of a West German military force. French prime minister René Pleven, hoping to scuttle the idea before it took hold, offered a counterproposal in October 1950: the Pleven Plan, calling for the creation of a multinational European army, composed of small contingents from each nation, as an adjunct to ECSC. Adenauer signed on, hopeful that this European Defense Community

(EDC) would, if successful, render further Allied occupation of West Germany superfluous.

The Pleven Plan, despite its eventual failure, reveals some interesting things about the Cold War attitudes of Paris, London, and Bonn. On 27 May 1952, the EDC Treaties were signed at Paris by the six signatories of the ECSC. Britain signed an additional protocol pledging to send assistance to any EDC member attacked by any nonsignatory, and both Washington and London swore to consider threats to the EDC as threats to their own security. But the French National Assembly held up ratification, and with Stalin's death and the end of the Korean War in 1953, the need for EDC appeared less urgent. By the summer of 1954, the French defeat in Indochina (Chapter 11) convinced the French army, beaten twice in fourteen years, that to surrender sovereignty over part of its forces would be dishonorable—a sentiment that found considerable support in the French Assembly, which after five years of relations with Adenauer was less concerned with a resurgent Germany than with the dangers of delegating sovereignty to a supranational body. As if these were not sufficient nails in EDC's coffin, Britain's consistent refusal to become a direct signatory to the agreement (in keeping with London's fidelity to isolation from the continent), not to mention the lack of any organized political body to control a multinational army, gave the assembly a multitude of pretexts for rejecting France's own proposal in August 1954. The USSR was delighted with what appeared to be a spoke in the wheel of the drive for German rearmament; yet EDC's failure was only the prelude to the admission of West Germany to NATO in 1955, a result which was not at all to Moscow's taste. The German question continued to defy settlement while refusing to go away.

STALIN AND THE GERMAN PROBLEM

After the failure of the Berlin Blockade, Soviet policy toward Germany proceeded along three tracks simultaneously. The first track involved the abandonment of the policy of plunder which Moscow had followed in its zone since 1945. Dismantling had never been particularly lucrative: entire German factories, cut into numbered sections and shipped east, sat rusting for months on rail sidings as the Soviet bureaucracy proved incapable of allocating and utilizing them. Now it stopped altogether, as Moscow became more interested in rebuilding rather than further destroying the German Democratic Republic, its new client state. If the existence of two Germanies could not be prevented, prudence seemed to dictate that one of them should be strengthened for incorporation into the Soviet system of buffer states.

Track two led through Eastern Europe, as the process of bringing the Soviet satellites into line intensified. By mid-1948, Poland, Czechoslovakia, Hungary, Romania, and Bulgaria were safely within the Russian orbit, while Yugoslavia remained just as safely outside it. As long as any chance existed that the Grand Alliance might yet serve some purpose, Stalin had shown a flexible willingness to tolerate noncommunist governments—provided that it could be demonstrated that they would maintain friendly relations with Moscow. But with the West revitalizing and unifying its zones of Germany, deviation from orthodox communism was no longer a viable option. Stalin spent his remaining years in an effort to ensure strict adherence to his wishes through a series of brutal purges and show trials.

Hungary felt the pinch first with the arrest of Joszef Cardinal Mindszenty in December 1948 following the refusal of the Hungarian Catholic Church to make concessions to the government. Tried for conspiracy and sentenced to life imprisonment, Mindszenty found refuge in the American legation in Budapest, where he became an international symbol of resistance to communism until he was permitted to emigrate to the United States in 1971. Similar charges of conspiracy were leveled against Hungarian foreign minister László Rajk in June 1949; his conviction was the signal for a wholesale purge of dissident Communists. That same month, Bulgarian deputy premier Traicho Kostov was arrested and charged with ideological deviation and high treason. With ten of his associates, he was executed in December.

For two years, possibly because Stalin was distracted by the Korean War, Eastern Europe lay quiet. When another round of purges began in 1952, the targets were predominantly Jewish. The vicious anti-Semitism that characterized Stalin's final year resulted in the liquidation of the Jewish intellectual elite of the communist parties of Czechoslovakia, Hungary, and Romania. First to fall was Ana Pauker, one of the principal architects of the communist takeover of Romania, purged from the Politburo and Central Committee secretariat in May 1952. That November the former general secretary of the Czechoslovak Communist party, Rudolf Slánský, was tried with thirteen other party leaders (nearly all Jewish) on charges of treason, espionage, and sabotage. Three were sentenced to life imprisonment; the others, including Slánský, were hanged and cremated. Their ashes were poured into the ruts of a dirt road outside Prague.

Two months later, Stalin announced the discovery of the "Doctors' Plot," involving an alleged conspiracy of a number of Jewish physicians in the Soviet Union to undermine the health of leading Soviet government and Party officials. Shortly thereafter, more than thirty Jewish leaders of the Hungarian Communist party were purged. There is no telling where all this would have stopped had not Stalin died of a stroke in March 1953. The Eastern European purges terrorized communist bureaucrats and politicians while cowing them into submission to every directive from Moscow, no matter how trivial its nature. Without question, Stalin's second track succeeded (at least according to his own standards): it provided him with a terrified but unquestioningly loyal Eastern European leadership, ready to serve on the front lines against a reinvigorated and newly dangerous Germany.

Stalin's third and final track targeted Germany itself. In September 1950, with the Korean War (for the time being) running in favor of the United

States, a meeting of Eastern European foreign ministers convened in Prague to discuss the dangers of German remilitarization. On 19 September, a Western communiqué had implied that West Germany would soon be contributing directly to Western defense. This conference issued the Prague proposals: German remilitarization should be forbidden, a unified German state should be constructed without delay, and all occupation forces should be withdrawn within one year of the signing of a German peace treaty. East and West Germany would have equal voice on a council charged with creating a new constitution for the entire country. Apparently, Moscow was prepared to make concessions, even to the extent of giving up its complete control over East Germany, in order to prevent West German rearmament.

The Prague proposals went nowhere. The Truman administration, having come under withering domestic political fire because of Yalta and its own previous willingness to negotiate with the Soviets, was unwilling to rise to Stalin's bait in the midst of the Korean War. Even had Washington been more responsive, there is no guarantee that such negotiations would have succeeded. By its warlike posture and belligerent language, Moscow had been able to consolidate its hold on Eastern Europe while concealing the extent of its military inferiority vis-à-vis the West. But that same conduct had encouraged the West to create a military alliance against Soviet expansion. Stalin, knowing that he had no intention of invading Western Europe (and assuming that Washington must know this as well), probably interpreted NATO as a mechanism designed to roll back Soviet gains in Eastern Europe. Truman, knowing that he had no intention of invading Eastern Europe (and assuming that Moscow must know this as well), saw Soviet opposition to NATO as designed to weaken and subvert Western Europe in preparation for either a military or a peaceful takeover. And so it went: each side was concerned with not only the *intentions* but the *capabilities* of the other. Intentions, of course, could always change, sometimes with devastating speed. It was prudent to presume that they would and to defend against capabilities.

Because of these suspicions, it was impossible in 1950 for the two sides to sit down and negotiate the key issue that divided them and divided Europe: the German problem. Moscow could not convince Washington that it was seriously alarmed about Western actions and wanted meaningful talks; Washington could not convince Moscow that it was seriously alarmed about Soviet intentions—and even if such assurances were believable, the Americans had by 1950 decided that a separate, rearmed Germany was preferable to a unified, neutralized one, given the degree of tension existing between the two armed camps in Europe.

These conditions also destroyed Stalin's final third-track initiative on the German question, launched on 10 March 1952. With the EDC Treaty almost ready for signature and a West German army seemingly about to spring out of the paving stones of Bonn, Molotov dispatched a note proposing four-power talks on German unification. This démarche went beyond the Prague proposals by declaring that as long as a unified Germany was neutral, Moscow would be willing to permit it to rearm. The note astonished Washington, which rejected it two weeks later, unwilling to jeopardize the fragile EDC in exchange for lengthy, acrimonious, and (in Washington's opinion) probably fruitless negotiations with the Soviets. Once again, nothing came of the initiative.

Was Stalin serious? Would he have surrendered control over East Germany in exchange for a neutralized, unified state? Adam Ulam believes that the danger of a large German army pointed eastward at a time before the USSR had been able to stockpile many atomic weapons was enough to force Stalin to make serious concessions. He points out that any German elections, whether supervised by the United Nations (as Washington expected) or by the four occupying powers (as Moscow wished), would inevitably have led to a noncommunist government. Even if all the East Germans had voted Communist, the West had 75 percent of the population—and the Communist share of the vote there had never reached 10 percent. It is, of course, possible that the Soviet action was a carefully orchestrated bluff, designed to derail EDC while bogging the West down in interminable German peace talks. But Washington's rapid rejection, understandable though it may have been, scuttled any chance of finding out. Although they could not say so publicly, Western leaders were uncomfortable with any prospect of a unified Germany, particularly a neutralized one, since this would deprive them of the advantages conferred by possession of the industrialized, densely populated western sector. Stalin's calling of their bluff could scarcely have been welcome. Even had they been willing to discuss the matter, a decision to sit down with Stalin would have been hazardous. With McCarthyism blackening the reputations of men as upright as George Marshall, and with a presidential election only eight months away, the prospect of direct talks with the USSR would have frightened any American politician. It would, as Ulam says, be nearly another decade before an American president could say, "Let us never negotiate out of fear, but let us never fear to negotiate."

THE PERSISTENCE OF THE GERMAN PROBLEM

Stalin's three tracks led not to a roundhouse in Berlin but to dimly lit sidings in the remote countryside of Cold War Europe. When he died in March 1953, the face of postwar Europe had been, in essence, fixed for the next thirty-five years. Eastern Europe was firmly within the Soviet camp, with the exception of Yugoslavia (with which Stalin's successors would bury the hatchet in 1955) and tiny Albania (whose alignment with China against the USSR in the 1960s was more humorous than dangerous). Marshall Plan aid had enabled Western Europe to rebuild its economies, and NATO provided it with a Cold War military shield against perceived Soviet ambitions and genuine Soviet capabilities. The legacy of bitterness and distrust between Washington and Moscow was so great that future efforts at détente would be halting, tentative, and unsatisfying. In the midst of it all stood Germany, the only nation (after Austrian reunification in 1955) divided by the iron curtain, a country of barbed wire, watchtowers, guard dogs, minefields, and armies poised to spring across heavily defended borders in defense of the status quo. As the world's attention wandered to Cold War disputes in Asia and the disruptions posed by the triumph of communism in China, every nation's leadership kept one eye focused on Germany. The German problem had still not been solved, and as long as it persisted, there would be no end to the Cold War.

6

The Communist Revolution in China, 1946–1950

As we have seen, both in its roots and in its origins, the Cold War was primarily a European phenomenon. It is not surprising, then, that conflicts in Europe dominated the first few years of the struggle and shaped the perceptions and policies of both sides. By the summer of 1949, however, a state of relative equilibrium had been achieved in Europe. The Soviets had consolidated their control over Eastern Europe, and the West had neither the will nor the inclination to challenge this hegemony. But further Soviet gains had effectively been blocked, while the Truman Doctrine, Marshall Plan, Berlin Airlift, and North Atlantic Treaty had seemed to restore both the initiative and the confidence of the West.

The illusion of Western success, however, was soon shattered by the news of momentous developments in Asia. On 1 October 1949, Chinese communist leader Mao Zedong proclaimed in Beijing the formation of a new socialist state called the People's Republic of China. The communist victory in the Chinese Civil War, and the establishment of a dynamic and militant socialist regime in the world's most populous nation, gave an enormous boost to the communist cause and set off shock waves of fear and alarm which reverberated throughout the Western world.

THE NATIONALISTS AND THE COMMUNISTS

For several decades prior to 1949, the forces of communism in China had been engaged in a bitter struggle with the Nationalist government of Chiang

Kai-shek (Jiang Jieshi). Throughout this struggle, at various points and in various ways, the Communists had received advice and assistance from the Soviet Union, while the Nationalists had been aided and supported by the United States. Neither superpower, however, had been fully or consistently engaged, and both were somewhat ambivalent about their Chinese clients.

The National People's Party, or Kuomintang (Guomindong), had been founded by Dr. Sun Yat-Sen in 1912, following the collapse of the last Chinese dynasty in the preceding year. Dedicated to the principles of nationalism and democracy, its fortunes had fluctuated during its early years, as China disintegrated into a chaotic assortment of autonomous territories ruled by competing warlords. By the 1920s, however, it had emerged as the leading force in the struggle to reunite China. The Soviets, anxious to align themselves with this national unification effort, sent agents to China in 1923 to help Sun reorganize and strengthen his movement. Sun's disciple, Chiang Kai-shek, was sent to Moscow to learn Soviet military techniques; he returned to create a Kuomintang (KMT) army with the assistance of Soviet advisors. Sun himself died in 1925, but Chiang went on to lead his new army on the Great Northern Expedition of 1926–1928, conquering some of the warlords and negotiating agreements with others. By 1928, China had been unified under the new Nationalist government, with its capital at Nanking (Nanjing).

Born into a petty noble family, Chiang Kai-shek had chosen a military career, and he remained essentially a military man throughout his political life. Surrounded by Western advisors, converted to Methodist Christianity, and married to an American-educated Chinese woman whose brother was a wealthy industrialist, Chiang at first seemed to represent a progressive, Westernizing, democratic trend. But the inflexible determination and ruthless militarism that had helped him unify his country did not serve him as well once he became its leader. Distrustful of the masses and uncomfortable with democracy, he soon turned his government into a repressive single-party dictatorship characterized by corrupt opportunism and reliance on military force.

Meanwhile, in 1921, a group of Marxist intellectuals had founded the Chinese Communist party (CCP), hoping to initiate a Bolshevik-style revolution in China. Assisted by Soviet agents, they had also joined the Communist International, or "Comintern," the Soviet-dominated organization designed to foster the spread of communism throughout the world. In 1923, on Comintern orders, the fledgling CCP allied itself with the KMT, actually joining the latter organization. This arrangement seemed to make sense: after all, from a Marxist-Leninist perspective, the Communists were natural allies of newly emerging nationalist groups in their struggle against Western imperialism.

The KMT-CCP alliance, however, was not destined to last. Alarmed by the growing strength of the CCP, and fearful that the Soviets were merely using him to pave the way for a communist takeover, Chiang turned against his erstwhile allies in 1926 and 1927. In 1926, he staged a *coup* in Canton (Guangzhou), arresting some of his Soviet advisors and removing many CCP leaders. The following year, with the tacit support of the Western capitalists, he unleashed a reign of terror in Shanghai, using local gangs to slaughter thousands of Communists. Moscow, having invested its hopes in the KMT, insisted that the CCP should maintain the alliance in spite of Chiang's persecution. This callous Soviet pragmatism, which would manifest itself repeatedly in the course of the next several decades, created a legacy of resentment and distrust on the part of the Chinese Communists toward their Soviet mentors. Chiang, meanwhile, showed no signs of conciliation: in 1931, once he had consolidated his control over most of China, he launched a series of "extermination campaigns" designed to rid his country of the communist presence once and for all.

It was in this period that the CCP, devastated and decimated, acquired a new leader and a new philosophy. Mao Zedong, who came from a peasant family in south central China, had developed both a belief in the untapped potential of the Chinese peasantry and an attraction to the Marxist notions of mass mobilization and class struggle. As an early member of the CCP, he did organizational work among the urban proletariat in Shanghai, but finding it frustrating and uninspiring, he returned in 1925 to his native Hunan province to work among the peasants. There he found that the local farmers were already forming associations, creating paramilitary organizations, and displaying a revolutionary mentality. He became convinced that, contrary to orthodox Marxist expectations, it was indeed possible to organize a socialist revolution that was based on and relied on the peasants. This conviction, combined with his dynamic leadership skills, his driving and restless intellect, and his unshakable faith in his own ability to transform society by organizing and educating the masses, would make him the dominant figure in twentieth-century China.

With the assistance and advice of a group of Soviet advisors, Mao and his comrades set up in south central China a "Soviet Republic," complete with its own laws, institutions, and even a primitive army. On four occasions from 1931 through 1933, they fought off Chiang's extermination campaigns, but a fifth campaign was so massive and well organized that they could not hope to survive it. In desperation, in October of 1934, the beleaguered Communists abandoned their territorial base, broke through the Nationalist blockade, and began a perilous yearlong flight with the KMT army in hot pursuit. This was the fabled Long March, one of the century's most colorful and heroic epic adventures. In October 1935, after 6,000 miles of constant danger and struggle, the vestiges of Mao's forces finally made it to the relative safety of Yenan, a town in northwestern China. There, shielded by the distance and terrain, they proceeded to regroup and reorganize, setting up a simple, egalitarian society among the sturdy rustic souls of this primitive, arid, and inhospitable region.

Although Chiang remained determined to crush the Communists, and in fact sent periodic bombing raids against Yenan, the looming war with Japan proved to be an inescapable distraction. Having forcibly annexed the northeastern Chinese province of Manchuria in 1931, the Japanese military had expanded its operations and increased its provocative belligerence. Chiang's decision to ignore the Japanese and focus on the Communists dismayed his own forces, and in December of 1936, some of them kidnapped the Nationalist leader and compelled him to form a "united front" for struggle against Japan. Under instructions from Moscow, the CCP agreed to join, and by 1937, when the conflict with Japan became an all-out war, the KMT and CCP were once again linked as "allies."

During the next eight years, despite their formal alliance, the KMT and CCP waged separate wars against Japan and struggles against each other. The Communists proved more effective: With their talent for organizing the peasants, and their experience at using guerrilla tactics to stave off Chiang's superior forces, they were better equipped to mount a serious resistance. Expanding across northern China and even into the Yangtze Valley, they became a painful thorn in the side of the Japanese invaders and occupiers. Their bravery and dedication, combined with the flexible reform policies invoked by the party leadership, helped them also to expand their support among the peasant masses.

Meanwhile the KMT army, committed to conventional warfare, was proving to be no match for the forces of imperial Japan. The Nationalist government, forced to flee from its power base by the Japanese conquest of eastern China, survived only by moving its headquarters deep in the interior to Chungking (Chongqing). Riddled with corruption and incompetence, it managed further to alienate the peasants by subjecting them to grain requisitions and forced labor. The United States, after joining the war in 1941, found itself increasingly ambivalent about its Nationalist allies. To Americans on the scene, Chiang appeared as a petty fascist dictator who was misgoverning his people, undermining the war effort, and squandering American aid. But to the U.S. public, and to his many supporters in the West, he was still the heroic leader of "Free China" in its struggles against Japanese militarism and Marxist-Leninist socialism.

Neither the Communists nor the Nationalists, it turned out, were able to win the war. Japan was defeated, not by the Chinese resistance, but by the gross overextension of its own forces and by the massive resources and devastatingly destructive technology of the United States of America. The Americans, therefore, had every reason to expect that they would play a leading role in determining the future of postwar China. But the Soviet Union, which joined the war against Japan only in its final stage, was also determined to play a role. As a result, the ongoing conflict between the Chinese Nationalists and Communists soon became part and parcel of the emerging Cold War struggles in East Asia.

AMERICAN ATTEMPTS AT MEDIATION

The Japanese surrender in August 1945 did not bring peace to China. As soon as the world war ended, in fact, civil war was in the air. For all intents and pur-

Mao Zedong (left) exchanging a toast with Chiang Kai-Shek during their negotiations in Chungking, August-October 1945. (Jack Wilkes/Life Magazine, Time Warner, Inc.)

poses, the "united front" between the KMT and the CCP had been a hollow façade since 1941, when Nationalist troops had ambushed and attacked the headquarters unit of the Communist New Fourth Army. By 1945, both sides had begun to gird and position themselves for a renewal of their hostilities once the foreign invader was gone. The actual conflict was delayed, however, by the maneuvering of the superpowers, neither one of which had a very firm grasp on the situation in China.

The Americans, largely ignorant of both the independent strength of the CCP and the strained nature of its relationship with Moscow, were anxious above all to prevent a civil war. Such a war, they feared, might give the Soviets a chance to extend their influence over communist-controlled territory in northern China, much as they were bringing eastern Europe under their control. The United States, therefore, labored mightily to create a coalition government, trying to preserve the "united front" that had long since ceased to exist. At the same time, however, the Americans gave continued aid and support to their wartime ally, the Nationalist government, which was seeking to crush the Communists and reassert its control over all of China.

Dependent as they were on American aid, the Nationalists had little choice but to play along with the "coalition" charade, even though their overriding goal was to destroy the CCP. General Patrick J. Hurley, the special U.S. emissary in China, arranged a series of face-to-face negotiations between Chiang and Mao in Chungking from August to October of 1945. For public consumption, the leaders agreed in principle to combine their forces and cooperate in support of human rights and representative government. Seldom have words meant less. Indeed, even as the negotiations went on, both sides were actively scrambling for territorial control in northern and northeastern China.

The Nationalists, with American support, at first seemed to gain the upper hand. At the behest of the United States, Japanese forces were ordered to surrender to the KMT army everywhere in China except in Manchuria, which had been designated at Yalta as a Soviet zone of operations. American transport ships and planes moved Nationalist troops quickly into China's major cities, and U.S. Marines were sent to northeastern China to help prevent Communist expansion in that area. When the CCP forces attempted to extend their control across northern China, the KMT leadership simply ordered the Japanese troops still there to forcibly resist them—an effective ploy, perhaps, but a public relations nightmare. Before long, using such tactics, the Nationalists had gained nominal control over most of China and effective control of almost all its cities and railways. The KMT army was three times as large as that of the CCP and, thanks to the United States, it was far better equipped. From all appearances, Chiang Kai-shek was once again emerging as the master of China.

But appearances proved deceptive. The Nationalists, relying as always on military force, had little real support among the Chinese people. Indeed, by using the hated Japanese to fight off the Communists, and by rampant profiteering in the reoccupied cities, they managed to forfeit whatever prestige they had accrued as the nominal victors in the war against Japan. By failing to carry out a meaningful land reform program, moreover, they left open the village gates to the CCP, which had worked so assiduously to earn peasant trust. And the Communists, despite their apparent weakness, were by no means without resources. Having mobilized the northern Chinese countryside against the Japanese, they had established a series of bases there from which they could operate effectively. Having fought Japan more convincingly than the KMT, and having implemented land and social reforms in the areas they controlled, they had won the allegiance of the local peasants. Furthermore, the Soviet occupation of Manchuria was providing them with a chance to move into that area and would eventually give them access to large amounts of weapons and supplies left behind by the Japanese.

The Soviets, however, were no more in touch with Chinese reality than were their American adversaries. Stalin, who neither fully understood nor fully trusted the CCP, seems to have habitually underestimated its potential strength. Ever the cautious pragmatist, he sought simultaneously to assist the Chinese Communists and remain on good terms with Chiang Kai-shek. In August of 1945, following through on an agreement made at Yalta, he even went so far as to conclude a Treaty of Friendship and Alliance with the Nationalist government, which ironically gave Moscow a certain stake in the survival of Chiang's regime. Nonetheless, during their actual occupation of Manchuria, Soviet troops gave aid to the CCP, allowing its forces to take control of certain positions and help themselves to Japanese equipment. But when American-assisted KMT forces defeated the Communists in south Manchuria late in 1945, Stalin once again urged the CCP to collaborate with the KMT. The communist reversals in Manchuria apparently convinced him that military confrontation was counterproductive and that Soviet interests would best be served by CCP-KMT cooperation. With Chiang's acquiescence, then, the Soviets extended their stay in Manchuria, withdrawing their last soldiers in May of 1946. From that point on, during the course of the ensuing civil war, they provided precious little aid or support to their Chinese communist comrades.

The United States, meanwhile, had not given up on its efforts to arrange for a coalition government in China. General George C. Marshall, wartime chief of staff of the U.S. Army, was sent to China in December of 1945 to arrange a truce between the CCP and the KMT. His mission, which lasted over a year, was not a happy one. Using the promise of U.S. aid, coupled with the threat of its withdrawal, he was able to get the Nationalists to agree to a cease-fire early in 1946. The Communists went along, if for no other reason than to buy time, but efforts to create a workable coalition made little headway. The CCP wanted a share of real power, and Chiang, ever fearful of communist subversion, was unwilling to grant them that. U.S. policy vacillated between even-handed mediation and support for the KMT, but in trying to have it both ways the Americans succeeded at neither. Continued American assistance to the Nationalists undermined Marshall's credibility with the CCP, and his belated embargo on arms shipments to Chiang had little real impact on the negotiations. By mid-spring, in fact, the truce had broken down, and by autumn of 1946, a full-fledged civil war was raging in Manchuria. In January of 1947, when Marshall returned to Washington to become secretary of state, it was obvious his mission had failed.

THE CHINESE CIVIL WAR

The Nationalists once again gained the apparent advantage in the early stages of the renewed civil war. Sweeping across northern China in 1946, the KMT army captured the major cities, controlled the railway lines, and even conquered Yenan, the longtime CCP headquarters. Communist leaders were forced to flee, and their sympathizers in the countryside were brutally rooted out by Nationalist soldiers and landlords. Deprived of its main bases, and scattered throughout the countryside, the CCP seemed to have been dealt a staggering and crippling blow.

But the communist defeat was less serious than it seemed. As experienced guerrilla warriors, the CCP forces had long since learned to retreat in good order and avoid direct confrontation when the odds were against them. And, having treated the peasants well when they were in control, the Communists could subsequently count on widespread popular allegiance. The Nationalists controlled the cities and railways, it is true, but these were almost like islands and bridges in the midst of a hostile sea. The KMT was little more than an occupying force, much as the Japanese had been, in most of northern China.

Besides, during the nine months of Soviet occupation, the CCP had managed to set up a new power base in Manchuria. There, as in northern China, they cultivated the peasant masses, carried out meaningful reforms, and organized the countryside for struggle on their behalf. There, for the first time, they could equip their troops with modern weapons, thanks to the unintended largess left behind by the Japanese. There, if the Nationalists would accommodate them, they were willing to make their stand.

By 1947, then, the battle for Manchuria had emerged as the central struggle of the Chinese Civil War. Perceiving his chance to destroy the CCP, Chiang committed his best troops to the Manchurian theater, ignoring the danger inherent in overextending his forces and fighting the Communists on their own turf. Under the skillful leadership of General Lin Biao, the CCP's "People's Liberation Army" retreated into the northeastern part of the province, avoiding direct combat and forcing the KMT army to extend its lines. Then, in July, they began a stunning counterattack, launching a series of raids which divided the Nationalist forces. Chiang, who had little trust in either the local Manchurian authorities or his own military commanders, insisted on calling all the shots from a distance. He refused to allow a retreat while there was still time, and as a result large elements of his army were trapped in the cities they had so recently occupied. Although the battle for Manchuria raged on until the fall of 1948, by the end of 1947 it was clear that the Communists were gaining the upper hand.

The Manchurian debacle surprised the United States, and American policymakers soon concluded that the Nationalist government was no longer capable of winning the civil war. Quite wrongly, however, they also assumed that the Communists could not win either, due to the size of Chiang's forces and the superiority of his equipment. Washington, therefore, braced itself for a protracted struggle which might lead to the division of China into communist and Nationalist entities. Preoccupied with Europe, the Truman administration was unprepared and unwilling to commit U.S. forces and massive

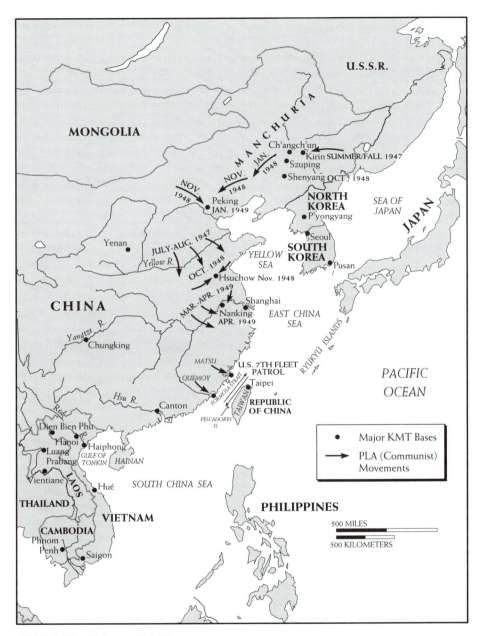

MAP 4 The Chinese Civil War

resources to Chiang Kai-shek's defense. But neither was it willing to abandon him entirely and face charges of "sellout" from the American "China Lobby." So the United States continued to send aid, pouring in good money after bad, with a fading hope that things would somehow work out for the best.

The Soviet leadership, ironically, was no more perceptive or prescient than the American policymakers. Rather than urging the Chinese Communists to follow up their victories, Moscow instead advised them to be cautious and to consolidate their position in Manchuria before attempting to move on. Soviet assistance to the CCP remained minimal at best, and Soviet relations with the Nationalist government continued unimpaired. As late as the summer of 1948, as they confronted each other in Germany over the status of West Berlin, neither superpower expected that the collapse of Chiang's government was imminent.

But imminent it was. By November of 1948, the Communists had conquered Manchuria, winning a smashing and decisive victory that changed the momentum of the civil war and shifted the strategic balance. The CCP not only showed that it could defeat the best KMT forces, it also captured from them large amounts of American-supplied equipment. Nationalist morale declined, while that of the Communists soared, to the extent that some KMT troops barely put up a fight, while others began defecting to the communist side. Meanwhile, during that same year, the Nationalist government had initiated an ill-conceived currency reform that accelerated the rampant inflation to such an extent that its money became virtually worthless. This, in turn, robbed Chiang of his support among the urban middle classes and capitalists, destroying the last remnants of his political base.

As the battle lines moved south, CCP soldiers received aid and sustenance from the peasantry, which was effectively mobilized by the party leaders to hamper the KMT. In October and November, a massive battle developed near the Huai River in the area north of Nanking. The Battle of Huai-hai, as it came to be known, pitted about half a million communist troops against a similar number of Nationalist soldiers. But hundreds of thousands of peasants aided the CCP, digging miles of tank traps to stop the KMT armored units. Chiang Kai-shek took personal command of his own troops but was unable to stave off defeat: When the dust had settled, the Nationalists had lost over 200,000 soldiers and had been cut off from contact with their units further north. By the end of the year, Beijing (then called Beiping) was surrounded by communist soldiers; in January of 1949, its KMT commander surrendered without a fight. The once and future capital of China had fallen into communist hands.

By early 1949, then, the Nationalists were in disarray. Their support had evaporated, their troops were being defeated, and their confidence was gone. Two decades of corruption, incompetence, oppression, and disaster had taken a heavy toll. Chiang himself temporarily "retired," in hopes that a new leader could strike a deal with the CCP, but this effort came to naught. The

Communists, now that victory was within their grasp, had no incentive to bargain. Although they were no less authoritarian and brutal than the Nationalists, they were better organized, better led, more idealistic, less corrupt, and more tuned in to the people's needs and concerns. In an earlier era, it might have been said that the "Mandate of Heaven" had passed to Mao Zedong.

THE COMMUNIST VICTORY AND ITS IMPACT

The capture of Beijing by communist forces at the start of 1949, coming on the heels of decisive CCP victories in Manchuria and Huai-hai, made it clear to the world that the Nationalists were on the run. By the end of April, communist troops had crossed the Yangtze River and captured Nanking, the Nationalist capital. The following month they seized the great port city of Shanghai. The KMT leaders moved south to Canton, where they set up a temporary headquarters, but by October they were forced to flee even from there. By May of 1950, when the fighting finally ceased, the Communists were in control of most of mainland China.

The Nationalists, meanwhile, had fled to Taiwan (also known in the West as "Formosa"), a large island located about 100 miles off the southeast China coast. Here, protected by the distance, and eventually by the U.S. Seventh Fleet, Chiang and his followers would regroup and reform. The communist victory was thus less than complete: based on Taiwan, the Nationalist government would continue to exist, and continue to press its claim as the legitimate government of China, throughout the Cold War era.

The communist victory was momentous nonetheless. In October of 1949, when Mao Zedong proclaimed the formation of the People's Republic of China, his new government could claim authority over more than half a billion people, one-fifth of all the human beings on the planet. Within just a few years, it seemed, the communist tide had swept over Eastern Europe and much of eastern Asia. From the Baltic to the Pacific, from the Arctic Ocean to the South China Sea, a vast land mass encompassing one-third of all humanity was now under communist rule. "The East is Red," proclaimed the Chinese Communists, and those words seemed to resonate ominously throughout the Western world.

The Chinese communist victory was a major defeat for the United States, and a serious political setback for the Truman administration. It came hard on the heels of reports that, in August 1949, the Soviets had exploded their first atomic device—years ahead of Western expectations. It also corresponded in time with the establishment of a separate, communist-dominated government in East Germany. Although the U.S. State Department issued a self-justifying "White Paper," defending its policies in China and exposing the corruption and incompetence of Chiang's regime, it also tended to portray Mao as a Soviet agent and Chinese communism as an extension of Moscow's reach. Before long, the administration was being blamed for "losing" China, and a "Red

Republican Senator Joseph McCarthy of Wisconsin.
(UPI/Bettmann)

scare" of epic proportions was sweeping the United States. In January 1950, a State Department official named Alger Hiss was convicted of perjury, in connection with charges that he had spied for the Soviets. The following month, Senator Joseph McCarthy of Wisconsin leveled accusations of "communist conspiracy" at the U.S. government itself, charging that over 200 known Soviet agents were at work in the Department of State. In this atmosphere, the Truman administration had little choice but to publicly redouble its efforts to counter the communist threat, especially in East Asia. Official recognition of communist China, which in normal circumstances would have been almost automatic, was delayed and eventually denied, while the United States used its leverage to ensure that the Nationalists on Taiwan, and not the "Reds" on the mainland, would continue to represent China in the United Nations.

Ironically, one of the main beneficiaries of Chinese communist success was Japan, the recently defeated enemy of America, China, and the USSR. In 1945, as the occupying power in Japan, the United States had embarked on a policy designed to demilitarize that country, destroy its war-fighting potential, decentralize its industry, and break up its military-industrial combines. American policymakers hoped and intended that Japan would be replaced as the central force in East Asia by a revived and refortified Nationalist China. But by 1947, these hopes had dissipated, and the United States was casting about for a new strategic approach. Japan, the erstwhile adversary, soon became an important partner in the anticommunist struggle and a key element in the U.S. "defensive perimeter." As a result, the Americans began to focus on the reindustrialization of Japan, abandoning their efforts to decentralize its economy, and helping to transform the island nation into a bastion of industrial capitalism in the western Pacific. By 1950, in an astonishing turn of events, Japan was on its way to becoming a crucial American ally, while China had become a bitter, implacable foe.

STALIN AND COMMUNIST CHINA

Meanwhile, the policies of the new Chinese government were doing little to mollify American and Western fears. In the wake of their victory, Mao and his comrades began to transform China by pursuing a radical program of socialist reform. Emulating the Soviet model, they set up parallel institutions in the government and Communist party and installed party leaders as the dominant figures in the state bureaucracy, the military, the trade unions, and the police. Non-Communists were included, but their effective power was limited. In the cities, the people were mobilized by mass campaigns directed against merchants, manufacturers, and the remnants of the Kuomintang. In the countryside, an extensive land reform program was initiated, complete with a "class struggle" against the former landlords. "Enemies of the people" were identified and persecuted, while a program of "thought reform" was instituted to modify the attitudes and behaviors of people who had been "contaminated" by the former regime. This latter process, often referred to as "brainwashing," helped create in the West an image of a regime that was even more fiercely totalitarian than Stalin's Soviet state. When Mao praised Stalin, and concluded a Treaty of Friendship and Alliance with the Soviet Union early in 1950, the worst fears of the Western world seemed to have been realized.

Curiously, the celebrating in Moscow was much more subdued than the Western wailing and hand wringing would seem to have warranted. Stalin, in fact, was clearly less than thrilled by the dramatic turn of events that had brought the Chinese Communists to power. He had, after all, established a solid working relationship with the Nationalists and had received important concessions in Manchuria from Chiang Kai-shek's regime. And Mao, despite

his outward show of allegiance to the aging Soviet leader, represented a potential rival for leadership of the communist world. Although the CCP, mindful
of its need for assistance from Moscow, had joined in the denunciation of Tito
when he quit the Soviet camp, the memories of the Yugoslav debacle were too
fresh in Stalin's mind for him to be entirely comfortable with any communist
leader who was independent of Moscow's control.

During 1949, then, as the CCP carried out its triumphal march to power,
Stalin maintained a posture of virtual neutrality. He chose not to recognize
Mao's regime, either when it occupied Beijing in January or when it captured
Nanking in April. Indeed, although many foreign envoys chose to stay in
Nanking, the Soviet ambassador followed the Kuomintang to its new headquarters in Canton. Only in October, once the People's Republic was formally declared, did the USSR officially recognize the new Chinese regime. By this
time, it had finally become clear to Stalin that the United States was not going
to rescue Chiang and that China's future was in the hands of Mao Zedong.

Even then, when Mao arrived in Moscow to negotiate a new treaty in
December of 1949, he was welcomed with something less than open arms. The
Chinese communist leader was greeted upon arrival by Foreign Minister
Molotov rather than Stalin himself, was referred to in the newspapers as "Mr.
Mao" rather than "Comrade Mao," and was treated more as a supplicant than
as a heroic partner. The negotiations were difficult, and it was not until
February of 1950 that an agreement was reached, thanks largely to the efforts
of China's new prime minister, the adroit and astute Zhou Enlai. The Soviets
agreed to provide limited credits and aid to their new allies and eventually to
return the railway and seaport concessions that had been granted them in
Manchuria by the Nationalists. For one of the few times in his career, Stalin
was compelled to relinquish gains that he had earlier obtained.

So, although the communist victory in China was a major setback for the
West, it was less of a boon to the USSR than Westerners then feared. Ironically,
it turned out, the affinities between the superpowers and their Chinese clients
had been more apparent than real. The Nationalists, it is true, maintained an
outward façade of parliamentary government, but Chiang was in no sense a
democrat, and his regime bore more resemblance to a European fascist dictatorship, or a Latin American military junta, than to a Western-style democracy. The Communists, to be sure, spoke the language of Marxism-Leninism
and professed allegiance to the principles of Soviet-style socialism. But they
were by no means Soviet puppets: They had come to power on their own, with
little support and even less encouragement from Stalin and his cronies. And
theirs was a peasant revolution, rural and antiurban in tone, which did not
entirely resemble either the proletarian dictatorship envisioned by Marx and
Lenin or the industrialized behemoth created by Joseph Stalin.

The Chinese Revolution, and the superpower involvement therein, set a
pattern that would be repeated at various times and places throughout the
Cold War era. Indigenous political groups, struggling for power within their

own country, frequently found it beneficial and expedient to define their causes in Western ideological terms. As often as not, one side would claim to be a vanguard of social democracy and communism—or, at the very least, a liberation movement devoted to the struggle against capitalist imperialism. The other side, typically, would profess to be a harbinger of liberal democracy and capitalism—or, at the very least, a bulwark of opposition to the spread of communist power. By identifying with one side or the other in a worldwide ideological conflict, they were able to invest their movements with an aura of idealism and morality: they were fighting not just for power but for righteousness and protection against an evil and oppressive foe. More importantly, perhaps, they were able to lay claim to the moral and material support, and sometimes even the armed assistance, of ideological brethren in the capitalist or socialist camp. As the overall leaders of these camps, the United States and the Soviet Union typically found themselves drawn into the fray, if for no other reason than to prevent the other side from gaining the upper hand. Internal rivalries and power struggles were thus distorted and transformed into component elements of an international ideological contest. And the Cold War, which had begun mainly in Europe but had soon reached a standoff there, increasingly became a global confrontation.

7

The Conflict over Korea, 1950–1953

The communist victory in China served to broaden the scope of the Cold War. The American policy of containment had been designed primarily to check the spread of communism in Europe and southwest Asia; it was not yet clear to what extent it applied to eastern Asia. Indeed, the Truman administration's preoccupation with Europe had been one of the key factors which had precluded U.S. military involvement in the Chinese Civil War. Extensive as they were, American resources were not unlimited, and conventional strategic wisdom said that they should not be diverted to support a land war in Asia. The Soviet Union, likewise absorbed with Europe, had not even been willing to supply any substantive aid to its Chinese communist comrades during their long struggle against Nationalist rule.

But Mao's revolution changed all that. Stalin, for all his caution, found himself compelled by the logic of events to make concessions and provide real assistance to the People's Republic of China. And the Truman administration, for all its focus on Europe, had been so severely wounded by the "loss" of China that it could not tolerate any new extensions of communist power anywhere in the world. As a result, during the course of 1950, a remarkable series of events propelled the American administration into precisely the situation it had so recently and so carefully avoided: a land war in Asia against the Chinese Communists. And the Cold War became a shooting war in a country called Korea.

NORTH AND SOUTH KOREA

The Korean peninsula juts out from southeast Manchuria, almost like an incomplete land bridge stretching three-fourths of the way to Japan. Only 100 miles from the westernmost Japanese islands, it has a short border with Russia and a long border with China. Partly as a result of its location, at the juncture of three great powers, it has had a troubled past, and its internal affairs have often been subject to outside interference.

From 1910 until 1945, in fact, Korea was under the dominance of imperial Japan. These were difficult years for the Korean people. On one hand, the Japanese sought to industrialize and modernize the peninsula: they built factories, roads, hospitals, and schools, improved sanitation and medicine, and transformed the Korean economy. At the same time, however, their rule was harsh and repressive. They exploited Korean natural resources, drained off the fruits of Korean labor, and set up a brutal police state to control the Korean people. The standard of living fell, as Korean workers were exploited by Japanese capitalists and Korean peasants increasingly came under the control of Japanese landlords. Korean laws and customs were banned, and Korean newspapers were suppressed. The nation of Korea was virtually transformed into a Japanese province called Chosen.

Japanese efforts to destroy the native culture, however, were not entirely successful. In some ways, they may even have been counterproductive, for they helped to spawn a national liberation movement among the Korean people. In 1919, emboldened by the Wilsonian call for national self-determination, a group of Korean intellectuals drafted a "Proclamation of Independence," and popular demonstrations were held all over Korea on the occasion of the funeral of the last Korean emperor. The movement was a failure: it was brutally suppressed by the Japanese authorities and conveniently ignored by the Western leaders who met that year in Versailles (Japan, after all, had been their wartime ally). But it did help lay the foundations for a nationalist movement in exile.

As the Japanese cracked down, hundreds of Korean patriots fled their country to plan its liberation. Many went to China, where they established at Shanghai a provisional government in exile that claimed to speak for "Free Korea." Some resettled in the United States, especially in Hawaii, and sought to win American support for their independence efforts. Influenced by American attitudes and values, they tended to define their movement in terms of Western liberal and nationalist ideals and to maintain contact with the Korean émigrés in China. A third group went to Soviet Russia, the newly established socialist state, which seemed to be the only major nation consistently to advocate the national liberation of oppressed colonial peoples. Disenchanted with the West, a number of young Koreans studied in Russia and were instrumental in forming the Korean Communist party in 1925.

During the 1930s, as Japan moved into Manchuria and then into China proper, the prospects for Korean independence seemed to grow even dimmer. With their land almost totally surrounded by Japanese-controlled territory, and their economy fully integrated into that of Japan, the Koreans became a forgotten people, increasingly forced to take Japanese names and speak the Japanese language. But in 1941, when Japan went to war against America and Britain, Korean hopes began to brighten: their oppressors had overextended their reach and sooner or later must fall. A further boost to Korean morale came late in 1943 when Allied leaders Roosevelt, Churchill, and Chiang Kai-shek, meeting in Cairo, declared their intention that postwar Korea should "in due course" become a free and independent state. Stalin added his assent at Tehran a few weeks later.

Unfortunately for the Koreans, things did not quite work out the way they might have hoped. In February of 1945, when the Allied leaders met again at Yalta, they discussed the possibility that postwar Korea might be placed under the joint trusteeship of the United States, Great Britain, Nationalist China, and the Soviet Union. No arrangements were made, however, for the liberation or occupation of Korea, and nothing was said about Korea in the secret agreement by which the USSR agreed to enter the war against Japan. In the ensuing months, anticipating a long and difficult struggle to conquer the Japanese islands, the Americans deferred making concrete plans for Korea, effectively consigning the peninsula to the Soviet zone of operations. Stalin, who rarely missed an opportunity to extend his influence, needed no further invitation. On 9 August, the day after his country declared war on Japan, he sent troops to invade both Manchuria and Korea. By 14 August, when the Japanese surrendered, Soviet forces had already occupied large sections of Manchuria and northern Korea.

The United States, caught off guard by the unexpected rapidity of this advance, became increasingly concerned that Korea would fall entirely under Soviet control. So in drafting General Order No. 1, the surrender instructions to be issued to the Japanese troops, U.S. officials inserted a provision dividing Korea along the 38th parallel of latitude. North of that line, Japanese forces would be expected to surrender to the Soviets; south of it, they would turn over control to the Americans.

Somewhat surprisingly, since the United States as yet had no presence in Korea, Stalin accepted this arrangement. Rather than occupying the entire peninsula, which he easily could have done, he agreed instead to divide it with the United States. At this point, he was still hopeful that the Americans might honor his request for a Soviet occupation zone in northern Japan, and this might well have explained his uncharacteristic restraint. At any rate, neither Moscow nor Washington saw the division as permanent; both agreed that Korea should be reunified once the occupation was over. But there was no clear agreement as to how the unification should take place or what sort of regime should govern the new Korea.

Since they were already on the scene, the Soviets were much better prepared to deal with Korea than were the Americans. Having at its disposal a
number of Soviet-trained Korean Communists, Moscow simply installed them
in positions of authority, rather than trying to rule northern Korea directly.
The Americans did not even arrive in Korea until three weeks after the war
had ended. Fearing that it might be controlled by Communists, they ignored
the "Korean People's Republic" which left-wing nationalists set up in Seoul.
Instead, showing manifest insensitivity, they at first attempted to administer
south Korea using Japanese officials. Within a few months, however, these
were replaced by Americans, whose job it was to run the show until unified
rule could be established.

But unified rule never came. With Cold War tensions increasing,
Moscow and Washington were unable to agree on a united government, and
the Koreans themselves were soon involved in a violent internal struggle for
influence and control. As a result, two separate regimes developed. In the
Soviet-occupied north, a communist-dominated provisional government was
set up in 1947. Its leader was Kim Il-song (born Kim Song-ju), a young Korean
Communist who had adopted the name of a legendary guerrilla fighter, and
who had himself been active in the Manchurian resistance against the
Japanese. Talented and energetic, but ruthless, ambitious, and cruel, he
would prove to be the most durable of all the Cold War leaders. His new
regime almost immediately began nationalizing industry and confiscating
landed estates, prompting thousands of people, including many industrialists
and landlords, to flee to the south.

In the south, meanwhile, as hopes for unity faded, the Americans finally
began turning over power to Koreans. The United States avoided imposing
economic reforms, preferring instead to set up a representative assembly, see
that elections were held, and then let the elected Korean officials decide their
own policies. Thanks partly to American influence, and partly to the influx of
capitalists and landlords from the north, southern politics came to be dominated by conservative and ultranationalistic forces. Their leader was an aging
nationalist named Yi Sung-man, known in the West as Syngman Rhee. Having
fled Korea in 1911, following the Japanese takeover, the Princeton-educated
Rhee had spent much of his life in exile, living in Hawaii and pushing the
cause of Korean independence. An eloquent speaker, effective organizer, and
strident anti-Communist, he returned to Korea after the war, created a political party, and conducted a vicious struggle against leftist elements in the
south. In the summer of 1948, after leading his party to victory in South
Korean elections, he became the president of a new "Republic of Korea"
which set up its headquarters at Seoul. In response, Kim Il-song and his comrades in the north declared the formation of a "Democratic People's
Republic" with its capital at P'yongyang.

The establishment of two separate and hostile regimes on the Korean
peninsula pleased no one. Each side talked of eventually unifying the country

under its own control. In the north, Kim Il-song moved systematically to eliminate his opponents and create a personal dictatorship. With continued Soviet
assistance, he also built up his military forces and launched an industrialization
drive. In the south Syngman Rhee, faced with widespread left-wing opposition,
made extensive use of martial law and brutal, authoritarian methods to quell
internal dissent. His government, nevertheless, was recognized by the United
States and admitted to the United Nations as Korea's sole representative.

The superpowers, meanwhile, began to disengage their forces now that
the rationale for occupation was gone. By the end of 1948, in fact, the Soviets
had withdrawn most of their soldiers, leaving behind a well-equipped North
Korean army and a cadre of political advisors and military technicians. The
Americans, aware that the military balance favored the north but unwilling (at
that point) to make a permanent military commitment to the south, pulled
out their troops during the course of the following year. They agreed to provide limited aid to Syngman Rhee's regime and equipment and training for its
army. But they avoided a major investment, fearful that Rhee might use it to
launch a war against North Korea. At the same time, they purposely left their
intentions concerning the defense of South Korea ambiguous, gambling that
the resulting uncertainty would deter a North Korean attack. It was a gamble
they were destined to lose.

THE OUTBREAK OF HOSTILITIES

The end of the Soviet and American occupations left behind in Korea a highly unstable situation verging on civil war. Periodic raids and attacks were
staged by both sides against each other, and each began to prepare for possible combat. In the south, Syngman Rhee vigorously pressed his claims for
increased U.S. aid, while cracking down even further on dissenters within his
own country. His popularity by this time was slipping, partly as a result of his
repressive policies and partly due to the rampant inflation that was afflicting
the South Korean economy. American support for the Seoul regime, moreover, was inadvertently called into question by the U.S. secretary of state in a
major address to the National Press Club in January of 1950. In this speech,
Dean Acheson outlined an American defensive perimeter in the western
Pacific which encompassed Japan and the Philippines, but not South Korea or
Taiwan. The secretary was referring to a global conflict, in which the United
States would be unable to defend the last two areas, and not to an invasion of
South Korea from the north. Still, his remarks had the unintended effect of
casting doubt on the administration's willingness to protect the south. The
Koreans could hardly help but take notice.

In the north, Kim Il-song continued to build up his military forces, creating a well-trained army of over 130,000 strong. His regime also began sending guerrilla warriors to infiltrate the south, while marshaling its tanks and
troops along the 38th parallel. By June of 1950, he had amassed a consider-

able force. Western analysts, however, discounted the possibility that he would actually invade without direct Soviet military support, and they presumed that Korea was as low on Moscow's priority list as it was on their own. So the West was caught off guard on Sunday, 25 June 1950, when the North Korean army crossed the border and launched a massive and well-coordinated attack against the forces of South Korea. The Korean War had begun.

At the time, it was generally assumed in the West that the North Korean forces were acting on orders from Moscow and that Stalin had decided either to test American resolve or to divert U.S. attention from Europe. Much later, claims would be made that the initiative came from Kim Il-song, who was convinced that he could conquer the south without direct Soviet involvement. There is little doubt, however, that Stalin knew what was going on and that the invasion could not have taken place without his consent. There is also little doubt that the Communists were counting on a quick victory, hoping that this would decrease the likelihood of U.S. military involvement.

At any rate, neither superpower appears to have been entirely prepared for the outbreak of hostilities. The Soviet Union, in protest against the UN refusal to admit the People's Republic of China in place of the Nationalist regime, had withdrawn its delegation early in 1950. It was not in a position, therefore, to counter American maneuvering in the Security Council, and it clearly had not anticipated the extent to which Truman would be able to use the UN to mobilize world opinion and legitimize U.S. military intervention.

The Americans, meanwhile, were in the midst of reconsidering their overall strategy when the North Korean invasion occurred. At the beginning of 1950, President Harry Truman had authorized the National Security Council to undertake a secret reassessment of U.S. policy in the wake of the successful Soviet atomic bomb test and the Chinese revolution. Its report, known as NSC-68, had been completed in April and reviewed by the president at that time. Portraying the Soviet challenge in primarily military terms, it called for a massive military effort on the part of the United States to counter this global threat. America must build up its conventional and nuclear forces, it asserted, and must be prepared to respond to communist adventurism anywhere in the world. Although NSC-68 was highly secret, and was not formally approved until September of 1950, it clearly had an impact on the Truman administration's reaction to the crisis in Korea.

As a result, although they were taken unawares by the news from Korea, American officials responded with remarkable speed and vigor. President Truman, who was home in Missouri when the war broke out, rushed back to Washington to deal with the emergency situation. Presuming that the Soviets were behind the attack, and smarting from widespread criticism of the recent debacle in China, he and his advisors immediately concluded that they could not afford to countenance a further extension of communist control. Both in domestic politics and in international relations, their credibility seemed to be at stake. A special session of the UN Security Council was hastily arranged on

25 June, and a resolution was pushed through calling for an immediate end to the fighting and withdrawal of North Korean forces from South Korean territory. General Douglas MacArthur, the head of the U.S. occupation forces in Japan, was ordered to send in supplies to aid South Korea and to protect American nationals trying to evacuate that country. Two days later, aided by the absence of the Soviet ambassador and the assistance of Secretary General Trygve Lie, the United States won Security Council approval of a resolution calling on UN member nations to assist the South Koreans in resisting the invasion from the north.

Events in East Asia were also moving swiftly. Even before the passage of the second UN resolution, President Truman had already authorized the use of American air and naval power to slow the communist advance. This, however, soon proved insufficient. The forces of South Korea, poorly trained and poorly equipped, were unable to deal effectively with the North Korean assault. By 28 June 1950, only three days into the war, the communist armies had captured Seoul. It appeared to be only a matter of time before they would overrun the entire peninsula. Two days later, following a quick trip to the combat zone, General MacArthur reported that the South Korean army could not hold out without the direct commitment of U.S. combat forces. Washington, concerned that the invasion might be a Soviet tactic designed to divert Western resources in anticipation of a major thrust elsewhere, had been hesitant to take such a step. On 30 June, however, President Truman decided he could wait no longer and authorized the employment of American ground troops. The civil war in Korea had become an international conflict.

The big question at this point was how the Soviet Union would react. The Americans' rapid response, and their ability to win UN approval for it, left the Soviet leaders with little room for diplomatic maneuvering. On 29 June, they officially disavowed any responsibility for the war and instead accused the South Koreans of having started the conflict by invading the north. They also issued a warning against foreign involvement in Korea's internal affairs, declaring their own intention not to intervene. Most importantly, they made no open movement to send in Soviet soldiers to assist the North Koreans. At the time, of course, in view of the sweeping successes enjoyed by Kim Il-song's armies, such assistance hardly seemed necessary. Still, as they would do so often during the course of the Cold War, the Soviets opted to show caution in a time of international crisis. For all their efforts to extend their influence, when push came to shove they were generally unwilling to run the risk of direct military conflict between the superpowers.

THE WIDENING OF THE WAR

The United States of America, however, had decided to take the risk. Although it was conducted under the auspices of the United Nations, the defense of South Korea was to be largely an American affair. President

Truman, in fact, had authorized the use of force without waiting for UN approval, and the United States quickly took the lead in organizing the war effort. On 7 July 1950, when the United Nations Command was officially created, it was immediately placed under American authority. Although sixteen UN member nations would eventually send soldiers, the United States provided fully half of the ground troops and most of the air and sea power. On 8 July, in a move that was to prove portentous, Truman appointed General Douglas MacArthur as commander-in-chief of UN forces in Korea.

During a long and spectacular career, General of the Army Douglas MacArthur had established himself as one of the leading military figures in American history. Brilliant and vain, eloquent and arrogant, self-confident and self-righteous, he had led the U.S. Army in the Pacific theater during World War II and had served since then as the Supreme Allied Commander in occupied Japan. There, wielding viceregal powers, he had carried through a forced revolution designed to transform imperial Japan into a bulwark of Western-style democracy against the expansion of communism in Asia. A rigid conservative and staunch anticommunist, he was convinced that U.S. policy focused too much attention on Europe, and too little on Asia.

When MacArthur assumed command, the situation of the South Koreans was desperate. The first several weeks of the war had witnessed a steady string of victories on the part of the North Koreans. The South Korean army, in devastation and disarray, was unable to regroup and mount an effective resistance. American units, which began arriving in July, were too small in number and too poorly equipped to be of much help. U.S. air power, which might have been used to slow the attacking forces, was instead directed against strategic targets in North Korea. And, although there was no massive uprising against Syngman Rhee, many South Korean students and workers at first welcomed the invaders.

By early August, the North Korean forces controlled the entire peninsula, except for a modest-sized "perimeter" in the extreme southeast around the city of Pusan. At this point, however, the strategic balance was beginning to shift. With their lines extended, and with increasing harassment from UN tactical warplanes, the North Korean forces found the going much more difficult. And they soon found themselves outnumbered: by the end of August, the steady influx of UN soldiers gave the defenders of South Korea a numerical advantage. The Pusan perimeter, fortified by U.S. tanks and protected by U.S. aircraft, held out against a determined North Korean assault. In early September, the offensive came to an end: the North Koreans had come close, but they had fallen short of the quick and total victory they sought.

Meanwhile, the UN command had secretly been making plans for a surprise counteroffensive of its own. General MacArthur, with vast experience in amphibious operations, had in early July conceived the idea of staging a surprise landing behind enemy lines. By the end of August, his plans were complete. On 15 September, in a daring and spectacular operation, United

Troops in combat during Korean War. (U.S. Army Photo)

Nations personnel began landing at Inchon, a port city on the Yellow Sea located 20 miles from Seoul and 180 miles behind the North Korean lines. The next day, another offensive was launched by the UN troops in the Pusan perimeter. Within two weeks, the South Korean capital had been recaptured, and the communist forces were in full retreat almost everywhere.

As the North Koreans fled in disarray, the Americans began to expand their original objectives. Instead of simply defending South Korea, they now resolved to move into the north, destroy the Kim Il-song regime, and unite the entire peninsula under Syngman Rhee's control. Late in September, Truman authorized MacArthur to cross the 38th parallel, provided there was no immediate threat of Soviet or Chinese intervention. Early in October, South Korean troops actually traversed the dividing line, while the Americans pressed the UN for formal approval of their plans to do the same. It came on 7 October, and on that same day American forces moved into North Korea. The effort to resist aggression was thereby transformed into a campaign to conquer the north.

During the next few weeks, as UN troops pushed deep into North Korea, it began to look as if their new goal would readily be achieved. By October 19, MacArthur's forces had conquered P'yongyang, and they were soon moving

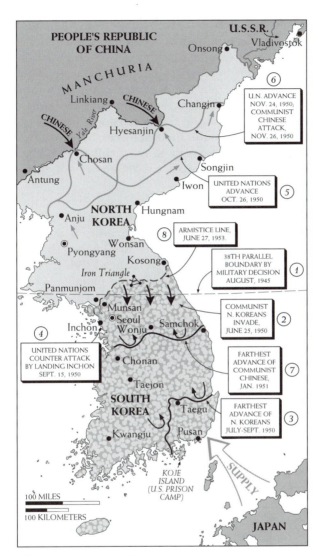

MAP 5 The Korean War

The following labels appear on the map:

U.S.S.R.

PEOPLE'S REPUBLIC OF CHINA

Vladivostok

Onsong

MANCHURIA

Linkiang

CHINESE

Changjin

Yalu River

CHINESE

Hyesanjin

6 U.N. ADVANCE NOV. 24, 1950; COMMUNIST CHINESE ATTACK, NOV. 26, 1950

CHINESE

Chosan

Antung

Songjin

Iwon

5 UNITED NATIONS ADVANCE OCT. 26, 1950

NORTH KOREA

Hungnam

Anju

Wonsan

8 ARMISTICE LINE, JUNE 27, 1953.

Pyongyang

Kosong

1 38TH PARALLEL BOUNDARY BY MILITARY DECISION AUGUST, 1945

Iron Triangle

Panmunjom

Munsan

2 COMMUNIST N. KOREANS INVADE, JUNE 25, 1950

Inchon

Seoul

Wonju

Samchok

4 UNITED NATIONS COUNTER ATTACK BY LANDING INCHON SEPT. 15, 1950

Chonan

7 FARTHEST ADVANCE OF COMMUNIST CHINESE, JAN. 1951

Taejon

SOUTH KOREA

Taegu

3 FARTHEST ADVANCE OF N. KOREANS JULY-SEPT. 1950

Kwangju

Pusan

SUPPLY

KOJE ISLAND (U.S. PRISON CAMP)

100 MILES

100 KILOMETERS

JAPAN

north toward the Yalu River that separates Korea from Manchuria. Ignoring counsels of caution from his superiors in Washington, the general pushed on toward what he hoped and expected would be a swift and total victory.

The invasion of the north, however, had placed Stalin and Mao into a situation not unlike the one faced by the Americans only a few months earlier. They had to decide whether to watch as their comrades were overrun by a hostile force or to intervene and run the risk of starting a world war. Stalin, cautious as ever, was unwilling to commit his own forces, but he was willing to support Chinese efforts to prevent North Korea's collapse. And the Chinese, fearful that MacArthur might not stop at the Yalu, were not disposed to sit by idly and watch their neighbor fall.

In early October, as South Korean troops began crossing the 38th parallel, Chinese foreign minister Zhou Enlai called in the Indian ambassador in the middle of the night to issue a pointed warning. If non-Korean forces should cross that line, he asserted, China would join the war. The UN Command dismissed this as a bluff and went ahead with its offensives deep into North Korea. Later that month, in a dramatic meeting between Truman and MacArthur at Wake Island, the general assured his president that Chinese forces would be slaughtered if they dared to intervene. Even as evidence mounted that China was massing forces north of the Yalu and had actually begun infiltrating soldiers into Korea, the UN commander remained undaunted. Promising grandly that the war would be over by Christmas, he prepared his final assault.

The Chinese, meanwhile, were mobilizing swiftly and sending personnel across the Yalu in ever-increasing numbers. To avoid an open declaration of war against the United Nations, they used a simple ruse: Chinese soldiers were portrayed as "volunteers" who were coming to the aid of their North Korean comrades. Their aid would prove most effective. In late November, just as MacArthur was starting his "final" offensive, Chinese "volunteers" began pouring into North Korea. The UN forces, caught unprepared, were severely routed, and by early December they were everywhere on the run. Desperate evacuation efforts managed to avert a total disaster, but most of North Korea was soon back under communist control. By Christmas, instead of going home, UN troops had withdrawn more or less to the 38th parallel. Once again, the momentum of the fighting had shifted dramatically, this time in favor of the Chinese and North Koreans.

THE DISMISSAL OF MACARTHUR AND THE STALEMATE IN KOREA

Now it was America's turn to face the specter of defeat. On 30 November, responding to the news of the massive Chinese intervention, President Truman gave a press conference in which he refused to rule out the use of nuclear weapons to halt the communist advance. This precipitated a flap between the United States and its allies, with British prime minister Attlee flying to Washington to secure assurances that the war would remain limited. And, although Truman declared a national emergency in mid-December, his administration was already starting to talk about a cease-fire and looking for ways to cut its losses.

MacArthur, however, had other ideas. Blaming his reverses on intelligence leaks and restraints placed on him by his U.S. superiors, he demanded the authority to widen the war by blockading communist China, bombing its industrial sites, and bringing in Nationalist Chinese troops to join the war in Korea. By this time, however, the Truman administration had abandoned its hopes of unifying Korea and was seeking a way out of the war. MacArthur's demands received little sympathy from U.S. military planners who, as General Omar Bradley would later suggest, saw an invasion of China as "the wrong war, in the wrong place, at the wrong time, and with the wrong enemy." For several months, the frustrated UN commander chafed as Washington moved increasingly to keep the war limited and seek a negotiated settlement. Finally, on 24 March 1951, he issued a statement containing a virtual ultimatum to the Chinese, in effect demanding that they either surrender to him or run the risk of "imminent military collapse."

MacArthur's statement was a contradiction of both U.S. and UN policy and, as such, was regarded by President Truman as an act of insubordination. Shortly thereafter, when a telegram from the general implicitly denouncing the administration's "limited war" policy was read in the United States Congress, the president decided he could tolerate no more. On 11 April, in a dramatic and controversial gesture, he announced that he was dismissing MacArthur from his military command. The move ignited a storm of protest in the United States, where the president's popularity soon sank to an all-time low, while the general returned to a hero's welcome of unprecedented proportions. But in Europe, where MacArthur was widely regarded as dangerous and uncontrollable, Truman's move was applauded and Allied fears relieved. And in Asia, where the battles were actually being fought, the terrible specter of all-out war had apparently been averted.

But the fighting in Korea dragged on. By June of 1951, UN forces had managed to halt the Communist advance, inflict severe casualties on the Chinese and North Koreans, and push them back across the 38th parallel. Rather than pressing their advantage, however, the Americans decided to halt their offensive and test the diplomatic waters. Several meetings were held between George Kennan, the Truman administration's leading Soviet expert, and Jacob Malik, the Soviet ambassador to the United Nations. Malik at first expressed reluctance to get involved, pointing out that the USSR was not a participant in the war. But on 23 June, during a UN broadcast, he gave a speech calling for the opening of peace talks in Korea and a cease-fire along the 38th parallel. This seemed to signal a shift in Soviet policy, and by 10 July discussions between communist and UN representatives were under way in Kaesong, a town not far from the front.

The wave of optimism that greeted these developments was rapidly dispelled. The talks soon bogged down over a variety of issues, while the fighting and bloodshed continued. And, even though some progress was made when the negotiations eventually resumed in nearby Panmunjom, the issue of prisoner repatriation remained an intractable one. The UN side simply would not agree to turn over to the Communists the many captured soldiers who did not wish to go back.

The impasse at the conference table was accompanied by a stalemate on the battlefield. With a cease-fire apparently in sight, both sides maneuvered for position, but neither seemed willing to risk an all-out offensive. Instead they dug themselves in behind heavily fortified lines, fighting occasional bloody battles at key tactical points, and carrying on a debilitating war of attrition for two more years. The deadlock would not be broken until 1953, and then only after some major changes had taken place in superpower leadership.

CHANGES IN LEADERSHIP IN WASHINGTON AND MOSCOW

The Korean War coincided with a substantial shift to the right among voters in the United States, who in 1952 elected their first Republican president since 1928. International relations and Cold War considerations played a prominent role. In the 1948 campaign, in line with the bipartisan approach to world affairs which had prevailed since Pearl Harbor, the Republicans had largely refrained from attacking the Truman administration on foreign policy issues. But Truman's unexpected triumph, followed in 1949 by the communist victory in China, had undermined this cooperative spirit, and it had since been blown to smithereens by the controversies surrounding the dismissal of General MacArthur and the tactics of Senator McCarthy (Chapter 6).

The presidential campaign of 1952, then, provided a forum for discussing and debating the perceptions and decisions that had shaped U.S Cold War policy. The Republicans, anxious to regain the White House after twenty years of Democratic rule, mercilessly blasted the Truman administration with the pithy slogan, "Korea, Communism, and Corruption." Truman himself did not seek reelection, and his party's candidate, Adlai Stevenson of Illinois, found it advisable to keep some distance between his campaign and the beleaguered administration. Pressure from the "McCarthyites" compelled moderate Republicans, including presidential nominee General Dwight D. Eisenhower, to run on a platform that deplored the "immoral policy of `containment' which abandons countless human beings to a despotism and godless terrorism." In the course of the campaign, Republicans called for a new policy of "liberation" that would free the "captive nations" and "roll back the iron curtain." Eisenhower, although he privately doubted its wisdom, publicly embraced this concept, while promising also to "go to Korea" and bring that war to "an early and honorable end." Although Stevenson ran a thoughtful and articulate campaign, he could not match the immense popularity of war-hero Eisenhower, who rode into office on a landslide.

Despite the fact that he often came across as a simple and loyal soldier, folksy and direct, Dwight David Eisenhower was in fact a complex man who possessed considerable skills as an administrator and a politician. Indeed, the fatherly "Ike" had an extraordinary talent for maintaining a kindly image while working ruthlessly behind the scenes to attain his ends and letting his subordinates take the rap for unpopular decisions and policies. As the wartime commander of Anglo-American forces in Europe, he had acquired valuable experience in dealing with the British, the French, and even the Soviets. As his administration progressed, he would come to play an increasingly visible and active role in implementing his foreign policy; but in the beginning, he left the outward conduct of diplomatic affairs largely in the hands of John Foster Dulles, his secretary of state.

A prominent international lawyer and foreign affairs expert, Dulles was also a strict Presbyterian and a stern moralist. He despised the atheistic Communists and saw the superpower struggle mainly in moral and ideological terms. Depicting the Soviets as fanatics bent upon world conquest, and convinced that the East-West conflict was largely irreconcilable, he had authored the sections of the 1952 Republican platform calling for the end of containment and the beginning of liberation. Once in office, he sought to devise a new foreign policy, based on an assertive and combative attitude toward the Soviets and the "Red" Chinese, combined with a willingness to go to the "brink" of nuclear war to secure American interests and prevent communist gains. Simultaneously, however, he allowed many experienced foreign service officers to be forced out of the department by McCarthyite accusations and innuendoes, even when he realized the charges were baseless. By the time Senator McCarthy was finally censured in 1954, significant damage had been done.

To a certain extent, men like Eisenhower and Dulles were boosted into their positions by a widespread belief that they were the ones best qualified to deal with Joseph Stalin. But in March of 1953, only six weeks after the inauguration of the new American president, the Soviet dictator confounded his Western adversaries one last time. He died.

The last few years of Stalin's reign had been marked by continued tensions, both in the USSR and abroad. The aging dictator, increasingly reclusive, refused to yield authority even as his faculties declined and his grip on reality loosened. Jealous of his powers, and neurotically suspicious of even his closest comrades, he began to prepare for yet another purge of "disloyal" elements, real and imagined.

His country, meanwhile, continued to reap the bitter harvest of his paranoid foreign policies. In his brutal efforts to secure the borders of the Soviet homeland and extend his influence in Eastern Europe and Asia, he had frightened his erstwhile allies and enemies into joining together against him. In relying so heavily on militarism, he had saddled his people with the largest peacetime military establishment in history. Most poignantly, perhaps, in seeking so belligerently to prevent "capitalist encirclement" he had awakened within the capitalist powers a virulent anticommunism. This in turn helped to advance the careers of those Western politicians who were most hostile to the USSR and to virtually ensure that any Soviet initiative would be regarded with extreme suspicion and distrust.

In October of 1952, for the first time in thirteen years, there convened in Moscow an official congress of the Communist party of the Soviet Union. The Nineteenth Party Congress turned out to be a somber and sobering event. On its eve, Stalin published a rambling treatise entitled *Economic Problems of Socialism in the USSR*, in which he called for continued emphasis on heavy industry, predicting that the capitalist world would soon be torn asunder by wars and confrontations among the imperialist nations. At the congress itself, for the first time in memory, the keynote address was given by someone other than Stalin: Georgi M. Malenkov, the dictator's principal lieutenant and current heir apparent. Stalin himself, looking white-haired and frail, attended the sessions only sporadically.

Then, in January 1953, an ominous development occurred. Soviet police arrested a group of Kremlin doctors and charged them with hastening the deaths of several high officials and conspiring with Western spies. A new and bloody purge, menacing even Stalin's closest comrades, was apparently in the works. Early in March, however, as the tension mounted, the dictator suffered a stroke. His deputies, less than anxious to find out what their mentor had up his sleeve, may well have taken their time about securing medical care. At any rate, they were by no means the only ones to breathe a sigh of relief on 5 March 1953, when Joseph Vissarionovich Stalin went to his final reward.

The passing of Stalin seemed to open the door for an easing of Cold War tensions. Western hopes that the dictator's death might create instability within the USSR failed to materialize, but a more moderate and flexible leadership did begin to emerge. Malenkov at first took over as head of both the Communist party and the Soviet government, but within a few weeks, as his comrades sought to preclude a return to one-man rule, he was compelled to relinquish the former post to Nikita S. Khrushchev. For the next two years, the USSR was governed by a "collective leadership," with Premier Malenkov serving as the principal spokesperson, while he and Khrushchev maneuvered for power behind the scenes.

Malenkov, an intelligent and sophisticated man who recognized that the policies of confrontation were straining his country's resources without adding to its security, moved quickly to defuse Cold War tensions so that more energy could be focused on domestic concerns. He abandoned claims that Stalin had made upon territory in northeast Turkey, and he sought to repair Soviet relations with Iran, Israel, Greece, and Yugoslavia. Internally, he strove to deemphasize heavy industry, increase production of consumer goods, and improve the standard of living. And, while calling for the peaceful resolution of international disputes, he moved away from the Stalinist line that conflict between communism and capitalism was inevitable. This helped pave the way for a cease-fire in Korea.

THE ARMISTICE AGREEMENT

By early 1953, both sides were determined to find a way out of the Korean quagmire. Eisenhower, who had promised in his campaign to end the war, and who had actually visited Korea a month before taking office, tried to break the stalemate in January by hinting that he might "unleash" Chiang Kai-shek and allow the Nationalists on Taiwan to invade mainland China. This heightened anxieties but produced no immediate breakthrough. After Stalin's death in March, however, the new Soviet leadership launched a "peace offensive," with Malenkov announcing that there were no disputes between the United States and USSR that could not be resolved by peaceful means. A few weeks later, in a similar spirit, Chinese premier Zhou Enlai offered a major concession on the prisoner exchange issue, suggesting that those prisoners who did not wish to be repatriated might be turned over to a neutral country.

The peace talks, which had temporarily been suspended, reconvened in April amid expressions of hope. But the new U.S. administration, inherently distrustful of any communist initiative, found the details of the Chinese offer unacceptable. An alternative plan, under which the prisoner exchange would be handled by a commission made up of personnel from neutral nations, was more to its liking. Several months of difficult negotiations ensued. In May, during a visit to India, Secretary of State Dulles implied that the United States might widen the war—and perhaps even use nuclear weapons—if no agreement were reached. In June, in an effort to sabotage the peace talks and preclude any form of repatriation, the South Korean government purposely allowed some 27,000 of its prisoners to "escape." In July, determined to achieve a more favorable cease-fire line, the Communists launched a massive and successful assault on a position called "Pork Chop Hill." But the talks proceeded all the while, and, on 27 July 1953, in an atmosphere of silence and resignation, the armistice was signed at Panmunjom.

The agreement ended the fighting, but it was only a cease-fire, not a treaty of peace. An international peace conference was convened at Geneva in 1954 to negotiate such a treaty, but its efforts in this regard came to naught, and it wound up focusing mostly on Indochina (Chapter 11). Formal talks at Panmunjom continued for decades, but these too accomplished little. The two Koreas were destined to remain bitter foes, heavily armed and hostile, for the rest of the Cold War era.

From a Korean perspective, the war, which had dragged on for three years, was an incredible disaster. Appalling devastation and slaughter were visited upon the country by the continual fighting and shelling and the massive aerial bombardments. At least four million people, the majority of them Koreans, were killed in what was elsewhere billed as a "limited" war. And yet neither side could claim victory; indeed, the final cease-fire line was not far from the original 38th parallel. In the long run, the South Koreans fared better: thanks to a mutual defense pact with the United States and massive American aid, they gained a measure of security and prosperity, although full freedom and democracy would continue to elude them for years. In the north, there was neither prosperity nor freedom, as Kim Il-song's dictatorial regime persisted in emphasizing military strength and internal repression throughout the Cold War and beyond.

Few nations, in fact, could take much satisfaction in the outcome of the war. The United States could claim to have saved South Korea from communist aggression and halted the momentum of communist advance. But it had failed to win the war and had suffered some embarrassing setbacks in the process. Furthermore, it had vastly extended its global commitments: in adopting NSC-68 it had expanded its containment policy into an anticommunist crusade, taken upon itself the role of world policeman, and condemned itself to huge new outlays in military spending. It had frightened its traditional allies, who were increasingly alarmed at the growing militarization of U.S. foreign policy. It had driven its major adversaries, the Soviet and Chinese Communists, into each other's arms. And it had, by implication, acquired some embarrassing new friends. Indeed, by rescuing Syngman Rhee and propping up Chiang Kai-shek, the United States seemed to signal its intention to support any regime, no matter how brutal or corrupt, that was faced with a communist threat.

The communist powers likewise had little reason to gloat. The People's Republic of China gained substantial credibility as a military power by holding its own against the mighty United States. But it also found itself more dependent than ever upon Soviet assistance and, thanks to implacable American hostility, shut out of both the UN and Taiwan. The Soviet Union, by remaining officially neutral, had seemed to have it both ways: it had tested Western resolve and diverted American resources without risking much in the process. But the results were hardly to Moscow's liking: The Korean War had triggered an American backlash that seemed to threaten the security of the USSR itself. As the United States poured vast sums into rebuilding, rearming, and defending West Germany and Japan, the Soviets once again found themselves surrounded by armed and hostile powers. They thus felt compelled to increase the size of their armed forces and engage in a long, debilitating arms race with the wealthier Americans.

Oddly enough, the chief beneficiaries of the Korean War were Germany, Japan, and Nationalist China, the three great losers of the conflicts that closely preceded it. The outbreak of hostilities in Korea gave added impetus to U.S. efforts, already under way, to transform Japan and West Germany into trusted friends and partners in the anticommunist cause. During the course of 1950, the United States overcame the fears of its reluctant European allies and got them to agree to the rearming of West Germany—a prospect that would have been unthinkable only a few years earlier. Japan, meanwhile, had become a staging ground for U.S. operations in Korea and a silent partner in the UN war effort there. On 8 September 1951, the Japanese reaped the benefits of the changing world scene when the United States signed a security treaty committing itself to their defense and, by the Treaty of San Francisco the following year, ended its occupation.

The Nationalist Chinese, largely written off by the West early in 1950, gained a new lease on life as a result of the war in Korea. The Americans sent their Seventh Fleet to protect Taiwan and began pouring in military and economic aid to support the beleaguered regime. They abandoned any thoughts of recognizing communist China, at least for the time being, and contrived to have the Nationalists retain their UN seat as the formal representatives of all of China. In 1954, the United States even went so far as to conclude a mutual defense treaty with the government of Chiang Kai-shek. But American aid had its limits: for all its support of Chiang, the United States consistently refused to help him launch a bid to reconquer the Chinese mainland.

Indeed, although the Korean conflict represented a widening of the Cold War, it also helped to establish the boundaries of that contest. The Soviets had been willing to allow and perhaps encourage adventurism on the part of their clients, but they were unwilling to commit their own forces, or to rescue protégés whose adventures went awry. The Chinese had shown that they were quite capable of protecting their own borders, but unwilling to extend themselves too far beyond, and wary of risking a nuclear attack upon their own territory. The Americans had demonstrated that they could effectively project their power and were prepared to do so to protect anticommunist regimes. But they would engage only in limited wars fought by limited means and would prefer to accept tactical setbacks rather than chance an all-out conflict. Their nuclear armaments might prove useful as deterrents or as threats but not as weapons of choice to be employed in actual combat situations. The memories of Korea, and the terrifying specter of a nuclear conflict, would supply both sides with a healthy dose of restraint during future Cold War confrontations.

8

New Leaders and
New Realities,
1953–1957

The years between 1953 and 1957 witnessed some important alterations in the overall environment of the Cold War. To some extent, these were the result of leadership changes in the United States and USSR, but they also were occasioned by several new realities in the circumstances that surrounded and defined the contest. One was the emergence of a growing bloc of nonaligned nations and movements, with no strong allegiance to either East or West. Another was the development on both sides of awesome new weapons of mass destruction that promised, within the foreseeable future, to alter the calculus of war, and to rob of any real meaning the concept of "victory" in a conflict between the superpowers. The new leaders, whatever their preconceptions, found themselves increasingly compelled to deal with the new realities.

THE "NEW LOOK" IN U.S. FOREIGN POLICY

The Eisenhower administration came into office in 1953 publicly committed to an anticommunist crusade. Almost immediately, however, it was confronted with a new situation: Stalin's death and replacement by leaders who appeared more reasonable. Unprepared for this turn of events, the Eisenhower team simply transferred its hostility to Stalin's heirs and responded very warily to Soviet peace initiatives. The president let it be known in April that, if the

Soviets wanted better relations, they would have to agree to permit free elections to unite Korea and Germany, withdraw their troops from Austria, allow the peoples of Eastern Europe to choose their own governments, and put an end to the communist-led rebellions going on in Southeast Asia. The U.S. leaders remained adamant even when Winston Churchill, a man with impeccable anticommunist credentials, proposed that the West adopt a more flexible approach to the new Soviet regime. To them the Soviet threat was both global and ideological, and any attempt to negotiate issues piecemeal smacked of compromise and concession.

As it turned out, however, there was more bark than bite to the new U.S. approach. The administration got an unexpected chance to test its commitment to "rolling back the iron curtain" in June of 1953, when anticommunist demonstrations and a general strike broke out in East Germany. The Americans openly encouraged the strikers and publicly supported their goals. But when the Soviets sent in soldiers and tanks to crush the strikes, the Eisenhower team did nothing. It became obvious that Moscow's peace initiatives certainly had their limits and that Washington was not prepared to intervene directly in the Soviet-occupied zone. The following month, the United States also agreed to a cease-fire in Korea, even though this meant that the communist regime would continue to rule the north. The "rollback" policy, when put to the test, proved to be little more than rhetoric.

Indeed, as these developments made clear, the Eisenhower administration was finding itself torn between two conflicting objectives. One of them, identified most closely with Secretary of State Dulles, was the anticommunist crusade, which involved using American power and influence to combat Soviet pressure anywhere in the world. This, as Truman's experience had shown, could be a very expensive proposition. The other, identified most closely with George M. Humphrey, the penurious new secretary of the treasury, was to reduce government spending and balance the federal budget. This could not be done without making big cuts in defense expenditures and trimming the vast military establishment inherited from Truman. "Rolling back the iron curtain," for all its emotional appeal, did not quite fit this picture.

Nonetheless, within the context of their self-imposed fiscal restraints, the president and his team strove mightily to achieve their Cold War objectives. One result of this was an increasing reliance on atomic weapons instead of conventional force. From a political perspective, nuclear armaments had two big advantages: they were relatively inexpensive, compared to the high costs of equipping and maintaining vast standing armies, and they enabled governments to avoid unpopular efforts to increase the number of troops, especially by military conscription. Voters, it seemed, were far less likely to complain about new weapons systems than about attempts to raise their taxes and draft their sons. Dulles himself alluded to these considerations in 1954, explaining a policy that came to be known as "massive retaliation":

> The total cost of our security efforts . . . could not be continued long
> without grave budgetary, economic and social consequences. . . . [T]he
> basic decision was to depend primarily on greater capacity to retaliate
> instantly by means and at places of our own choosing. As a result it is now
> possible to get and to share more basic security at less cost.

Charles E. Wilson, the U.S. secretary of defense, put it much more succinctly:
nuclear arms provided a "bigger bang for the buck."

This "new look" in U.S. defense policy did effect substantial reductions
in military expenditures. Within a few years, the U.S. defense budget
decreased by almost a third, while the country doubled its supply of nuclear
weapons and began producing large numbers of behemoth B-52 bombers
capable of delivering these weapons to targets in the USSR. The president, in
fact, professed to see "no distinction between conventional weapons and
atomic weapons," and in 1955 he suggested that the latter should be employed
"just exactly as you would use a bullet or anything else." The trick, according
to Dulles, was "to get to the verge without getting into war," using these instruments for leverage without actually having to employ them. This technique,
known as "brinkmanship," was characteristic of Dulles's approach to Soviet-
American relations.

But "massive retaliation" had its limits. The threat of a nuclear response
might have real credibility in some areas, such as the defense of Western Europe,
where vital U.S. interests were perceived to be at stake. But as the Soviets developed their own nuclear capacity, it hardly seemed likely that the United States
would risk an atomic war in situations where its own security was not directly
threatened. Some way had to be found to counter Soviet advances in circumstances where a nuclear response was neither appropriate nor credible.

The Eisenhower administration tried several creative approaches. One of
these was to rely increasingly on "covert operations" performed by the Central
Intelligence Agency (CIA). Under the direction of Allen W. Dulles, the secretary of state's brother, the CIA subverted leftist governments in Iran (1953) and
Guatemala (1954). A second tactic was to send military advisors to supplement
anticommunist forces. As the French withdrew from Indochina following the
victory of the communist-led Vietminh in 1954 (Chapter 11), the Americans
began sending personnel to help organize and train the noncommunist South
Vietnamese army, deluding themselves into thinking that this would be an
inexpensive and painless way to stop the spread of communism.

A third device was the formation of military alliances aimed at blocking
communist advances in certain vulnerable areas. If NATO could serve as an
effective vehicle for the defense of Western Europe, Dulles reasoned, then
similar alliances might prove useful in "trouble spots" like Southeast Asia and
the Middle East. In 1954, largely on U.S. initiative, the Southeast Asia Treaty
Organization (SEATO), made up of the United States, Britain, France,
Australia, New Zealand, Thailand, Pakistan, and the Philippines, was formed.

Unlike NATO, however, it provided no military guarantees, calling only for mutual consultation in the event of aggression. Furthermore, its title belied its composition: key nations of Southeast Asia were not members of SEATO, and most of its members were not in Southeast Asia! In 1955, the Americans went along with Britain in forming the Baghdad Pact, which incorporated Turkey, Iraq, Iran, and Pakistan into a new alliance system (later known as the Central Treaty Organization, or CENTO). This alliance, if anything, proved counter-productive, for it helped to alienate the Egyptians and other Arab nationalists, thus opening the way for increased Soviet influence in the Middle East.

Ironically, these new U.S. policies were all designed more to prevent Soviet expansion than to liberate "captive nations." They amounted, in effect, to an extension and institutionalization of the containment policy which had been adopted by Truman and criticized so vociferously by Republicans. Furthermore, despite the fact that John Foster Dulles tended to regard other nations' attempts at compromise or neutrality as immoral, the Eisenhower administration was finding it had little choice but to trim its sails and accept the harsh realities of an ambiguous world order. As a result, by 1955 the "new look" in U.S. foreign policy had come to bear a rather striking resemblance to the old.

KHRUSHCHEV AND THE WEST

Meanwhile, Soviet Cold War policy was also changing shape. Premier Georgi Malenkov, who in 1953 introduced a "new course" designed to spur the domestic economy and improve relations with the West, came under increasing fire from Kremlin hardliners as a result. Military leaders and champions of heavy industry, fearful that their resources would be diverted to the consumer economy, made common cause with Malenkov's chief rival, Communist party boss Nikita Khrushchev. In February 1955, Malenkov was forced to resign and was replaced as premier by Defense Minister Nikolai Bulganin. The chief beneficiary of this was Khrushchev, who had already emerged as the dominant force in the Kremlin.

Nikita S. Khrushchev, a hard-bitten party *apparatchik* who had risen from obscure poverty to become one of the world's most powerful leaders, soon proved to be a flexible and creative innovator who was not afraid to challenge traditional assumptions. Crude, uncouth, and lacking in social graces, he nevertheless blended crafty wit, clever spontaneity, formidable ambition, and energetic opportunism in a mixture baffling to both colleagues and adversaries. Before long he turned against the hardliners and, adopting many of Malenkov's policies, began to devise a new course based on "peaceful coexistence" with the capitalist world and efforts to court the nonaligned nations.

May of 1955 witnessed a flurry of diplomatic activity, as Khrushchev began to put his stamp on Soviet foreign policy. Early in the month, the USSR put forth an arms control proposal which included, for the first time, some serious innovations. It foresaw the creation of a permanent monitoring system, with foreign inspectors stationed at major airports and seaports, and along major highways and railways, in each of the superpowers. By calling for a ban on nuclear testing and the gradual reduction of nuclear stockpiles, it put the Eisenhower administration in an awkward spot. Many U.S. officials, including Secretary of State Dulles, were so committed to "massive retaliation" that they had no real interest in reducing their nuclear arsenal. And, faced with a huge Soviet preponderance in conventional forces, American military planners were loath to bargain away the U.S. nuclear advantage. The Americans, with the ambiguities of their position suddenly exposed, scrambled to find an effective response to the initiative from Moscow.

Later that month, following NATO's decision to admit West Germany and anticipating the imminent conclusion of the Austrian State Treaty, the foreign ministers of the Soviet bloc nations met in Warsaw at Khrushchev's initiative to chart a collective response. The result was the formation of a military alliance consisting of Poland, Hungary, Czechoslovakia, Bulgaria, Romania, the USSR, and eventually East Germany (see Map 3, p. 74). This agreement, known as the "Warsaw Pact," would act as a counterweight to NATO and would place over six million soldiers under Soviet command in Eastern Europe. Unlike the Western alliance, however, it served an additional purpose: it provided a convenient pretext for the continued presence of Soviet troops in Eastern Europe and thus a handy mechanism for keeping this region firmly under Moscow's control. This was indeed a strange alliance: during its entire history, the Warsaw Pact would use its military forces only against its own members!

That same month, Khrushchev and his comrades took a major step to ease international tensions by suddenly agreeing to a peace treaty with Austria which, like Germany, had been divided into zones of occupation since World War II. Originally, it had been intended that Austria would be included in an overall settlement with Germany, because the two had been one country from 1938 to 1945. But since such an agreement was beyond reach in 1955, the "Austrian State Treaty" was negotiated as a separate pact. As a result of this treaty, all occupying powers agreed to remove their forces, and Austria became a neutral and independent country. This was a major concession for the Soviets, for it meant giving up territory that had been under their control. But it did give them some advantages. It compelled the Western powers also to remove their forces from Austria, thus eliminating NATO's land contact with Hungary and decreasing it with Yugoslavia. And it showed that Moscow could be reasonable, thus undermining the Western hardliners and paving the way for direct talks between Soviet and Western leaders. Shortly thereafter, Khrushchev and Bulganin made a state visit to Yugoslavia, where they initiated a limited rapprochement with the troublesome Tito regime.

One result of all this activity was the first summit conference of the Cold War era, which took place at Geneva in July 1955. The British and French had been pushing for such a meeting and Eisenhower, overriding Dulles's reservations, had agreed to go along. He was joined by Khrushchev and Bulganin from the USSR, Premier Edgar Faure of France, and Britain's Anthony Eden. A number of issues were discussed, and, despite the apprehensions of both sides, a spirit of good will prevailed.

The most dramatic event of the summit was Eisenhower's unexpected "open skies" proposal, designed to steal the spotlight from Moscow's arms initiatives. Speaking directly to Khrushchev and Bulganin, without previously informing them of his intent, Eisenhower put forth a scheme by which the superpowers would exchange blueprints of their military force dispositions and allow each to make regular flights over the other's territory. It was a bold diplomatic stroke, but, as Eisenhower himself later admitted, there was little likelihood that the USSR would accept. For one thing, since the location and nature of most U.S. installations was already public knowledge, Moscow stood to gain much less than Washington from the information exchange. For another thing, since the Americans had a big lead in atomic weapons and long-range bombers, the Kremlin was disinclined to expose its relative weakness. Unwilling to forgo the secrecy that helped offset this weakness by keeping his foes guessing, Khrushchev derided the plan as a "very transparent espionage device" and refused to give it serious consideration.

In terms of substance, not much was accomplished at Geneva. An impasse was reached over Germany, with Moscow refusing to consider reunification until West Germany had been disarmed, and little real progress was made in other areas. In psychological terms, however, the conference was a success: the talks were cordial, the leaders got along well, and cultural and economic ties between East and West were improved. Later that year, as the USSR decreased the size of its army, returned a naval base to Finland, and extended diplomatic recognition to West Germany, the "spirit of Geneva" appeared to be working well. And in November, when the peripatetic Khrushchev announced in India that "the socialists and the capitalists have to live side by side," the age of "peaceful coexistence" seemed to be on its way.

Difficulties, of course, remained. This became clear at a foreign ministers' conference in the fall of 1955, when Foreign Minister Molotov and Secretary of State Dulles found they could agree on nothing in the absence of their more congenial bosses. Tensions in the Third World, where Moscow was beginning to gain influence, also served to cast some shadows on the after-summit glow. The legacy of distrust, it became apparent, could not be dispelled simply by improving relations among leaders.

MOSCOW AND THE NONALIGNED NATIONS

Khrushchev's overall strategy appears to have been based on a genuine belief in the superiority of the Soviet system, combined with a very real concern about the cataclysmic power of nuclear weapons. Like Malenkov, he rejected the Stalinist notion that war was inevitable and instead concluded that all-out war must by all means be avoided. At the same time, however, he made it clear in both word and deed that he intended to work by "peaceful" means for the eventual destruction of capitalism and triumph of world communism. His approach thus mirrored in some respects the West's containment policy: in time, he reckoned, the inherent contradictions and conflict within the capitalist system would cause it to self-destruct, and people the world over would follow a variety of paths to arrive at a socialist future.

Since direct conflict with the West would place the USSR and the world in dire peril, Khrushchev opted instead for indirect confrontation in what was coming to be known as the "Third World." As the peoples of Asia and Africa began to assert their independence from Western control, Moscow sought in various ways to win their friendship and support. National liberation movements and nonaligned nations often found the Soviets willing to provide them with arms and advisors, as well as financial aid. Taking his cue from Leninist theory, Khrushchev treated these movements and nations as natural allies of the industrial proletariat in their struggles against capitalist imperialism. In so doing, he deftly managed to maneuver the United States, a nation born of anticolonial revolution and dedicated to national self-determination, into the role of defender of the status quo and opponent of revolutionary nationalism.

Khrushchev's approach was especially relevant to Asia, where Moscow sought to exploit anti-Western sentiments in former European colonies like India and Indonesia. In these nations, as elsewhere in the Third World, the nationalist movements predated the Cold War and existed independently of superpower rivalries. This explains why it was always difficult to analyze Third World revolts using Cold War terminology, and why it was often inaccurate to portray uprisings around the world as merely functions of the global rivalry between Washington and Moscow.

India, the "crown jewel" of English monarchs, had gained its independence in 1947 after years of nonviolent marches and hunger strikes, led by an Oxford-educated Hindu lawyer and saint named Mohandas ("Mahatma") Gandhi. The immense religio-cultural chasm that divided Hindu from Muslim had made it necessary to divide the subcontinent into a Hindu nation (India) and a Muslim nation (Pakistan). For reasons totally unrelated to the Cold War, the two nations had been born as mortal enemies.

Jawaharlal Nehru, a close associate of Gandhi, ruled India as prime minister from 1950 until his death in 1964. Brooding yet lively, morbid yet energetic, Nehru strove to create a more stable world free from the danger of nuclear war. Only in such a world could impoverished nations like India, to say nothing of those still trapped in colonial bondage, develop their resources to build better lives. To that end, he adopted a foreign policy of nonalignment, taking a leading part in the 1955 Conference of Nonaligned Nations at Bandung, Indonesia, and linking himself with leaders like

Nasser, Nehru, and Tito. (UPI/Bettmann)

Indonesia's Sukarno and Egypt's Nasser in promoting a third path between capitalism and communism.

Pakistan would have none of this. Its foreign policy was largely determined by its rivalry with India, with which it contested rights to the former princely state of Kashmir. While India carved out a centrist course, Pakistan linked its fortunes to the United States, from which it enjoyed significant amounts of military and developmental aid. Moscow stepped in to provide the same sort of aid to India, with Khrushchev and his successors dispensing a substantial amount of technical and economic assistance. Ironically, the USSR ended up supporting India, the world's largest democracy, while Washington backed authoritarian Pakistan. Such was the logic of the Cold War!

Indonesia, formerly the Dutch East Indies, had also gained independence after World War II. In 1927, a civil engineer named Ahmed Sukarno had founded the Nationalist party to seek expulsion of the Dutch. When

Japan surrendered in 1945, the Nationalists had quickly proclaimed a sovereign state called Indonesia, naming Sukarno president. They had then proceeded to wear down the Dutch in an exhausting four-year struggle. By 1949, Sukarno headed a chain of islands nearly 3400 miles long, with a population approaching 100 million people, most of whom were Muslim.

Like Nehru, Sukarno embraced nonalignment. In April 1955, while the Soviets and the Western powers were still trying to make arrangements for their summit conference at Geneva, Sukarno hosted a different sort of summit meeting in Bandung, Indonesia. The Bandung Conference brought together leaders from twenty-nine nations, mostly in Asia and Africa, which considered themselves part of neither the Soviet bloc nor the Western world. Their purpose was to establish a "nonaligned movement," beholden to neither East nor West, which would pursue an independent course. Along with Sukarno, India's Nehru, Yugoslavia's Tito, and Gamal Abdel Nasser of Egypt all sought a leading role.

The Bandung Conference founded the nonaligned movement and stamped Sukarno as a leader aspiring to global stature. But unlike Nehru, Sukarno was not motivated by visions of stability and peace. He was a thoroughly romantic revolutionary who dreamed of nations on fire with the fervor of forceful change, a man enthralled by the spiritual purification to be derived from righteous action, the Ignatius Loyola of nonalignment. The Americans, who distrusted Nehru and disapproved of Nasser, regarded Sukarno with the sort of horrified fascination displayed by a jungle traveler confronting a cobra. But the Soviets, anxious to woo the nonaligned nations and undermine the West, established close ties with him. Indonesia became a Soviet client and would remain so until the mid-1960s, when an unsuccessful war with Malaysia and a failed military coup would lead to the eclipse of Sukarno and a murderous campaign of suppression against the Indonesian Communists. By 1967, Sukarno would be removed, and General Suharto, whose anticommunist crusade had slain over 100,000 people and filled Indonesia's rivers with headless corpses, would emerge as military strongman and lead Indonesia into the Western camp.

The Indonesia story demonstrates the limits of nonalignment. It was all very well for a nation like Indonesia or India to pose as the leader of a third alternative, but to translate this posturing into effective action was a different story entirely. Indonesia was a client state, first of the East, later of the West, and client states cannot truly be nonaligned. As long as the emerging nations of Asia and Africa needed economic and military aid from the superpowers, not only their alignment but also their very independence would be compromised.

These events would also show how treacherous it could be for Moscow to go fishing in the troubled waters of the nonaligned nations. Even where the Kremlin did make inroads, as in Indonesia, there was no guarantee the influence would last. Once Sukarno was removed, Moscow's influence would be gone, and a substantial Soviet investment would be washed down the drain.

Still, in the mid-1950s, Soviet attempts to gain influence among the non-aligned nations appeared to be bearing fruit. Moscow was acquiring important friends in India and Indonesia and was even making headway in Egypt (see below). As the Kremlin extended economic and military aid to selected countries in Africa and Asia, Soviet stature in the Third World seemed to be on the rise.

KHRUSHCHEV AND STALIN'S LEGACY

In 1956, his standing enhanced by an impressive performance on the international stage, Khrushchev turned his attention to the Twentieth Party Congress which met in Moscow in February. There, in a highly publicized speech, he modified the Marxist tenet that war was inevitable and issued a call for "peaceful coexistence" between different social systems. The highlight of the gathering, however, was his dramatic "secret speech." Late in the evening of 24 February, delegates were summoned back to the conference hall for a special closed session to which no outsiders were admitted. Beginning around midnight, the party leader proceeded to deliver an astonishing four-hour address which methodically exposed and denounced the crimes of Joseph Stalin. He accused the late dictator of having created a "cult of personality," ordered the torture and murder of many loyal party members, and imprisoned legions of innocent people. He also blamed Stalin for terrible "mistakes," such as leaving his country disastrously unprepared for war and causing the Soviet break with socialist Yugoslavia. The delegates, many of whom (like Khrushchev) had been loyal supporters of Stalin, were shocked and stunned by the candor and content of this address.

The speech, it turned out, was hardly a secret for long. Copies were distributed among party members, to be read at private meetings throughout the USSR, and by June the U.S. State Department had obtained, translated, and published a version in the West. Khrushchev no doubt intended the address as a conscious break with the past and as part of a move against his internal "Stalinist" rivals. But this speech, along with his other pronouncements at the Twentieth Party Congress, also had a wider significance: by disassociating the Soviet system from the violent abuses of its Stalinist past, Khrushchev aimed to make it a more attractive model for the developing nations of the future.

At first it appeared that the congress might lead to a further easing of anxieties. In April, the Cominform, created in 1947 to help Moscow maintain its influence over other communist parties, was formally dissolved. That same month Khrushchev made a state visit to Britain—his first trip to a major Western power. In June, the recalcitrant Molotov stepped down as foreign minister, although he, Malenkov, and several other Khrushchev rivals would remain members of the Party Presidium until the following year. This was followed by a visit to Moscow from Yugoslavia's Tito, who was welcomed with open arms. These developments, coming on top of Khrushchev's call for "separate roads to socialism" and his renunciation of Stalinist terror, seemed to indicate that the USSR was willing to improve relations with the West and relax its grip on Eastern Europe.

Despite the Kremlin's softer line, however, the Warsaw Pact nations were still dominated largely by disciples of Stalin. In denouncing their mentor, Khrushchev had undermined them and thus set the stage for dramatic developments in Poland and Hungary.

In July 1956, in the Polish city of Poznán, a bloody clash occurred between rioting factory workers and city police. Before long, as the crisis threatened to escalate into a nationwide liberation movement, the Polish government began removing hardline officials and replacing them with "moderates" who were not linked directly with Soviet control. On 19 October, Wladislaw Gomulka, who had been purged by Stalin as a "Titoist" and only released from prison in 1955, was selected as first secretary of the Polish United Workers' (Communist) party. Alarmed, Khrushchev flew to Warsaw and threatened to use Soviet troops to keep the Polish leaders in line. Gomulka, with broad support among the Polish workers, was able to hold his own by warning of massive popular resistance to any such attack. Rather than face a possible war in Poland, the Kremlin leader backed down and, reassured that Gomulka would not take Poland out of the Soviet bloc, agreed to work with the new Polish leader.

In Hungary, however, things did not work out so well. Encouraged by the Polish success, students in Budapest began to demonstrate on 22 and 23 October for the return to power of the reform-minded premier Imre Nagy, who had been forced out of office the previous year. The Soviet Union sent planes and tanks to help put down the riots, but this merely stoked the fires of revolt, and Hungarian "freedom fighters" soon clashed in the streets with units of the Red Army. Nagy returned as premier and, with Moscow's consent, on 27 October formed a new government that included prominent non-Communists. The next day, the Soviets began to withdraw their forces from Budapest. Khrushchev had once again shown a willingness to compromise and to allow an East European nation to pursue its own road to socialism.

But the Hungarians, unlike the Poles, were unwilling to settle for partial autonomy. The demonstrations continued, amid demands for further reforms and real independence from Soviet control. Bowing to popular pressure, on 1 November Nagy announced that he would establish a multiparty government, declare his nation's neutrality, and withdraw Hungary from the Warsaw Pact. This created a sense of euphoria in Hungary and the West, but the celebrations were short-lived. On the morning of 4 November, Soviet tanks began rolling into Budapest, and Red Army soldiers were soon battling with the thousands of Hungarian resisters who took to the streets to defend the Nagy regime. János Kádár, the head of the Hungarian Communist party, announced the formation of a new government and appealed to Moscow for military aid to "smash the dark forces of reaction." Within a week, the resistance had been

The Hungarian uprising of 1956. (UPI/Bettman)

crushed, thousands of Hungarians lay dead, and Kádár was in firm control. Nagy sought asylum in the Yugoslav embassy, but he was eventually talked into leaving, arrested, and executed by the Soviets.

The West was caught flatfooted by the brutal suppression of the Hungarian revolt. The United States and Britain, deeply at odds over the simultaneous Suez crisis (discussed below), were incapable of a joint response. John Foster Dulles, who had cancer surgery on the eve of the Soviet invasion, was likewise incapacitated. The imminence of the U.S. presidential elections, which took place on 6 November, complicated things still further. But even without these distractions, there was little real chance that the Americans or their allies would actually intervene. Western speeches and radio broadcasts had encouraged the Hungarian rioters and led some to think that help might be forthcoming from the United States. But the logistics of providing aid would have been so complex, the dangers so great, and the chances of success so slim, that it was never seriously considered. When push came to shove, as the events of 1956 made clear, the West was unprepared to interfere directly within the Communist bloc.

Nevertheless, the tragic events in Hungary had a devastating impact on international relations, destroying the climate of hope that had been created by Khrushchev's initiatives. The Soviet intervention was formally denounced by the United Nations, while Western leaders and citizens expressed shock and outrage at the brutal and bloody affair. Several hundred thousand Hungarians managed to flee their homeland and take up residence as refugees in the West. This was all accompanied by a certain retrenchment within the communist world, as a harsher attitude toward the West seemed to reemerge. Both Tito and Gomulka gave their tacit support to the Soviet move against Hungary, and Khrushchev himself publicly adopted a tough and unapologetic stance. "When it is a question of fighting against imperialism," he announced on the last day of 1956, "we can state with conviction that we are all Stalinists."

THE SUEZ CRISIS, 1956

In late October of 1956, while Moscow was preoccupied with the Hungarian revolt and the United States was in the final stages of its presidential election campaign, a major crisis erupted in the Middle East. The immediate cause of the crisis was an Israeli invasion of Egypt and rapid intervention by Britain and France on the Israeli side. But the underlying factors that engendered these events, and served to make the region a tinderbox throughout the Cold War period, were the dependence of the West on Mideast oil, the rise of Arab nationalism, and the existence of a Jewish state in the midst of the Muslim world.

It just so happened that the world's most extensive oil reserves were located in the Middle East. The vast petroleum deposits of Saudi Arabia, Iraq, and other Persian Gulf lands were of crucial importance to the industrial economies of Western Europe and Japan. In World War II, the Japanese had attacked America largely because of their need for oil, and Germany's inability to supply its armored units and airplanes with gasoline had ensured its defeat. Notwithstanding the large domestic petroleum resources of both the United States and USSR, victory in the Cold War might well depend on access to Middle Eastern oil.

The rise of Arab nationalism was a direct result of the formation of Israel in 1948 and Arab humiliation at Israeli hands in the war that followed (Chapter 5). For decades, the Arab world had been torn by dynastic rivalries which pitted the Hashemite monarchs of Jordan and Iraq against the ruling dynasties of Egypt and Saudi Arabia. However, in the wake of the military debacle of 1948–1949, new political forces had arisen to oppose these traditional regimes, hoping to overcome the divisions among Arabs by creating secular governments dedicated to the destruction of Israel. Ironically, since Israel was supported at first by both the United States and the USSR, and since Marxism, with its denial of the spiritual dimension of human existence,

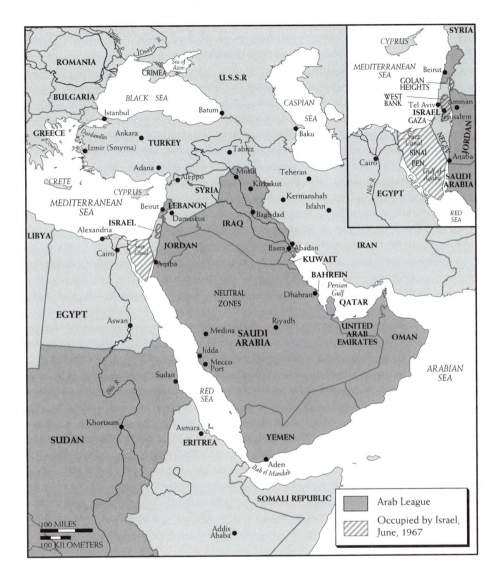

MAP 9 The Middle East

remained an alien philosophy among the Muslim peoples of the Middle East, these new forces were at first both anti-Western and anti-Soviet.

The most notable changes had taken place in Egypt, largely as a result of the Egyptian army's humiliation in 1948–1949 and Britain's continuing control of the Nile Valley and Suez Canal. In July 1952, Egypt's King Farouk had been overthrown by a group of military officers led by General Mohammad Naguib and Colonel Gamal Abdel Nasser. In 1955, Nasser attended the Bandung Conference and initiated contacts with Third World nationalist leaders. By this time, it was obvious that he aspired to continue the longstanding Egyptian struggle against the Hashemites for leadership of the Muslim world and to take advantage of anti-Zionist sentiments to unite the Arab peoples. By late 1955, Nasser saw himself as a potential leader of the nonaligned movement and unifier of the Arab world. Egypt charted a neutralist course, while Washington and Moscow watched uneasily.

Concerned that Nasser might turn to the USSR for assistance, America offered substantial aid to Egypt and, in conjunction with Moscow, pressed the British to accommodate Nasser's demands for full sovereignty over the Suez Canal (see Map 9, p. 131). When the British agreed to leave in 1954, the Americans hoped that Nasser would join the Baghdad Pact and align Egypt with the West, but longstanding regional rivalries prevented this. In September 1955, Nasser tried to outflank Baghdad and Washington by agreeing to sell cotton to the USSR in exchange for Czech weapons. Moscow then opportunistically advanced itself as the champion of Arab nationalism against American and British imperialism, and its guns promised to give Egypt the power to stand up to Israel.

Washington and London, hoping to keep Nasser out of the communist camp, agreed in 1955 to provide funding for an immense Egyptian power and irrigation project called the Aswan High Dam. But in the spring of 1956, Nasser recognized communist China, in protest against a U.S. decision to let France sell to Israel arms originally intended for NATO. The Americans responded by withdrawing funding from the dam project on 21 July. Five days later Nasser nationalized the Suez Canal, intending to use its tolls to build the dam. The Soviet government quickly announced that it would provide the financial and technical assistance so precipitately withdrawn by the West. Britain and France now saw Nasser as an unstable demagogue, ready to hold hostage the oil and other products passing through the canal whenever he—or Moscow—decided that such action would be appropriate.

Nasser, who was not at all unstable, became the de facto leader of the Arab world, and Syria and Jordan drew closer to Egypt. But Arab nationalism now posed a direct threat to European prosperity, and Israel feared for its continued existence should Nasser succeed. Therefore, in the fall of 1956, Britain, France, and Israel conspired to attack Egypt, reasoning that a preventive war was called for on the assumptions that Nasser was planning to cut off Europe's oil supplies (which was unlikely, given his need for revenue from the canal) and then attack Israel. The arrangements were concealed from Washington, largely because its courtship of Nasser had irritated and frightened London and Paris. The conspirators seem to have concluded that there was little risk of Soviet intervention on Egypt's side, since events in Poland and Hungary were monopolizing Khrushchev's attention.

The Israelis invaded Egypt on 29 October. As agreed, the British and French then intervened to "restore order," although their true purpose was to recapture the canal and remove Egypt as a threat to Israel's existence. But they failed to take the canal in heavy fighting involving airborne and amphibious forces. The Americans, whose aerial espionage had detected Israeli preparations two weeks before the assault, were annoyed. They feared that the real winners in a prolonged war would be the Soviets and their Arab nationalist clients and therefore obtained UN resolutions prescribing the cessation of hostilities and the withdrawal of all invading troops. The USSR, fearing an Egyptian defeat and happy to embarrass Britain, joined the United States in condemning the aggression. London and Paris were forced to agree to a cease-fire on 6 November and a pullout in the ensuing months.

The crisis passed, but its impact upon the Western alliance was devastating. British prime minister Anthony Eden was forced to resign, and U.S. president Eisenhower had been placed in the uncomfortable position of disavowing America's closest allies while supporting Nasser and Khrushchev. The Europeans' failure to seize the canal proved mortifying, and their inability to act militarily in the absence of U.S. support clearly foreshadowed the steep decline of Europe's influence in the Middle East.

No one came out of Suez untarnished. Moscow may have won points with the Arabs by backing Egypt, but its military impotence in the Middle East was striking. For his part, Nasser had nowhere to turn for assistance other than the USSR, but he was hardly enthusiastic about the prospect. This marriage of convenience would last until the mid-1970s when Anwar Sadat's abrogation of the Soviet-Egyptian friendship would terminate a relationship with which neither side had been comfortable. The Soviets would remain outsiders in the region, unable to match Washington's potential influence.

To make matters worse, Moscow's hypocrisy in condemning the aggression was exposed simultaneously by the Soviet suppression of the Hungarian uprising, while Washington's was demonstrated when the United States sent Marines into Lebanon less than two years later. The Eisenhower Doctrine (1957), in some ways an extension of the Truman Doctrine, offered military and economic assistance to any Middle East nation facing communist subversion. It would be invoked in July 1958 when General Abdel Karim Kassem, backed by Iraqi Communists and Arab nationalists, overthrew the Hashemite monarchy in Iraq. Eisenhower responded by landing Marines in Lebanon to protect that country and Jordan from similar coups. The superpowers were obviously more than willing to use force when their own interests were at stake.

THE ARMS RACE AND THE SPACE RACE

Not only did the various crises of 1956 serve to derail the movement toward East-West détente, they also undermined the position of Khrushchev himself. Hardliners like Molotov, incensed at his denunciation of Stalin and disturbed by the Hungarian debacle, made common cause with Malenkov and others whose influence had waned. In June of 1957, while Khrushchev was in Finland, his foes decided to strike. A majority of the Party Presidium, including Malenkov and Molotov, voted to oust him from his position as first secretary. Returning quickly, the besieged Soviet leader fought back, insisting that he could be removed only by the Party's Central Committee which had elected him. With the help of Defense Minister Georgi Zhukov, who dispatched aircraft to bring its members quickly to Moscow, Khrushchev was able to convene the Central Committee and have it reaffirm his position. He then had his chief rivals demoted to obscure posts: Malenkov became manager of a power station in Kazakhstan, and Molotov was made ambassador to Mongolia.

Khrushchev's victory over the "Anti-Party Group," as it came to be known, did not give him unfettered power. Even after he assumed the office of premier in March 1958, thus consolidating control of both government and party in his own hands, he found it necessary to maintain the support of various elements and factions. His foreign policy reflected his ambivalent position. On one hand, he sought to restore the momentum to improvement of East-West relations, which had been interrupted by the events of 1956. On the other hand, in order to mollify the hardliners in his own entourage and enhance his credibility as a world leader, he found it useful to resort to belligerent speeches and displays of military muscle. In so doing, he helped to undermine his own efforts at détente and accelerate the arms race with the West.

In the early 1950s, both the USSR and the United States had begun developing a new generation of nuclear weapons that were far more powerful than the relatively primitive bombs that had obliterated Hiroshima and Nagasaki. Those original devices had been based on nuclear *fission*, a process that involved splitting uranium atoms to release the energy stored in their nuclei, creating a chain reaction of devastating force. After the successful Soviet atomic test in 1949 had destroyed the U.S. monopoly, President Truman had authorized his scientists to begin work on a new type of bomb based instead on nuclear *fusion*. Physicists calculated that it would be possible to release even greater amounts of energy by fusing together the atoms of hydrogen isotopes. Within a few years, they had completed their work. Using an atomic fission bomb to produce the million-degree temperatures needed to initiate such a reaction, American scientists achieved the first "thermonuclear" explosion in November of 1952. The force of this blast was equivalent to over three million tons of TNT—hundreds of times greater than the most devastating weapons hitherto produced. The age of the hydrogen bomb had arrived.

The following year, to the chagrin of their Western adversaries, the Soviets exploded their own H-bomb, showing that they were closing the gap in developing destructive technologies. In their ability to mass-produce nuclear weapons, however, and to deliver them to distant targets, they remained well behind the United States. In 1953, the Americans possessed over a thousand atomic bombs—at least ten times as many as the Soviets had—and they were building a fleet of B-52 bombers capable of reaching the USSR. Under Eisenhower and Dulles, as the Americans emphasized "massive retaliation," their lead continued to grow, and they even began building "tactical" nuclear weapons designed for battlefield use.

Khrushchev's response to all this was to try to deceive the West by creating the impression that the Soviets had far more weapons than they actually possessed. He thus sought to enhance his nation's power position by exaggerating its strength. In June of 1955, for example, the Soviets impressed observers with the large number of new long-range bombers that were flown over Moscow on Aviation Day. In fact, they only had a small number of bombers, but they created an impression of having many more by flying the same planes several times over the city.

The impact of this obfuscation, however, was merely to add fuel to the arms race. In the United States, critics began to raise fears that there existed a huge "bomber gap" favoring the USSR. In order to get a better handle on Soviet capabilities, Eisenhower ordered the development of a new type of aircraft, the U-2 spy plane, which was designed to elude interception by flying long distances at very high altitudes. Within a few years, U-2 overflights of the USSR would demonstrate that the "bomber gap" existed in reverse and that the United States actually had a substantial lead in the number of long-range bombers. But, for fear of compromising the U-2, the administration could not reveal this information. Besides, the very fact that the USSR possessed bombers capable of delivering nuclear bombs against the United States left Americans feeling vulnerable. Programs of civil defense, complete with the construction and designation of "fallout shelters" to house survivors of an atomic attack, were started across the land. Never again would U.S. citizens feel completely secure: the horrible specter of nuclear war was intruding on America.

Jet bombers, however, for all their destructive capacity, were not an ultimate weapon. They were piloted by humans, took many hours to reach their targets, and were to some extent susceptible to enemy defense. Much more fearsome were new unmanned rocket systems, capable of delivering nuclear payloads from one side of the world to the other. These intercontinental ballistic missiles (ICBMs) were destined to become, in just a few years, the very symbols of the nuclear arms race.

On 26 August 1957, the USSR announced that it had successfully tested the world's first ICBM. This was a stunning achievement: for the first time, the Soviets had beaten the United States in developing a major weapons system.

But even more shocking news came several weeks later. On 4 October 1957, Soviet scientists launched into orbit an artificial earth satellite known as Sputnik I, from a Russian word meaning "fellow traveler." The space race was on, and the USSR had the lead!

This was an enormous setback for the West. It undermined the Americans' faith in their science and technology and even their educational system. Before long critics were claiming that U.S. grammar schools did not teach enough arithmetic and that American science and mathematics education was woefully lacking in comparison with that received by Soviet students. In the developing nations, it added greatly to the prestige of the USSR, which had shown that a poor nation could make enormous strides in a rather short time by following the socialist path.

The U.S. space program, embarrassed by its apparent lag, began speeding up efforts to launch its own artificial earth satellite. But in December of 1957, one of America's new Vanguard missiles blew up on its launching pad, further compounding the national sense of humiliation and frustration. Only in January of 1958 did the United States finally join the Soviets in space, when a team of scientists led by Wernher von Braun, a missile expert who had helped develop the German V-2 rockets during World War II, successfully propelled a small satellite into earth orbit.

By this time, however, the Americans' self-confidence had been shattered. In November of 1957, the Soviets had launched Sputnik II, a much larger satellite that carried a dog on board. The USSR obviously had booster rockets that were much more powerful than anything the United States had developed. Dire warnings of a "missile gap" were issued throughout the land, as critics of the administration warned of imminent danger. In fact, no such "gap" ever existed: the Soviets, having decided to await further technological advances before investing heavily in ICBMs, built only a small number of their primitive early missiles. But the Americans did not know this, and Khrushchev skillfully exploited their fears by trumpeting his country's nonexistent lead.

Ironically, Khrushchev's clever deceptions and saber-rattling speeches gave an unintended boost to the U.S. military-industrial establishment. Anxious to secure increased funding for new weapons systems, Pentagon planners were only too eager to buttress their case by pointing with alarm to the "missile gap." Eisenhower, who of course had access to information provided by the secret U-2 flights, refused to panic, but U.S. nuclear forces did grow substantially during the next few years.

More important than their numbers, however, was the impact of the Soviet missiles on the perceived strategic balance. If the USSR had rockets that could launch a dog into space, it clearly had the capacity to deliver nuclear warheads against the United States, and to do so much more quickly than long-range bombers could. Not only did this destroy what was left of the American sense of security, it also called into question the viability of the NATO policy of using the threat of a U.S. nuclear response to deter a Soviet conventional attack. American presidents could no longer threaten to use atomic weapons with impunity, and their allies could no longer be quite so confident of U.S. nuclear support in the event of a Soviet invasion. Crossing the nuclear threshold was now even riskier than ever, since it could well lead to vast devastation in the United States itself.

By the late 1950s, then, the Cold War was becoming a permanent state of affairs. On one hand, hobbled by historic hostility and divided by deep distrust, the two sides were unable to resolve their differences and arrive at an accommodation. On the other hand, faced with the terrifying consequences of a nuclear confrontation, neither could seriously contemplate the elimination or incapacitation of its enemy. They thus found themselves maneuvering for advantage in a complex and volatile environment, striving all the while to manage their rivalry so it did not destroy them both.

9

The Perpetuation of the Cold War, 1957–1961

By 1957 it was clear that, despite the openings presented by Stalin's death and the hopes generated by Khrushchev's secret speech, the Cold War had become an enduring phenomenon. During the next few years, both sides would seek to defuse the conflict, sometimes by bluster and sometimes by accommodation. For a while, it appeared as if real progress was being made, but the legacy of distrust, combined with superpower meddling in Africa and the unfortunate U-2 incident of 1960, would preclude any real détente and result in the perpetuation of the Cold War.

THE QUESTION OF GERMAN NEUTRALITY

For a time in the mid-1950s, while the world was absorbed with events like Khrushchev's attack on Stalin, the rebellions in Poland and Hungary, and the Suez Crisis, the German Question had seemed to fade into the background. But it was not destined to stay there for long. In October 1957, just a few days after the Soviet Union launched "Sputnik," the world's first artificial satellite, Polish foreign minister Adam Rapacki proposed the establishment of a "denuclearized zone in Central Europe," consisting of Poland, Czechoslovakia, and both parts of Germany.

The Rapacki Plan was a response to a NATO decision to rearm West Germany. In 1956, West German chancellor Konrad Adenauer had asked the West to provide his nation with bombers, artillery, and missiles that could give it a nuclear capability if properly configured and armed. The missiles would not be delivered until 1980, but the bombers and artillery were deployed at once, and European leaders began to think twice about the possibility of German neutrality. In the United States, George Kennan suggested that the West press for neutralization of all of Central and Eastern Europe, using as a bargaining chip the possible "nuclearization" of West Germany. Former Secretary of State Dean Acheson retorted that this would be very dangerous, since a neutralized Germany would float between East and West, raising the specter of renewed German efforts to dominate Europe. In addition, the withdrawal of U.S. troops might make it possible for the USSR to communize Central Europe through internal subversion.

Whatever advantage Americans might hope to derive from it, the prospect of West Germany becoming a nuclear power brought Moscow up short and prompted some serious thinking in the Communist bloc about ways to head off this horror. The Rapacki Plan provided a thoughtful and attractive alternative to the remilitarization of Germany and a possible first step toward resolving the German Question.

In 1958, however, the United States formally rejected the Rapacki Plan on the premise that Western troops in Germany, unless equipped with nuclear weapons, would be at the mercy of the vast Soviet conventional forces in Central and Eastern Europe. Washington also pointed out that the plan would require the West to give up something it might wish to do (arming West Germany) while requiring the Soviets to refrain from doing something they had no intention of doing (arming Poland, Czechoslovakia, and East Germany). In reality, as Michael Beschloss has pointed out, the West had little to lose, since it was *not* planning to give nuclear weapons to Bonn, while a nuclear-free zone in Central Europe involving some sort of international monitoring might have weakened Soviet control over Poland, Czechoslovakia, and East Germany. At any rate, Moscow gained a propaganda advantage from the proposal, but since the attention of the world was largely diverted by Sputnik, even that advantage was limited.

Still, the West's decision to rearm West Germany, and its rejection of the Rapacki Plan, pointed up an uncomfortable anomaly in its approach to Central Europe. Whatever Western leaders might say in public about the tragedy of a divided Germany, in private they were just as happy to keep it that way, and they were by no means enthralled with any notion of unification that would entail German neutrality.

Konrad Adenauer, who served as West German chancellor from 1949 until 1963, consistently opposed Soviet offers to reunify and neutralize Germany despite his unabashed patriotism. His motives were complex. He was convinced that any reunited Germany must be firmly tied to the West if it hoped to avoid a repetition of the Nazi nightmare, given what he considered the Germans' ingrained tendency to behave so terribly as to unite the world against them. As a Rhenish Catholic, he despised the East German *Saupreussen*

Adenauer and de Gaulle. (UPI/Bettmann)

("sow Prussians"), considering them Eastern European militarists with marginal ties to the West. He also feared that, since most East Germans were Protestant and socialist, his Catholic and capitalist Christian Democratic Union would probably be voted out of office in a reunified nation. His reluctance to surrender West German gains presented Moscow with an imposing roadblock, but even had he been more forthcoming, other Western leaders would have been difficult to convince.

The United States, led by President Eisenhower, wanted to tie any reunited Germany to NATO and the European Economic Community (EEC), failing which it preferred continued division. In 1954, when Moscow had offered a united Germany from which all foreign troops would be withdrawn, under some sort of system which would perpetuate East Germany's socialist accomplishments, the United States had not been interested. France, preoccupied with its collapsing empire, wanted closer economic ties with West Germany but remained troubled by the prospect of a reunified, rearmed, economically powerful Germany dominating Central Europe—even if that nation was firmly allied to NATO. Once Charles de Gaulle came to power in 1958, French opposition became more pronounced; Gaullists were skeptical of NATO's usefulness under the doctrine of massive retaliation, which posited an all-out nuclear response to any conventional Soviet attack on Western Europe. Most Frenchmen found it hard to believe that any U.S. government would risk the incineration of America to defend Paris against communism. De Gaulle accordingly sought closer ties with West Germany through the EEC and the Franco-German Friendship Treaty of 1963. Nor would Britain be any more likely to embrace Soviet initiatives: twice already, in 1917 and 1941, the intervention of the New World had saved the Old from German domination. London would follow America's lead on the German Question, regardless of whether a Conservative or a Labour government sat in Whitehall.

KHRUSHCHEV'S BERLIN ULTIMATUM, 1958–1959

By mid-1958, then, German reunification and neutralization lay dead in the water, and the Rapacki Plan floated motionless alongside. Khrushchev spent the early months of that year consolidating his power: in March he ousted Premier Bulganin and assumed that office himself, ending any pretense of collective leadership. That autumn he once again addressed the German Question. On 10 November, he declared his intent to sign a peace treaty with East Germany that would force the Western powers to negotiate access rights to West Berlin directly with the East German government. Washington, London, and Paris quickly replied that their rights in West Berlin were guaranteed by the 1945 Yalta agreements, which predated the creation of East Germany. On 27 November, Khrushchev promised no alteration in Berlin's status for a period of six months, during which negotiations should lead to the withdrawal of all foreign troops and UN recognition of Berlin as a free city. Eisenhower was willing to consider this, as long as both East and West Berlin were included and all access routes were patrolled by the UN; but Khrushchev wanted to turn East Berlin over to East Germany. His lengthy note abandoned previous Soviet insistence on reunification and neutralization: the unfortunate existence of two Germanies could be accepted, but the anomalous occupation of Berlin must end. The note carried the tone of an ultimatum: six months and out, or else.

Khrushchev hoped to use this threat as a negotiating tool to prevent West Germany from deploying nuclear weapons. If West Germany were to withdraw from NATO and East Germany from the Warsaw Pact, Germany would be effectively neutralized even if it were not reunified. But Khrushchev had bluffed too often, having threatened to use rockets during the Suez and Lebanon crises. Eisenhower, who knew the real limitations of the Soviet nuclear arsenal from U-2 espionage data, did not believe Moscow would go to war over Berlin. The six-month deadline baffled him, since he was unaware of Khrushchev's fear that the Sino-Soviet split was widening and would soon become public. For the time being, Beijing endorsed the 10 November note, being favorably inclined toward anything that would worsen relations between Moscow and Washington; but Khrushchev wanted results quickly, while he could still derive some leverage from the eroding Chinese alliance.

In the spring of 1959, a mild war scare afflicted the United States as the 27 May deadline approached. Eisenhower handled the situation skillfully, denying the existence of any real crisis, secure in the knowledge that the Soviet nuclear capability was exaggerated, and consistently demonstrating both his willingness to negotiate and his refusal to panic. He did, of course, have contingency plans: if the deadline passed and East Germany tried to cut off access to West Berlin, he was prepared to initiate a new airlift and sever relations with Moscow. But he doubted this would be necessary, and his doubts were well placed. London and Paris pushed for a summit meeting to settle the issue; Eisenhower and Secretary of State Dulles (then dying of cancer), wishing to avoid a meeting with Khrushchev unless there were guaranteed results, countered with the offer of a conference of foreign ministers in Geneva. It convened on 11 May, after Khrushchev hinted that his Berlin deadline would not expire as long as the meeting was proceeding satisfactorily. Simultaneously, he invited Eisenhower to visit the USSR, and the tension began to lift.

Eisenhower decided in July that if the foreign ministers' conference showed progress, he would invite Khrushchev to America for a few days in September. He asked Robert Murphy, his special representative, to convey the suggestion to Soviet first deputy premier Frol Kozlov, who was in New York to open Soviet art and technology exhibitions; Vice-President Richard Nixon was set to open comparable U.S. exhibitions two weeks later in Moscow. Unfortunately, Murphy was unaware of the linkage between the offer of the visit and the progress of the conference. He delivered an unconditional invitation, which Khrushchev accepted on 22 July. The Soviet leader announced that he would come in September for *ten* days and tour the entire country. Eisenhower, who had not bargained for this, was utterly exasperated and complained that the mix-up would not have occurred had Dulles been alive. Khrushchev, however, was exhilarated: a face-to-face sojourn with Eisenhower on U.S. soil would underline for the entire world the equality of status between the United States and USSR which he had sought to confirm through bluster and bluff since 1953.

Nixon arrived in Moscow the day after Khrushchev's acceptance. Under the circumstances, his journey took on a significance well beyond its original purpose. As Nixon and Khrushchev toured the kitchen of a "typical American home" exhibit, they needled each other, traded thinly veiled insults, and extolled the virtues of their respective systems. The "Kitchen Debate," captured on film, did wonders for Nixon's image in the United States and both stimulated and amused Khrushchev, who enjoyed the rare occasions on which adversaries stood up to him in blunt, earthy terms. For his part, Nixon recalled years later that of all the statesmen he had known, none had a "more devastating sense of humor, agile intelligence, tenacious sense of purpose and brutal will to power" than Khrushchev. This peculiar combination of crude Russian peasant and shrewd politician would shortly become the first Russian head of state to visit the United States.

KHRUSHCHEV'S TRIP TO AMERICA

On 15 September 1959, Premier and Mrs. Khrushchev arrived in Washington for a twelve-day visit which fascinated the world. The Soviet leader spent his first ten days meeting U.S. politicians and film stars, touring New York, Los Angeles, San Francisco, and Pittsburgh, discussing hybrid corn with Iowa farmer Roswell Garst, and publicly bemoaning his inability to visit Disneyland (security forces could not guarantee his safety among large crowds). Antipathy to the Soviet Union was of course widespread, and not everyone was friendly. Conservative columnist William F. Buckley suggested dyeing the Hudson River red so that Khrushchev could sail into New York Harbor on a sea of blood, but this novel suggestion was never implemented.

At the end of the visit, Khrushchev and Eisenhower spent two days in private talks at Camp David, the presidential retreat in Maryland's Catoctin Mountains. As might have been expected, the boisterous, earthy Ukrainian and the businesslike, impatient Kansan did not become close friends. Khrushchev's indirect effort to raise the subject of U.S. relations with China has intrigued historians ever since; apparently, he was laying the groundwork for a future attempt to barter Soviet help in scuttling China's nuclear program for a Western pledge to deny such weapons to West Germany and Japan. Although Eisenhower was aware of the deepening Sino-Soviet rift, he did not accept the gambit. But he did raise the German Question on the second day, persuading Khrushchev to cancel his Berlin ultimatum in exchange for a presidential promise to seek a fair solution in the near future and to endorse a summit meeting of the four great powers. Khrushchev, delighted, invited the entire Eisenhower family to visit Russia in June 1960 and flew back to a hero's welcome in Moscow.

On the face of it, the trip produced modest results, but on a less tangible level its effects were significant. Khrushchev had demonstrated his equality with Eisenhower and had defended Soviet interests with vigor and skill; his stature in his own government was enhanced considerably. Eisenhower, entering the final year of his presidency, now believed that Khrushchev was a man

Eisenhower and Khrushchev at Camp David in September 1959.
(United States Army)

with whom he might work for a truly lasting peace that would constitute his final legacy to his country and the world. The Soviet people, proud of their leader's achievement, hoped for a restoration of the wartime friendship with America which many remembered wistfully, while the Americans, getting a close look at the first communist leader ever to visit their shores, sensed with some surprise that Khrushchev was not a monster but a man, and not an entirely unpleasant man at that. The visit helped to stabilize U.S.-Soviet relations and furnished a benchmark against which later such trips would be judged. What did it matter that the German Question had not been settled? No one had thought it would be, and at least it had been rendered less explosive. Further progress could be expected at the summit in 1960.

THE NUCLEAR TEST BAN ISSUE

One of the key issues to be discussed at the summit was the banning of nuclear tests. During the 1950s, as both superpowers tried out their nuclear bombs, there had arisen a growing concern about the deadly fallout these explosions caused. World attention had been drawn to the problem in 1954, when a huge U.S. H-bomb test in the western Pacific rained radioactive fragments upon a boat full of Japanese fishermen, poisoning them with radiation sickness. Before long, scientists and luminaries like Albert Einstein and Albert Schweitzer were calling for an end to such tests. The Soviet arms proposal of 10 May 1955 advocated a ban on nuclear blasts, and, in the U.S. presidential campaign of 1956, candidate Adlai Stevenson proposed a joint moratorium on the testing of hydrogen bombs. Unfortunately for Stevenson, Moscow compromised him by endorsing his proposal. And the Eisenhower administration, which was using its tests to develop a new generation of weapons, remained opposed to any moratorium.

By the following year, however, the international clamor had become so strident—and so damaging to the U.S. image—that the administration began to rethink its position. Even Secretary of State Dulles, who had little use for arms control, gradually changed his tune as it became clear that U.S. opposition to a test ban was giving Moscow an edge in the court of world opinion. The Soviets, meanwhile, were scoring public relations points by periodically offering to suspend their nuclear tests for two or three years, provided the United States would follow suit.

At first the Americans, who were working on a "clean" bomb that was relatively fallout-free, had tried to finesse the issue by floating a counterproposal hedged with provisions unacceptable to Moscow. But on 31 March 1958, the Soviets, having just finished a series of nuclear tests, announced the voluntary suspension of their own testing program and invited the United States to join them. Their timing was superb. The Americans, on the verge of beginning their own series of tests, refused to go along and thus offended world opinion. To save face, Eisenhower called for a conference of technical experts from East and West to devise an inspection and detection system. After some hesitation, Khrushchev agreed, and in the summer of 1958 technicians from the United States, Britain, and the USSR met at Geneva and designed a workable approach. Eisenhower, sensing a chance to restore his nation's lost prestige, invited the Soviets to meet and negotiate a comprehensive test ban treaty, beginning on 31 October. For good measure, he announced that the United States (which was completing its own test series) would cease testing for a year beginning on that date. The British soon followed suit. The Soviets finally agreed to the talks, and, after a few quick tests in early November, they announced their own moratorium. Hopes were raised the world over, as it began to look as if a test ban was within reach.

But difficulties remained. It was true that the nuclear powers had decided to stop contaminating the planet with fallout, at least for the time being, and this was cause for hope. And indeed, for almost three years no atomic tests by either side were detected. Moreover, in a key concession made early in 1959, the United States and Britain agreed to decouple the test ban from other arms issues. But the talks, held in Geneva, soon ran into a stumbling block. The United States announced that the detection system worked out by the experts was deficient in one key respect: it could not identify small nuclear tests conducted underground. This flaw did not prove fatal, but it did delay things for almost a year, as negotiators looked for a way around the problem. Finally, early in 1960, the United States and Britain suggested that the ban apply only to above-ground tests and underground blasts large enough to be detected with existing seismic equipment. Joint research could then seek technical advances to pick up smaller explosions. In March, the Soviets agreed, provided that both sides declare a moratorium on underground tests while the detection research was proceeding. In principle, the Western powers were willing to accept this, and there was reason to believe that remaining issues could be resolved at the Paris summit, scheduled to begin in May.

THE U-2 AFFAIR

Both Eisenhower and Khrushchev had wanted a summit earlier in the year, but French president Charles de Gaulle managed to delay it until after an atomic test in February 1960 made France the fourth member of the nuclear club, so he could host the meeting in Paris as an equal of the other three. Standing six feet five in a nation whose average man was a foot shorter, de Gaulle dominated France both physically and politically. Having resurrected French honor from the ignominy of collaboration with Nazi Germany in the 1940s, he returned from retirement in 1958 to rescue French democracy and eventually to extricate his country from a debilitating war in Algeria (see below). In the process, he implemented a new constitution and presided over the rapid modernization of one of Europe's most traditional societies.

To the Germans, de Gaulle was a formidable adversary turned potential ally; to the Soviets, a bemusing combination of farsighted statesman and strutting peacock; but to the British and Americans, he was an arrogant and ungrateful ally whose tenacious defense of French grandeur was neither understood nor appreciated. Frosty, suspicious, and eloquent, he stood not only for French dignity and sovereignty but also for a Europe positioned between Washington and Moscow, a Europe of independent nations and integrated economies, a Europe in which the United States and Britain possessed neither permanent interests nor a permanent place. He remembered Eisenhower fondly as an American general who had treated him and his country with respect, and he made it clear that if push came to shove, France would side with the West. But he insisted on an equal say in U.S. strategic decisions, being unimpressed with Soviet bluffs and suspecting that if the Cold War ever turned hot, it would be through American miscalculation rather than Russian aggression. In 1966 he would take France out of the NATO military command, asserting French sovereignty while remaining America's ally from (as he saw it) a position of equality. In 1960, holding the atomic bomb, he could play his hand to the limit and infuriate both sides with his penchant for unyieldingly independent action.

So de Gaulle had his way. The summit would convene in Paris on 16 May. Meanwhile, there was work to be done. Khrushchev had hoped for a summit before the end of 1959 because he intended to announce a Red Army troop reduction of 1.2 million men in January 1960. This move, undertaken to cut costs, would deprive him of elbow room for concessions at Paris and would put him under pressure from Kremlin hardliners to stand firm against the West. Given de Gaulle's intransigence, he was forced to make this disclosure well before the summit. Ironically, this attracted Eisenhower's attention and helped convince him that Khrushchev was ready to make serious moves in the direction of arms control. With real progress being made on the nuclear test ban issue, it appeared that the summit would furnish the occasion for Eisenhower to end his long career with a meaningful arms control measure and for Khrushchev to cap the arms race so that the Soviet economy could redirect its emphasis to consumer goods.

Inspections posed the most challenging remaining obstacle, since the U.S. Senate would be reluctant to ratify any treaty if it looked like the Russians could cheat. Given the closed nature of Soviet society, American compliance would be easier to judge than Russian. Since 1956, however, Eisenhower had received high-quality, top-secret photographic intelligence as to the nature and extent of the USSR's ballistic missile deployment. These photographs were provided by the CIA's U-2 reconnaissance planes, which could be expected to afford superb monitoring capability between the signing of a test ban and the anticipated deployment of a U.S. spy satellite in the early 1960s.

The U-2 was designed to cruise at 70,000 feet, far higher than any other aircraft and well above the 45,000-foot maximum range of the best Soviet surface-to-air missile. It carried huge cameras equipped with telescopic lenses that permitted continuous photography of a strip of land 750 miles wide. Taking off from bases in Japan, Pakistan, Turkey, West Germany, and Norway, it could traverse the USSR from any direction with a range of 4,750 miles. Beginning with its first mission on 4 July 1956, the U-2 flew only on the explicit orders of the president, who assisted the CIA and Department of Defense in target selection. The plane was so secret that America's own National Security Agency tracked its initial flights over Russia without knowing what it was. Its photographs convinced Eisenhower that as late as January 1960 Moscow had not a single operational ICBM, and the knowledge that the USSR was engaged neither in planning a nuclear attack nor in accelerating its weapons production helped the president to resist post-Sputnik demands for a vast missile buildup.

Eisenhower could not, of course, disclose the source of his information, any more than Moscow could tell the world about the U-2. Khrushchev was outraged by the flights, but to publicize them would be to admit that Soviet antiaircraft weapons could not defend the world's largest nation against repeated violations of its airspace. He lodged a generalized protest after the first flights in 1956 but remained silent thereafter. As a retired military officer, Eisenhower knew that it was only a matter of time before the Soviets developed a weapon that could bring the U-2 down, and when Khrushchev accepted his invitation to come to America, he suspended all flights over Russia for an indefinite period. Had that prohibition continued a few more months, the course of the Cold War might have been changed radically.

CIA director Allen Dulles asked in the spring for resumption of the U-2 missions, and Eisenhower, anxious for all possible insight into Soviet deployments prior to the summit, reluctantly agreed. Two presummit runs were authorized; the first, on 9 April, proceeded without incident. But the second, on 1 May, was reported missing. Soon the USSR announced that a U.S. plane had crashed in Soviet territory. Assuming that the pilot, a CIA operative named Francis Gary Powers, had either been killed in the crash or committed suicide per instructions, the United States put out a cover story that the plane was a weather flight that had strayed off course. In Moscow, Khrushchev faced a crisis. Holding off hardliners who wanted to use the incident as a pretext for canceling the summit, he decided to expose the wrecked aircraft as a spy plane. After further U.S. denials, he revealed that the pilot had been captured alive (for Powers had parachuted to safety and declined to take his own life). He hoped thus to put Eisenhower on the defensive and force him to apologize for intelligence services which had exceeded his orders—a standard defense mechanism used by politicians for ages. Khrushchev could then accept the apology and proceed to the summit in triumph, while Eisenhower would fly to Paris with egg on his face.

It was a promising scenario, and it unfurled flawlessly for a few days. The difficulty was that Khrushchev's solution to his dilemma placed Eisenhower in one of his own. If he denied authorizing U-2 flights, it would appear to the world that the U.S. president had so little control that his subordinates could trigger a major crisis without his knowledge. And Khrushchev might have more surprises up his sleeve: Who knew what Powers had said under interrogation? If Eisenhower lied, Khrushchev might be able to throw the lie back in his face. On the other hand, if he told the truth, he would become the first U.S. president to admit that his nation practiced peacetime espionage. It was difficult to imagine how Khrushchev could sit down with him in Paris and welcome him to Russia after such a disclosure, particularly since the Soviet leader had repeatedly assured his colleagues and people that Eisenhower was a man who could be trusted.

Either way, it was a gamble. Eisenhower chose the option for which his entire career as a military officer had conditioned him. He put out a statement to the effect that the U-2 flights had been carried out under his general orders and might continue until the USSR agreed to reciprocal inspection of bases and installations. With that revelation, the U-2 affair took on a different dimension, putting an end to the recent thaw in the Cold War and rupturing personal relations between Khrushchev and Eisenhower.

THE COLLAPSE OF THE PARIS SUMMIT

Khrushchev was beside himself. Eisenhower's decision to resume U-2 flights had placed him in a tough position; the crash of the 1 May flight and the pilot's survival (neither of which have ever been fully explained) presented him with an enticing opportunity; now the president's astonishing decision to accept personal responsibility for acts of espionage held him up to ridicule and left him few options. He responded with an emotional tirade which left little doubt that the Paris summit was in danger. Had he known that Eisenhower had instructed that the presidential plane, Air Force One, be equipped with high-resolution cameras for use during the president's travels within the USSR, his reaction may have been even stronger.

Still, something might be salvageable in Paris. The Soviet Presidium authorized Khrushchev to get there early; if he could obtain a public apology from Eisenhower, the summit and the president's trip to Russia might yet go forward. On 14 May, he arrived in Paris and conferred the next day with de Gaulle, who told him flatly that he could not expect a head of state to apologize for routine espionage, and with British prime minister Harold Macmillan, who was no more helpful. Macmillan was more eager than Eisenhower or de Gaulle to settle the German Question, but he had worked with both men during World War II and had no intent of letting Britain be used as a cat's paw for Khrushchev. Meanwhile, Eisenhower's famous temper was beginning to flare. He was convinced that Khrushchev was using the U-2 incident as a pretext to wreck the summit and even considered calling it off himself. By the evening of 15 May, the summit seemed stillborn.

The next day the roof fell in. As de Gaulle opened the conference, Khrushchev demanded the floor and read a lengthy statement denouncing the United States, withdrawing his invitation to Eisenhower, and suggesting that the summit be postponed for six to eight months—until a new American president was inaugurated! Eisenhower replied that the flights would not resume while he was in office, and de Gaulle defended the United States by calling attention to a Soviet satellite which flew over France eighteen times a day. Khrushchev insisted on an apology for the sake of his country's honor and his own internal political situation (an admission which startled the U.S. delegation). Macmillan made an emotional plea that all the intense effort of the past two years should not be cast aside, but the meeting broke up in tur-

Khrushchev, flanked by foreign minister Gromyko and defense minister Malinovsky, denounces the United States at the abortive Paris Summit in May 1960. (AP/Wide World Photos)

moil. Khrushchev refused to meet again without some expression of U.S. regret, and by the next evening, it was clear that the summit was ruined.

The results were devastating. Khrushchev, both genuinely angry and under great pressure at home, had clearly written off Eisenhower; he would postpone further attempts to solve the German Question and slow the arms race until a new man sat in the White House. Years later he would claim that he never again enjoyed full control of his government after the U-2 affair. The episode, and especially Eisenhower's admission of responsibility, had undercut Khrushchev's authority by playing into the hands of Soviet hardliners and "metal-eaters" (who pushed for a massive military buildup). It exacerbated tensions between Moscow and Beijing, and contributed to pressures on

Khrushchev to strengthen the Soviet global posture, thus helping to lay the groundwork for the Berlin and Cuban crises of 1961 and 1962.

For his part, Eisenhower was enraged and frustrated, feeling that Khrushchev was wrecking his hopes for a peaceful world on the shoals of an impossible demand. He may also have privately regretted his own decision to let the U-2 fly so close to the summit. He was, however, heartened by de Gaulle's unequivocal support. The French president, a fatalist who had expected little from the conference anyway, was incensed at Khrushchev's conduct. He returned to the Elysée Palace to continue wrestling with the Algerian snarl and make plans for closer ties with West Germany. Finally, Harold Macmillan's devastation at the summit's collapse was unfeigned. Less than four years after the Suez debacle, London was liquidating its African and Middle Eastern empires and was openly yearning for a Soviet-American rapprochement. Britain was reduced to a supporting role in Cold War drama, a fact that would be underscored in 1962–1963, when Skybolt, EEC, John Profumo, and Kim Philby (Chapter 10) would drive further nails into the coffin of British world leadership.

THE COLD WAR COMES TO AFRICA

Meanwhile, as the superpowers' attention was focused mostly on Europe, a vast sea change was taking place on the continent to the south. The great colonial empires of Britain, France, Spain, Belgium, and Portugal were beginning to disappear, as the African nations one-by-one made good their independence. Hitherto, neither superpower had shown much interest in Africa. But the newly independent nations would provide a tempting Cold War target, with some prized for mineral wealth, others for strategic location, and all for their votes in the UN General Assembly, where the Soviet bloc was grossly outnumbered. Decolonization offered Moscow the opportunity to alter the balance, and Khrushchev was not one to let such a chance go by.

In 1959, Khrushchev's government established an Africa Institute and hired distinguished historian I. I. Potekhin to direct it. By then it was obvious that many African nationalists, resentful toward Europe after decades of domination, were ill-disposed toward the West and inclined toward socialism. These considerations, along with Khrushchev's strategy of weakening the West by wooing the Third World, led the USSR to establish the People's Friendship University in Moscow in 1960 and to present itself as the natural ally of liberation movements.

Washington looked askance at the potential expansion of Soviet influence, but it had few vital interests in Africa. U.S. policy toward Africa was, therefore, ambivalent. There was some support for nationalism, such as Eisenhower's rebuke of the Suez invasion in 1956 and Senator John Kennedy's 1957 speech urging the French to leave Algeria. But neither Eisenhower nor Kennedy articulated any consistent policy toward African liberation. The decolonization of Africa coincided with the most intense phase of the U.S. civil rights movement (1955–1965), and no U.S. government could move more forcefully to promote rights for Africans than it was moving to promote them for African-Americans.

The Cold War's impact on Africa, therefore, was localized in a handful of emerging nations. Wherever Moscow decided to push, Washington, with its containment mentality, would usually push back. The Americans were opposed to colonialism and thus were glad to see the empires fall, but they were also closely tied to the European nations whose empires were crumbling, and they were loath to see the Communists gain a foothold anywhere.

The ambiguities of the U.S. approach were nowhere more evident than in Algeria, the largest of France's North African colonies. In 1954, a number of radical nationalist groups, composed of disenchanted urban professionals and veterans of the French army, had merged to form the *FLN* (National Liberation Front), which then launched an All Saints' Day uprising in forty-five Algerian cities on 1 November 1954. The French, having recently been embarrassed in Indochina (Chapter 11), were in no mood to capitulate again or to surrender their most desirable overseas possession. France thus sent 750,000 troops to Algeria in a war which lasted over seven years. That level of commitment required the conscription of large numbers of men who had little sympathy for colonialism. Marked by widespread atrocities on both sides, the conflict was labeled *la sale guerre,* "the dirty war."

At first the FLN disdained communist aid and turned for help to other Islamic countries: Tunisia, Morocco, and Nasser's Egypt. Moscow backed the FLN out of a desire to embarrass France, and the French Communist party followed suit, but prospects for communizing an independent Algeria were never strong. Marxism's materialistic philosophy proved no more attractive in Islamic Algeria than it had in Islamic Egypt, and the Algerian Communist party remained the orphan stepchild of the Algerian war.

In Washington, the war was viewed with concern—not because of potential communist inroads, but because of its destabilizing effects on France, a key U.S. ally. Senator Kennedy's 1957 speech asking France to quit Algeria made it clear this would be in the best interests of France itself. The Eisenhower administration backed the French halfheartedly. When de Gaulle assumed power in 1958, it appeared that the situation might stabilize. De Gaulle studied the issue, temporized, waffled, and earned the title "prince of ambiguity" for his indiscernible posture. After an abortive coup in Algiers in January 1960, he tilted against independence, provoking the *FLN* to turn to Moscow and Beijing for aid. This in turn prodded de Gaulle to negotiate with the rebels, and the war would finally end with Algerian independence in 1962.

In supporting the Algerian rebels, the Soviets managed to embarrass France, but they did not gain much else. Throughout the Cold War years, Algeria would remain friendly to Moscow but would never become in any sense a member of the "Communist bloc," and would vote as it pleased in the

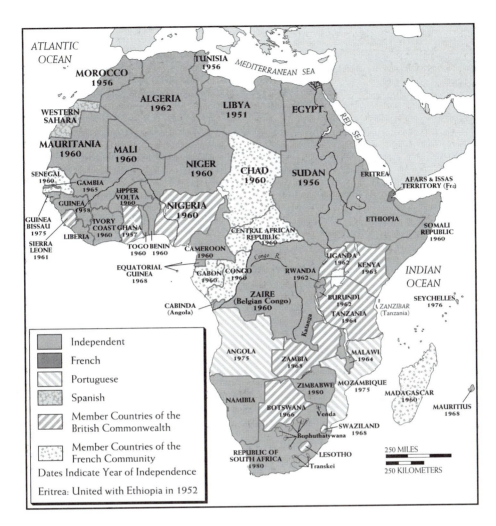

MAP 6 Africa

UN. Algeria remained beholden to no one. With Tunisia following a similar course, and Morocco drawing closer to the United States, the independence of North Africa would carry with it no distinct Cold War advantages for the USSR.

Neither, for that matter, would the concurrent rebellion in the Congo, Belgium's only colony, which had not been prepared for self-government. In 1957, a British decision to give independence to Ghana (formerly the Gold Coast) galvanized African aspirations for self-rule. One year later de Gaulle visited the French Congo, which bordered the Belgian colony, to campaign for votes in favor of autonomy and further association with France in an upcoming referendum. His wartime prestige had been strong in central Africa, and his visit inspired a Congolese cultural association known as ABAKO to transform itself into a political party.

ABAKO was led by Joseph Kasavubu, deputy of the Congolese prophet Simon Kimbangu, who had died in a Belgian prison in 1951 after thirty years of captivity and who was rumored to be advising Kasavubu from beyond the grave. More terrestrial leadership came from Patrice Lumumba, a young postal worker who attended an All-African Peoples' Conference in Ghana in December 1958 and returned preaching pan-African solidarity in the struggle against imperialism. Lumumba assumed leadership of the Congolese National Movement, which stood for centralization after independence, in opposition to federalist regional leaders like Kasavubu and the wealthy Moïse Tshombe of mineral-rich Katanga province. On 4 January 1959, the prohibition of an ABAKO meeting in the colonial capital of Léopoldville triggered widespread riots in an area plagued by increasing African unemployment. More than a hundred Congolese were killed, and the Belgian government panicked.

Belgians suddenly saw the possibility of an Algerian-style colonial war and began to pay heed to the Congo's drain on the Belgian economy. King Baudouin promised the Congo independence following a period of constitutional reform, but when a meeting was held in Brussels in January 1960 to plan the transition, the Belgians were shocked to hear all Congolese representatives ask for immediate independence. The Congolese in turn were astonished when Belgium granted the request, setting 30 June 1960 as independence day. Lumumba was Belgium's favorite Congolese politician, and, when his movement won a plurality of seats in the Congo's first national election, he was installed as prime minister with Kasavubu as president. The Belgians appear to have hoped that the new government would remain dependent on Brussels and that white Belgians would continue to exercise broad authority in the Congo. The Congolese appear to have hoped for independence and modernization under stable leadership.

None of these hopes were realized. Five days after independence, Congolese troops mutinied against their Belgian commanders. This crippled the new government and terrified European residents, who appealed to

Brussels to return and protect them. The resulting reintroduction of Belgian troops muddied the waters even further. On 11 July 1960, Tshombe pulled Katanga out of the Congo; its foreign business community wanted no part of a centralized Congolese regime and was willing to bet the wealthy province could make it on its own. Belgium supported Tshombe with a regular armed force under a Belgian commander. South Kasai province, where the Belgian diamond company *Forminière* was influential, seceded in turn on 8 August.

Facing the double danger of a disintegrating nation and the resumption of Belgian control, Lumumba asked for help from the UN, the United States, and the USSR. The sudden power vacuum in a country with huge strategic mineral resources threatened to make tropical Africa a theater of the Cold War. To keep the superpowers at arm's length, the United Nations sent in a peace-keeping force. UN secretary general Dag Hammarskjöld, a man who combined traits normally associated with corporate executives, backroom political vote mechanics, devout Lutherans, and introspective Scandinavian mystics, would labor mightily to stabilize the Congo from then until he died in a highly suspect plane crash in September 1961.

Lumumba feared that UN involvement would solidify the Congo's partition, since Katanga and South Kasai were likely to be reliant on Belgium and the United States if they became independent. Short on options, he turned to Moscow for assistance, but this discredited him in Western eyes and led to the collapse of his fragile coalition. This action, coupled with his affection for pan-Africanism, led to the widespread belief in the West that he was a closet Communist. On 5 September, he was dismissed by Kasavubu and replaced by Joseph-Désiré Mobutu (later Mobutu Sese Seko), the pro-Western head of the Congolese armed forces. The Congolese parliament supported Lumumba, but the UN forces denied him access to transportation and communication facilities, thereby confirming Kasavubu's action.

For months there was no effective central government in the Congo. Lumumba's ally, the Belgian leftist soldier of fortune Antoine Gizenga, was able to establish a pro-Soviet government at Stanleyville in October 1960. Lumumba was on his way there on 25 November when he was arrested by Congolese troops, turned over to his enemies in Katanga, and eventually murdered in February 1961. The Soviets quickly made him a pan-African Marxist martyr, renaming Moscow's People's Friendship University in his honor. But Lumumba was a nationalist and a centralizer rather than an ideologue, and in this way was similar to Ghana's Kwame Nkrumah, Tanzania's Julius Nyerere, Zambia's Kenneth Kaunda, and Kenya's Jomo Kenyatta. All these men emerged from African elites to lead their lands to independence, and all were far more interested in self-rule than Cold War ideology.

At any rate, Soviet efforts to gain a foothold in the Congo were doomed. With Lumumba gone, Moscow placed its dwindling hopes on Gizenga, but the latter would be defeated and arrested in 1962, ending the Stanleyville regime. Russians were as European as Belgians, and just as unwelcome in the Congo.

When a small Soviet expeditionary force arrived in Stanleyville and began to persecute anti-Lumumba elements, it aroused nearly universal hostility and had to be escorted out of the Congo by UN forces. Within a few years, Katanga would rejoin the Congo, and the Western-oriented Mobutu would take control of the country, rename it Zaïre, and rule it for more than a generation.

Zaïre's tragic birth pangs proved that imperial withdrawal could actually lead to increased foreign intervention. They also showed that the UN, although it never lived up to its original expectations, could play a positive role in a very difficult situation. It managed to prevent the Belgians from reoccupying the Congo, escort the Soviets out, keep the Congolese economy from collapsing, and obstruct Katanga's secessionist efforts, while avoiding direct European or American intervention. The Congo also showed that Africa was not immune from the conflicts of the Cold War. Although the USSR suffered a setback in the Congo, it nonetheless would step up its involvement elsewhere in Africa and continue to court the newly emerging nations.

THE U.S. PRESIDENTIAL CAMPAIGN OF 1960

As the dream of détente deteriorated and the Congo dissolved into disarray, the United States geared up for its 1960 elections. With the nation in a recession and Richard Nixon the likely Republican nominee, the fight for the Democratic nomination drew a surfeit of senators: Kennedy, Johnson, Humphrey, and Symington, all much younger than Eisenhower and all eager to blame him for the collapse of the Paris summit and the perpetuation of the Cold War. One must, of course, avoid going *too* far, as Kennedy discovered when he accused Eisenhower of irresponsibility in refusing to apologize to Khrushchev. The gaffe brought avalanches of irate letters cascading onto Kennedy's desk, and as the other contenders hastened to vilify Khrushchev, the Massachusetts senator trimmed his sails to the wind. Handsome, intelligent, and articulate, he was the front-runner throughout the campaign and won the nomination on the first ballot in Los Angeles in July. The Republicans duly nominated Nixon the following month.

Slowly the limelight began to shift away from Eisenhower, which, given the continuing decline in his fortunes, was probably a good thing. After the cancellation of his Russian visit, the president decided to tour several Pacific nations, including Japan. The announcement of his visit coincided with a parliamentary debate over the renewal of the Japanese-American Security Treaty, and this, combined with the unpopularity of Japanese prime minister Nobosuke Kishi and the disclosure of the presence of U-2 aircraft in Japan, led to massive anti-American demonstrations. It became necessary to cancel Eisenhower's visit, and, as he sailed for Taiwan, the People's Republic of China thoughtfully began shelling the offshore islands of Quemoy and Matsu. A grim and exasperated president, looking every one of his seventy years, returned to Washington on 25 June. One week later the Soviets shot down another American spy plane.

This was not a U-2 but a modified B-47 bomber, called the RB-47. On 1 July, it vanished along the north coast of the USSR; Khrushchev soon announced that it had violated Soviet airspace and had been destroyed. Two survivors were in Soviet custody. In fact, the plane had been thirty miles *outside* Soviet airspace, but this could not be revealed without compromising American monitoring installations. As the UN Security Council debated the matter, an American C-47 got lost in the Pacific and strayed over the Kurile Islands. The Russians failed to bring it down, but Eisenhower might well have been tempted to cross the Wright Brothers off his list of American heroes. Ironically, the escalating tension played into the hand of Nixon, who trumpeted his modest foreign policy experience as vice-president for eight years. At forty-seven, he was only four years older than Kennedy, but the American people might decide that the world situation required the election of the more experienced candidate. Khrushchev, fearing that release of Powers and the two RB-47 airmen might aid in the election of Nixon, whose politics he despised, kept them under lock and key until after the election.

That September, Khrushchev again visited the United States, this time not as Eisenhower's guest but as a head of state on his way to address the UN General Assembly on its fifteenth anniversary. His sojourn bore out Marx's assertion that history repeats itself as farce. Because of threats against his life, Khrushchev was restricted to Manhattan (a curious refuge for someone in danger), but he made the most of it, embracing Fidel Castro at Harlem's Hotel Theresa, entertaining the press with a variety of quips and crudities, and vilifying Eisenhower (who spoke at the assembly's opening session and left quickly). When Prime Minister Macmillan addressed the assembly and mentioned Khrushchev's behavior in Paris, the Soviet leader, seated with the USSR's delegation, heckled the speaker repeatedly and finally took off his shoe and pounded it on the desk. The assembly president broke his gavel trying to regain order, whereupon Khrushchev and Foreign Minister Gromyko began to pound their fists on their desks in a consistent rhythm. By this time, America's image of the Soviet leadership had changed dramatically: the reasonable Khrushchev of September 1959 had been superseded by the uncouth buffoon of September 1960.

The 1960 election was very close. That the Democrats could win in such a volatile international climate may be attributed to several factors, including the persistent recession and Kennedy's offer of support to the jailed civil rights leader, Dr. Martin Luther King, Jr., which helped attract many African-American voters. But Kennedy was also able to turn the global situation to his advantage by alleging the existence of a "missile gap" between the USSR and the United States. He charged Eisenhower and Nixon with having designed a defense budget so penurious that it starved the American missile program. Meanwhile, he claimed, the Soviets were turning out ICBMs in large numbers.

There was no "missile gap," but Kennedy didn't know that and Eisenhower didn't think he could tell him. To prove that the Soviet missile program was actually *behind* that of the United States would require the publication of U-2 photographs and other highly sensitive intelligence information, some of it from sources behind the iron curtain. Rather than compromise such sources, Eisenhower kept silent. Nixon was narrowly defeated in November (which didn't totally displease Eisenhower, who never thought much of Nixon), and Kennedy found out for himself upon taking office in 1961 that the "missile gap" was imaginary.

By then Khrushchev was ready to extend an olive branch to the new president. He offered to release the two RB-47 fliers if Kennedy promised not to exploit them for propaganda purposes and not to authorize any more flights over Soviet territory. The president agreed and was able to announce the release at his first news conference. (Powers would be exchanged for Soviet agent Rudolf Abel in 1962.) Kennedy hoped that, despite their obvious differences, he would be able to find some common ground on which he and the Soviets could begin to dismantle the more dangerous structures of the Cold War. If espionage flights had been the chief issue, he would have been halfway home. But two far more serious problems awaited him: a new communist regime in Cuba and the omnipresent German Question. Together they would intensify the Cold War and imperil not only the political futures of Kennedy and Khrushchev, but the very existence of life on earth.

10

Crisis and Coexistence, 1961–1964

The Cold War's most dangerous phase coincided roughly with the presidency of John Kennedy, who began his term in 1961 with a ringing inaugural address. "In the long history of the world, only a few generations have been granted the role of defending freedom in its hour of maximum danger," he exulted. "I do not shrink from this responsibility—I welcome it." During the next few years, as he became locked in a deadly war of nerves with Moscow, and as his European allies began to edge out of the U.S. orbit, Kennedy would have ample opportunity to rue those words.

Later, the tragic circumstances of his death would lead first to a romanticization of his life and legacy, and later to a reaction focusing mainly on his incessant pursuit of women. Both do violence to historical fact. Kennedy kept his public and personal lives separate at a time when journalistic restraint made it possible to do so; he occasionally crossed the separation line, but no more so than other public figures had done. As for the myth of Camelot, it was a frothy confection which no one in the White House took seriously. Kennedy was no crusading liberal: He was a pragmatic politico who disdained ideology and openly sought the middle way. His foreign policy was that of a staunch Cold Warrior who loathed communism, feared nuclear war, and was anxious to alleviate Third World discontents so that Moscow could not capitalize on them. He was convinced that Russia had started the Cold War—and determined that America would finish it!

THE BAY OF PIGS FIASCO

Kennedy inherited from his predecessor a major problem in Cuba, where a revolutionary regime had come to power in 1959. Since the Spanish-American War, the United States had treated the island nation as part of its sphere of influence and maintained close ties with various Cuban leaders. In the 1950s, however, the dictatorship of Fulgencio Batista had brought large-scale investment by organized crime and turned Cuba into a playground for wealthy Yanquis (a Latin American term for U.S. residents). This was resented by many Cubans, who held Washington responsible for their misery. On 26 July 1953, Fidel Castro, a Jesuit-educated, upper-class *pistolero* with a law degree from the University of Havana, launched a seemingly quixotic revolution with an attack on an army barracks. Castro stood for agrarian reform, reduced dependence on the sugar harvest, and the purification of Cuban society from Yanqui influence and corruption. This puritanical revolution caught the Cubans' fancy, and Castro's forces slowly gained ground. Batista's army suffered morale problems and melted away after several demoralizing defeats at the hands of Castro's forces. On New Year's Eve, 1958, Batista fled to Miami. The 26th of July Movement took power eight days later.

By July 1960, a split between the United States and Cuba was evident. Castro's forthright anti-Yanquiism and leftist reforms, coupled with the presence in his entourage of Marxists like his brother Raúl and Ernesto "Che" Guevara, led the Eisenhower administration to cut off sugar imports from Cuba. Diplomatic ties were severed in January 1961. Moscow indicated its willingness to buy large quantities of Cuban sugar (a commodity which Russians consume in huge quantities), and Cuba tilted toward the Soviet camp.

Moscow thus gained an ally ninety miles south of the Florida Keys, and an "unsinkable aircraft carrier" in the Caribbean, while the United States acquired a persistent headache. Communist Third World expansion had come to America's backyard! However, thousands of anti-Castro Cubans had fled the island in 1959–1960, giving the United States a pool from which to form a counterrevolutionary invasion force. Eisenhower had given preliminary assent to a CIA plan to depose Castro, sketched on lines similar to the overthrow of Jacobo Arbenz in Guatemala in 1954, when a small-scale insurgency composed of Guatemalan dissidents, CIA pilots, and a ramshackle radio transmitter had forced a leftist regime from power. Shortly after taking office in 1961, Kennedy gave final approval to what would become known as the Bay of Pigs invasion.

Kennedy had no qualms about trying to oust Castro, provided he could get away with it. His advisors were divided concerning Moscow's probable reaction. Some believed that if it could be done swiftly, Khrushchev would be unlikely to move; America had clear military superiority in the Caribbean, and Latin America was an area of peripheral interest to the USSR. Others feared

Fidel Castro and his comrades. (Andre St. George/AP/Wide World Photos)

Moscow *would* move, not in the Caribbean but in Central Europe, around Berlin, where the Soviets had a huge military advantage.

Despite the German Question's propensity for turning up everywhere (like the proverbial bad penny), few in Washington doubted that the invasion scheme was feasible. But it wasn't, and the failure to examine it critically would lead to a debacle. The CIA assumed that anti-Castro feeling in Cuba was so strong that a successful landing would trigger massive street riots and defections from the Cuban army. Under such conditions, a brigade of fewer than 3,000 Cuban exiles could provide the spark to ignite revolution. U.S. involvement would be limited to two preinvasion air strikes to disable the Cuban air force; the pilots would be CIA agents posing as Cuban defectors, flying planes painted to look like they were stolen from the Cuban air force. If things went wrong, the brigade could melt into the mountains and begin guerrilla warfare. Castro himself had done this in 1956 with sixteen associates; two years later they had toppled the regime.

What was wrong with this plan? Nearly everything. There was no reliable evidence of widespread anti-Castro feeling in Cuba; indeed, most of Castro's foes were either in exile or in prison. The island was so large that a quick *fait accompli* with a small invasion force was implausible, yet such an outcome was needed to forestall a Soviet response. If the initial air strikes failed to destroy the Cuban air force, the invasion force could be cut to pieces—but there was no backup plan to cover this contingency. Finally, although the original landing (Operation TRINIDAD) was to occur at a site from which the brigade could take refuge in the mountains, the revised plan (Operation ZAPATA) would bring it ashore at Playa Girón (the Bay of Pigs), from which the mountains were inaccessible. This change was apparently never made clear to Kennedy or other key officials. Still, basic military analysis would have shown the plan's absurdity, and the failure to provide such analysis was the fault of the U.S. government.

On 12 April 1961, three days before the air strikes were to begin, Soviet cosmonaut Yuri Gagarin became the first person to orbit the earth. This Russian space triumph turned Washington's mood sepulchral. If successful, the landing in Cuba would turn the tables on Moscow, but ZAPATA was, in the words of one witness, "a perfect failure." The first air strike, on 15 April, saw six B-26 bombers with Cuban air force insignia destroy less than half of Castro's fighter planes. Kennedy, who had reduced the number of bombers from sixteen to six, then canceled the second strike. The CIA objected and was told to call the president, but, perhaps fearful that he would scrub the entire operation, they waited until the morning of 17 April and then asked him to have the U.S. aircraft carrier *Essex* provide air cover for the landing. No such request had previously been broached; indeed, Kennedy had recently received a cable from a U.S. Marine officer confirming that the invaders expected no U.S. military support. Kennedy denied the request for air cover, and the operation failed.

The Bay of Pigs invasion was quickly enshrouded in myth. The invaders were routed: 114 were killed; 1,189 were captured; the rest escaped by sea. By 19 April it was over, and recriminations began. Kennedy was furious at the CIA, which he felt had misled him, but he squelched any public headhunting by assuming full blame as "the responsible officer of the government." He then replaced Allen Dulles as CIA head and ordered a housecleaning of the agency. Some of those let go would later surface as members of the unit that broke into the Watergate Hotel, setting in motion the events leading to President Nixon's resignation.

CIA apologists later claimed that, had proper air cover been provided, the operation would have succeeded. This is dubious, given the plan's inherent weaknesses and the fact that air cover was requested only at the last moment. Kennedy's defenders saw him as blameless, but even he admitted it

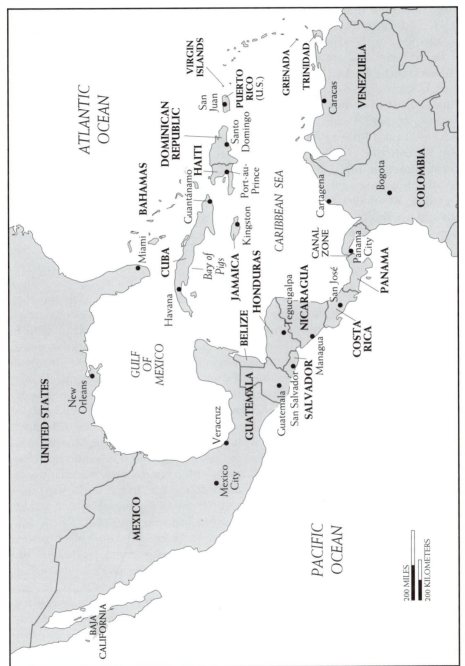

MAP 7 Central America and the Caribbean

was a mistake to cancel the second air strike. Had he lived longer, he might have concluded that his main error was in approving the plan without a rigorous study. Eisenhower, too, bears some responsibility for initially sanctioning the plan, but it is hard to imagine the organizer of the Normandy invasion of 1944 giving final approval to a scheme that would likely have failed even had everything worked.

U.S. prestige, to say nothing of America's self-image, had not been lower since Pearl Harbor. Between Gagarin and Playa Girón, April 1961 was a month Washington would rather forget. Astronaut Alan Shepard's 5 May suborbital space flight did little to revive the administration's good humor, particularly with Khrushchev's unexpected acceptance of Kennedy's February invitation to a summit meeting. The Soviet leader had delayed his response for over two months, but now, reckoning that Kennedy would be on the defensive, and regarding Kennedy's Bay of Pigs performance as evidence of indecisiveness, Khrushchev was ready to meet his second U.S. president and once again come to grips with the German Question.

THE VIENNA SUMMIT, JUNE 1961

Of all the Cold War summits, the Vienna meeting of 3–4 June 1961 was the most unfortunate. The participants got along badly, and misperceptions growing out of their talks led to two major crises: a serious one over Berlin in 1961 and a potentially catastrophic one in Cuba in 1962. In the two years following this meeting, war between the superpowers was a real possibility.

Kennedy and Khrushchev found they spoke different languages: not only Russian and English, but different political languages as well. Kennedy was a pragmatist who considered ideologically motivated people to be feckless and impractical. Having watched Khrushchev maneuver on the world stage, he judged that the Soviet leader was the same sort of man. But Khrushchev, while recognizing politics as a "merciless business" at which he could be quite ruthless, had an idealistic faith in Marxism which verged on the romantic. It had, after all, lifted him out of poverty and allowed him to rise to the top position in the USSR. It was also, in his view, the "wave of the future" which would triumph over capitalism because it was more just and equitable. Kennedy's first error was in thinking that Khrushchev was just as skeptical of grand designs as he was. Then, when he realized this was not the case, he thought he could argue ideology with the Soviet leader. The result was a series of talks that were tense, grinding, and often curt.

Beyond the two leaders' communication problems lay the grave issues which divided them. Some were less vexing than expected. Kennedy was clearly in an awkward spot concerning Cuba, thanks to the Bay of Pigs, but Khrushchev took a fairly detached view: Castro was not a true Marxist, no matter what he said, and Cuba was no more a threat to the United States than Turkey was to the USSR. Laos (Chapter 11) was at the forefront of Kennedy's

Kennedy and Khrushchev in Vienna, June 1961.
(UPI/Bettmann)

mind, but the Soviet leader showed little interest in the subject. These, of course, were peripheral issues. When the talks turned to Berlin, the centrality of the German Question was evident once more.

By 1958, Khrushchev had given up the idea of a reunited and neutralized Germany, opting instead for a peace treaty with East Germany as a lever to remove the Western Allies from Berlin. He had repeatedly postponed his own deadlines and allowed Kennedy several months to formulate a new U. S. position. Now he faced a great opportunity to intimidate the young president, fresh from disaster in Cuba, and force a settlement on Berlin. He was under pressure from Kremlin hardliners, the Chinese, and his own political instincts. He had not reached the pinnacle of Soviet power by flinching from pressing home an advantage.

Kennedy, startled by the vehemence of Khrushchev's demands on Berlin, countered with a consistent argument: America was in West Berlin not by force but by agreement. Moscow's desire to alter the balance of power was disturbing and dangerous. Khrushchev proposed a limited compromise in the form of an interim accord, by which the superpowers would indicate their intent to turn the problem over to the Germans. But Kennedy, sensing that it could undermine U.S. credibility to accept such a bargain in the wake of the Bay of Pigs debacle, would have none of this.

The conversation then turned ugly. Khrushchev stated that he wanted peace, but it seemed Kennedy wanted war (a word rarely used in diplomatic discourse). Kennedy, taken aback, replied that the responsibility for forcing change rested with Moscow. Noting that "the calamities of war will be shared equally," the Soviet premier vowed to sign a treaty with East Germany by December 1961 unless Washington accepted an interim agreement. Grimly, Kennedy rejoined that "if that is true, it's going to be a cold winter." Never before in the Cold War had such words been spoken between the superpower leaders; even Truman's April 1945 dressing down of Molotov cannot compare with Vienna.

The lessons of Vienna were ominous. Kennedy, dismayed by his inability to persuade Khrushchev of U.S. resolve, was sobered. He knew that, after the Bay of Pigs and Vienna, the United States must respond firmly to any challenge over Berlin, but he didn't know how much firmness would produce an acceptable result. Khrushchev returned from Vienna certain that Kennedy was no match for him. He saw at the summit a callow, unseasoned young man, born to wealth and accustomed to deference; there was no category of person with whom Khrushchev would be less sympathetic. Yet he also saw in Kennedy a belligerence he had not sensed in Eisenhower, and the mixture of immaturity and pugnacity gave him pause. That combination had gotten Kennedy into trouble at the Bay of Pigs, and it might get him into trouble again over Berlin. The dangerous difference was that, while Cuba was not worth a nuclear conflict, Germany might be. With the American feeling cornered and the Soviet sensing an opportunity, Central Europe could become a very unpleasant place in the wake of the Vienna summit.

THE BERLIN WALL, AUGUST 1961

The perilous game of superpower chess continued after Vienna. On 8 July, Khrushchev rescinded the 1.2-million-man cut in Soviet army strength he had announced in January 1960. Kennedy countered with his own version of Truman's 1947 "all-out speech" on Greece and Turkey. In a televised address on 25 July, he asked Congress for authority to call up U.S. reserves and disclosed plans for a large military buildup, including preparations for an encore of the Berlin airlift. The most arresting parts of the speech dealt with measures to provide fallout shelters in the event of a nuclear war. Kennedy's intent was to persuade the Kremlin that America, if pushed, would go to war rather than retreat from Berlin.

With a showdown looming, both sides examined their options. It had occurred to Washington as early as March 1961 that East Germany might move to close the border between East and West Berlin in order to staunch the steady hemorrhage of refugees. Ever since the end of the blockade, people could go from one part of Berlin to the other simply by walking through the Brandenburg Gate; 40,000 East Berliners crossed every day to and from jobs in West Berlin. It was a hole in the iron curtain, through which passed many of the most talented people in East Germany. More than 2,500,000 had used this escape hatch since 1949.

Two key U.S. senators, Mike Mansfield and J. William Fulbright, speculated openly during summer 1961 that the border could easily be closed. Fulbright opined that the Soviets could do so without breaking any written agreement with the United States. Michael Beschloss has raised the possibility that such comments may have been planted by Kennedy to alert Khrushchev to a viable solution. In early August, when asked at a press conference about Fulbright's statement, the president declined to warn the USSR against a border cutoff, using language that indicated little interest in the refugees but deep interest in the status of West Berlin. At least one secret channel was available by which Kennedy could have issued the same sort of caveat he had sent during the Bay of Pigs invasion, when he had warned Moscow against exploiting the opportunity to move against Berlin. No such warning came from the White House that August.

On the other side of the iron curtain, Walter Ulbricht, head of East Germany's ruling Socialist Unity party, had been lobbying Khrushchev for months to let him close the border. On 31 July, he suggested that the air corridors from Berlin to West Germany should be cut in order to keep refugees from leaving. Khrushchev rejected this, fearing it might lead to war, but agreed finally to let Ulbricht seal the border with barbed wire; if the West did not try to break through, the wire could be replaced by a wall.

Construction began at midnight on 12 August. The first news reached Washington six hours later—a graphic display of how rudimentary communication still was in 1961. The U.S. response was a thunderous silence. The State Department, having long feared that the Soviets might renew their 1948 blockade, had not prepared for the possibility that West Berlin would be isolated from *East* rather than West Germany. Kennedy's advisors urged restraint, and National Security Advisor McGeorge Bundy pointed out the obvious propaganda advantages Ulbricht had handed the United States. The president himself made no comment on the subject for a week. His critics complained that he should have ordered American forces to destroy the barrier before it hardened into a wall, as began to happen three days after the wire was strung. His defenders replied that such action would have led to war. Neither seemed to consider that, if the wire was cut, the East Germans could simply restring it

Construction of the Berlin Wall, 1961. (UPI/Bettman)

the next night, or else string it *inside* the border so that the Americans would have to invade in order to cut it! It is hard to conceive of a U.S. response that would have prevented the completion of the Berlin Wall, short of coming to terms with Moscow and withdrawing from West Berlin. And there is no reason to believe that this was contemplated at the time.

Besides, the Berlin Wall conferred real benefits on both sides. Although it did not solve the German Question, it certainly defused it. Khrushchev was able to stem the flow of East German refugees and to defang the critics who had long pressured him to deal resolutely with Berlin. At the same time, the West got a propaganda windfall from this highly visible symbol of communism's repugnance. And Kennedy could breathe easier, sensing that Khrushchev had perceived the U.S. resolve not to leave Berlin and had shown the dexterity to effect a workable compromise. If Kennedy had not urged Fulbright to signal that a border cutoff was acceptable to Washington, he probably should have. The Berlin Wall was one of the few Cold War milestones that actually benefited both sides. Berliners, of course, with their city divided in two, could derive little comfort from their lot. And the accelerating nuclear arms race would continue to make the world a very dangerous place.

THE U.S. ARMS BUILDUP AND THE SOVIET RESPONSE

When Kennedy took office in 1961, the United States had a huge lead in deliverable nuclear weapons, with many times more operational ICBMs and long-range bombers than the USSR. Kennedy, however, had promised during his campaign to reinvigorate American leadership, regain the Cold War initiative, and close the "missile gap" that allegedly favored Moscow. Therefore, even though that "gap" was soon shown to be nonexistent, his administration accelerated the weapons-building programs begun under his predecessor, increasing the numbers of missiles far beyond those that Eisenhower had considered more than adequate. The decision was made to build and deploy 1,000 of the new solid-fuel Minuteman ICBMs and as many as 41 nuclear submarines, each carrying 16 Polaris missiles capable of reaching the USSR. When added to the fleet of over a thousand strategic bombers, these would give the United States by the mid-1960s an overpowering "triad" (land-based missiles, submarine-launched missiles, and bombers) of awesome destructive power, far beyond anything the USSR could hope to have operational by then.

Kennedy's secretary of defense was Robert S. McNamara, a man with dazzling managerial skills, an unrelenting attention to detail, and a ruthless bent for efficiency and rationality. McNamara seized control over the sprawling military bureaucracy, antagonizing the Pentagon brass as he rode roughshod over their most beloved traditions and cherished weapons systems. Undaunted by precedent or sentiment, and possessing the full support of his president, he imposed a sweeping new strategic vision, even as he presided over a nuclear arms buildup of staggering proportions.

Like many European statesmen and U.S. defense experts, McNamara felt that the Dulles doctrine of "massive retaliation"—calling for a full-scale American nuclear response in the event of Soviet aggression—had lost its credibility. Its rigidity also seemed to tie the hands of U.S. presidents by forcing them to choose in a crisis between nuclear Armageddon and surrender. He thus promoted a policy of "flexible response," designed to provide decision makers with options for gradual escalation of hostilities in the event of a conventional attack by Soviet forces in Central Europe. In 1962, he would also announce a new nuclear strategy known as "counterforce," which implied that U.S. weapons would be launched not against Soviet cities but only against military targets. Since a counterforce attack would not kill tens of millions of people (and thus ensure a massive response), it seemed to be more plausible that a president might actually employ it.

From a Soviet perspective, however, the combination of the U.S. nuclear buildup and counterforce retargeting seemed to indicate that the Americans were moving toward a "first-strike capacity." This meant that the United States, with a well-coordinated attack upon Soviet military targets, might be able to destroy Moscow's ability to retaliate and thus render the USSR defenseless. Whether or not the Americans were actually seeking this capability, the Soviets saw little choice but to protect themselves against it.

For financial reasons, Moscow had decided not to invest in large numbers of first-generation ICBMs, preferring to wait until more sophisticated weapons could be produced. Khrushchev instead had relied on bluster and deception to exaggerate Soviet strength, thus contributing inadvertently to America's massive overreaction. With an economic base much smaller than that of the United States, the Kremlin leader could not hope to match the U.S. buildup without sacrificing his prized programs to improve Soviet agriculture and consumer goods production.

In October 1961, to reassure his NATO allies of U.S. resolve in the wake of the Berlin Wall crisis, Kennedy authorized Deputy Secretary of Defense Roswell Gilpatric to reveal to the world the extent of U.S. superiority. The "missile gap" had been exposed as a sham by McNamara in February, but no specific comparisons had been made. Gilpatric now delineated in brutal terms the precise correlation of forces: The U.S. nuclear arsenal consisted of 5,000 warheads, while the Soviets possessed 300, and the USSR deployed only 6 ICBMs capable of reaching the United States (although it also had submarine-based missiles that could do so).

Gilpatric's speech not only conveyed Kennedy's message (Soviet pressure on West Berlin eased noticeably); it also disarmed and humiliated Khrushchev. No longer could he rattle rockets and issue impressive ultimata to anyone who threatened Soviet interests. To make matters worse, Kennedy himself observed in a March 1962 magazine interview that under certain conditions, the United States might launch a nuclear first strike against the USSR. Khrushchev, sobered, looked for an area of the world that annoyed Kennedy as much as Berlin annoyed him. He found Cuba.

THE CUBAN MISSILE CRISIS

Kennedy had admitted in Vienna that he had made a mistake at the Bay of Pigs, but he didn't promise not to try again. Perhaps his talk about a mistake simply meant that next time he would not fail. Given Washington's obvious hatred for Castro, and a failed CIA attempt to overthrow or kill him called "Operation MONGOOSE" (of which Moscow was aware), an American invasion of Cuba seemed plausible to the Soviets. Thus, Kennedy's arms buildup,

Gilpatric's speech, and the Cuban situation all led Khrushchev to conclude by spring 1962 that the USSR should station nuclear missiles in Cuba. He had two immediate aims: to defend Cuba against a U.S. invasion and to redress the strategic balance by locating Soviet missiles close to America. He had in mind medium-range SS-4s, with a range of 1,200 miles, and intermediate-range SS-5s, which could travel about 2,500 miles; neither could reach the United States from the USSR but both could do so from Cuba. Khrushchev's plan to visit the UN in November suggests another possible motive: he may have intended to reveal the missiles in Cuba at that time and use the resulting leverage to reopen the German Question from a more favorable negotiating position.

In summer 1962, the Soviets offered, and Castro accepted, up to forty missile launchers, each equipped with two missiles and one nuclear warhead. Delivery and installation would occur between August and November. This decision, however, was based on faulty assumptions. Underrating U.S. surveillance techniques, Khrushchev thought the missiles could be delivered and set up in secret. He assumed that even if Kennedy learned of the process, he would conceal it from the American people until after the November congressional elections, by which time the missiles would be operational. He expected Kennedy to accept the missiles in Cuba as Moscow had accepted U.S. Jupiter-C missiles in Turkey. All these expectations proved false.

For his part, Kennedy did not consider the impact on Moscow of the Gilpatric speech and other American rhetoric. He had no appreciation of Khrushchev's fear of an invasion of Cuba, since he knew he did not plan to invade. He never suspected Moscow might place missiles in Cuba, so he did not convey the sort of precise warning he had issued over Berlin. When CIA director John McCone reported in August that Cuba was receiving from Russia large shipments that probably included missiles, neither Kennedy nor McNamara believed it. Nor did CIA analysts, who processed over 2,000 reports of missiles arriving in Cuba but discounted them because many such reports proved phony. Even accounts from CIA agents in Cuba were not considered credible—until they reported eighty-foot cylinders being carried on trucks that couldn't make turns without slicing off mailboxes! This got Kennedy's attention and led him to issue warnings to Moscow on 4 and 13 September, but it was too late for Khrushchev to stop an operation already more than half completed. And neither Kennedy nor his advisors ever considered what to do if the Soviets ignored the warnings.

The U.S. congressional election campaign was now under way, and Republican senator Kenneth Keating was charging Kennedy with covering up evidence of Soviet missiles in Cuba. Administration officials denied the charges since their evidence, like Keating's, was anecdotal, and since they did not believe Khrushchev would take the risk. Then, on 14 October 1962, the U-2 again flew into the midst of the Cold War. A flight over Cuba by Major Rudolph Anderson brought back clear photographic evidence of missile launcher construction. McGeorge Bundy informed Kennedy on the morning of 16 October. The Cuban Missile Crisis was on.

The U.S. response was prepared by a group of key officials and advisors meeting in utmost secrecy. For the first few days, the president was a sporadic participant in their daylong meetings, keeping to his announced schedule of appointments and appearances; he began to meet regularly with the "ExComm" (Executive Committee of the National Security Council) only on Saturday, 20 October. By that time, the group had proposed and the president had agreed that the U.S. objective should be the removal of the *missiles*, not the Castro regime. Three options had been identified. The first, which Kennedy dismissed as unworkable, was to negotiate removal of the missiles: what could he offer to induce Moscow to withdraw? The second was a conventional air strike to destroy the missiles, and the third was a naval blockade or "quarantine" to prevent warheads and other weapons from reaching the island. The option Khrushchev had thought most likely—to accept the presence of the missiles—was not even considered. According to Bundy, the reasons were not strategic: the missiles did not alter the global balance, and America had been vulnerable to nuclear attack for years. Rather, they were political: Soviet missiles in the Western Hemisphere, ninety miles from the United States, would be intolerable to the American people. Nothing short of decisive action would be acceptable to them.

Kennedy decided on Sunday for the third option, against the advice of many, if not most, of the ExComm. The deciding argument was that an air strike could not guarantee removal of more than 60 percent of the missiles. It would have to be followed by additional strikes and probably an invasion. By contrast, the quarantine offered a first step which could always be escalated if it proved ineffective. Kennedy himself, despite his naval background, had little confidence in naval interdiction, but he chose this option because it seemed the lesser of two evils. He disclosed the presence of the missiles and the imposition of the quarantine in a nationally televised address at 7:00 P.M. on Monday, 22 October.

Concurrently, the United States began a massive military buildup in south Florida. Nothing was done to conceal it, both because it would have been futile to try and because it was important that Moscow see what was going on. Khrushchev, startled by Kennedy's reaction, stalled for time. For two days, Soviet spokesmen were authorized to answer inquiries with nothing more than standard public relations responses. Kennedy's address had made much of Soviet secrecy and duplicity and of Foreign Minister Gromyko's failure to disclose the missiles when he had met with the president a few days earlier. This approach assured Washington the unanimous backing of NATO and the Organization of American States, as well as several African nations, which denied landing and refueling rights to Cuba-bound Soviet aircraft.

On Tuesday, 23 October, Khrushchev warned that Soviet submarines would sink the U. S. blockaders, and the world watched in spellbound terror as Cuba-bound Soviet vessels approached the American ships. The next day, however, the crisis eased, when the Soviet ships stopped and turned back rather than run the blockade. Khrushchev, it turned out, had been bluffing! Afraid that his ships would be boarded and searched, and thus reveal Soviet military secrets, he had decided to avoid confrontation. This meant that the game was up, since Cuba could not survive a blockade and Khrushchev was obviously unwilling to escalate the crisis. By nightfall, it was clear the missiles would be removed, and the rest of the crisis was spent working out the conditions. But plenty of tension and danger remained.

A long letter from Khrushchev arrived at the U.S. embassy in Moscow at 4:30 P.M. local time on Friday, 26 October. Transmitted through Soviet channels, it did not reach Washington for eight hours. As in the Berlin crisis of 1961, slow communications led to irksome delays (although Bundy implied that the message may have been delayed by Kremlin officials hostile to its contents). Had it arrived more quickly, much of the next day's tension and aggravation might have been avoided. In any case, it was remarkably forthright. Khrushchev claimed the missiles were deployed for defensive purposes only, but admitted he could not convince Kennedy of this. He stated flatly that nuclear war was out of the question and proposed that he would send no more weapons to Cuba in return for a U.S. promise not to invade the island. The letter (released in 1973) ended with a now-famous passage that encapsulated Khrushchev's emotions and fears:

> If you have not lost your self-control and sensibly conceive what this might lead to, Mr. President, we and you ought not now to pull on the ends of the rope in which you have tied the knot of war, because the more the two of us pull, the tighter that knot will be tied. And a moment may come when that knot will be tied so tight that even he who tied it will not have the strength to untie it . . . Let us not only relax the forces pulling on the ends of the rope. Let us take measures to untie the knot.

The letter clarified several things. Khrushchev obviously knew that the quarantine was effective; he knew that America's massive superiority in the Caribbean precluded him from using force to break it; he knew from Kennedy's prior warnings that to bring pressure on West Berlin could lead to nuclear war; he knew that he could not fire his Cuban missiles without *ensuring* nuclear war; and he knew that nuclear war was unacceptable. In such circumstances, he could only haggle over terms. The terms he offered were clearly insufficient for Washington, since they did not assure the withdrawal of the missiles. But they did form the basis for an eventual understanding.

The letter's full implications were not immediately grasped at the White House, where tired men wrestled with their own worst fears. Saturday, 27

October, proved the most trying day of the crisis. As the ExComm convened at 9:00 A.M., Radio Moscow broadcast a second letter from Khrushchev. This one upped the ante, offering for the first time to remove the missiles from Cuba but demanding in return both a no-invasion pledge and the removal of fifteen U.S. Jupiter-C missiles from Turkey. The obsolete Jupiters were set to be withdrawn once Polaris submarines were deployed in the eastern Mediterranean, but Kennedy did not want to remove them under the gun. Unfortunately, he realized, the request would look reasonable to the rest of the world, which would not understand his willingness to risk total war over such a trivial item. Indeed, Kennedy would not have run the risk and would have accepted the bargain had he been unable to find a way around it.

What did the second letter imply? Was Khrushchev still in charge in the Kremlin? Apparently, on Friday Khrushchev was afraid that an invasion of Cuba was imminent; that day's letter thus sought a quick solution. On Saturday, the situation appeared less menacing, and the Turkish missile demand was added. But no one in Washington knew this at the time. While the ExComm was puzzling over the letters, a U-2 on a routine Pacific mission accidentally strayed into Soviet airspace. The Red Air Force scrambled but allowed the plane to return; a U.S. first strike was unlikely to occur in such a remote area. Kennedy, who had ordered such missions canceled at the outset of the crisis, remarked, "There is always some son of a bitch who doesn't get the word." His sense of humor was notably absent that afternoon when word arrived that another U-2, this one on an authorized overflight of Cuba, had been detected—and this one had been shot down!

Washington, needing to know the operational status of the Cuban missiles, was sending U-2s over Cuba several times a day. This one was piloted by Major Anderson, the man who had brought back the photos showing the first solid evidence of missile deployment. General Stepan Grechko, commander of Soviet air defenses on Cuba, tried to reach General Issa Pliyev, commander of all Soviet forces there, for authorization to bring down the U-2. Unable to reach Pliyev, he gave the order on his own; the plane was shot down and the pilot killed. Soviet defense minister Rodion Malinovsky wired a rebuke to Grechko, but the damage had been done. Khrushchev was staggered by the incident, and Kennedy, though careful not to react with an inflammatory public statement, began to wonder how long he could wait before ordering an air strike that would probably lead to an invasion. He assumed the incident was a deliberate provocation and became suspicious of Khrushchev's intentions. Those intentions, it turned out, were pacific: a cable from Castro begging Moscow to launch a nuclear strike against the United States arrived that afternoon and was ignored.

At this point, Washington turned creative. McGeorge Bundy, backed by Attorney General Robert Kennedy, proposed that the first letter be accepted as a basis for agreement. The United States would pledge not to invade Cuba, provided the missiles were withdrawn. The second letter would simply be ignored. Concurrently, ABC reporter John Scali was sent to meet with Alexander Fomin, a Soviet embassy official who was really a KGB (Soviet state security) agent. The two had already served as an unofficial channel between Kennedy and Khrushchev earlier in the crisis; now Scali, briefed on Saturday's events, read Fomin the riot act. He told him to inform Khrushchev that the United States was resolved to remove the missiles and that an invasion of Cuba was near. Robert Kennedy delivered a similar warning to Soviet ambassador Anatoly Dobrynin, coupled with a private assurance that, once the crisis was resolved, the Jupiters would be removed from Turkey. This could not, however, be part of the bargain: the understanding must be secret.

The strategy worked. At 9:00 A.M. Washington time on Sunday, 28 October, Radio Moscow broadcast another letter from Khrushchev. Accepting the U.S. assurance that Cuba would not be invaded, he would have the missiles dismantled and returned to the USSR. No mention was made of the U.S. missiles in Turkey. The Cuban Missile Crisis was over, and the Cold War was changed irrevocably.

Although both Kennedy and Khrushchev had acted prudently during the crisis, determined to prevent nuclear war, the danger was nonetheless real. Unbeknown to Washington, the Soviets already had thirty-six operational nuclear missiles and nine short-range tactical nuclear weapons in Cuba. Had America launched an air strike, at least some of these would have survived, and a U.S. invasion would have been needed to finish the job. Since there were 43,000 Soviet troops in Cuba (and not 10,000, as the CIA thought), a U.S. landing would doubtless have led to bitter fighting and mass casualties. And, given the presence of Soviet tactical "nukes" and the difficulties of maintaining contact between Cuba and Moscow, it could well have escalated into an all-out war between the superpowers.

The Cuban Missile Crisis frightened the world and brought few tangible gains for either side. Khrushchev, although defeated, could claim publicly that he had saved Cuba from invasion and privately that he had gotten U.S. missiles out of Turkey. But to risk nuclear war over such small stakes was hardly the path of wisdom. Kennedy gained much domestic popularity and international respect, although all he had accomplished was to restore the status quo. His no-invasion pledge was honored by later presidents despite its lack of binding force: it was predicated upon international inspection of Cuba, which Kennedy knew that Castro would never grant. Binding or not, the pledge proved a godsend to Castro, whose regime was destined to outlast the Cold War, and even the USSR!

The crisis also carried several key lessons for Moscow. For one thing, U.S. naval power, not nuclear weapons, had proven decisive, making the quarantine effective and leaving the Soviets short of options. If they wanted to hold their own in future crises, they would have to build a navy to match. For another, Khrushchev's attempt to close the missile gap cheaply and quickly had failed, since the United States would not abide nuclear rockets on its doorstep.

If the Soviets wished to achieve nuclear parity, they would have to follow the arduous and expensive path of building their own vast fleet of ICBMs.

STRESSES AND STRAINS IN THE WESTERN ALLIANCE

During the missile crisis, America received strong public support from its European allies, but in private these allies were disturbed by U.S. failure to consult them on key decisions. This was especially true of France's de Gaulle, who had for some time been advocating an independent course. Against U.S. wishes, he had made France a nuclear power, shrugging off gibes at the size of his *force de frappe* by noting that nuclear powers were Great Powers, no matter how small their arsenals. Convinced of the need for Franco-German cooperation, he continued French participation in the European Economic Community, despite his dislike for its structure. Under his influence, a prosperous Western Europe was beginning to ponder the limits of NATO and to consider a possible role as a third force between Washington and Moscow.

De Gaulle's fixation on national sovereignty was viewed as anachronistic by the White House, which saw Britain, France, and West Germany as junior partners in a U.S-dominated alliance. But America's view of his ideas as antiquated relics of old world chauvinism begged the question posed by nationalism's persistent appeal. Collective security organizations like NATO and the UN might be of limited value in specific situations, but they could never, in de Gaulle's view, earn the affection and dedication of Europeans accustomed for centuries to celebrate their differences, not as defects but as sources of strength.

To de Gaulle, nationalism and sovereignty were not limiting factors. Any organization that respected national identities and gave a leading role to *all* Great Powers could claim his support. He sought not the equality of all nations but the rightful participation of powerful states like France, Britain, and West Germany in all decisions affecting the future of Europe. After all, the United States could not garrison Europe forever, and its insistence on defending Europe by threatening a nuclear strike on the USSR simply meant that Moscow, if it wanted to move west (which de Gaulle doubted), would do so only under conditions designed to preclude U.S. retaliation. It therefore behooved Europe to maintain friendly ties with the United States, while seeking its own identity as a third force.

London, like Washington, at first underestimated de Gaulle. But by 1962 it was clear that the Algerian albatross no longer adorned the neck of France. With a nuclear capability, a thriving economy, and effective, farsighted leadership, Paris seemed ready to make its own way in the Cold War. Harold Macmillan's British government accordingly sought to join the EEC, an option consistent with Kennedy's expressed hope of more closely uniting Europe and America in economic as well as political affairs. But while Britain saw its decision as an effort to draw closer to a dynamic France, de Gaulle interpreted it differently.

In the first place, he didn't want England *too* close to France. It was one thing for London to participate in decisions affecting Europe, but quite another for it to dilute French domination of the EEC. In the second place, the British demanded special arrangements to protect their own agriculture and the economies of their Commonwealth associates. De Gaulle and other European leaders justifiably believed that, if special privileges were granted every member, the EEC would never work. In the third place, he interpreted Britain's decision to seek entry as evidence of its intention to act as a stalking-horse for the United States. He had long resented the Anglo-American treatment of his Free French movement in World War II, and now he saw the British desire to join the EEC as one more manifestation of the English-speaking powers' arrogant ambition to dominate the world.

Negotiations progressed throughout 1962, culminating in a devastating turn-of-the-year for British Prime Minister Macmillan. At a conference with Kennedy in Bermuda just before Christmas, he learned that the United States was pulling out of its joint effort with Britain to develop the Skybolt missile. Kennedy preferred to use the cheaper American-built Polaris, and since the United States controlled the nuclear material used in Polaris warheads, the decision reduced Britain to a dependent nuclear power. This blow to British pride was followed on 14 January 1963 by de Gaulle's blunt, cruelly disappointing announcement that France would veto British entry into the EEC.

As if these disasters were insufficient, two scandals titillated Britain in summer 1963. First, Kim Philby, a top official of the British espionage service (MI-6), defected to the USSR. Then it was alleged that Secretary of State for War John Profumo had shared state secrets with call girls Christine Keeler and Mandy Rice-Davies, who in turn had passed them on to their Soviet clients. Macmillan, besieged, resigned in October. His replacement, Sir Alec Douglas-Home, would then lose the 1964 election to Harold Wilson's Labour party by the slimmest of margins.

Konrad Adenauer, at 87, preceded Macmillan into retirement by three days. *Der Alte* had narrowly won the 1961 election and then hung on for two more years, long enough to sign a Franco-German Friendship Treaty early in 1963. The United States also changed leaders that year, owing to Kennedy's murder in Dallas, but de Gaulle soldiered on, pursuing his vision of a "Europe from the Atlantic to the Urals" that would include a less belligerent Russia. But this concept, which was far ahead of its time, had made little impact on Moscow or Washington by the time de Gaulle retired in 1969.

THE LIMITED TEST BAN TREATY OF 1963

Meanwhile, in the wake of the Cuban crisis, both Washington and Moscow had begun to contemplate changes that could prevent a repetition of the 1962 brush with eternity. Renewed talk of a nuclear test ban circulated through both capitals, but vexing issues like on-site inspections continued to defy easy solution. To improve communication channels, so sadly primitive during the missile crisis, a "hot line" was installed to link the White House and the Kremlin. The brainchild of nuclear scientist Leo Szilard, it was not a telephone but a circuit composed of telegraph lines and teleprinters that ran through London and Scandinavia. It was appallingly slow by modern standards and did not allow for voice contact, but it was a big improvement over conditions in 1962.

Perhaps the greatest change took place in John F. Kennedy. Pampered and privileged in his youth, he had long since learned that life is not always happy. Back surgery in 1954 had nearly killed him and left him in constant pain; his wife had miscarried a girl in 1956, and seven years later their second son had lived for scarcely a day. Now the harrowing October of 1962 left him questioning Cold War dogmatics, while his skyrocketing popularity gave him room to maneuver. On 10 June 1963, he gave the finest speech of his life at American University in Washington.

Eloquent, resonant, and in parts poetic, the "Peace Speech" (as Kennedy called it) articulated a peaceful man's abhorrence of war and proposed that a reexamination of Cold War attitudes was imperative if humanity hoped to avoid annihilation. The speech promised that America would not conduct atmospheric nuclear tests as long as other nations refrained from doing so. It sought to develop broad public backing for a test ban treaty and to impress Khrushchev with Kennedy's commitment to détente with the USSR. Coming from a master of Cold War oratory, the speech startled and inspired many, both within the United States and abroad.

Then, a few weeks later, the president visited Berlin. Arriving on 26 June to commemorate the fifteenth anniversary of the 1948 airlift, Kennedy was greeted by over a million people, gathered in a plaza within sight of the Wall. Carried away by the emotion of the moment, he delivered a bitterly anticommunist valedictory, toying with the crowd and ending with the words: "Today, all free men, wherever they may live, are citizens of Berlin. And therefore, as a free man, I take pride in the words, 'Ich bin ein Berliner.'" He thus became a hero to the Germans and a source of somber reflection to Konrad Adenauer, who speculated that despite fifteen years of democratic rule, Germany might someday give its devotion to another Hitler.

Fortunately, this lapse into Cold War rhetoric did not derail the test ban talks. Khrushchev was as concerned as Kennedy about atomic fallout and was eager to conclude a treaty that would put his country on an equal footing with America. After the United States had dropped its demand for on-site inspections, Moscow agreed to what would become the Limited Test Ban Treaty, signed on 5 August 1963. It forbade atmospheric tests by its signatories (the United States, USSR, and Britain—but not France) but allowed underground blasts, since these were hard to detect without inspections. It did not halt, or even slow, the arms race, since both sides could still develop new weapons through underground testing. But it did deal effectively with the fallout problem, and it showed that it was possible for the superpowers to work out an arms agreement.

EXIT KENNEDY, EXIT KHRUSHCHEV

The Test Ban Treaty, although limited, did provide a sense that superpower relations were improving. That impression deepened in the next few months, partly due to U.S. Senate ratification of the treaty in September and partly because the German Question was quiescent. South Vietnam now took center stage, with Buddhist demonstrations, a military coup (Chapter 11), and Kennedy's gnawing fear that the United States was being drawn into a highly dubious venture. But he also believed, recalling Khrushchev's diffidence over Laos in 1961, that Southeast Asia was too peripheral to superpower interests to cause an escalation of the Cold War.

In November, the president turned to domestic politics. To patch up a quarrel between Texas Democrats, he traveled to San Antonio and Dallas on 22 November and ran into an ambush. Debates still rage over whether a single gunman or a crossfire took his life, but not about the result: he died within minutes of being shot in the head, and the presidency passed to Lyndon B. Johnson.

In domestic affairs, Johnson was a superb political operator, a man of both close-range and long-distance vision, a tough yet compassionate figure who blended skeptical pragmatism with a strong stream of idealism. But his experience in foreign affairs was limited, and he lacked Kennedy's mental flexibility and willingness to grapple with unconventional solutions. Fiercely anticommunist, he would instinctively deepen U.S. involvement in Vietnam and would prove less willing to continue along the path of cooperation initiated by the test ban.

Khrushchev was devastated by the events in Dallas. He broke down when Gromyko told him the news and wept the next day while paying his respects at the U.S. embassy. He feared for the future of détente and lamented the premature death of an adversary with whom he had shared more than one serious crisis and whom he felt he had begun to understand. No doubt, as his seventieth birthday approached, he was also reminded of his own mortality. He did not know that his own career would soon come to an end.

In the final year of his rule, Khrushchev kept a low profile in world affairs. In the interests of superpower relations, he quietly tried to restrain the Vietnamese Communists, but failing this he again showed little concern for Southeast Asia. In March 1964, a rumor spread in the United States that he had either been removed from office or died of heart failure, but it proved premature. During the American presidential campaign, the Soviet leader kept silent, hoping to do nothing that might help the right-wing Republican nominee, Barry Goldwater. But by election time, Khrushchev himself was gone, forcibly retired on 14 October by a Presidium conspiracy fronted by Leonid Brezhnev and Alexei Kosygin, but orchestrated by party ideologist Mikhail Suslov. Although Khrushchev's failures in foreign affairs, particularly in Cuba and Berlin, were cited as reasons for his fall, a more proximate cause was his plan to restructure the Soviet Communist party—a threat to the standing and careers of many party functionaries.

Khrushchev's fall, and his replacement by Brezhnev as party first secretary and Kosygin as premier, gave a huge boost to the Soviet military establishment. For all his bluster, Khrushchev had been reluctant to commit vast resources to a massive military buildup, for fear this might derail his plans to improve the consumer economy. Brezhnev and Kosygin had no such qualms. Having received strong support from the military in their effort to topple Khrushchev, they would preside over a sustained weapons buildup of epic proportions. This would enable the USSR to surpass the United States in numbers of strategic missiles, but it would exact a frightful toll on the overall Soviet economy.

Brezhnev, a Khrushchev protégé who had risen through the ranks by maintaining an image of quiet competence while building a powerful base, lacked his predecessor's flair for the dramatic. Colorless and unimaginative, yet determined and effective, he imbued the Soviet leadership with an aura of stability, prudence, and pragmatism. A skilled machine politician, he would manage by patronage and consensus, satisfying the various elements of his coalition while consolidating his power and undermining his rivals. In domestic affairs, he would clamp down on dissent and jettison the more extreme initiatives of Khrushchev (including the anti-Stalin campaign and the party restructuring), while continuing his predecessor's general political thrust. In foreign policy, as relations with communist China deteriorated, he would eventually seek to improve relations with the West, pursuing his version of détente while continuing the relentless arms buildup.

So within a single year, from October of 1963 to October of 1964, West Germany, Britain, the United States, and the USSR all changed leaders. Meanwhile, the focus of the Cold War was beginning to shift—away from Europe and toward Southeast Asia.

11

Vietnam War and Cold War, 1964–1970

When Lyndon Johnson became president of the United States, Southeast Asia was one of his lowest priorities. His ambitious domestic agenda included civil rights laws, a war on poverty, and a wide range of measures designed to remake America into a "Great Society." Soviet leader Brezhnev, preoccupied with consolidating his power and building his nation's strength, also had little interest in the region. Soon, however, the struggle for Southeast Asia, in progress since World War II, was destined to become the focal point of the Cold War.

THE STRUGGLE FOR SOUTHEAST ASIA

The events of World War II, from the Japanese conquest of Southeast Asia through the final defeat of Japan, had touched off a series of indigenous revolts in Western colonies like Malaya, the Philippines, and Indochina. These movements predated the Cold War, existing independently of the superpower rivalry, but they were exploited by participants in the Cold War and eventually were absorbed into it. Since these movements were anti-Western in nature, and since Communists usually played a leading role, they often received support from Moscow and opposition from the United States.

In the British colony of Malaya, apparently on instructions from Moscow, the Malayan Communist party had launched an anti-British rebellion in 1948. But because of the Maoist orientation of the Malayan Communists, the USSR had eventually lost interest, and the rebels were left on their own. Faced with a manhunt conducted by 40,000 British regulars, the revolutionaries (who never numbered more than 5,000) resorted to hit-and-run attacks. These caused extensive damage but failed to destroy the economy. By late 1953, the rebellion had been confined to isolated jungle areas, and in 1956, the British granted independence to the colony without incident. The revolt was disbanded in 1960.

Communists fared no better in the Philippines, which had been a Spanish colony before 1898 and a U.S. possession from then until 1946. During World War II, when the islands were occupied by Japan, there had been formed a *Hukbong Bayan Laban sa Hapon,* or People's Anti-Japanese Army. After liberation (1944) and independence (1946), President Manuel Roxas had driven the "Huks" underground, where they formed the *Hukbong Mapagplayang Bayan* (People's Liberation Army). The Philippine Communist party had joined the Huk revolt in 1948, but Moscow had remained aloof, reluctant to challenge the United States in an area where it maintained major military bases. Nonetheless, the Huks had developed into a strong military force by 1950, largely due to governmental ineptitude and the attraction of their ideas for the peasantry. The tide turned when the CIA threw its support to populist defense secretary Ramón Magsaysay. By the mid-1950s, thanks to Magsaysay's popularity with the peasants and middle class, massive U.S. aid, and lack of Soviet or Chinese help, the Huks were defeated. Magsaysay, at five feet eleven inches a giant among the small-statured Filipinos, became a folk hero and is still revered in many parts of the Philippines, remaining a staunch U.S. ally until his death in a plane crash in 1957.

French Indochina, a large colony that included the lands of Laos, Cambodia, and Vietnam, presented a unique case. Of all the outbreaks of the Cold War in Southeast Asia, by far the most serious occurred there, where a shared border with China and a lack of effective governmental resistance foreshadowed results very different from those in Malaya and the Philippines. France had ruled Indochina since the nineteenth century but had failed to suppress the region's ancient cultures. Demands for liberation had been articulated as early as 1919, when a young Vietnamese Communist named Nguyen Tat Thanh, later called Ho Chi Minh ("he who brings enlightenment"), tried to gain accreditation at Versailles as a spokesman for Indochinese independence. A former merchant seaman and an expert pastry chef, Ho was a quiet, resourceful Communist who led by example, not pontification. Two decades later, he and a small group of associates, including Pham Van Dong and Vo Nguyen Giap, would create the Vietnam Doc Lap Dong Minh (League for Vietnamese Independence), or "Vietminh," at the May 1941 plenum of the Indochinese Communist party.

During World War II, Vietminh fought on the Allied side, receiving arms and aid from the Americans, who saw it as a useful underground resistance movement against the Japanese occupation forces. In December 1944, Vietminh guerrilla units were formed under the command of Giap, a young

French-educated high school history teacher with a law degree from the University of Hanoi. Giap hated the French, who had guillotined his sister-in-law and allowed his wife and child to die in a French prison in 1943. Many of those who joined his units were non-Communists, who rallied to Vietminh because it was the only effective agency aiming at liberation and independence.

Although the Japanese were annoyed by Vietminh's guerrilla tactics, when they surrendered in August 1945, their troops in Indochina had never been defeated. Rather than turn over their weapons to the French, these troops surrendered to Vietminh, which was composed of Asians like themselves. Thus, on 2 September 1945, the tiny, frail figure of Ho Chi Minh addressed a rally of 400,000 people in Hanoi, proclaiming Vietnamese independence in an address deliberately modeled on the U.S. Declaration of Independence.

But real independence proved elusive. Ho anticipated support from America, the first colony to defeat a colonial power, but Truman's anticommunism and desire to back France undermined that hope. Indochina was divided into two occupation zones, under Britain in the south and Nationalist China in the north. The British, against their better judgment, allowed France to move back into the south, while the impending civil war in China soon forced Chiang Kai-shek to call his troops home.

Vietminh now hoped that the French would make a deal rather than wage a costly and lengthy colonial war. Ho believed that if Paris was offered economic concessions and the preservation of French property in Indochina, it might recognize Vietnamese independence. This was not a totally naive position, given the attitude of Jean Sainteny, chief of French intelligence in south China, who saw military reimposition of French colonial control as problematic at best. Two months of talks resulted in the Ho-Sainteny Accords of 6 March 1946, under which France would recognize Vietnam as a "free state with its own government, parliament, army, and finances." Vietnam would become part of an Indochinese Federation and the French Union. France would station 25,000 troops in the north until the end of 1952; in return, Vietminh would end its guerrilla war in the south. But the Ho-Sainteny Accords were doomed from the start. The only reason Paris let Sainteny sign them was to gain unopposed entry of French troops into the north, so that France could eventually destroy Vietnamese independence. Similarly, the reason Ho agreed to the accords was to buy time in which to consolidate his hold by destroying all opposition and to give Giap time to prepare his forces for battle.

By fall 1946, the accords' inadequacy was clear. Incidents between Vietminh and French troops multiplied, and on 23 November the French cruiser *Suffren* bombarded the Vietnamese quarter of the port of Haiphong, killing at least 6,000 and perhaps as many as 20,000 people. On 19 December, Vietminh soldiers in Hanoi killed 37 Frenchmen, in response to which French forces attacked and took the city. Ho, seriously ill throughout the previous

Ho Chi Minh (left) and Vo Nguyen Giap (right) plan strategy. (Black Star)

week, escaped out a back window as the French came in the front door. The First Indochina War had begun.

Ho Chi Minh, waging a struggle for independence and self-determination, expected at least a modicum of international support. But Cold War politics quickly dashed his hopes. The United States encouraged Paris to persevere in its anticommunist course, and London, though favorably disposed toward Vietnamese independence, followed suit. Stalin, true to his spheres-of-influence concept, ignored the conflict in Indochina, and the Chinese Communists were too busy with their own civil war to be of any help.

Despite the solitary nature of its struggle, Vietminh gave the French all they could handle and more. By 1952, the territory under French control was smaller than in 1947. Vietminh greatly increased its military strength and began to conduct large-scale offensive operations. Giap and Ho refused to use their main forces in open encounters, preferring to focus on building up an army and fearful of direct conventional battles against the French. Meanwhile, following the communist victory in China in 1949, the Chinese sent substantial aid to Vietminh, so that by 1952 Giap had a well-equipped regular army of 300,000 men with which to oppose 150,000 French and 300,000 colonial troops.

By late 1953, after seven years of fruitless attempts to defeat Hanoi, the French people had good reason to question the high cost in money and lives of their leaders' chosen course. That policy as of fall 1952 had cost 90,000 casualties and 1.6 trillion francs, twice the amount of Marshall Plan aid to France. Maintaining a force of 150,000 men in Asia also kept France weak in Europe. Add to this the fact that French economic recovery was lagging behind that of Germany, and it is easy to see why even those of undoubted patriotism began to question the war.

By early 1953, both Giap and French general Henri Navarre were seeking to break the deadlock. Giap launched a drive toward Laos in hopes of enticing the French to defend it and, in so doing, to overextend their supply lines. Navarre decided to block Vietminh's advance by garrisoning a dismal little village called Dienbienphu, which sat astride a major road linking Vietnam and Laos. Nothing could have pleased Giap more. By March 1954, he had surrounded it with 40,000 regulars, armed with large numbers of antiaircraft guns and howitzers concealed in caves beneath dense foliage. The French had fewer than 20,000 men in their garrison. They didn't know that the concealed artillery could put Dienbienphu's airstrip out of operation, nor did they realize that Vietminh porters could supply enough ammunition to sustain continuous artillery fire and massive infantry attacks. Giap attacked on 13 March 1954 and assured himself of victory in five days by taking all three French strongpoints in the northern hills. From 18 March to 7 May, the French held out, but their fate was sealed.

Meanwhile, Paris had decided to seek a settlement that would extricate France from Indochina. In February, Britain, France, the United States, and USSR had agreed to a conference at Geneva starting on 26 April, ostensibly to discuss Berlin but really to focus on Indochina. Some French officials, unreconciled to the loss of their colony, asked the United States to intervene to save Dienbienphu. Their allies in Washington, including Secretary of State Dulles and Vice-President Nixon, suggested various actions, including massive air strikes, infantry landings, and the use of tactical nuclear weapons. But President Eisenhower, who feared a land war in Asia and possessed that sense of proportion common to the greatest generals, refused to consider this lunacy. He responded to the suggestion of nuclear strikes with a characteristic outburst: "My God, you boys must be crazy. We can't use those terrible things on Asians twice in ten years!" Instead he endorsed Dulles's call for a political and military effort to destroy communism in Southeast Asia, knowing that neither the British nor the U.S. Congress would go along. Dienbienphu fell to Vietminh on 7 May 1954.

Now the French military position was hopeless. On 17 June, socialist Pierre Mendès-France took over as premier, threatening to resign if a peace settlement were not concluded by 20 July. In Geneva, he, Soviet foreign minister Molotov, and Chinese foreign minister Zhou Enlai worked out a plan to divide Indochina into four states: North Vietnam, South Vietnam, Laos, and

Cambodia. North Vietnam would be ruled by Vietminh, while South Vietnam would be a democracy, led by the anticommunist politician Ngo Dinh Diem. The two would be divided at the 17th parallel, as suggested by Molotov; elections to reunify Vietnam under one government would be held in 1956. Laos and Cambodia would become independent and neutral nations under coalition governments. Vietminh foreign minister Pham Van Dong, faced with the loss of Chinese support, reluctantly came on board. The United States placed no obstacle in the way of a settlement but took a strong interest in South Vietnam. On 20 July 1954, as Mendès-France's deadline ran out, the First Indochina War ended with the signing of the Geneva Accords.

Mendès-France had won at Geneva a far more favorable pact than the French had any right to expect, yet this could not assuage the effects of defeat on the French Empire. Conversely, Ho Chi Minh felt betrayed by the USSR and China, who settled for much less than Giap had won on the battlefield. Zhou Enlai was the real winner: he got a divided Vietnam, which was much more to China's liking than a united and potentially troublesome southern neighbor. He would have preferred to leave France in full control of Indochina, since this would prevent the United States from intervening there and threatening China, as it recently had in Korea. But Zhou, one of the most superb diplomats in modern history, was not inclined to chase chimeras. Cosmopolitan, suave, and ruthless, resolute yet amazingly flexible, he would defend the interests of his nation for more than a generation, and he would take what he could get. If in the process he outmaneuvered Moscow, played false with Vietminh, and played ball with Mendès-France, that was all to be expected in the Cold War, a complex struggle in which neither ideology, nor nationalism, nor the balance of power could fully explain the behavior of a diplomat or a nation. Zhou's machinations guaranteed that, while Vietminh had succeeded in expelling the French, it had failed to unify Vietnam. That would have to wait until 1975.

THE COLD WAR IN VIETNAM AND LAOS

Ho Chi Minh's initial effort to unify Vietnam had failed, but the verdict was not yet final. Vietminh had earned enormous respect by liberating Vietnam from the French. In the south, to overcome this, Ngo Dinh Diem would have to build a regime that could, by its behavior, demonstrate that the country was better off in its hands. Diem's nationalist credentials were impeccable, but he did not appreciate the need for drastic social reforms to destroy the vestiges of French colonialism. Even if he had, his government lacked support among the masses, the police, and the army, and thus was not equipped to execute reforms that would harm the interests of entrenched social and political groups.

After Geneva, Ho waited with scant optimism for the 1956 elections, which he anticipated would never be held. Diem had denounced the Geneva

Accords while the ink remained moist; both he and his U.S. sponsors knew that an election so soon would be won by Vietminh. Their joint opposition ensured that it would not take place. Diem's rule in the south, therefore, evolved through three stages: 1954–1955, during which he managed, against all expectations, to maintain himself in office; 1955–1957, during which his government created a strong belief in its capability for constructive action; and 1957–1963, during which disenchantment with Diem grew, resulting in a consistent erosion of his support.

Ngo Dinh Diem was an enigma. His modern authoritarian ideas, emotional fondness for medieval monarchic concepts, and professed belief in democracy created a complex outlook which defies simple labels. A devout Catholic in a Buddhist land, a lifelong bachelor with monastic tendencies, and an honest man whose family and advisors were hopelessly corrupt, Diem was one of the century's most unusual leaders. Hating both communism and colonialism, he erred in believing that once both were expelled his new nation would be free. Yet his reluctance to alter the old colonial structures discredited him in the eyes of the poor, while his democratic principles alienated the army and worried the Catholic Church. Ho Chi Minh too was hated and mistrusted by many, but he enjoyed an extensive base of support which allowed him to enact broad social and economic reforms. Diem never built that base.

In 1957, Moscow suggested a permanent partition and the admission of both Vietnams to the UN. Washington, reluctant to recognize a communist regime in the north, rejected the offer. That decision proved to be a calamity for South Vietnam, which subsequently suffered through fifteen years of war, only to lose in the end. Had Eisenhower accepted the deal, Ho would have been frantic with despair over yet another sellout by his "friends." In hindsight, of course, the United States should have accepted the bargain. But in the context of the Cold War, both Moscow's offer (in hopes of holding on to what it had) and the U.S. rejection (in hopes of rolling back the Geneva Accords) are understandable. Superpower interests took precedence over those of both Vietnams.

For several years, Ho discouraged armed attacks against the Diem regime, considering the situation unripe for insurrection. However, following Mao Zedong's famous "East Wind over West Wind" speech in Moscow in 1957, calling for communist insurgencies, he began to change his mind and eventually to believe that armed revolt was the only way to reunify Vietnam. In 1959, he authorized the formation of "Viet Cong" (VC) guerrilla units in the south, and in 1960 they created the National Liberation Front (NLF), in a ploy reminiscent of the 1941 formation of Vietminh. The United States supported Diem against the Viet Cong, even though he was a dictator, because he was anticommunist. In reality, *both* Vietnams were one-party states, with a few opposition parties as window dressing. Both had secret police, rigged elections, ubiquitous propaganda, and political reeducation camps. They differed

MAP 8 Vietnam and Its Neighbors

in their economic and social systems, and in South Vietnam's openness to religious diversity—which, ironically, would pose an enormous problem for Diem.

North Vietnam's eventual decision to launch a revolt in the south had a profound impact on neighboring Laos. A mountainous, sparsely populated, destitute country whose capital city of Vientiane had only two traffic lights in 1963, Laos controlled a network of roads, fords, and pathways called the Ho Chi Minh trail—the only route by which North Vietnam could send supplies and personnel to the south. The Geneva Accords had stipulated that Laos remain neutral, but this was easier said than done.

Since the early 1950s, Laos had been effectively divided. Most of the country was under the nominal sway of a neutral coalition government led by Prince Souvanna Phouma, a world-class bridge player who once made a three-no-trump contract by discarding three aces. This bent for taking amazing risks was part of his complex character. His half brother, Prince Souvanouvong, a Communist, led a Vietminh-style army called the Pathet Lao which controlled two northern provinces. The United States backed two other factions, one standing for pro-Western neutrality and another, headed by CIA protégé Phoumi Nosavan, standing for militant anticommunism and destruction of the Pathet Lao. Hanoi, which needed extensive use of the Ho Chi Minh Trail to conduct its insurrection in the south, tried to maintain a low profile and work through the Pathet Lao.

Souvanna Phouma did his best to construct a government of national unity. In December 1960, however, Washington's favorite, Phoumi Nosavan, broke a U.S.–sponsored cease-fire and captured Vientiane, pushing Souvanna Phouma into the arms of the Pathet Lao. A communist counterstroke in March 1961 routed Phoumi's forces and opened all of Laos to attack. John Kennedy, the new U.S. president, now faced the prospect that Laos might fall to the Communists, enabling North Vietnam to outflank South Vietnam. He considered military intervention, but the Joint Chiefs of Staff, traumatized by the Korean experience, insisted that commanders of any U.S. troops in Asia must be authorized to use nuclear weapons. Loath to permit that, Kennedy dispatched Averell Harriman, former ambassador to London and Moscow, to seek a compromise in Laos.

Harriman, nicknamed "Crocodile" for his tendency to snap at those guilty of fuzzy thinking, had decades of experience in dealing with Communists. Seventy years old and increasingly deaf, he could still work eighteen-hour days for weeks on end without suffering any loss of efficiency. Harriman quickly reached several conclusions. The neutralist course was the only one that might enable the United States to avoid war in Laos. Khrushchev did not want war in Laos, both because he thought it would fall to communism anyway and because issues such as Berlin were far more important. Zhou Enlai did not want to provoke a Korean-style U.S. intervention but was willing to run risks in Laos in the belief that Washington would not intervene. Ho Chi Minh wanted a communist Laos, but not at the cost of provoking American or

Chinese intervention. There was room for maneuver, and Harriman made sure that Kennedy saw it.

Now Laos became even more entangled with the Cold War. The Bay of Pigs debacle in April 1961 convinced Kennedy that he could not afford another humiliation at communist hands. He decided to back Souvanna Phouma's neutralist approach in hopes of achieving a negotiated settlement. When he met Khrushchev at Vienna in June, their standoff over Berlin was tempered by their agreement that Laos was not worth a conflict and that a neutralist solution was acceptable to both. The issue dragged on for the rest of 1961, with endless negotiations at Geneva leading even the impassive Andrei Gromyko to grouse that "One cannot sit indefinitely on the shores of Lake Geneva, counting swans." A breakthrough came in May 1962, when Pathet Lao pressure led Kennedy to send the Seventh Fleet to the Gulf of Thailand and U.S. ground forces to Thailand. Simultaneously, Souvanna Phouma initiated direct talks, setting a 15 June deadline for success (as Mendès-France had done in 1954).

Moscow, Beijing, and Hanoi now concluded that a settlement was less risky than continued military pressure. They decided to put Laos on the back burner, apparently reasoning that if Vietnam were united under communist control, Laos would become communist anyway. On 11 June, Souvanna Phouma announced the formation of a government of national unity. Agreements were signed in Geneva on 23 July, reaffirming Laotian neutrality and setting a schedule for removal of all foreign forces. The neutral regime continued to wink at Hanoi's use of the Ho Chi Minh Trail, but in all other respects the arrangement held up until 1975, when Hanoi's victory in Vietnam would bring the Pathet Lao to power in Laos.

Meanwhile, U.S. aid to South Vietnam was increasing markedly. Kennedy's administration kept elevating the number of American military advisors, from 300 in January 1961 to 16,000 by the summer of 1963. Various U.S. military initiatives, like the 1962 Strategic Hamlet Program, had little effect on the insurgency. Then Diem ran afoul of the Buddhist majority (70 percent of the population). For years, he had funneled government posts, land, and power to the Catholic minority. In summer 1963, the militant United Buddhist Church, led by a nationalist monk named Thich Tri Quang, took advantage of government repression to stage a series of provocations aimed at uniting South Vietnamese nationalists to overthrow Diem and return to traditional Vietnamese values by expelling the United States.

Buddhist hunger strikes in May led the regime to declare martial law in several places. Then, on 11 June 1963, a Buddhist monk knelt on a Saigon street, had himself drenched with gasoline, and committed suicide by lighting a match. He was followed over the next few weeks by a number of emulators, and images of burning monks shocked the world. Diem's sister-in-law callously offered to furnish fuel for what she termed "the next barbecue." Appalled, Kennedy insisted that Diem compromise, but even had he been willing, caving in to U.S. pressure would have destroyed his credibility and played into the hand of the Buddhists. As government atrocities mushroomed, Diem on 20 August imposed martial law nationwide and suspended all civil liberties.

Kennedy was no happier with the war than he was with Diem. The Strategic Hamlet Program was a failure, and Viet Cong strength in the south was growing. Kennedy began talking about installing a government in Saigon that would ask the United States to pull out. In the fall, American ambassador Henry Cabot Lodge and CIA operative Lucien Conein conveyed Washington's wishes to certain key military leaders. Diem got wind of this and devised a counterplot, involving a phony revolt that would result in the murders of Lodge, Conein, and the military plotters. Unfortunately for Diem, his closest military advisor, who was supposed to put this plan into effect, was part of the plot against him. On 1 November 1963, the government was overthrown. Diem and his brother, assured of safe conduct by the rebels, were arrested and murdered (according to General Duong Van Minh, they committed "accidental suicide"). A military dictatorship now ruled in Saigon.

Three weeks after the coup, John Kennedy followed the Ngo brothers to the grave. His replacement, Lyndon Johnson, was not interested in a government that would ask the Americans to leave. He wanted instead to "nail the coonskin to the wall," to inflict a decisive defeat on the communist side in the Cold War. If the response had been up to Nikita Khrushchev or Zhou Enlai, some sort of compromise might have been reached. Russia and China, after all, had sold out their comrades before. But the response was in the hands of Ho Chi Minh, and it was not long in coming.

THE AMERICAN INVOLVEMENT IN VIETNAM

Lyndon Johnson's main concerns after taking office were getting elected in 1964 and achieving his domestic agenda. As for Vietnam, he was leery of altering the Kennedy commitment and hopeful that the revolt could be put down swiftly and communism contained. If the war went badly and he tried to get out, conservative lawmakers would hold up his social programs until he gave the Pentagon what it wanted. But if he escalated the conflict, he would alienate key senators like Mike Mansfield, J. William Fulbright, and Richard Russell. He also needed *them* for his social legislation, and they wanted America out of Indochina.

Hanoi's position was also delicate. Annoyed by Khrushchev's disinterest in their struggle and resentful of his efforts to get them to abandon it, the North Vietnamese Communists (Lao Dong party) tilted toward Beijing late in 1963. But China was Vietnam's age-old enemy, and Mao Zedong had his own agenda. He urged Ho to fight a war of attrition, reasoning that it would tie both North Vietnam and the United States down to a long, expensive conflict.

This gave Mao a way to fight America without risking a repetition of Korea, where U.S. technology had claimed a million Chinese lives. Hanoi distrusted Mao's advice and was reluctant to alienate Moscow by increasing its support for the Viet Cong against Khrushchev's wishes. But to let the Viet Cong wither and die was to give up hope for reunification and to tolerate an indefinite U.S. presence in Indochina. Finally, on 28 March 1964, the Lao Dong Party opted to fully support revolution in the south by sending in regular units of the North Vietnamese Army (NVA). For this, it needed the arms Mao could supply, and its tilt toward Beijing continued.

The first NVA units reached the south in August. At the same time, Washington was concluding that it would have to bomb North Vietnam and mine its harbors to cut off its support for the Viet Cong. Congressional approval was obtained through passage of the Gulf of Tonkin Resolution, following an alleged attack by North Vietnamese patrol boats on U.S. surveillance ships in that body of water. Seizing this opportunity, the Johnson administration asked Congress for extensive authority to use military force in Southeast Asia. The resulting resolution, passed by voice vote in the House of Representatives and by 98-2 in the Senate, authorized the president to "take all necessary steps, including the use of armed force, to assist any member . . . of the Southeast Asia Collective Defense Treaty requesting assistance in defense of its freedom." It was a blank check for U.S. military action.

Direct American involvement in the Vietnam War posed a dilemma for Beijing. The Chinese Communists split between those who thought China should draw closer to Moscow and prepare for war against the United States, and those who feared that such action would only delay the revolutionizing of Chinese society. Mao backed the latter faction, depicting American weapons as "paper tigers" and holding that China, which could not really compete with the industrial West, must rely on its own revolutionary spirit for survival. Lin Biao, head of the Chinese People's Liberation Army and a close ally of Mao, endorsed this line in his 1965 article, "Long Live the Victory of People's War." In late 1965, China detached itself from Vietnam and other external affairs, concentrating on an internal upheaval known as the Great Proletarian Cultural Revolution (Chapter 12). Beijing continued to supply Hanoi with arms and encouragement, but nothing else. North Vietnam was on its own.

After Johnson's victory in the 1964 election, most of his advisors favored mass bombing of North Vietnam. Many Americans, including some of the president's main critics, were certain that Southeast Asia was vital to U.S. interests. Secretary of State Dean Rusk went so far as to link it to the German Question, contending that the U.S. guarantee of West Berlin would lose its credibility should South Vietnam fall. Still, the president walked a cautious path until February 1965, when a Viet Cong raid on U.S. military advisors at Pleiku convinced him to initiate bombing. By mid-February, the United States was engaged in Operation ROLLING THUNDER (whose name came from the Christian hymn "How Great Thou Art"), a systematic bombing campaign which would continue until 1968.

The bombing, far from sapping Hanoi's morale, inspired it to greater effort. The first shipments of Soviet and Chinese arms to the Viet Cong down the Ho Chi Minh Trail took place in late 1964. Early the next year, CIA reports indicated that VC strength was increasing exponentially and that a communist victory could not be ruled out. The rebel threat to the U.S. air base at Danang led Johnson to grant the request of General William Westmoreland, commander of American forces in Vietnam, for two battalions of marines, despite the opposition of the U.S. ambassador, General Maxwell Taylor. Once American troops were committed, Johnson would find it impossible to resist further requests. By the end of 1965, troop levels had reached 184,300, with another 200,000 on the way. In pursuing this course of action, the president committed the United States to a land war in Asia while misleading the American public as to the scope of the commitment. The sense of betrayal fostered by this duplicity would contribute greatly to the antiwar protests of the late 1960s.

In making this extensive troop commitment, Johnson had no reason to fear the sort of Chinese intervention that had occurred in Korea. China by 1966 was knee-deep in the Cultural Revolution, and Moscow's postwar record indicated that Soviet military action was unlikely. But the limited war in Vietnam carried all the liabilities of limited war in Korea: significant U.S. casualties, a stalemate with no prospects for quick victory, and the sense that the military was being unduly restricted by civilian politicians. Democracies find it easier to fight total war than limited war, as Truman's experience had shown.

As in Korea, a lack of clear war aims plagued the U.S. command. Westmoreland tried to win a war with no well-defined goals and no consensus on what would constitute victory, short of the total destruction of communism in Vietnam. He fought a conventional war against a guerrilla insurgency, hoping that he could kill enough of the enemy to drive North Vietnam to negotiate. But he had no way of knowing how many deaths that would take and no awareness of the level of Ho Chi Minh's commitment to the war. U.S. forces killed Vietnamese by the thousands, and total communist deaths between 1961 and 1975 surely exceeded a million. But the Lao Dong party believed it could raise at least 250,000 new recruits *each year* and that America simply couldn't kill that many. The U.S. goal was fuzzy and probably unattainable.

As for negotiations, it was difficult to envisage a plausible bargaining scenario. Vietminh had come to Geneva in 1954 sure that its Dienbienphu victory would bring it a unified nation, only to have Moscow and Beijing sell it out and divide Vietnam. But Ho Chi Minh would not make the same mistake twice. North Vietnam had consciously adopted a long, painful process to conquer the south. Hanoi had no expectation of quick victory, and the war from its perspective was not a stalemate but an endless chain of small encounters designed to weaken America's will. This strategy slowly succeeded, a fact implicitly recognized in Lyndon Johnson's rueful comment: "If I were Ho Chi Minh, I'd never negotiate."

ESCALATION WITHOUT VICTORY, 1965–1967

Hanoi's ability to resist the U.S. onslaught derived from a number of factors. First was the simplicity of its goal: to reunify Vietnam by expelling the Americans and conquering the south. The Lao Dong party was thus able to focus the nation's energies on an understandable and attractive objective. Great sacrifice would be required, but the end was concrete in nature and easily imaginable: no one believed that the Americans would stay forever, and no one thought South Vietnam could long survive their departure. Inspired by this goal, the Communists persevered for years despite terrible hardship.

Second, North Vietnam's economy could not be destroyed by bombing. An agrarian nation with few industrial areas, it could hardly be "bombed back to the Stone Age," as General Curtis LeMay suggested. Compared with America, it was already there. Hanoi's weapons were furnished by its allies: trucks and AK-47 rifles from China; tanks, planes, and surface-to-air missiles from Russia. They were produced at facilities in those nations and thus lay beyond the reach of U.S. bombing.

Third, the NVA followed the same strategy it had used against France: employ guerrilla tactics against a superior foe until you can entice that foe into a situation where you have the advantage. NVA commander Vo Nguyen Giap knew how to fight set-piece battles and knew that he would lose them unless he could select the proper time, place, and conditions. Time was on his side, and his skills far surpassed those of U.S. generals reluctant to part with methods honed on European plains in the 1940s and Korean hills in the 1950s. The Communists' ability to live off the land and mix with the local people made it impossible for the United States to force them to fight a conventional war until it was in their interest to do so.

So when the U.S. government sent American marines ashore at Danang on 8 March 1965, it was confronting an adversary much better prepared and much more focused on attainable objectives than Washington realized. As if this were not dangerous enough, almost at once an antiwar movement began in the United States. On 24 March, the University of Michigan was the site of a "Teach-In" against the war, as classes throughout the day were devoted to the situation in Vietnam. Johnson's decision two weeks later to let U.S. combat troops engage in offensive operations was met with an antiwar rally in Washington organized by a radical group called "Students for a Democratic Society," or SDS. On 15 May, a National Teach-In took place on campuses in all fifty states, and that October, antiwar protests were conducted simultaneously in forty American cities. The war was becoming the defining feature of

Johnson's administration, imperiling the consensus needed for his Great Society reforms. Yet thus far the reaction was out of proportion to the American involvement. By year's end U.S. troop strength in Vietnam stood at 184,300, and only 636 American soldiers had been killed. Later increases in casualties and draft calls would turn the antiwar movement into the most extensive grass-roots protest in American history.

In November, a small U.S. detachment moving through the Ia Drang Valley was ambushed by an NVA regiment. After a three-day battle, 240 American soldiers had been killed, a total which shocked Defense Secretary McNamara and angered Johnson; but the NVA counted 1,800 dead and a like number seriously wounded. This decided an internal dispute between Giap and General Nguyen Chi Thanh, who felt the United States could be defeated by conventional means: casualties on that scale were unacceptable to Hanoi. From then on, the NVA would avoid large battles in favor of Giap's hit-and-run tactics. Westmoreland failed to make a similar adjustment, and American military fortunes began a barely perceptible decline.

On Christmas Day, 1965, Johnson suspended Operation ROLLING THUNDER to give Hanoi a chance to seek a negotiated settlement. He received no response and resumed the bombing on 31 January 1966. The next few months proved difficult. The Senate Foreign Relations Committee opened televised hearings on the war four days after the bombing resumed; Secretary Rusk doggedly defended the U.S. position against skeptical witnesses and suspicious senators. Two months later National Security Advisor McGeorge Bundy, disturbed over the rapid increase in U.S. troop commitment, resigned. He was replaced by Walt Whitman Rostow, an inflexible Cold Warrior and a true believer in the virtues of strategic bombing. Meanwhile, Senator Wayne Morse tried to get the Senate to repeal the Gulf of Tonkin Resolution but failed by a vote of 92–5. Most senators still felt the war was winnable, and those who didn't were reluctant to withdraw authority from a president in the midst of a conflict.

The mood of the country was both more and less warlike than that of the Congress. U.S. casualties were still fairly low, and most people, if they thought about the conflict at all, considered it an unpleasant necessity akin to the Korean War. The "Baby Boom" generation, however, had different ideas. They were beneficiaries of the new housing, schools, and roads of the postwar era; the GI Bill had given their parents access to better education and jobs; they had responded to Kennedy's youth and vigor and had joined the Peace Corps, Johnson's War on Poverty, and the Civil Rights Movement. Their parents found their sexual mores and rock music disturbing. This generation now had to answer draft calls for the Vietnam War, and they were convinced neither of its value nor its morality.

No single response to the war came from the Baby Boomers. Some enlisted eagerly, some were drafted reluctantly, some sought escape in student deferments or conscientious objector status, some (given Johnson's odd decision not to call up the reserves) enlisted in the reserve forces to avoid combat, and a few fled to foreign lands. Many took part in antiwar protests, which grew in size and frequency throughout the 1960s. For Lyndon Johnson's generation, the sight of thousands of Americans demonstrating in the streets against U.S. policy was deeply disturbing. Totalitarian regimes could repress such protests, but a democratic society had to respond in some way to popular pressure. In April 1966, Johnson called on Ho Chi Minh to make peace in return for $5 billion in aid and a huge development program. Hanoi responded with silence. On 1 May, the United States bombed Viet Cong camps in Cambodia for the first time, and the antiwar demonstrations at home continued.

By early 1967, American troop levels in Vietnam had risen to 385,300. Six thousand U.S. soldiers died there in 1966, bringing the war's total to 6,644. General Westmoreland continued to seek a military victory but could not find a strategy to cope with Giap's guerrilla warfare. Defense Secretary McNamara, horrified at the growing death toll and suspicious of the accuracy of the U.S. military's "body counts," advised Johnson to deescalate the conflict and seek a negotiated settlement. He was eased out of office in late 1967. That September, Johnson offered the San Antonio Formula: the bombing of North Vietnam would stop as soon as talks began. Hanoi had other plans, and the war went on.

Bombing of the north intensified, as did aerial defoliation of the south: huge quantities of potent herbicides, including the carcinogenic Agent Orange, were sprayed over jungles throughout South Vietnam to deprive the enemy of cover. Antipersonnel raids by B-52 bombers produced areas of destruction similar to that of an atomic blast. Body counts showed colossal casualty rates among communist forces. None of it seemed to make a difference. Johnson, desperate for a way out, met Soviet premier Kosygin in a strange one-day summit in Glassboro, New Jersey, in summer 1967. But nothing came of the talks, because neither Russia nor China had as much influence over Hanoi in 1967 as they had exercised in 1954. The Lao Dong party was resolved to fight until the United States withdrew and then to continue its subversion of the south.

Meanwhile, American support for the war was eroding rapidly. In April, an antiwar protest in New York drew over 100,000 people, and six months later 50,000 marched on the Pentagon. The antiwar movement, though growing larger by the day, was never united, save in seeking the end to U.S. involvement in Vietnam. Liberals who saw the war as a mistake, radicals who opposed capitalism, and pacifists who hated violence, all came together to try to force Johnson to end the war.

Johnson responded by questioning his critics' patriotism and trying to prove that the war was being won. But U.S. troop levels at the end of 1967 were 485,600, and the death toll for that year was 9,377, bringing the total for the war to 16,021. Intelligence showed that, despite this huge effort, North

Vietnamese and Viet Cong control continued to grow in the south. As 1967 ended, the validity of American strategy and public support for the war hung by slender threads. Ho Chi Minh would cut them in 1968.

THE TET OFFENSIVE

In Vietnam, the Lunar New Year, or "Tet," was the year's main holiday. For several years, a truce had been observed so that both sides might celebrate in peace. The Americans expected a low level of hostilities during this period. Had they known more Vietnamese history, they might have recalled that an earlier ruler had routed invading Chinese troops who were observing Tet festivities in 1789. On 21 January 1968, nine days before Tet, the NVA baited its trap, laying siege to a remote U.S. outpost at Khe Sanh. This was done to draw American forces away from South Vietnamese cities, exposing them to Viet Cong attack.

It was not a terribly clever ploy, but Westmoreland fell for it. He redeployed U.S. forces toward Khe Sanh, presuming the cities would be safe during Tet. It would have been just as logical to assume that Khe Sanh would be safe, but Westmoreland's logic stopped short of that conclusion. On 30 January, the first day of Tet, the Viet Cong invaded thirteen provincial capitals, captured the ancient imperial capital of Hué, and used nineteen commandos to attack and briefly occupy parts of the U.S. embassy in Saigon. The attacks came without warning, and in the subsequent judgment of a West Point textbook on military history, the Tet Offensive was an American intelligence disaster equivalent to Pearl Harbor.

By late February, order was restored. Westmoreland portrayed Tet as a Viet Cong defeat, and in a military sense it was. The VC lost their best people, and the North Vietnamese who replaced them turned what had been a largely indigenous southern movement into a subsidiary of the NVA. The VC's casualties were horrendous, and they failed to hold any of the cities they had attacked. Hanoi's real objective, however, was not a military one. Giap said later that he had hoped to spark uprisings throughout South Vietnam by showing that the Americans could not protect its people. Clearly, that goal was not attained. Ironically, Hanoi *did* succeed in influencing U.S. public opinion, which it had not set out to do!

Tet proved to be Johnson's political death knell, not because it turned most Americans against the war (public opinion polls showed the contrary), but because it confirmed two key groups in their convictions. The antiwar movement had always seen the war as unjustified, immoral, and/or not in the U.S. interest. But others felt that Johnson was not waging the war effectively and that American troops were being asked to fight with one hand behind their backs. Tet verified this belief and turned this group against continued U.S. involvement. Deprived of this support, with his domestic agenda in ruins, Johnson now faced a challenge for the Democratic presidential nomination

Vietnamese Children running from napalm attack. (UPI/Bettman)

from Senator Eugene McCarthy, whose entry into the primary races in November 1967 had been greeted with polite disdain. Tet turned him into a viable candidate, as those who were upset with Johnson now saw a vote for McCarthy as a way to send the White House a message.

On 27 February, Westmoreland made public a request for 206,000 more troops. The shock to the nation was even deeper than the trauma of Tet. After years of duplicity in its portrayal of the situation in Vietnam, the Johnson administration seemed ethically bankrupt. Even worse, Americans began to realize that, despite what they had been promised, a victorious end to the war was nowhere in sight. CBS news anchorman Walter Cronkite observed that the war was likely to end in a stalemate, and a few days later he broadcast a secret CIA estimate that, at present levels, the war could last a century. Johnson had been fatally wounded at "Credibility Gap," and on 12 March McCarthy nearly buried him, losing the New Hampshire primary by fewer than 300 votes out of 50,000 cast. Four days later Senator Robert Kennedy, brother of the slain president, entered the Democratic race, splitting the anti-war vote but providing the peace movement with a candidate far more formidable than McCarthy. That same day, a U.S. platoon massacred nearly 500 women and children in a remote village called My Lai. The news was hidden for twenty months.

On 26 March, Johnson assembled the Senior Advisory Group on Vietnam, a panel of statesmen and experts whom he consulted often. As recently as November 1967, they had advised him to stand firm. Now, headed by presidential troubleshooter Philip Habib and Dean Acheson, who as Truman's secretary of state had helped lead the nation into the Korean War, they overwhelmingly recommended disengagement. Johnson was stunned and bitter. Five days later, on 31 March, he addressed the nation and announced that he would not seek another term. Vice-President Hubert Humphrey entered the race as Johnson's heir, despite his own misgivings about the war.

NIXON TAKES COMMAND

In April 1968, it seemed the war might soon be over, but more than half the U.S. combat deaths in Vietnam still lay ahead. The year itself turned into an unimaginable horror. Peace talks opened in Paris on 12 May, but no real progress was made. Robert Kennedy was murdered on 5 June, moments after defeating Humphrey and McCarthy in the California presidential primary. In events unrelated to Vietnam, American civil rights leader Martin Luther King was gunned down on 4 April; student and working-class riots in May nearly toppled de Gaulle's regime in France; the USSR invaded Czechoslovakia in August to destroy Alexander Dubcek's reformist government; and in Mexico City in October, President Gustavo Díaz Ordaz's troops opened fire on a crowd of demonstrators and killed more than 300, two weeks before the start of the Olympic games.

A dazed world turned its eyes to U.S. presidential politics. Former Vice-President Richard Nixon won the Republican nomination in July, narrowly defeating California governor Ronald Reagan. Humphrey prevailed over McCarthy to become the Democratic nominee, but not before antiwar protests during the party's convention in Chicago turned brutal. Scenes of police clubbing protesters and rioters looting stores were telecast throughout the world, seriously weakening the moral credibility of both the antiwar movement and the Chicago police, and damaging the Democrats so badly it was hard to see how Humphrey could win.

Amazingly, he nearly did. Torn between loyalty to Johnson and his own conscience, he missed a splendid chance at the convention to reconcile with the Kennedy forces by denouncing the war, an act which would have isolated McCarthy and reunified the party. Not until late September would Humphrey voice a willingness to seek a quick end to the war. Johnson did his part by halting Operation ROLLING THUNDER on Halloween night, sparking a surge to Humphrey five days before the election. Assisted by George Wallace of

Alabama, who ran as a third-party candidate and split the pro-war vote with Nixon, Humphrey closed to within a percentage point; but Nixon held on and narrowly won the election. As 1968 mercifully ended, U.S. troop levels in Vietnam stood at 536,000. Deaths that year totaled 14,589, the highest single-year total of the war.

By 30 April 1969, American troop strength peaked at 543,300. Nixon, despite his militaristic campaign rhetoric, had no intention of escalating the conflict; nor did he envision a quick pullout. Resolved not to become the first U.S. president to lose a war, he wanted to remove troops gradually while strengthening South Vietnam with a flood of military equipment. That material would be used by local forces rather than by Americans, a concept enshrined as a worldwide principle in the "Nixon Doctrine" of July 1969. At the same time, the CIA's "Phoenix" program employed infiltration techniques to cripple the Viet Cong's operations through the unmasking and (in many cases) killing of approximately 60,000 VC agents in the south.

Nixon's phased withdrawal began with the removal of 25,000 troops in June and was soon incorporated in the Pentagon budgets by Defense Secretary Melvin Laird. This annoyed National Security Advisor Henry Kissinger, who felt that scheduled troop pullouts deprived him of negotiating leverage with Hanoi. Laird also coined the term "Vietnamization" to describe the execution of the Nixon Doctrine in Southeast Asia. Despite Johnson's 1964 campaign pledge that "We don't want American boys to do the fighting for Asian boys," South Vietnam had not begun drafting eighteen-year-olds until Nixon took office, while Americans of that age had been fighting in Vietnam since 1965. Vietnamization, of course, had its enemies, including the U.S. antiwar movement (which saw it as a delaying tactic) and South Vietnamese president Nguyen Van Thieu (who considered it a betrayal of America's commitment). Thieu undermined the Paris peace talks so well that Nixon lost interest in them and dispatched Kissinger to meet secretly in February 1970 with Hanoi's special emissary, Le Duc Tho. It would take nearly three years for those secret talks to pay off.

Clearly Nixon's strategy would take time, and America was growing impatient. Ho Chi Minh's death in September 1969 had no impact on North Vietnam's bargaining posture; on his deathbed, the world's most famous pastry chef enjoined his successors to avoid another Geneva conference in which Moscow and Beijing could once more sell the Lao Dong party down the Mekong River. The antiwar movement continued, sponsoring nationwide "moratorium" demonstrations on 15 October, followed by a huge march on Washington on 15 November. A day later, the *New York Times* published the first accounts of the March 1968 My Lai massacre. As 1970 began, U.S. troop levels were down to 475,200, but total American dead now exceeded 40,000. Nixon wanted a break in the stalemate, and he wanted it quickly.

His impatience mirrored that of the American people, and it led to a widening of the war. Throughout the 1960s, North Vietnam had made skillful use of the Ho Chi Minh Trail, which ran through neutral Laos and Cambodia. NVA and VC units had often taken refuge in camps just across the border to avoid pursuit by U.S. forces. In March 1970, a military coup deposed Cambodia's neutralist Prince Sihanouk, replacing him with pro-American general Lon Nol. The United States at once pressured Lon Nol to expel the NVA and VC forces, and on 30 April Nixon announced an American invasion of Cambodia to close down the camps and supply routes. The Vietnam War now became the Second Indochina War, and U.S. campuses erupted in protest. The Ohio National Guard fired on one such demonstration at Kent State University, killing four students and sending ripples of revulsion across the nation. Several more students were killed at Jackson State University in Mississippi that same week. Many colleges canceled classes and exams, either in protest against the war or as a sign of helplessness in the face of angry students.

American operations in Cambodia ended on 30 June. Six months later, Congress prohibited the use of U.S. combat troops in Laos and Cambodia. But the Ho Chi Minh Trail was still open, and American forces were still mired in South Vietnam. Desperate to find a way out, Nixon and Kissinger increasingly placed their hopes on détente with China and Russia, hoping that Beijing and Moscow could help them end the war.

12

China, SALT, and the Superpowers, 1967–1972

By the late 1960s, in several respects, the world strategic balance seemed to be shifting in Moscow's favor. As a result of a massive weapons buildup, the Soviet Union was rapidly closing the gap between itself and the United States, at least in the area of land-based strategic missiles. Meanwhile, the United States was finding itself sinking ever more deeply into the morass of Vietnam, expending its resources and credibility in a war that was becoming increasingly unpopular and tearing apart the fabric of American society. As the U.S. military effort failed to bring a quick victory, and as the war dragged on with no end in sight, the aura of American superiority seemed to be vanishing into the jungles and swamps of war-torn Southeast Asia.

Despite the American setbacks, however, the appearance of Soviet gain was both illusory and deceptive. The economy of the USSR continued to falter, as the efforts of Brezhnev and Kosygin to modernize production and increase the supply of consumer goods proved ineffective and inadequate. In strategic terms, the Soviets might be catching up, but in economic terms, they were falling further behind the industrialized West and Japan. And even their strategic gains were being offset by the emergence of a formidable new foe, as they increasingly came into conflict with their erstwhile communist allies in the People's Republic of China (PRC).

THE SINO-SOVIET SPLIT

The antagonism between the Soviets and the Chinese had both historical and ideological roots. In the nineteenth century, the imperial Russian government had taken advantage of weakness and turmoil in China to impose unequal treaties, thus helping itself to territory previously claimed by the Chinese. Although the Soviet government renounced such treaties after it came to power, no land was ever returned, and there remained large disputed areas along the 4,000-mile border between the two countries. Then, during the long struggle between the Chinese Communists and Nationalists, the Soviet leaders often seemed to side with the Nationalists, urging the Communists to collaborate with their adversaries even at the risk of extermination. Even during the Civil War of 1946–1949, Mao Zedong and his comrades received only limited support from Moscow and on occasion found it necessary to reject Stalin's advice that they work out some accommodation with the Nationalist regime. And Mao's brand of communism, based on mobilization of the peasant masses, was significantly at odds with the more traditional model of a Marxist-Leninist proletarian vanguard espoused by the USSR.

At first, in the full flush of fervor following the Chinese communist victory in 1949, such differences mattered little. Mao would need massive aid to build his new society, and the obvious place to turn was to the USSR. He thus initiated a policy of "leaning to one side," aligning the PRC clearly with the USSR and traveling to Moscow in December of 1949 to negotiate with Soviet leaders. Stalin, for his part, was outwardly receptive to a Sino-Soviet alliance, whatever his private misgivings may have been about a potentially powerful socialist state that was not under his control. The "Treaty of Friendship and Alliance," which took two months to negotiate, was finally signed on 14 February 1950. It provided for a thirty-year alliance during which the Soviets agreed to provide the equivalent of $300 million in credits to assist in Chinese development, as well as the equipment needed for a number of construction projects. Although this aid only amounted to about one-tenth of what Mao thought he needed, it was welcomed as a first step.

During the course of the 1950s, then, the USSR did provide significant aid and assistance to the PRC. During the Korean War, although they avoided sending combat troops or military advisors, the Soviets supplied the Chinese with technological support and sold them military hardware, including several submarines and a number of MiG fighter aircraft. The USSR quickly became China's main trading partner, accounting for roughly half of all Chinese foreign commerce. The Soviets sent thousands of advisors and technicians to China, trained thousands of Chinese in Russia, provided industrial plans and expertise, and helped to construct several hundred industrial projects in China. Throughout the decade, at least until 1958, the Chinese borrowed heavily from Soviet experience and expertise and clearly sought to emulate the Soviet model—even to the point of adopting their own "Five-Year Plan" for rapid industrialization.

It was not long, however, before the shine of socialist solidarity had begun to fade. As early as 1955, in fact, there were several indications of troubled waters ahead. At the Bandung Conference of nonaligned nations (Chapter 8), to which the Soviets were not even invited, the Chinese began to pursue an independent course in foreign policy, seeking to establish themselves as leaders of the emerging nonaligned movement. That year also witnessed the purge and suicide of Gao Gang, the Chinese Communist party boss in Manchuria, who was accused of trying to carve out an independent kingdom there and was resented by Mao for his close association and identification with Moscow.

As long as Stalin was alive, Mao was willing to accept a secondary role as junior partner to the Soviet dictator, but he accorded Stalin's successors no such esteem. In 1956, when Soviet leader Khrushchev attacked Stalin and called for peaceful coexistence with the West, the Chinese leader was horrified. After all, China was still following the Stalinist model, and Mao resented Khrushchev's denigration of Stalin's activities and personality cult. Besides, the Chinese Communists had only recently concluded a bloody struggle in Korea against the United States, which continued to recognize the Nationalist regime on Taiwan as the legitimate government of all of China. From the perspective of Beijing, peaceful coexistence with the West was little more than a sellout of socialist standards.

It took several years, however, for the growing divergence between the two communist giants to become an open rift. Throughout 1957, they managed to present a united front, with Chinese premier Zhou Enlai traveling to Eastern Europe early in the year to help shore up the Soviet position, and Soviet party boss Khrushchev promising late in the year to provide the Chinese with an atomic bomb. But in 1958, the façade of unity began to crumble. In August, without consulting Moscow, Mao suddenly abandoned the Soviet model and launched his nation on the "Great Leap Forward," a campaign of mass mobilization designed to transform China posthaste into a society based on huge peasant communes which would supervise production in both agriculture and industry and control almost every aspect of people's lives. Along with this, there was initiated a cult of Mao that was even more extreme in its veneration than the Stalin cult which Khrushchev had so forcefully condemned. The following month, when the Chinese precipitated a crisis with the United States by shelling the Nationalist-controlled island of Quemoy, five miles off their coast, the Soviets conspicuously failed to support them.

Although Moscow and Beijing did manage to conclude a new economic agreement early in 1959, Sino-Soviet relations continued to deteriorate. In July, after it had become obvious that Beijing would not consent to Soviet control over atomic warheads in China, Khrushchev canceled his earlier offer to furnish the Chinese with a nuclear bomb. In September, when border clashes broke out between China and India, the Soviets sided diplomatically with India, a neutral democracy whose friendship Moscow was trying to cultivate. That same month the Chinese watched in dismay as Khrushchev visited the United States and held cordial talks with Eisenhower. A follow-up visit by the Soviet leader to Beijing failed to placate the Chinese, who had been mortified at the sight of their supposed socialist ally collaborating openly with their most powerful imperialist enemy.

The split became an open rupture during the course of 1960. By this time, the Great Leap Forward had proven a dismal failure, and the Chinese economy was in desperate straits. The Soviets, having seen their advice rejected and their experience ignored, showed little sympathy for the Chinese plight. Khrushchev traveled to India early in the year to sign a treaty which involved very generous economic aid to China's Asian rival. In May, he began withdrawing Soviet advisors and technicians from China, signaling the end of Sino-Soviet cooperation. Beijing made indirect attacks upon the USSR by criticizing Yugoslavia, with which Soviet relations had recently improved. Moscow responded with verbal assaults against Albania, which was openly moving into the Chinese camp.

In the early 1960s, the temporary eclipse of Mao Zedong and ascendancy in Beijing of moderates led by Liu Shaoqi resulted in a short-lived easing of tensions between China and the USSR. The most radical aspects of the Great Leap Forward were forsaken, and Soviet-style economic practices were reinstated. But the atmosphere was soon soured by Khrushchev's renewed campaign against Stalinism, begun in Moscow at the Twenty-second Party Congress in October of 1961. Zhou Enlai, who attended as head of the Chinese delegation, responded by ostentatiously placing a wreath on Stalin's grave and then departing early.

Following this incident, relations continued to worsen. In 1962, an acrimonious border dispute occurred during which Soviet officials encouraged Muslim peoples in northwestern China to depart for Soviet territory. In October of that year, Chinese disgust over Soviet capitulation in the Cuban Missile Crisis, coupled with Moscow's sympathy for India in a Sino-Indian border war which began that same month, effectively destroyed any hopes for Sino-Soviet rapprochement. By 1963, the two sides were publicly attacking each other, and not just their Yugoslavian and Albanian comrades, while border clashes were becoming increasingly frequent. In July of that year, their "Treaty of Friendship and Alliance," moribund since 1960, was dissolved. The socialist schism was official and complete.

During the middle 1960s, the two communist titans squared off against one another as competitors for leadership of the socialist world and the allegiance of communist parties in nonaligned states. The ideological war of words heated up, with each side accusing the other of various heresies, and with the Chinese even going so far as to portray the Soviets as fascists and imperialists. Mao weighed in with a bitter diatribe entitled "On Khrushchev's

Phony Communism and Its Historical Lessons for the World." In a number of places throughout the Third World, communist parties split into pro-Soviet and pro-Chinese factions. The fall of Khrushchev in October of 1964, which coincided with the successful testing of China's first atomic bomb, was welcomed by Chinese leaders and helped bring about a temporary thaw in Sino-Soviet relations. The new Soviet premier, Aleksei Kosygin, traveled to Beijing early in 1965 but failed to achieve any lasting measure of cooperation. Before long, the two nations were once again at odds, and the USSR was beginning a buildup of military forces along its border with China.

At the end of 1965, there began in China the immense series of internal convulsions that came to be known as the "Great Proletarian Cultural Revolution." For the next few years, the Chinese virtually withdrew from the arena of international affairs, as their energies were focused inward. Determined to prevent his revolution from following the path of bureaucratic elitism that he perceived in the USSR, Mao emerged from semiretirement to lead yet another mass mobilization campaign to transform the consciousness of the Chinese people. Universities were shut down, industrial enterprises were closed, and legions of youthful "Red Guards" were employed to force bureaucrats and professionals to work in the fields. The Soviet system was vilified, and the Soviet embassy in Beijing was even besieged by the rampaging Red Guards early in 1967.

MUTUAL ASSURED DESTRUCTION
AND MISSILE DEFENSE SYSTEMS

Sino-Soviet bitterness did nothing to slow the relentless nuclear arms race between the superpowers. In 1967, the United States completed the ICBM buildup begun in the Kennedy years, deploying the last of its thousand Minuteman missiles. The American lead, however, was beginning to evaporate. Between 1965 and 1968, the Soviets, producing new ICBMs at an unprecedented rate in the wake of Brezhnev's accession, more than tripled their operational long-range missiles, achieving a total of 950 by early 1969.

Although American officials were surprised by the rapidity of the Soviet missile buildup, which far exceeded U.S. intelligence predictions, they did not at first see it as a threat to U.S. security. Indeed, Defense Secretary McNamara had come to believe that international peace was best secured by a situation of "mutual assured destruction," in which each side possessed the wherewithal to obliterate the other in response to any attack. This condition, known by the terribly apt acronym of "MAD," would theoretically preclude either superpower from launching an attack by making such an action suicidal. It might also help slow the arms race, since a numerical lead in such a situation appeared to offer little real advantage. Besides, as McNamara and his colleagues were well aware, progress in the development of so-called MIRVs (multiple independently targeted reentry vehicles) would eventually make it possible for each missile to deliver a number of nuclear warheads against a variety of enemy targets.

Of far greater concern to Washington was the rapid Soviet development of an antiballistic missile (ABM) system designed to defend against nuclear attack. Such a system, if it were extensive enough, could potentially destroy the MAD balance of terror by giving one side or the other hope of surviving a nuclear counterattack. Once a nation had an effective ABM system in place, it could launch a surprise strike without necessarily committing suicide. Furthermore, the deployment of such a system might well give a boost to the arms race, encouraging each side to deploy massive numbers of rockets and warheads so as to potentially overwhelm its adversary's missile defense.

Washington was appalled, then, in 1966, when U.S. intelligence discovered evidence that the Soviets were constructing an ABM system around the city of Moscow. As pressures mounted for America to build its own ABMs, Johnson and McNamara instead tried a different tack. They began a concerted effort to convince the Soviet leaders that it would be far cheaper and safer to negotiate upper limits on their nuclear stockpiles than to engage in a costly and dangerous race to develop missile defenses.

In June 1967, following a brief visit to the United Nations in New York, Soviet premier Kosygin met with President Johnson and his aides in Glassboro, New Jersey (selected because it was precisely halfway between the UN and the White House). Although the Glassboro summit achieved no breakthroughs with respect to the Vietnam War (Chapter 11), it did help set the stage for important future developments in the arena of arms control. During the course of the meeting, Defense Secretary McNamara delivered an impassioned plea to the Soviet leaders to restrict their ABM development, arguing that it was bound to trigger a massive and expensive new arms race that would undermine each side's security and sap its resources still further. Although Kosygin remained unmoved, contending angrily that defensive systems were "moral" and offensive ones were not, the logic nonetheless had an impact on Soviet planners, helping to pave the way for serious efforts at strategic arms limitation.

Gradually, then, the two superpowers began to feel their way toward arms control. In 1967, they signed an accord banning nuclear weapons from outer space. That same year, although he reluctantly approved development of a U.S. ABM system, McNamara decried the "mad momentum" by which each side's weapons programs encouraged and incited the other. In 1968, a Nuclear Non-Proliferation Treaty, designed to prevent additional nations from joining the nuclear club, was signed by the United States, USSR, Britain, and numerous other countries (although not by France and China). Soviet foreign minister Gromyko then announced that Moscow was ready to engage in preliminary discussions about restricting strategic weapons. By August, private plans were being made for President Johnson to visit the USSR in order to help initiate the opening round of strategic arms limitation talks.

But the visit never came. Instead, a series of developments took place that eventually changed the nature of the Cold War and dramatically altered relations between the superpowers.

THE INVASION OF CZECHOSLOVAKIA
AND THE BREZHNEV DOCTRINE

The first of these events was the Soviet invasion of Czechoslovakia in August 1968. Early that year Antonin Novotný , a heavy-handed dictator who had ruled his nation with an iron fist since 1953, was compelled to step down as leader of the Czechoslovak Communist party. He was replaced by Alexander Dubcek, a reform-minded Slovak who soon began to implement a series of measures designed to institute a form of "democratic socialism" in the country. Basic civil rights were expanded, freedom of the press was permitted, and steps were taken toward democratization of the political system. This "Prague Spring," as it was called, inspired much excitement and sympathy in the West, but it also engendered deep consternation among Soviet leaders, who feared that the zeal for reform might threaten their hold on all of Eastern Europe.

Moscow sought in various ways to halt this trend and to bring the situation back under its control. A face-to-face conference in late July between the Soviet and Czechoslovak leaders, followed by a meeting in early August of Eastern European party bosses, seemed to ease the crisis but did not result in a solution that was fully acceptable to Moscow. Hopes for a peaceful settlement were soon to be cruelly dashed. On the evening of 20 August, fearful that the Czechoslovak experiment might spread to the other satellites if it remained unchecked, the Kremlin launched a sudden military invasion of its socialist neighbor and ally. Once again, as in Hungary in 1956, the world was treated to the brutal spectacle of Soviet troops and tanks moving in to reassert hegemony over a neighboring country. The democratic movement in Czechoslovakia was crushed, Dubcek and his colleagues were forced to rescind their reforms, and the reformers themselves were gradually removed from all positions of power. The following April, Dubcek was replaced by Moscow-loyalist Gustáv Husák, who proceeded to bring the wayward Soviet ally firmly back into line.

This invasion had a number of far-reaching effects. In the long run, by allowing the USSR to maintain and consolidate its control over Eastern Europe, it may have helped to give Moscow the security it needed to improve its relations with the West. In the short run, however, it cast a pall over international relations and seriously undermined the public stature of the USSR. In the resulting climate of anti-Soviet outrage, Lyndon Johnson—whose presidency had already been ruined by the Vietnam War—had little alternative but to cancel his trip to Russia and leave it to his successors to deal with arms control. Meanwhile, in an ominous coincidence, both superpowers were successfully testing new multiple-warhead missiles that threatened to accelerate

Soviet tanks in Prague, 1968. (UPI/Bettmann)

the arms race by allowing each side rapidly and inexpensively to increase its destructive capabilities.

Even among Communists, the Soviet invasion of Czechoslovakia was greeted with considerable hostility. The communist parties of Western Europe joined the chorus of those condemning the Kremlin for its naked and brutal intervention. Some socialist nations, like Romania and Yugoslavia, also took pains to express their displeasure, while others reluctantly expressed support for the actions taken by Moscow. Most concerned of all were the Chinese, whose relations with the USSR had been deteriorating steadily; they could not help but be frightened by the Kremlin's proclivity for interfering forcibly in the affairs of its socialist neighbors and to wonder if they might well be next on the list.

Sino-Soviet relations were further damaged by the subsequent promulgation of the "Brezhnev Doctrine." In late September, an article in *Pravda*, the official newspaper of the Soviet Communist party, stressed that decisions made by leaders in communist countries "must damage neither socialism in their own country nor the fundamental interests of the other socialist countries." In November, speaking in Poland, Soviet party boss Brezhnev added that "when . . . forces hostile to socialism seek to reverse the development of any socialist country," this becomes "a common problem and concern of all socialist countries." Although Brezhnev would later deny the existence of any formal doctrine, there was little doubt, in Beijing or elsewhere, that the Soviet leaders were asserting the right to intervene in the affairs of other communist countries whenever they felt that the interests of socialism were threatened.

The Soviet invasion of Czechoslovakia had ominous implications for Sino-Soviet relations, for it illustrated Moscow's willingness to use its military forces to suppress other socialist nations which dared to behave independently. The Brezhnev Doctrine further exacerbated Chinese fears by providing a rationale for such intervention, which from Beijing's perspective was little more than naked Soviet imperialism. Before long, these tensions and fears were destined to erupt into direct military confrontation.

THE SINO-SOVIET BORDER WAR OF 1969

From 1966 through 1968, as it went through the throes of its Cultural Revolution, the People's Republic of China largely ignored the outside world. By 1969, however, that revolution's fury was mostly spent, and the People's Liberation Army was being employed to restore some semblance of order. In the midst of this process, the Chinese leaders were once again forced to turn their attention to international affairs. In an atmosphere charged with tensions resulting from the Soviet invasion of Czechoslovakia, the Sino-Soviet territorial disputes and occasional border clashes became increasingly dangerous, and soon they would degenerate into bona fide armed conflict.

On 2 March 1969, fighting erupted between Soviet and Chinese forces on Damanskii (Zhen Bao) Island, in the Ussuri River along the Russo-Manchurian border. This was more than just another frontier incident: at least thirty-one Soviet soldiers were killed in the initial conflict. Within a few weeks, the Soviets struck back with overpowering force, as each side blamed the other for initiating hostilities. The following month, further fighting broke out along the northwestern border of China, on the disputed boundary between Xinjiang (Sinkiang) province and Soviet Central Asia. Before long, both sides were rapidly increasing the size of their border forces. In August, the Soviets hinted broadly that nuclear weapons would be employed in a Sino-Soviet conflict, and the Chinese started building shelters and girding for war.

As it turned out, neither side really stood to benefit from a war. The Chinese, even with their vast population, could scarcely hope to win in a full-fledged showdown with a nuclear superpower. And the Soviets, even if they did win, could hardly expect to be able to occupy and control a defeated and embittered China. In September, therefore, Premier Kosygin traveled to Beijing to meet with his counterpart Zhou Enlai and defuse the volatile situation. Negotiations began in October, and the two sides started pulling back from the brink of armed conflict.

The specter of war, however, made a lasting impact upon the leaders of both countries. For the Soviets, who found themselves compelled to maintain vast military forces along the Chinese frontier, it strengthened their determination to normalize the situation in Europe and stabilize relations with the West. For the Chinese, it brought home with unavoidable clarity the extent of their isolation and the danger of their situation. Now, as their troubles with Moscow increased, the masters of China started to give serious consideration to a notion they would have found unthinkable only a few years earlier. They began to contemplate a rapprochement with the long-despised leader of the imperialist camp, the United States of America.

THE ROOTS OF DÉTENTE

Early in 1969, while Soviet-Chinese antagonisms were intensifying, a new administration was establishing itself in Washington. Richard Milhous Nixon came to the White House with a well-earned reputation as a devout anti-Communist and a militant Cold Warrior. Inherently suspicious and insecure, he had reached the pinnacle of American politics by dint of his unfettered ambition and unbridled opportunism. Ironically, although these characteristics would eventually bring his presidency to an early and unhappy end, they would serve him well in his relations with the communist world.

Nixon was ably assisted in foreign policy matters by Henry A. Kissinger, his national security advisor and future secretary of state. A university professor and a student of great power politics, Kissinger was convinced that the superpower rivalry could and should be managed so as to protect the interests of both sides and that peace could be maintained by establishing a balance of power based on mutual self-interest. Brilliant, vain, secretive, and clever, he was hampered little by scruples about ideology or human rights and was thus well-disposed to work with Nixon in steering U.S. policy toward détente with Russia and China.

Détente between East and West was hardly a new idea. In the late 1950s, under the banner of "peaceful coexistence," Soviet leader Khrushchev had managed to take some limited steps toward reducing tensions between Washington and Moscow. In the mid-1960s, as Western Europe had begun to move out of the U.S. shadow, there had been several efforts to achieve a measure of East-West rapprochement. In 1966, French president Charles de Gaulle, in a series of initiatives designed both to increase French influence and to normalize conditions in Europe, had visited Moscow, established closer ties with Eastern Europe, and withdrawn French forces from the unified NATO command. That same year there had come to power in West Germany a coalition government which, under the auspices of Chancellor Kurt Kiesinger and Foreign Minister Willy Brandt, had cautiously begun to pursue a new *Ostpolitik* (Eastern Policy) based on improved relations with the Soviet bloc. The Soviets, sensing an opportunity to drive a wedge between Western Europe and the United States, had encouraged such initiatives, and Leonid Brezhnev had pointedly called for a European security arrangement based

on international recognition of the conditions and boundaries that had existed since World War II. In the meantime, both the Warsaw Pact and NATO had
begun seeking ways to stabilize the military situation in Central Europe, while
Moscow and Washington had warily started inching toward arms control negotiations. But the Soviet invasion of Czechoslovakia in August 1968 had undermined these early efforts, scuttling a planned summit meeting between
Johnson and Kosygin and postponing the onset of arms limitation talks.

By the time Nixon came into office, then, little real headway had been
made. But the new president was convinced that progress was possible, and he
spoke in his inaugural address of "a new era of negotiation" in which nations
would "cooperate to reduce the burden of arms, to strengthen the structure
of peace." He and Kissinger were destined to go beyond the previous initiatives and to implement a revised détente policy designed to deal with new
geopolitical realities.

One of these was the fact that, for the first time, the Soviets were on the
verge of strategic parity with the United States. Although during his campaign
Nixon had vigorously advocated American strategic superiority, once in office
he found it expedient to lower his sights and tone down his rhetoric. The vast
scope of the Soviet arms buildup, combined with the enormous expenses of
weapons production and the destabilizing potential of new technologies, convinced him and Kissinger that it was preferable to try to limit Soviet arms
through negotiation rather than commit unlimited resources to maintaining
a U.S. lead.

The other new reality was the relative decline in American power and
prestige which resulted from the U.S. debacle in Vietnam. Having promised
to extricate his nation from this conflict, Nixon would go on to initiate a gradual withdrawal of American forces from Southeast Asia and a scaling back of
U.S. military commitments around the world. In July 1969, he put forth the
so-called Nixon Doctrine, calling for American friends and clients (like Japan
and Iran) to rely less on the United States and to assume the primary role in
their region's military defense. By encouraging the Soviets to moderate their
own behavior and restrain their Third World clients, détente could help maintain stability during and after the U.S. disengagement.

The Soviets, meanwhile, had their own reasons for moving toward
détente. For one thing, like the Americans (and everyone else on the planet)
they had an obvious stake in preventing nuclear war and slowing the arms
race. For another thing, their growing conflict with China made it imperative
for them to seek some stabilization and relaxation of tensions on their
Western front. For a third thing, their economy continued to stagnate, and it
was becoming apparent that progress in this area would require increased
trade and access to Western technology.

Questions of equality and recognition may also have played a prominent
role in Moscow's thinking with respect to détente. For reasons of both security and status, the Soviets were naturally anxious to have their hard-won gains

in the Second World War, including the revised boundaries of Eastern Europe and the permanent division of Germany, receive international recognition. Likewise, as their mammoth weapons buildup moved them toward parity with the United States, they were anxious to have their newly achieved status "locked in" by an international agreement. Otherwise, the Americans, with their enormous resources and technological advantage, could always launch a new arms buildup that would leave the USSR behind. And, of course, there was the matter of national pride. Equality with the West had been a goal of Russian leaders for centuries: to be dealt with as an equal, and to have its equal status recognized in international agreements, would be no small triumph for the Brezhnev regime.

There was a major difference, however, between the Nixon and Brezhnev approaches to détente, and this involved the issue of "linkage." Nixon and Kissinger expected that, in return for concessions in the realms of trade and arms control, the Kremlin could be induced to alter its conduct, restrain its expansionism, and rein in its belligerent clients. They especially hoped that Moscow would agree to pressure Hanoi to accept a negotiated settlement in Vietnam. And, in fact, Soviet influence may have been instrumental in getting the North Vietnamese to come to the bargaining table in Paris in 1968 (Chapter 11). For the most part, however, the Soviets resisted American efforts at linkage, assuming and expecting that the superpowers would continue to confront one another in areas where their interests clashed, even as they negotiated agreements on issues (such as arms control) where their concerns might coincide. They did not insist that the United States pull out of South Vietnam before arms talks could begin, and they saw no reason why they should reduce their aid to North Vietnam, or modify their behavior in Africa and the Middle East, to accommodate Washington's concerns. Besides, if they were to maintain their leadership of the world Communist movement in the face of the Chinese challenge, they had little choice but to continue their support for Third World communist parties and "national liberation movements."

As a result of all this, despite the fact that there was strong support for détente in both Moscow and the West, progress was rather slow. Early in 1969, the Soviets informed the new administration that they were ready to negotiate on a broad range of issues, including arms control and antiballistic missiles (ABMs), but they also made it clear that they were opposed to linkage. The Nixon people, for their part, were anxious to shore up relations with Western Europe and review their own military policy before sitting down to talk. They also decided to press for congressional approval of an American ABM system, to be known as "Safeguard," which finally squeaked through the Senate in August after a long and heated public debate. This in turn gave the Soviets pause, and it was not until November of 1969 that arms control negotiations began.

The Strategic Arms Limitation Talks (SALT) were destined to become the centerpiece of the quest for Soviet-American détente. There would be seven separate sessions, each lasting several months, which would meet alternately in Helsinki and Vienna over the next two and a half years. The official Soviet delegation was headed by Deputy Foreign Minister Vladimir S. Semenov, while the American team was led by Gerald C. Smith, the director of the U.S. Arms Control and Development Agency. At various points, however, the "real" negotiations were conducted behind the scenes by a private White House channel involving National Security Advisor Kissinger and Soviet ambassador Dobrynin.

There were four major obstacles that had to be addressed before real progress could be made. First was the issue of linkage, which Moscow eventually finessed by compromising in practice but remaining firm on principle. Second was the presence in Europe of U.S. nuclear missiles which, since they could reach the USSR, the Soviets wanted to count as part of the American strategic arsenal. In the interest of progress, however, Moscow finally agreed to defer discussion of these to future talks. Third was the development of MIRVs, or multiple-warhead missiles. Although both sides wanted to restrict or ban their deployment, negotiations foundered on the issue of verification—the traditional bugaboo of U.S.-Soviet arms limitation talks. In the end, no agreement on MIRVs would be reached, leaving a major lacuna in the eventual SALT I accords. Finally, the two sides clashed over the connection between defensive and offensive weapons. Anxious to forestall a new arms race in missile defense systems, Moscow proposed that negotiators should first conclude a separate ABM agreement, while the United States preferred an integrated and comprehensive treaty that would cover both ABMs and ICBMs. In a compromise arrangement announced on 20 May 1971, they ultimately decided to work toward a separate ABM treaty while negotiating a simultaneous accord restricting offensive arms.

Even then, a number of difficult issues remained. One was the question of how many ABM sites would be permitted to each side. Another was the issue of whether submarine-launched ballistic missiles (SLBMs) should be included in the treaty limiting offensive arms. Negotiations, therefore, continued for another year, and final decisions were not reached until Nixon's historic visit to Moscow in May of 1972. By then, however, the international situation would be substantially altered by two dramatic developments: détente in Europe between West Germany and the USSR and rapprochement in Asia between the United States and China.

WILLY BRANDT AND *OSTPOLITIK*

In October of 1969, as Washington and Moscow prepared for negotiations to limit strategic arms, there came to power in the Federal Republic of Germany a new government that was committed to East-West détente in Europe. As the longtime mayor of West Berlin, Willy Brandt had become a symbol of freedom to many Germans, East and West. As leader of West Germany's Social

Democratic party (SPD) since 1958, he had also become a symbol of innovation and reform. As foreign minister in Kurt Kiesinger's coalition government from 1966 to 1969, he had cautiously sought to improve West German relations with the Soviet bloc. Now, as chancellor, he began to push with a vengeance his precedent-shattering "eastern policy," or *Ostpolitik*.

The thrust of Brandt's new policy was to forsake as unrealistic the goal of German reunification, futilely proclaimed for two decades by his Christian-Democratic predecessors, and to work toward greater cooperation with the East. This meant accepting the political realities of Europe, including communist control of East Germany, no matter how unpleasant they might seem. As mayor of West Berlin in 1961, Brandt had watched in angry frustration as the Berlin Wall went up without effective opposition from Washington. Now, with his American allies bogged down in Vietnam, and with Soviet domination of Eastern Europe reinforced by the Brezhnev Doctrine, Brandt concluded that his government had little to gain by clinging to things that it had long since lost. So he attempted to turn weakness into an advantage, making concessions to the Soviets and East Germans in return for stability and normalization in Central Europe.

His first step was to put forth the notion of "two states in one nation," accepting the reality of Germany's political division. His next step was to have his government sign the Nuclear Non-Proliferation Treaty, in effect forswearing any West German effort to acquire its own nuclear weapons, thereby easing Soviet fears of a rearmed and hostile Germany. Since his own Western allies were opposed to a nuclear-equipped Federal Republic, Brandt's concession made good diplomatic sense, and it opened the door to improved relations between Bonn and Moscow.

Brandt's next move was to seek accommodation with some of the Eastern bloc countries. He offered to negotiate treaties with Poland and the USSR which would implicitly recognize the territorial gains that these countries had made at German expense at the end of World War II, and he proposed a trade agreement with Czechoslovakia. He even offered to negotiate a nonaggression pact with East Germany, although the latter refused to consider this unless and until the Bonn government granted it full diplomatic recognition. Nevertheless, in March of 1970, on an invitation from East German prime minister Willi Stoph, he visited the Democratic Republic and was greeted by large, friendly crowds. His talks with Stoph made little progress, but the fact that they occurred was an achievement in itself.

Brandt's initiatives presented Moscow with a historic opportunity. For years, the Soviets had sought to obtain international acceptance of the political and territorial adjustments that had resulted from World War II. These included, among other things, the USSR's annexation of territories along its western frontier, the transfer to Poland of part of prewar Germany, Moscow's sphere of influence over Eastern Europe, and the division of Germany into two separate states. Now that all this seemed to be within his grasp, Brezhnev was more than willing to do business with West Germany and even to pressure his East German allies into going along.

The Soviets, therefore, accepted Brandt's offer to negotiate, and the two sides moved quickly toward agreement on a nonaggression pact. The Treaty of Moscow, signed on 12 August 1970, did more than simply renounce war and proclaim détente between the two nations. It recognized as permanent the existing boundaries of Europe, thus affirming the loss of German territory east of the Oder-Neisse Line. It also acknowledged the existence of two separate German states, and it opened new trade channels between the USSR and the Federal Republic. Twenty-five years after the end of World War II, the Soviets and Germans finally reached an accord. The treaty was a triumph for Brezhnev and a major accomplishment for Willy Brandt: a significant step had been taken toward resolving the German Question!

Similar talks were conducted between West Germany and Poland, and a similar pact was concluded in December of 1970. Chancellor Brandt traveled to Warsaw to sign this treaty, which also confirmed Polish territorial gains east of the Oder-Neisse Line. The most moving and inspirational moment of this trip was Brandt's visit to the Warsaw ghetto memorial, where he humbly and poignantly paid homage to the victims of the Third Reich. The Germans, it was apparent, had come a very long way.

There remained, however, the problem of Berlin. The West Germans liked to consider West Berlin as part of their country, though it was physically separated from the rest of the Federal Republic, while the East Germans recognized East Berlin as their capital. Berlin had been both a flashpoint and symbol of the Cold War for a generation; resolving its problems would not be easy.

In March 1970, in the wake of Brandt's visit to East Germany, discussions began among the four occupying powers as to the status of Berlin. These "quadripartite" talks, as they were called, at first made little progress, in part because the East Germans refused to cooperate unless and until their government received full diplomatic recognition. It was not until May 1971, when Erich Honecker replaced Walter Ulbricht as the head of the East German Communists, that any real headway was made. Honecker proved to be less intransigent than his predecessor and more willing to follow the wishes of Moscow, which by this time had decided that its interests in détente far outweighed the East German desire for recognition. The Kremlin was anxious to secure final ratification of the Treaty of Moscow, which was being held up in the West German parliament pending an agreement on Berlin. And it needed a Berlin settlement in order to pave the way for realization of a long-held Soviet dream: an all-European security conference which would legitimize the status quo in Europe.

The resulting Berlin Accords, signed on 3 September 1971, were a compromise that fully satisfied neither side. The West Germans obtained a Soviet guarantee of free access to West Berlin and recognition of their important

economic and cultural ties with the city. They even gained the right to negotiate on the city's behalf. But their desire for full political integration of West
Berlin into the Federal Republic was rebuffed. The East Germans, forced to
defer their hopes for diplomatic recognition, gained little more than a relaxation of tensions and the gratitude of Moscow. Still, the agreement was a milestone for both the Germans and the Soviets, since it would open the way for
the Basic Treaty of 1972 between East and West Germany and for the
European Security Conference that would open at Helsinki in 1973. And, significantly, it moved the issue of Berlin, which had bedeviled East-West relations since the end of World War II, off center stage of the Cold War.

THE SINO-AMERICAN RAPPROCHEMENT

Even more remarkable than the relaxation of tensions in Central Europe was
the improvement of relations between Beijing and Washington. Since the days
of the Chinese Revolution and the Korean War (Chapters 6-7), America and
communist China had been bitter and implacable foes. During the 1950s,
Washington had viewed "Red China" as a dangerous and brutal Soviet satellite, while Beijing saw the United States as the imperialist warmongers who
stood behind the Nationalist regime on Taiwan. Chinese "volunteers" fought
American GIs during the Korean conflict, and the two nations almost came to
blows in 1954 and 1958 over Beijing's shelling of the Nationalist-controlled
offshore islands of Quemoy and Matsu. Even during the 1960s, when the rift
between Moscow and Beijing became increasingly apparent, there was no
thaw in relations between China and America. The United States continued
to deny recognition to the PRC, to block its entrance into the UN, and to prop
up the masters of Taiwan as the rightful rulers of China. American involvement in the Vietnam War, coupled with Chinese aid to Hanoi, effectively precluded any rapprochement, while the excesses of the Cultural Revolution
seemed to confirm U.S. fears about the nature of Mao's rule.

By 1970, however, the world scene was changing. American withdrawal
from Vietnam, and the corresponding decline of U.S. power in Asia, had
major implications for both countries. For Beijing, it meant that the
Americans were no longer as serious a threat, and it raised concerns that the
power vacuum created by U.S. withdrawal would be filled by the USSR. For
Washington, it opened up the prospect that China might serve as a counterweight to prevent Soviet expansion as the American presence declined.
Beijing's open hostility with Moscow, combined with increasing signs of
U.S.–Soviet détente, left the Chinese terribly isolated and vulnerable—and
even fearful that the two superpowers might conspire against them. And
Washington, eager to gain greater leverage in its relationship with Moscow,
was looking for ways to exploit the Sino-Soviet split.

The upshot of all this was what came to be known as "triangular diplomacy": a complex three-way relationship between China, the United States,

and the USSR. Slowly and cautiously, Washington and Beijing began to signal one another that they were interested in making contact and eventually improving relations. In November of 1968, shortly after Nixon's election, Chinese premier Zhou Enlai had issued a call for renewed diplomatic talks with the United States, to begin in Warsaw in February of 1969. The president-elect at once agreed. Nixon was a staunch Cold Warrior who over the years had earned a reputation of unrelenting hostility toward the communist world, especially toward communist China. But he was also a pragmatic opportunist who was willing to change course abruptly when he saw an advantage in doing so, and by this point he had come to the conclusion that improved relations with China could work to America's benefit. His strong anti-Communist credentials, in fact, would prove to be a blessing, for they protected him against charges of being "soft on communism" as he moved to establish dialogue with Beijing.

As it turned out, a few days before the Warsaw talks were set to begin, the Chinese abruptly backed out. This appeared to be a protest against the recent defection to the United States of a Chinese official, but it also may have reflected the ongoing power struggle in Beijing between Premier Zhou, who favored Sino-American rapprochement, and Chairman Mao's heir apparent Lin Biao, who opposed it. At any rate, this proved to be only a temporary setback, as the violent border clashes and intensification of Sino-Soviet hostilities during the course of 1969 gave Beijing added reasons to approach the United States. Nixon, meanwhile, was discreetly asking Presidents de Gaulle of France, Ceausescu of Romania, and Yahya Khan of Pakistan to convey to the Chinese his desire for better relations. He also took a series of economic and diplomatic steps designed to signal his interest in a relaxation of tensions. As a result, in January of 1970 (eleven months late), discussions finally began in Warsaw between Chinese and American diplomats.

But the road to rapprochement was a rocky one. On 1 May 1970, the United States invaded Cambodia, expanding the Vietnam War in an effort to destroy communist "sanctuaries." The Chinese once again canceled the Warsaw talks, and Mao delivered a stinging condemnation of the U.S. "aggressors." During the next few months, public relations between the two countries degenerated even further. Nixon, however, persisted in his quest. In October, he told *Time* magazine that it was his personal goal to visit China before he died. Later that month in Washington he asked Yahya Khan, who was about to visit Beijing, to transmit his willingness to send a key official to meet with the Chinese. The following day, during a reception for Romanian president Ceausescu, he made public reference to the "People's Republic of China." This was an important signal, for previous U.S. presidents had avoided using in public the official name of the country Americans knew as "Red" or "Mainland" China. The Chinese got the message. In December, the Pakistanis informed Nixon that Zhou Enlai was willing to meet with the president's personal representative, and Mao Zedong advised visiting American writer Edgar

Zhou Enlai and Richard Nixon in Shanghai, 1972. (UPI/Bettmann)

Snow that he would welcome a visit from Nixon himself. In January 1971, the Romanians conveyed to Washington a similar message from Zhou.

The real breakthrough in Sino-American relations came in 1971. In March, the Nixon administration removed all restrictions on travel to China, and in April it further eased restraints on trade. That same month, in a highly publicized good will gesture, the Chinese invited the U.S. table tennis team to the world championship matches in Beijing. Zhou Enlai himself met with the American players, spoke of a new relationship between China and the United States, and consented to a reciprocal visit to America by the Chinese team. This "ping-pong diplomacy" helped set the stage for further dramatic developments.

On 15 July 1971, in a televised address, President Nixon made the stunning announcement that he had accepted an invitation to visit China in the next ten months. It turned out that, during a visit to Pakistan the previous week, Henry Kissinger had slipped away from reporters and made a clandestine trip to Beijing, where he held lengthy talks with Zhou Enlai and even met Chairman Mao. Items of mutual interest were discussed, disputes over Taiwan and China were smoothed over, and the groundwork was laid for Nixon's visit.

The president's announcement created great excitement in the United States, but it also had serious international repercussions. Obsessed with secrecy and fearful of leaks, Nixon and Kissinger had concealed the latter's trip from the USSR, American friends, and even the U.S. State Department. The

Chinese Nationalists on Taiwan felt abandoned and betrayed, as did longtime American supporters of "Free China." Japan, the main U.S. ally in Asia, was shocked and dismayed that it had not been consulted and began to reconsider its heavy reliance on Washington. The USSR, fearful that its two chief adversaries might collude against it, began moving more briskly toward détente with the West. By September, agreement had been reached in the talks on Berlin, and progress was being made on SALT. Negotiations toward a Nixon-Brezhnev summit meeting were accelerated, and in October it was announced that the U.S. president would visit Moscow in the spring of 1972.

At the same time, several remaining obstacles to Sino-American rapprochement were being cleared away. In September 1971, Lin Biao, the main Chinese opponent of improved relations with Washington, was killed in a plane crash attempting to escape to the USSR after an abortive coup attempt. In October, Kissinger made another visit to Beijing to hold further talks with Zhou and help prepare for Nixon's visit. Meanwhile, despite U.S. advocacy of a "two Chinas" approach that would have seated both the Nationalists and Communists, the United Nations voted to expel the Taiwan government and replace it with the People's Republic.

The official state visit of President Nixon to the PRC, which took place during the last week of February in 1972, was important more for its symbolism than for its diplomatic accomplishments. Accompanied by television cameras and myriad reporters, Nixon flew to China, met with officials, attended the ballet, and visited the Great Wall. In his private talks with Chinese leaders, however, little progress was made toward resolving the issue of Taiwan, the one great stumbling block to normal relations. The United States did acknowledge the view, held by both the Communists and Nationalists, that there should be only one China and that it should include Taiwan. The Americans also agreed that they would eventually remove their military forces from Taiwan, as tensions in the area subsided. But they were not yet ready to withdraw formal recognition from the Nationalist regime. The Chinese for their part made it clear that full diplomatic relations, and expanded trade agreements, could not be established until this recognition was withdrawn. This impasse would delay normal relations for almost seven years.

Still, whatever its diplomatic value, the symbolic significance of Nixon's trip was enormous. The "Shanghai Communiqué," which was issued upon the president's departure, committed each side to work toward the normalization of relations and the relaxation of tensions in Asia. The euphoria was palpable, as longtime bitter foes agreed to work together to keep the peace and resolve issues of mutual concern. This trip, and Nixon's visit to Moscow the following May, seemed to signify to the world the end of the age of confrontation and the beginning of the era of détente.

13

The Heyday of Détente, 1972–1975

During 1972 and the first half of 1973, it looked as if the Cold War was coming to an end. President Nixon's celebrated visit to China in February 1972 was followed by a whole host of hopeful developments. In May, Nixon traveled to Moscow, where he and Soviet leader Brezhnev signed a number of historic agreements, including several major arms control treaties. In December, a "Basic Treaty" was concluded between East and West Germany. Early in 1973, U.S. involvement in the Vietnam War ended. That summer Brezhnev and Nixon met again, this time in Washington, and the multinational Conference on Security and Cooperation in Europe began in Helsinki. All the basic elements of the Cold War—the German Question, the status of Eastern Europe, the contest for Asia, and the nuclear arms race—seemed headed toward resolution.

Before long, however, it became apparent that détente had promised more than it could deliver. The Middle East crisis of fall 1973 once again brought the superpowers to the brink of armed conflict. American meddling in Chile, and the resumption of the fighting between North and South Vietnam, made it painfully obvious that the East-West rapprochement did not extend to the Third World. Difficulties and delays in the arms control talks, along with public clashes over trading status and human rights, also helped to sour the good will. Still, the basic framework of détente would remain in place throughout the 1970s.

THE FOUNDATIONS OF DÉTENTE, 1972–1973

Even before Richard Nixon made his dramatic trip to China, preparations had begun for a U.S.–Soviet summit conference to be held in Moscow in May 1972. It was destined to be one of the most productive and consequential summit meetings of the Cold War era. As the first visit by an American president to the USSR since World War II, and the first such peacetime visit ever, it also had great symbolic significance. More than any other event, it came to represent the dawn of the age of détente.

Getting to the summit, however, was no easy task, for there were several major hurdles blocking the way. One was the fact that the strategic arms limitation talks (SALT) were incomplete: several crucial issues remained unresolved as the Moscow meeting approached. Since the signing of the SALT treaties was to be the centerpiece of the summit, this was no small nuisance. The other problem was the ongoing Vietnam War, which escalated in the spring of 1972 and threatened to scuttle the whole show.

The two major unsettled questions in the arms control talks involved the number and nature of ABM sites to be permitted each side and the issue of whether the arms limitation treaty should encompass submarine-launched missiles (SLBMs) as well as the land-based ICBMs. The Americans had backed away from an earlier proposal to limit ABM sites to one for each national capital and were pushing for an agreement that would permit the construction of ABM systems (like the one they were building) to defend land-based missiles. They had also begun pressing to include SLBMs in the offensive arms control pact, in part because of Pentagon insistence that something be done to restrain the rapid Soviet buildup in this area. Having already been far surpassed by the USSR in numbers of ICBMs, the U.S. military was anxious to prevent a similar development with regard to SLBMs. But Moscow, upset that the Americans were raising new demands in the final stages of negotiation, was cool to these U.S. initiatives.

As the summit approached, the pressure mounted to reach agreement. Henry Kissinger met with Soviet officials in Moscow, and with Ambassador Dobrynin in Washington, in a persistent effort to break the logjam. Meanwhile, the SALT negotiators in Helsinki redoubled their efforts and continued to hold sessions even while the Moscow summit meeting was actually going on. The ABM issue was essentially resolved in April, but the final decision on SLBMs was reached only at the summit itself, with the active participation of Nixon and Brezhnev.

A potentially more serious problem arose out of the Vietnam War. At the end of March, the North Vietnamese launched a major offensive, and the United States responded with massive bombing of North Vietnam and mining of Haiphong harbor. At one point, several Soviet ships in the harbor were damaged, and a number of casualties inflicted. Nixon announced the escalation only two weeks before his scheduled Moscow trip, and there was widespread expectation that the summit might be canceled. But the Soviet leaders, although they publicly condemned the American bombing, proceeded with the conference. In their eyes, détente was too important to be jeopardized by linkage with other issues.

The Nixon-Brezhnev summit thus took place as scheduled in Moscow from 22 to 30 May 1972. It was as rich in achievements as it was in imagery. Agreements were signed on items such as the basic principles of U.S.–Soviet relations, measures to prevent the accidental outbreak of nuclear war, an upgrade of the Washington-Moscow "hot line," and scientific and cultural connections. The groundwork was laid for a major U.S.–Soviet Trade Agreement, to be concluded later that year. But the most important measures signed in Moscow were the Treaty on the Limitation of Anti-Ballistic Missile Systems (the "ABM treaty") and the Interim Agreement on the Limitation of Strategic Offensive Arms ("SALT I").

The ABM treaty limited each side to two defensive missile sites: one to guard its capital, the other to protect ICBMs. Since the USSR had already built one to shield Moscow, and the United States was constructing one to defend missiles in North Dakota, this would give each the opportunity to duplicate the other's system. In fact, however, neither would seek to do this, and a protocol restricting each side to one ABM site would be added in 1974.

SALT I was a temporary measure, designed to constrain each superpower from building ICBMs beyond 1972 levels for five years, during which time a permanent accord was to be negotiated. At U.S. insistence, limits were also placed on the numbers of submarine-launched missiles, although the pact was worded so as to allow for completion of those under construction and replacement of older land-based missiles by SLBMs. This made it possible for the Soviets to agree to an SLBM limit without having to sacrifice their current building program.

The final pact left the USSR with a preponderance of 1,618 to 1,054 in ICBMs and a 950-to-710 edge in SLBMs. This apparent Soviet advantage caused great consternation among U.S. "hawks" and became a problem when the treaty was submitted to the U.S. Senate for ratification. Senate approval finally came in September 1972, but only after Senator Henry Jackson had added an amendment stating that future arms control treaties must not leave the USSR with a numerical lead. The fact was, however, that SALT I did not include long-range bombers, U.S. missiles in Europe, the missiles of America's NATO allies, or multiple-warhead missiles (MIRVs)—all areas where the West had a big advantage. But Jackson and his supporters were deeply distrustful of both the Nixon and Brezhnev governments, and they wanted to ensure that their concerns were taken into account more fully during future talks.

The Moscow summit was also intended to pave the way for progress elsewhere. In particular, Nixon and Kissinger hoped that, in combination with the Sino-American rapprochement, it might encourage North Vietnam to compromise and thus help the United States extricate itself from Southeast Asia.

Indeed, a few weeks after the conference, Soviet president Nikolai Podgorny visited Hanoi, conveying new U.S. proposals to the North Vietnamese and urging them to work toward a negotiated settlement. But there were few immediate results. Long and difficult negotiations remained, and thousands of bombs would be dropped on North Vietnam, before a truce would finally be arranged in January 1973.

Détente in Europe, however, did get a boost from the Moscow meeting. At the conference, the two sides agreed to work together on plans to hold a Conference on Security and Cooperation in Europe (CSCE) and to begin talks on mutual and balanced force reductions (MBFR) between NATO and the Warsaw Pact. Gradually, in the wake of the summit, they began to implement these plans.

The CSCE was a longstanding Soviet goal, having been first proposed back in 1954 by Molotov, and an important element of Brezhnev's foreign policy. Although the existing boundaries in Eastern and Central Europe, and by implication the Soviet domination of this area, had recently been recognized in a series of bilateral treaties, Moscow was anxious to have them sanctioned by a multinational agreement. This would institutionalize Soviet hegemony in Eastern Europe, bring communist East Germany into the family of nations, and provide formal Western recognition of the political and territorial gains made by the USSR in the 1940s, while serving as the international peace conference that had not yet occurred in the wake of World War II. For obvious reasons, the United States was much less excited about such a conference, but Nixon had agreed to go along in the interests of détente and on the understanding that MBFR talks would also take place. Preliminary discussions began in August 1972, and these laid the groundwork for the Helsinki conference which would open the next summer.

Unlike the CSCE, the MBFR undertaking was a NATO initiative, based largely on Western European security concerns. Since the mid-1960s, U.S. senator Mike Mansfield had been championing a resolution advocating unilateral withdrawal of most American forces from Europe. Fearful that it might someday pass, NATO leaders in the late 1960s had begun to push for talks with the Warsaw Pact that would lead to force reductions on both sides. The Nixon administration supported this approach. The Soviets at first were hesitant, seeing the initiative as designed mainly to prolong the U.S. presence in Europe, but in 1972 they agreed to go along with parallel CSCE and MBFR talks. Preparations for the latter began in January 1973, and the talks opened in Vienna in October. They were destined to drag on inconclusively for years.

Meanwhile, real progress was made on relations in Central Europe. On 3 June 1972, the nonaggression pacts which West German chancellor Willy Brandt had previously negotiated with Poland and the USSR went into force, and the final protocol of the Berlin Accords was signed. Although these agreements had been worked out earlier (Chapter 12), their activation added to the sense of momentum created by the Moscow summit and helped set the stage for direct negotiations between East and West Germany.

In August 1972, the same month that preparatory talks began for the CSCE in Helsinki, East and West German officials started meeting in Berlin to work out a treaty between the two states. Although the resulting "Basic Treaty," concluded in December of that year, did not meet the East German goal of full mutual recognition and normalized relations, it did provide for an exchange of "permanent missions" between the Federal and Democratic Republics. It expanded commercial and cultural ties, committed each side to respect the other's boundaries, and cleared the path for both to apply for UN membership. It also paved the way for treaties between West Germany and a number of Eastern European states, and for formal recognition of East Germany by most Western nations, during the next few years.

THE AMERICAN WITHDRAWAL FROM VIETNAM

Across the Atlantic, Nixon was still searching for a way out of the Vietnam quagmire. His Vietnamization policy had worked no better than Americanization had, and the Ho Chi Minh Trail was still open, despite the South Vietnamese army's 1971 efforts to cut it by invading Laos and Cambodia. At home, support for the war was evaporating. Americans had been shocked by revelations at the trial of Lieutenant William Calley for atrocities in My Lai, where a 1968 operation designed to kill VC agents had instead wound up massacring nearly 500 civilians. And they had been offended by the "Pentagon Papers," a secret study of the war commissioned in 1967 by Robert McNamara and published by *The New York Times* in 1971. These documents, illegally photocopied and leaked by Defense Department analyst Daniel Ellsberg, painted a devastating portrait of U.S. duplicity in a systematic effort to deceive the American people about the situation in Vietnam.

Nixon's visits to Beijing and Moscow had reflected his hope that Hanoi's suppliers could bring pressure on the Lao Dong party to negotiate. But Ho's heirs were not interested, and despite Podgorny's visit to Hanoi, there were few signs that North Vietnam was in a receptive mood. This war was between the United States and North Vietnam, and, if a settlement was to be reached, it would be due to their own actions and reactions.

As the 1972 presidential election approached, Nixon and Kissinger adopted a two-track strategy to bring peace before election day. One track consisted of intensified secret talks with North Vietnamese emissary Le Duc Tho, mostly held in the Paris apartment of Jean Sainteny, the persistent diplomat who had helped arrange the abortive Ho-Sainteny Accords of 1946 (Chapter 11). The other track involved heightened military pressure. On 15 April 1972, American B-52s pounded Hanoi, prompting mass antiwar protests in the United States. One month later the U.S. Navy laid mines in Haiphong harbor and other North Vietnamese ports.

In October, it appeared that the two-track approach had paid off. Le Duc Tho, anxious for an end to the bombing and certain of Nixon's reelection, abandoned Hanoi's demand that South Vietnam's president Thieu resign and a coalition government be set up in Saigon. He would take the best terms he could get (which, prior to the election, might be very good) in exchange for a respite during which a final assault could be prepared. Kissinger offered total American withdrawal while North Vietnamese forces remained in place in the south. This was a major concession, but it was also unavoidable since, as James Olson and Randy Roberts have pointed out, "Ten years of war and the greatest expenditure of firepower in history had not dislodged them." Thieu objected strenuously, sensing a U.S. sellout and threatening not to sign the treaty unless major changes were made. With the election a few days off, Kissinger stated publicly that "peace is at hand," but Nixon's landslide reelection came and went without a peace agreement.

Nixon tried to bring Thieu around by secret promises of U.S. support in case the treaty was violated, but by this time Hanoi had decided to play off Saigon against Washington. Le Duc Tho was called home for consultations on 13 December. Nixon quickly dispatched an ultimatum to North Vietnamese premier Pham Van Dong, directing him to "resume serious negotiations within 72 hours or suffer the consequences." On 18 December, the United States began the eleven-day "Christmas Bombing," a massive aerial assault against virtually every strategic target in North Vietnam. Hanoi got the message: Le Duc Tho returned to Paris on 8 January, and on 27 January the Paris Peace Accords were signed, ending U.S. involvement in the Second Indochina War. Washington agreed to stop bombing the north and remove its forces from the south, while Hanoi promised not to renew its attack on the Saigon regime and to return all American prisoners of war. In the end, the United States kept its bargain, but North Vietnam did not.

THE FALL OF ALLENDE IN CHILE

In retrospect, the summer of 1973 can be seen as the high-water mark of détente. With the German Question apparently settled, and with U.S. involvement in the Vietnam War finally ended, the stage was set for continued progress toward stability and cooperation between East and West.

In June Leonid Brezhnev traveled to Washington for his second summit conference with Nixon. Although it was neither as dramatic nor productive as the previous year's Moscow extravaganza, it was nonetheless a major event. Discussions encompassed a wide range of issues, from arms control to concerns about China and the Middle East. A number of agreements were signed, including one on the peaceful uses of atomic energy and another calling for the prompt conclusion of a permanent arms control pact ("SALT II") to replace the temporary SALT I accord. Especially heartening was the "Agreement on the Prevention of Nuclear War," by which the two nations

Leonid Brezhnev and Richard Nixon. (UPI/Bettmann)

pledged to enter into "urgent consultations" should a conflict between other countries threaten to draw them into an atomic showdown.

The mood, as indicated by the joint communiqué issued at the end of the conference and by statements of officials on both sides, was one of cooperation and good will. It was Brezhnev's first visit to the United States, and he took advantage of the opportunity to meet with Nixon, not just in Washington and at Camp David, but also at the president's home near San Clemente, California. Mutual respect and harmony were the watchwords of the day, and even the spreading Watergate scandal failed to dampen the enthusiasm, since the Senate hearings were recessed during Brezhnev's visit.

On 3 July 1973, shortly after the summit ended, there opened in Helsinki the long-awaited CSCE. Thirty-five nations, including the United States, Canada, and all the European countries save Albania, were represented there. Even though it would take several years for the final accords to be concluded, the very fact that the meetings had begun enhanced the climate of collaboration. Further momentum was added in September of that year, when the UN admitted both East and West Germany.

It was not long, however, before disturbing developments began to dim the glow. In the fall of 1973, a significant crisis in Chile and a major conflict in the Middle East would make it abundantly clear that détente had its limits and that superpower collaboration did not include the Third World.

Since 1970, a Marxist professor of economics, Salvador Allende, had been serving as president of Chile. The existence of a freely elected Marxist president in the Western Hemisphere (or anywhere in the world) was anathema to Washington. Indeed the CIA had managed to prevent his election in 1964 by pouring money and energy into Chilean politics, and it had sought to do so again in 1970 by funneling massive aid to his opponents and bribing Chilean legislators. Even after his election, Washington had continued its campaign against him, cutting off Chile's foreign credit and recalling outstanding loans. The resulting cash shortfall had led to serious inflation, exacerbated by Allende's policy of providing massive pay increases for the poor in an effort to stimulate the production of consumer goods.

By 1973, then, Chile's economy was in shambles. Inflation reached 566 percent and impoverished the middle class. The price of copper fell steadily on the world market, undermining Chile still further. Moscow furnished a great deal of fraternal rhetoric but almost no financial assistance; Brezhnev was already underwriting one weak Latin American economy in Cuba, and he had learned the lessons of the Cuban Missile Crisis. Chile was even further from the Kremlin than Cuba and far more difficult to defend in the event of trouble. During the course of that year, a series of strikes by engineers, physicians, and finally truckers undermined Allende's capacity to govern to the point that the Chilean military stepped in. A junta seized power on 11 September 1973, following a siege during which Allende committed suicide. The United States was delighted with the coup, while the Soviets, who were realistic enough to understand that "peaceful coexistence" had its limits, were nonetheless dismayed to lose a potential client in the Western Hemisphere. Moscow was, however, distracted by preparations for the following month's Yom Kippur/Ramadan War, a conflict which marked the culmination of years of tension and warfare in the Middle East.

THE CRISIS IN THE MIDDLE EAST

During the 1960s, the Middle East had increasingly become an area of Cold War contention. Israel had emerged as a modern, Europeanized republic in the midst of an underdeveloped region. Its highly trained and motivated population, the vast financial aid given it by Western governments, the state of siege raised against it by the Arabs, and the vivid memory of the Holocaust had blended to create an advanced, militaristic society at once self-confident and fearful. Guerrilla raids across its frontiers had sharpened its siege mentality. Meanwhile, Egyptian president Nasser's fear of Israel had caused him to divert into the military vast sums which might have aided his social revolution and to turn Egypt into a police state. It had also led him to close cooperation with Moscow, which had sent large amounts of military aid and thousands of technicians to Cairo. As Nasser had modernized Egypt's military forces with substantial Soviet aid, the West had supplied Israel with the weapons of war, creating a local arms race—and a very dangerous situation.

More dangerous still was a new Soviet Middle East strategy. The overthrow of Soviet client Abdel Karim Kassem in Iraq in 1962 had convinced Moscow that regional and familial rivalries could quickly negate its political gains. The Kremlin had, therefore, adopted a coalition strategy designed to minimize the damage from inter-Arab squabbles. The best way to do this was to portray Zionism as the common enemy of all Arabs, with U.S. imperialism cast in the role of its banker. This new propaganda offensive poisoned the debate with overtones of anti-Semitism and nudged Washington closer to Israel. More significantly, the new Soviet stance transformed the Middle East from a peripheral into a central theater of the Cold War and laid the foundations for a severe international crisis in the event of a new war between Israel and Egypt. The stage was set for a superpower showdown.

The new Soviet strategy contained both a danger and an incongruity. The danger was that it increased the likelihood of war; the incongruity was that Moscow was backing the side most likely to lose. Perhaps the Soviets did not accurately assess the situation, or perhaps they reasoned that even an Arab defeat might serve their interests by creating anti-American hostility in the oil-rich Arab countries. At any rate, the new Soviet line had encouraged the Arab states to take a firmer stance toward Israel, in the hope that the USSR would intervene militarily if war broke out. Moscow intensified its anti-Zionist propaganda and seemed to be inviting the Arabs to act.

Repeated border incidents between Israel and Syria led to a crisis in May 1967. On 13 May, Moscow informed Nasser that Israeli troops were massing on the Syrian border. Although this proved false, Nasser decided to use the occasion to enhance his prestige in the Arab world. He may not have envisaged an all-out war, but that is what he got. In the ensuing days, he committed Egyptian forces to the Sinai Peninsula and demanded removal of its UN peace-keeping force. On 22 May, Egypt blockaded the Gulf of Aqaba. Levi Eshkol's Israeli government reaffirmed its peaceful intentions, and Washington urged caution on all parties. These responses intrigued both Moscow and Cairo. Apparently, the Kremlin overplayed its hand on 28 May: Soviet premier Kosygin seems to have assured Nasser that if war should ensue, Moscow would keep Washington distracted. He did not specify how this would be done.

The Soviets may have believed that they could make such a promise without having to fulfill it. Nasser, however, apparently thought the Arabs could hold their own against Israel, as long as the United States was neutralized. He, therefore, escalated the crisis by signing a mutual defense pact with Jordan on 30 May and issuing a strong denunciation of Israel's lack of action on the Palestinian refugee problem. Iraq and Kuwait joined the developing alliance

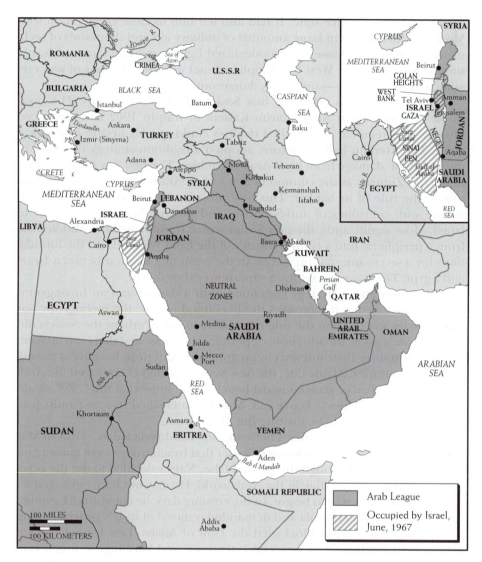

MAP 9 The Middle East

on 4 June. But Israel was not about to sit back and let the Arabs attack. In a preemptive strike two hours before dawn on 5 June, Israeli jets destroyed the Egyptian air force on the ground.

The Israeli first strike made Tel Aviv look aggressive, and the Egyptian army had been prepared to ride out the initial wave. Presumably, Israel's obvious aggression would disconcert the Americans, who would in some way be restrained by the USSR. But Israel's predawn strike deprived Nasser of the Arab world's only truly modern military force, and since the Arabs were forced to operate without air cover, the "Six-Day War" was one-sided from the start. The Israelis took the entire Sinai Peninsula and the eastern bank of the Suez Canal, while quickly expelling Syria from the Golan Heights. They offered King Hussein of Jordan an informal separate peace, which he realized he could not accept if he wished to remain in power. The price he paid for refusing this offer was Israeli occupation of the most valuable portion of his kingdom, the West Bank of the Jordan River.

By the time the UN Security Council arranged a cease-fire on 11 June, the Arab states had lost huge territories, much of their productive capacity, and their political self-respect. Arabs would bear the scars of 1967 for decades, with Israel occupying the Sinai until 1979, and the West Bank and Golan Heights for many years thereafter. The Arab defeat would also give a powerful impetus to the Palestinian guerrilla movement, as militants took over the Palestine Liberation Organization or PLO (created in 1964). And it would lead Nasser to conclude that his only chance for victory in the future lay in drawing Moscow into the actual fighting—a prospect from which Brezhnev understandably shrank.

Israel was exhilarated by its swift victory. It enjoyed its new-found leverage over the Arabs: if the losers wanted their lands back, they would have to recognize Israel's right to exist. King Hussein was willing to negotiate on this basis, but the PLO, annoyed at Jordan's conservatism and fearful of a breach in the united Arab front against Israel, tried to assassinate him in June 1970. On 6–9 September, Palestinians highjacked four commercial jets and flew them to northern Jordan, hoping to sabotage negotiations with Israel by blowing them up.

Hussein resolved to expel the Palestinians from Jordan and turned his army loose on them in what the PLO would call "Black September." In response, on 19 September, Syria invaded Jordan in defense of the PLO. America then came to Jordan's defense: Nixon issued a warning to Moscow and put the U.S. military on a partial alert. But Syria pressed on, and a desperate Hussein asked Washington to help arrange for Israeli air support. Support from the Jewish state would certainly have destroyed Hussein's moral authority within his kingdom and would no doubt have led to Egyptian and possibly Soviet intervention. Unwilling to run such a risk, Nixon on 21 September declared that the United States would help Jordan if it could not halt Syria alone and would keep both Moscow and Cairo out of the fighting. In fact, Moscow was even then trying to curb the Syrians, and the next day their forces began to withdraw from Jordan.

Nasser, who had acceded to Soviet demands to begin talks with Israel through the UN, mediated a settlement between Jordan and the PLO a few hours before he died of a heart attack on 28 September 1970.

Nasser was succeeded by his longtime friend and vice-president, Anwar Sadat, who had filled the role of heir apparent mainly because he seemed to pose no threat to his chief. To the general public, he seemed a rather indolent, good-natured fellow whose most striking attributes were his dark skin and deep voice. But Sadat's apparent lack of political ambition concealed a shrewd, calculating military officer who had earned his rank as a demolitions specialist in World War II and who had never lost his taste for the dangerous life. He would indulge that taste consistently between his accession to power in 1970 and his assassination by Islamic fundamentalists in 1981.

Sadat quickly determined that Egypt could no longer afford a permanent state of war with Israel. Some sort of compromise was needed, and only Washington could exert sufficient pressure to bring Israel to the bargaining table. Sadat laid the groundwork by ousting Soviet military advisors in 1972 and adopting a more equivocal stance between the United States and USSR. But once he had done this, the United States showed little willingness to press Tel Aviv, so he continued to accept Soviet weapons, as did Syria. Obviously, something more spectacular was needed to get Nixon's attention.

By the end of June 1973, Sadat and Syrian president Hafez Assad had formulated a rough plan of operations against Israel; they brought Hussein on board in September and obtained Saudi support for an oil embargo against any nation supporting Israel. Sadat warned that war was imminent in a 28 September speech, but the outbreak of the conflict inexplicably surprised Israeli intelligence. War began on both fronts on 6 October—for the Jews, Yom Kippur (the Day of Atonement), and for the Muslims, the tenth of Ramadan, the anniversary of Muhammad's conquest of Mecca.

At first, Egypt and Syria achieved remarkable success, but this was later neutralized and then reversed by massive U.S. arms shipments to Israel. The Americans opted for this course after Israeli prime minister Golda Meir warned Nixon that Israel would win, no matter what methods it needed to employ. Fearful that Israel might possess and use an atomic bomb, the United States decided to provide conventional weapons in large quantities in hopes that they would prove sufficient. This decision, combined with Egyptian and Syrian hesitation (possibly because they had not expected to achieve such stunning success and were uncertain as to how to proceed), permitted Israel to recover and push back the invaders. Moscow responded by urging Sadat to seek a truce and placing three airborne divisions on alert. By 23 October, the Israelis were within twenty miles of Damascus, and the Egyptian Third Army was surrounded on the west bank of the Suez Canal.

Nixon, seeing his opportunity, quietly informed Sadat that the United States would seek a negotiated settlement and would not permit the Third Army to be destroyed. The United States and USSR worked together in the Security

Council to obtain approval of resolutions calling for a cease-fire and peace talks, but Israel refused to comply. The Soviets quickly ordered a full alert of all their airborne forces and threatened to send peace-keeping troops to the region with or without American cooperation. Nixon, who wanted to avoid a joint intervention and maintain America's role as the one nation with influence on both sides, authorized a worldwide alert of all U.S. conventional and nuclear forces.

The resulting crisis, although it ended quickly and did not receive the dramatic publicity of the Cuban Missile Crisis, was in some respects more dangerous. In 1962, the Soviet air and rocket forces had been on full stand down after 24 October, and the U.S. military alert had been limited to conventional forces. In 1973, both the Soviet air force and the Strategic Rocket Forces were placed on full alert, and the U.S. move to DEF CON 2 (the maximum state of readiness short of all-out war) explicitly included nuclear forces. In 1962, the destinies of the United States and USSR had been largely in the hands of Kennedy and Khrushchev, while in 1973 Nixon and Brezhnev were to some extent at the mercy of Sadat and Meir. And the Egyptian president and Israeli prime minister were hardly models of restraint: one had just initiated a war with no perceptible provocation; the other had hinted that she might end that war by resorting to nuclear force!

In any event, the crisis subsided in less than forty-eight hours. The USSR, like a poker player whose imprudent bet has been raised by a strong opponent, quickly folded its hand. And Israel, bowing to American pressure, agreed to accept a cease-fire. On 25 October, Moscow supported U.S. proposals for a UN peace-keeping force, and on 28 October, Egyptians and Israelis negotiated directly for the first time since 1956. The resulting disengagement would permit the reopening of the Suez Canal in 1975.

The Yom Kippur War was the first true test of the value of détente in a major East-West crisis. The results, at best, were mixed. On one hand, improved relations and bilateral conventions did nothing either to avert the crisis or prevent it from escalating dramatically. Although the Soviets knew in advance of the Arab attack, they were constrained neither to restrain their Arab friends nor to consult beforehand with the United States. Détente did not deter either superpower from providing vast supplies of weapons to its clients; nor did it stop Nixon from resorting to nuclear brinkmanship. On the other hand, as Moscow and Washington both avowed in the wake of the crisis, the enhanced understanding and communications between them may well have helped to bring the war to an expeditious end and to prevent it from becoming a far more catastrophic conflict!

PROGRESS AND PROBLEMS IN EAST-WEST RELATIONS, 1974–1975

The Middle East crisis of October 1973 cast a chill over the warm glow of détente and splashed icy water on the overheated expectations kindled by the spectacular summits of 1972 and 1973. It also led to a cold winter in many

Western countries, as the Organization of Petroleum Exporting Countries (OPEC), led by oil-rich Arab nations irate over Western support for Israel in the Yom Kippur War, imposed an effective embargo on oil shipments to Israel's friends. Fuel shortages, sharp price increases, and lowered thermostats followed. They were accompanied by a perceptible cooling of the international climate.

By June of 1974, when Nixon and Brezhnev met in Moscow for their third summit conference, the early enthusiasm for détente had long since begun to fade. A deadlock in the ongoing SALT negotiations had dashed early hopes that a SALT II treaty might be concluded at this meeting. The mood was subdued and somber. Several minor agreements were signed, but in many respects, the summit was overshadowed by domestic developments in both the United States and the USSR. In the midst of the conference, Soviet dissident and world-renowned physicist Andrei Sakharov announced that he was beginning a hunger strike, thus calling world attention to the ongoing oppression and human rights abuses within the USSR. By clumsily cutting off the efforts of U.S. networks to telecast stories on Sakharov, the Soviet authorities merely added to their reputation for heavy-handed repression.

Far more detrimental to détente was the worsening Watergate mess in Washington. During the presidential campaign of 1972, several of Nixon's minions had been apprehended breaking into the Watergate complex headquarters of the Democratic National Committee to repair implanted bugging devices. To prevent political damage, Nixon and his associates sought to cover up the scandal and in so doing worked to obstruct the U.S. justice system. By summer of 1974, the House Judiciary Committee was holding hearings which would lead to a recommendation for impeachment of the president of the United States. The Watergate affair both emboldened Nixon's enemies and undermined his foreign policy effectiveness; during the Moscow summit talks, he seemed agitated and distressed. On 9 August, only five weeks after his return from Moscow, he resigned his office rather than face impeachment proceedings. The Brezhnev regime, with limited appreciation for American political and legal sensitivities, could only surmise that anti-Soviet forces in the United States had finally managed to destroy the architect of détente.

Nixon's replacement was Gerald R. Ford, a man with limited experience in foreign affairs. Ford retained the services of Henry Kissinger, who in 1973 had become secretary of state as well as national security advisor, and together they sought to continue the policies of rapprochement. A summit meeting was promptly arranged between Ford and Brezhnev, and in November 1974 the two leaders met at the Russian Pacific port of Vladivostok.

Somewhat unexpectedly, the Vladivostok summit served to breathe new life into the sagging spirit of détente. To the pleasant surprise of Ford and Kissinger, the Soviets were anxious to negotiate seriously with the new administration, and in the months before the summit they made concessions designed to overcome the impasse in the SALT II talks, finally agreeing to give up their edge in strategic missiles in return for limits on strategic bombers and MIRVs. At Vladivostok, the two leaders agreed in principle to place a ceiling of 2,400 on the total number of "launchers" (strategic missiles and long-range bombers) permitted each side and a sublimit of 1,320 on the number of these that could be equipped with multiple warheads. This was a major break-through, for it seemed to remove the key obstacle to an arms control agreement and to set the stage for a speedy conclusion of the arms talks in Geneva. Brezhnev and Ford happily began making plans for another summit the next spring, at which it was foreseen that the SALT II treaty would be signed.

No such conference ever occurred. Early in 1975, superpower relations once again turned sour. Partly this was due to unexpected snags in the SALT talks, as negotiators bickered about whether U.S. cruise missiles (low-flying, long-range missiles that could be launched from planes outside Soviet territory) and Soviet "Backfire" bombers (medium-range aircraft which could be modified to reach the United States) should be included in the overall limit on strategic weapons systems. But the climate was also affected by a rupture in trade negotiations between Moscow and Washington and by disturbing developments in Southeast Asia.

By 1975, the prospect of increased trade between the United States and USSR had lost its appeal to many Americans. One reason for this was the "great grain robbery" of 1972. Taking advantage of the spirit of détente and the Nixon administration's desire to sell off U.S. grain surpluses, the Soviets had cut a deal to buy vast amounts of American grain at prices well below market level over the next three years, assisted by extremely generous credit terms. By decreasing the supply of American grain, this in turn helped to drive up U.S. domestic prices, and embarrassed American officials had to admit that they had been outsmarted.

A more serious problem had resulted from the efforts of opponents of détente in the U.S. Congress to force the Soviets to improve their human rights performance in return for economic concessions. During 1973 and 1974, as Congress considered trade reform measures that would extend most-favored nation (MFN) status to the USSR, Senator Henry Jackson and Representative Charles Vanik put forth a proposal to refuse the Soviets such status until they agreed to ease restrictions on the emigration of Jews. The MFN arrangement, which would have given the USSR the same commercial rights as America's most privileged trading partners, was a central feature of the U.S.–Soviet Trade Agreement which had been negotiated in 1972 after the Moscow summit.

The "Jackson-Vanik Amendment," cleverly designed to attract the support of American Jews, human rights advocates, and foes of détente, became a major international issue. Moscow protested vehemently that it amounted to an unwarranted intrusion in its internal affairs, as well as a breach of the trade agreement. Throughout 1974, as the bill made its way through the U.S. Senate, the Nixon and Ford administrations had sought to work out a compromise arrangement acceptable to both congressional and Soviet leaders. In the end, however, their efforts came to naught. The Soviets were willing to make quiet concessions in order to get the troublesome amendment removed, but they did not want to give the impression of caving in to U.S. demands. When a related bill was amended to put severe limits on the amount of credit the USSR could receive, Moscow apparently decided that MFN status was no longer worth the price and repudiated the U.S.–Soviet Trade Agreement in January 1975. A severe blow was dealt to détente, and the beleaguered Soviet Jews gained nothing.

Events in Southeast Asia likewise served to weaken the structure of East-West rapprochement. The Vietnam settlement, which had seemed so promising in 1973, had started to come undone by the middle of 1974. In violation of their agreement with the United States, the North Vietnamese began to infiltrate large numbers of soldiers into the south. The Americans appealed to Moscow but to little avail: the Soviets were both unwilling and unable to restrain the Hanoi regime. Détente may have helped the United States extricate itself from Vietnam, but it could not prevent the communist side from continuing that war. Nixon, handicapped by the Watergate scandal, had been further constrained when Congress overrode his veto in November 1973 to pass the War Powers Act, restricting a president's ability to commit troops to combat without asking Congress for a declaration of war. His successor, Gerald Ford, had no intention of honoring Nixon's pledge to Thieu to intervene militarily if Hanoi violated the Paris Accords.

After two years of preparation, North Vietnam in early 1975 launched its final offensive, the "Ho Chi Minh Campaign." It was a huge conventional operation against a South Vietnamese army riddled with corruption and skeptical of its ability to resist. Major strategic targets throughout the south fell in March, while communist forces in Laos (the Pathet Lao) and Cambodia (the Khmer Rouge) made significant gains. Phnom Penh fell to the Khmer Rouge on 17 April, while Saigon was taken by North Vietnam on 30 April and renamed Ho Chi Minh City. Ho's dream of a unified Vietnam had finally come true! North Vietnamese units then entered Laos to assist the Pathet Lao in its final campaign, which would conclude successfully in October 1975, ending the Second Indochina War.

Americans waited for the dominoes to fall, but they didn't. The loss of Southeast Asia to communism had only a modest effect on the Cold War. Moscow and Beijing transferred their seemingly endless quarrel to Vietnam, which became a Soviet client, and Cambodia, which was supported by China. The ultramodern U.S. naval base at Cam Ranh Bay was turned over to the Soviets, who made little use of it. Clearly, it was too simplistic to view events in this region purely in Cold War terms. Superpower rivalry continued in Southeast Asia, but it was only one of the factors affecting that area and not necessarily the most important.

Still, the fall of Saigon in April 1975, coming on top of the renunciation of the U.S.–Soviet Trade Agreement in January, did help derail hopes for another Ford-Brezhnev summit. It was followed in May by the Khmer Rouge seizure of a U.S. merchant ship called the Mayaguez. The resulting American raid created a short-lived crisis, placing a further strain on East-West relations. The time was hardly propitious for a visit to the United States by the leader of the communist world.

A summit meeting of sorts did take place in July of 1975, when both Ford and Brezhnev traveled to Finland to sign the Helsinki Accords. Accompanied by Secretary of State Kissinger and Foreign Minister Gromyko, the two super-power leaders took advantage of this occasion to hold bilateral discussions. They agreed, in general, to continue the process of détente and the pursuit of a comprehensive SALT II accord. Their meeting was preceded closely by a dramatic "Apollo-Soyuz" coupling in outer space between orbiting U.S. astronauts and Soviet cosmonauts, which added to the overall impression of international good will.

The main significance of the gathering, however, was the Helsinki Final Act. After two years of work, CSCE participants had managed to reach agreement on issues ranging from the inviolability of international borders to improved trade among European nations to freedom of expression and emigration for all European peoples. On 1 August 1975, leading officials from thirty-five countries assembled to sign the Final Act. This was truly a historic event, for it marked the successful culmination of efforts at détente in Europe and, in many respects, the final European peace settlement of the Second World War. It also marked the fruition of West Germany's *Ostpolitik*, although ironically its architect, Willy Brandt, had the previous year been forced by scandal to resign as German chancellor.

In some respects, the Helsinki Final Act was a crowning achievement for Soviet foreign policy, for with it Moscow achieved its long-sought goal of gaining broad international recognition for the new boundaries and territorial adjustments that had resulted from World War II. In other respects, however, it worked to the Soviet leaders' disadvantage, for in order to get an agreement they had consented to language on human rights and individual freedoms (included in "Basket Three" of the Final Act) that would be used against them by internal dissidents and external foes.

Meanwhile, détente, which had begun like an express train, was coming to resemble a roller coaster. Each vital achievement seemed to entail a slow, painstaking climb, while major setbacks often came at breakneck downhill speed. The superpowers, to be sure, had found ways to communicate and collaborate in areas of mutual concern. But the Cold War was far from over.

14

The Decline of Détente, 1975–1979

In the latter half of the 1970s, the bonds of East-West rapprochement increasingly became unraveled. The continuing development of weapons technologies, along with superpower clashes in the Third World and confrontations over human rights, combined to reverse the momentum established earlier in the decade. By 1976, President Ford and Secretary of State Kissinger were studiously avoiding the use of the word "détente," and the Carter administration, which took office the following year, likewise deemphasized this term. Progress continued in areas such as U.S.–Chinese relations and strategic arms negotiations, at least until 1979. But by the decade's close, a series of crises and revolts, culminating in the Soviet invasion of Afghanistan in December 1979, had combined to put an end to the era of détente.

EUROCOMMUNISM, ANGOLA
AND THE DECLINE OF DÉTENTE

The Helsinki Accords, despite their historic significance, did not end East-West tensions in Europe. Indeed, these tensions were exacerbated in the mid-1970s by a phenomenon known as "Eurocommunism." Communist parties in several Western European states, particularly Italy and France, began making electoral gains, in part by asserting their independence and visibly distancing themselves from Moscow. This worried the Americans, who feared that the

Western alliance would be compromised if Communists achieved high positions in NATO countries. At first, it cheered the Soviets, but soon they became wary of maverick communist movements that might sabotage détente without bringing any real extension of the USSR's influence. Moscow's experience had shown time and again that it was often easier to deal with capitalists than with communists it could not control.

The most serious challenges arose from events in Portugal. In 1974, following the "Revolution of Flowers" which overthrew the fascist dictatorship of Marcelo Caetano, a military coup had brought to power Vascos dos Santos Gonçalves, a leftist military officer who soon brought Communists into his government and established close ties with Moscow. By 1975, amid rumors that this NATO nation might soon let the Soviet navy use its seaports, Washington had become increasingly nervous about the situation. Ford and Kissinger both warned Moscow to stay out of Portuguese affairs, and the Soviets, who had helped to finance the local Communists, apparently got the message. When the tide turned against Gonçalves in the summer of 1975, they did little other than rant against Western "interference" in Portuguese events. Rather than jeopardize détente and risk confrontation in an American sphere of influence, Moscow stood by as Gonçalves was deposed in August and a communist-led uprising in November was suppressed.

The Soviets were less cautious, however, in dealing with the Portuguese West African colony of Angola (see Map 6, p. 153). In 1975, as Gonçalves's government moved to liberate its African colonies, Moscow stepped up its aid to the Popular Movement for the Liberation of Angola (MPLA), a Marxist group which was engaged in a civil war against various forces backed by the Americans, South Africans, and others. Eventually, it even helped airlift 160,000 Cuban troops into the region, thus enabling the MPLA to gain the upper hand by early 1976. The U.S. Congress, unwilling to risk "another Vietnam," refused to let the administration send in American troops to help the anticommunist forces. So the Angolan civil war dragged on. It was destined to last until 1990, when the Cubans and South Africans would finally withdraw as the Cold War neared its end.

The Angolan debacle caused great concern in Washington, not because U.S. security was threatened, but because American policymakers thought they detected a new departure in Soviet strategy and a major new Soviet Third World offensive. Hitherto, they reasoned, the USSR had actively intervened primarily in regions along its periphery and had been very reluctant to try to extend its power to distant regions. Now, under the cover of détente, it seemed to be acting much more boldly. From Moscow's perspective, however, the Angolan initiative was merely a continuation of its traditional practice of aiding national liberation movements throughout the world, providing them with Soviet arms and assistance and letting the soldiers of client states bear the brunt of the battle. It was in no way inconsistent, the Soviets assured their American critics, with the spirit of détente.

Be that as it may, the Angolan affair was a setback for superpower relations. In the United States, former California governor Ronald Reagan mounted a serious bid for the republican presidential nomination, accusing Ford and Kissinger of having allowed the USSR to surpass America as the world's number one power and gaining broad support from conservative and anticommunist quarters. In March 1976, in an effort to shore up his right flank, Ford announced that he would no longer use the word "détente," and Kissinger began using tough talk about stopping Soviet expansionism. Efforts to make progress in the SALT negotiations were virtually placed on hold, as relations with Moscow were sacrificed in favor of domestic politics.

Ford survived the Reagan challenge, but he did not fare as well in the general election. Tarnished by the Watergate legacy and his subsequent pardon of Richard Nixon, and weakened by conservative attacks on his foreign policy during the battle for nomination, the president began the race with a huge deficit in the polls that he never quite made up. In defending détente during a televised debate, he made the egregious error of denying that Poland was under Soviet domination, thus forfeiting his presumed edge over his rival in foreign policy expertise. In November of 1976, Jimmy Carter, the former governor of Georgia, was elected president by a narrow margin.

HUMAN RIGHTS AND THE DECLINE OF DÉTENTE

Although Jimmy Carter was probably the least "hawkish" of Cold War presidents, at least in the early years of his term, his election caused consternation in Moscow. The Soviets had learned that, despite the prevalent perception that Democrats were "softer" on communism, it was easier to work with pragmatic and realistic Republicans who were willing, like themselves, to put national interest before ideology in dealing with world problems. They did not know what to make of Carter, a born-again Christian peanut farmer who seemed poised to push American policy in a different and destabilizing direction. And they were scarcely reassured when he chose as his national security advisor Zbigniew Brzezinski, a Polish émigré and hardline anti-Soviet scholar.

The new president was an enigma, not only to the Kremlin, but also to many in his own country. Raised in the rural South, he had earned an engineering degree from the U.S. Naval Academy and later served as governor of Georgia. He had a deep and abiding Baptist faith, which profoundly affected his outlook, and a prodigious capacity for processing information. In running for president, he had turned his inexperience into an advantage by depicting himself as an outsider, contrasting his own integrity with the duplicitous ways of Washington. But once he was in office, his aura of moral rectitude would hamper his relations with both the Kremlin and the Congress, neither of which was used to a president who put principle ahead of pragmatism.

U.S.–Soviet relations in the early stages of the Carter administration were dominated and damaged by two major issues: arms control and human rights. Although Carter was deeply dedicated to each of these concerns, he wanted to treat them as separate entities. In practice, however, they tended to become intertwined, often to the detriment of both.

On arms control, the new administration pushed quickly for reductions and limits far beyond those agreed to at Vladivostok. Cyrus Vance, the new secretary of state, was sent to Moscow in March 1977 to put forth some new U.S. proposals. They called for extensive cuts in strategic weapons and MIRVs, drastic reductions in "modern" ICBMs (like the USSR's mammoth new SS-18), and curtailment of plans for new types of ICBM (such as the projected American MX). The United States was particularly concerned about the Soviet SS-18 missiles, which were large enough to carry many warheads and potentially accurate enough to destroy American ICBMs in their underground silos.

The Soviets, who had put years of effort into negotiating a SALT II treaty that now seemed within reach, were dismayed that the Carter team wanted to scrap much of this and start over with a new and sweeping proposal. Brezhnev, who had overcome stiff opposition from his own military to the "equal ceilings" agreement at Vladivostok, was in no mood or position to make further concessions. He thus rejected the new U.S. approach and insisted that continued discussions must be based on the tentative accords already reached in the SALT II negotiations. The result was a setback for the arms talks, deterioration in East-West relations, and an impression in Moscow that the new U.S. administration was both unsophisticated and insincere.

This impression was further enhanced by the Carter approach to human rights. Internal dissent, which had been simmering in the USSR for years, had gotten a major boost from the human rights provisions of the Helsinki Final Act of 1975. Prominent Soviet dissidents formed self-styled "monitoring groups" and issued open letters, publicly accusing their government of violating the accords. The Brezhnev regime responded by exiling several of the dissenters and by trying to clamp down on contacts between those who remained and the Western press.

Carter, who was both genuinely concerned for human rights and anxious to maintain the support of hard-line Democrats like Senator Jackson, calculated that he could launch a major initiative in this area without damaging U.S.–Soviet relations. He was wrong. His administration made public statements critical of Soviet and Eastern European authorities, put increasing stress on human rights in U.S. radio broadcasts beamed to the communist bloc, and sent letters of support to leading Soviet dissidents. In March 1977, the president even held a highly publicized White House reception for Vladimir Bukovsky, a recently exiled dissident. The Kremlin responded by evicting or harassing several Western journalists and arresting a number of dissenters for alleged collaboration with the CIA. At one point, in reply, Carter felt compelled to issue a personal statement denying that detained dissident Anatoly Shcharansky had ever been associated with U.S. intelligence. But this did not help Shcharansky, who was convicted of treason and sentenced to hard labor. Nor did it satisfy the Soviets, who protested American interference in their internal affairs and warned Washington that continued U.S. support for anti-Soviet "sedition" would undermine détente.

Carter, nonetheless, persisted in his policies, insisting that his concern for human rights was a matter of global principle and not directed specifically against the USSR. He did, in fact, cut aid to several U.S. clients for human rights violations. But Brezhnev had little understanding or appreciation of Carter's Christian idealism. From his perspective, the American human rights campaign was little more than an attempt to embarrass the Soviet government and weaken its hold on Eastern Europe.

The human rights imbroglio intensified in fall 1977 when a new round of CSCE meetings, designed in part to evaluate the success of the Helsinki Final Act, opened in Belgrade. Moscow hoped to use this occasion to rejuvenate and consolidate détente, but the United States wanted to focus on how nations were complying with the document's humanitarian provisions. Prior to the conference, Washington issued a report, deeply resented in Moscow, which graded the USSR and other Communist bloc nations on their human rights performance, giving them poor marks. The conference was dominated by rancorous debates on this issue. Despite Soviet objections, and the private concerns of several U.S. allies, the Americans managed to establish as a legitimate international concern the internal human rights practices of nations which had signed the Helsinki Accords.

CONFRONTATION AND CONFUSION IN EAST AFRICA

Carter's human rights crusade did not always work to U.S. advantage. This was especially true in the Horn of Africa, where Ethiopia was an American friend and neighboring Somalia a Soviet client (see Map 6, p. 153). The Somalis, who were culturally and ethnically similar to the Ethiopians, had gained their independence in 1960. But part of Somalia, the Ogaden, had been given to Ethiopia during previous colonial partitions. The Somalis wanted it back. They were courted by Moscow, which coveted the access to the Indian Ocean which air and naval bases in Somalia could provide.

Soviet aid to Somalia had begun in 1963 and intensified after a military coup brought Colonel Mohammed Siad Barre to power in 1969. The USSR built an air base inland and a major naval facility at the port of Berbera. By the mid-1970s, more than 2,000 Soviet technicians were stationed in Somalia. This balanced the U.S. ties with Ethiopia and Saudi Arabia, which between them controlled much of the Red Sea coast. But in 1974, a military coup overthrew Ethiopian emperor Haile Selassie, and power passed to a Marxist colonel named Mengistu Haile Mariam. The United States, already in the process of transferring its naval and telecommunications facilities to a newly acquired base on the Indian Ocean island of Diego Garcia, had no desire to subsidize a Marxist regime. So in February 1977, America denounced the Mariam government for human rights violations and cut off all aid. Moscow thus gained a splendid opportunity to construct a network of clients in Ethiopia, Somalia, and South Yemen (which had become Marxist in 1967 as a result of a Yemeni civil war), ringing the southern entrance to the Red Sea.

If ideology were the dominant factor in international relations, this alliance could have been fashioned overnight. But if the history of the late twentieth century points to anything, it is the remarkably enduring attraction of nationalistic and ethnic rivalries. Somalia, seeing an opportunity to regain the Ogaden, broke its alliance with Moscow and invaded Ethiopia. Soviet forces were expelled from Berbera and replaced by American advisors, but Carter's scruples were offended by the invasion, and for reasons of both principle and public relations the United States refused to ship arms to the Somali aggressors. The USSR supplied Ethiopia with huge quantities of weapons, while Cuba sent troops to repel the Somali assault. This unprecedented direct Soviet intervention in Africa led to an uneasy stalemate, as Moscow refused to permit a counterassault by Ethiopia, which was having its own problems with an uprising in its province of Eritrea.

The conflicts in the Horn of Africa would eventually lead to a monstrous human tragedy. By the late 1980s, both Ethiopia and Somalia would be in desperate straits, with their economies in shambles, their social fabrics weakened by years of combat and hardship, and famine stalking their lands. As the Cold War came to an end in 1991, Ethiopia would overthrow its Marxist government and Somalia would oust the military dictatorship of Siad Barre. Superpower interest in the area had been dictated by its proximity to the Indian Ocean (for Moscow) and the Red Sea (for Washington). The wild card in the deal was Jimmy Carter's absorption in issues of human rights, which led the Americans to offend both sides and bewilder their friends in the region.

PEACE BETWEEN EGYPT AND ISRAEL

Although it was making inroads in Africa, the Kremlin could take little comfort from concurrent events in the Middle East. At first, the Carter administration, reversing the Nixon-Ford policy, sought to include the USSR as a partner in resolving the Arab-Israeli conflict. In October 1977, the two superpowers even issued a joint statement calling for renewed peace talks in Geneva. But the following month Egyptian president Anwar Sadat stunned the world by traveling to Jerusalem, setting in motion a process that would lead to peace between Egypt and Israel, an enhanced U.S. role, and a steep decline in Soviet influence in the Middle East.

Sadat's initial victories in the Yom Kippur/Ramadan War of 1973 (Chapter 13), despite his later reverses, had won him immense acclaim in Egypt. This position of strength enabled him to embark on a dramatic new course. He had already concluded that peace with Israel was an economic necessity and that a new war might well reveal whether rumors that Israel had a nuclear device were accurate. Disinclined to obtain this information in such a direct manner, he set out to work for peace.

Thus, on 20 November 1977, Sadat flabbergasted the world by making a surprise flight to Jerusalem and a speech to the Israeli parliament (Knesset). In Menachem Begin, Israel's recently elected prime minister, he found both a tenacious adversary and a prudent statesman. Begin, whose ancestry was Polish, had headed a Jewish terrorist organization in the 1940s and had masterminded the bombing of Jerusalem's King David Hotel in an effort to force British withdrawal. Worse still in Arab eyes, he had planned and executed a 1948 massacre of Arab villagers at Deir Yasin. Courtly and devout, passionately protective of Israeli independence and incorrigibly realistic regarding means to attain that end, his patriotic credentials were impeccable. Just as Nixon was one of the few U.S. politicians who could open the door to China, Begin was one of the few Israelis with the moral leverage to negotiate with an Egyptian. Their November meeting, while not without vociferous disagreements, was highly promising.

Begin, in return, flew to Egypt on 25 December for further discussions. Israel was ready to trade occupied land for peace with Egypt, since destruction of the common anti-Israeli front would give Tel Aviv unprecedented security. The talks which followed underscored the bankruptcy of Soviet Middle East strategy and the success of U.S. efforts to exclude Moscow from any real role in the region. Begin and Sadat agreed from the outset that any permanent settlement would have to be facilitated and guaranteed by the United States. With Carter acting as mediator, the two leaders held a twelve-day marathon meeting at Camp David in September 1978. They agreed on a framework for a peace treaty and established a three-month deadline for its conclusion.

The Israeli Knesset grudgingly authorized a military pullback from Sinai, but peace talks stalled over Egypt's efforts to tie the full resumption of diplomatic relations to Israel's willingness to relax its control over Palestinians in Gaza and the West Bank. The deadline passed without a treaty. Jews in Israel did not care to admit that Palestinians wanted freedom as much as they did, while Egyptians and other Arabs did not realize how much Israel's security concerns stemmed from the experience of Nazi genocide and the longstanding Arab-Israeli tension. Finally, Carter himself flew to Cairo and Jerusalem to negotiate final arrangements between Sadat and Begin. The Egyptian-Israeli treaty was signed in Washington on 26 March 1979. Through it all, the USSR had been little more than a bystander, eliminated from any substantive role in the peace process.

Sadat, Carter, and Begin. (AP/Wide World Photos)

THE CHINA CARD,
THE AMERICA CARD, AND THE VIENNA SUMMIT

Superpower relations, meanwhile, were severely complicated by a split in the U.S. government between Secretary of State Vance and National Security Advisor Brzezinski. With the apparent blessing of their president, the two men pursued contradictory policies while struggling for preeminence within the administration. Vance and his colleagues stressed cooperation with the USSR and worked to preserve détente. Having failed in their early attempt to get Moscow to assent to deep cuts in strategic arms, they fell back to the Vladivostok approach and worked to conclude a SALT II treaty based on the Brezhnev-Ford agreement. Brzezinski, however, disliked and distrusted the Soviets and felt that Vance and arms negotiator Paul Warnke were too soft and accommodating. He favored confrontation with Moscow, and to this end he pushed for an accelerated U.S. arms buildup and further rapprochement with the People's Republic of China.

At first, the secretary of state seemed to gain the upper hand. Carter, who saw himself as a man of peace and was determined to end the arms race, decided not to link progress on SALT with Soviet behavior in Ethiopia or elsewhere. Siding with Vance, he concluded that arms control was too important for U.S. interests to be used as a reward or punishment. The negotiations thus continued throughout 1978, despite the gradual worsening of superpower relations, and made enough progress so that by the end of the year agreement was close at hand.

The president decided, however, that he must also respond to the Soviet geopolitical challenge, and here he turned to Brzezinski. In an undisguised effort to "play the China card," the national security advisor went to Beijing in May 1978. There he met with Chinese leaders, joined them in criticizing the USSR, and renewed efforts to improve economic and diplomatic ties between America and communist China. In December, the dramatic announcement was made that Washington and Beijing would establish full diplomatic relations, effective 1 January 1979. The United States simultaneously agreed to sever its formal ties with the Nationalist government on Taiwan, though a number of informal connections would remain.

The normalization of U.S.–Chinese relations was followed closely by a highly publicized visit to America by Chinese vice-premier Deng Xiaoping. The diminutive and astute Deng, a veteran of the Long March and survivor of three separate purges, had emerged as China's effective leader in the wake of the 1976 deaths of Zhou Enlai and Mao Zedong. A seasoned pragmatist, he had overcome the machinations of the radical left and had launched China on a course of modernization, experimentation with free market incentives, and further accommodation with the West. Arriving in Washington in late January 1979, he charmed almost everyone, delighting conservatives by denouncing the Soviet "hegemonists." Then, soon after his return home, China launched a sudden invasion of Vietnam, its communist neighbor to the south.

Although China had aided Hanoi during its long war against the United States, relations between the two had deteriorated greatly since the end of that war. Vietnam had drawn closer to Moscow, while the Chinese had aligned themselves with communist Cambodia. Matters had finally come to a head late in 1978, following the conclusion of a formal alliance between Moscow and Hanoi in November. In December, Vietnam invaded Cambodia, proceeding to drive from power the murderous regime of Pol Pot and the Khmer Rouge, which since 1975 had killed over a million people with its radical deurbanization campaign. In January 1979, the Vietnamese installed a moderate communist government in Phnom Penh. But the fighting was far from over. In February, the Chinese invaded northern Vietnam, intending to "punish" Hanoi for its aggression and help the beleaguered Khmer Rouge. Deftly playing the "America card," Deng Xiaoping had informed his U.S. hosts of his intentions and then timed the Chinese attack to follow close on the heels of his visit, thus giving the impression that Washington had acquiesced. Although the Americans had privately tried to dissuade Deng from his plans, in public they did not condemn the Chinese invasion unequivocally, opting instead for an "even handed" approach to the conflict. Furthermore, in a move that made a mockery of Carter's human rights crusade, they continued to recognize and send arms to the genocidal Khmer Rouge.

Predictably, these events cast a pall over Soviet-American relations. Indeed, the December announcement of mutual U.S.–Chinese recognition came at a time when arms negotiators seemed close to an agreement, and plans were being discussed for a January summit in Washington to sign the SALT II accords. But the events of early 1979 chilled the international climate, and, although both Carter and Brezhnev wanted a summit, the time was just not right. Furthermore, the remaining arms control issues proved more troublesome than expected. It was not until May, following tedious work by negotiators in Geneva, augmented by private correspondence between Brezhnev and Carter and numerous meetings between Vance and Dobrynin, that a final accord was reached.

The long-delayed summit finally took place in June of 1979. Although it had originally been planned for Washington, in deference to the declining health of the aging Soviet dictator the meeting was held in Vienna. Both leaders attached great importance to the event. At their initial encounter, in fact, the atheistic Brezhnev declared to the deeply religious Carter that "God will not forgive us if we fail." And, at the signing ceremonies for SALT II, the leader of the free world warmly embraced the head of the Communist bloc.

The SALT II treaty was, of course, the heart of the Vienna summit. Coming almost five years after preliminary agreement had been reached at Vladivostok, it nonetheless followed the general understandings that had been achieved at that meeting. A ceiling of 2,400 was placed on the aggregate number of strategic launchers permitted to either side, with a reduction to 2,250 after 1981. The number of these which could be equipped with MIRVs was set at 1,320. Long-range bombers fitted with cruise missiles were to be counted as multiple-warhead vehicles and limited to 28 cruise missiles each. For verification purposes, each side agreed that it would not interfere with the other's technological efforts (such as the use of spy satellites) to monitor compliance.

The conclusion of the SALT II accords marked the culmination of a decade of negotiations which had begun in November 1969 with the original arms control talks in Helsinki. The process was far from perfect, and in some cases it may have actually created pressures to develop and build new weapons, either as bargaining chips or as sops to hardliners and military brass in order to win their support. The results, too, were less than conclusive: Each side was left with a vast nuclear arsenal of awesome destructive capability, far in excess of what might be needed for legitimate defensive purposes. Each weapons system continued to possess its own momentum, its own logic, and its own avid supporters. The arms control treaty was a finite and limited device, designed primarily to prevent a future escalation of the arms race rather than to reduce or eliminate existing stockpiles. Still, the agreement did seem to show that, despite their conflicting interests and their often dangerous global competition, the two superpowers were capable of reaching agreement on overriding issues of mutual concern.

The Vienna summit and the SALT II treaty also marked the pinnacle of the career of Leonid Ilyich Brezhnev. In internal affairs, he had increasingly consolidated his power, methodically removing his opponents inside the government and repressing the dissidents outside. In 1977, he had taken over the position of Soviet president while maintaining his post as general secretary of the Communist party. He had thus become the official head of state, as well as the effective ruler. That same year, he had also managed to implement a new constitution, updating and replacing the old "Stalin Constitution" of 1936. In foreign affairs, he had staked his reputation on the simultaneous pursuit of defense and détente, and he had apparently won. By virtue of its relentless arms buildup and its tenacious negotiations, the USSR had achieved a recognized position of diplomatic and strategic equality with the United States. The Soviet Union's territorial gains in World War II, and its domination of Eastern Europe, had been widely recognized and accepted in international accords. Brezhnev himself had met, and negotiated as an equal, with three American presidents. Under him, the USSR had become not just a military giant that was feared the world over but also a respected and accepted member of the world family of nations, symbolized by the fact that it was scheduled to host the 1980 Olympic Summer Games in Moscow.

Ironically, these achievements turned out to be illusory. By the time Carter and Brezhnev met in Vienna, forces were already in motion that would undermine SALT, the spirit of détente, and even the USSR itself. The SALT II treaty was fated never to be ratified, and détente would be doomed by the end of the year.

THE "ARC OF CRISIS" AND THE "WINDOW OF VULNERABILITY"

Even before Carter and Brezhnev met at Vienna in June 1979 to sign the SALT II accords, détente was in serious trouble. The main reason for this was a growing American perception that Moscow was using it to gain the advantage, both in Third World influence and in strategic weapons capability.

The previous four years had indeed witnessed a string of communist triumphs. In 1975, Communists had taken power in South Vietnam, Laos, and Cambodia. In 1976, the Soviet-backed MPLA had gained the upper hand in Angola. In 1977, the Kremlin had acquired an important new client in Ethiopia. In 1978, in a development that attracted scant notice at the time, a Marxist regime had come to power in Afghanistan. Early in 1979, a noncommunist but anti-Western revolution had toppled the shah of Iran, and a simultaneous crisis between South and North Yemen had eventually led to increased Soviet influence in both. Proponents of détente might argue that these were mainly localized rivalries, that they mostly involved forces that were not under Kremlin control, that the antagonists were more interested in getting Moscow's weapons than in joining the Soviet bloc, and that these ventures were doing more to drain the USSR's resources than to increase its influence. But to worried hardliners like Brzezinski, there was an "arc of crisis" stretching from Afghanistan, through the Persian Gulf, and down into eastern Africa. In this area, as well as in Southeast Asia and central Africa, it looked to many as if Communism was on the march.

Of even greater concern to American officials was the continuing Soviet arms buildup. Partly because of his own proclivities, and partly to ensure the support of the Soviet military for his pursuit of détente, Brezhnev had spent vast sums on weaponry, and by the late 1970s the USSR had actually surpassed the United States in several important categories. Most worrisome of all was the mammoth new SS-18 missile, a far more potent weapon than any previous Soviet ICBM. In terms of throw-weight, or weapons carrying capacity, the SS-18 could carry larger and more numerous warheads than any U.S. missile, and it was accurate enough to deliver these warheads near enough to its target to destroy or incapacitate a hardened underground missile silo. This made it potentially a first-strike weapon. Although the SALT II treaty would limit the SS-18s to ten warheads each, it also allowed the USSR to retain 308 of these missiles. Theoretically, by launching just 211 of them in a surprise first-strike attack, the Soviets could deliver 2,110 nuclear warheads, or two against *each* of America's 1,000 Minuteman and 54 Atlas ICBMs, thus destroying virtually the entire U.S. fleet.

For several years, an unofficial "Committee on the Present Danger," composed of leading U.S. hardliners and opponents of détente, had been warning publicly of just such a scenario. By demolishing the American ICBMs, it was feared, the Kremlin could deprive the United States of the ability to retaliate against the USSR's remaining strategic missiles, and thus leave American leaders in a terrible predicament. They could still use their nuclear submarines and bombers to retaliate against Soviet cities, but this would only invite a counterattack against U.S. population centers. If, however, they chose not to retaliate, they would in effect be giving Moscow a free hand to use its vast conventional military forces to launch unstoppable offensives in Europe, Asia, or the Middle East. The danger would decrease in the mid-1980s, it was assumed, when America's accurate new MX ICBMs and D-5 SLBMs were scheduled to come on line. Until that time, however, there would purportedly exist a "window of vulnerability," during which the U.S. land-based nuclear deterrent was very much at risk.

The "window of vulnerability," like the missile gap of the late 1950s, had far more political than strategic significance. It was a classic "worst case" scenario, ascribing to the Soviet weapons a far greater reliability than they usually had and overlooking the enormous technical difficulties of launching and coordinating such a mammoth attack. Critics of this concept further noted that, while ICBMs accounted for the vast preponderance of the USSR's nuclear capability, they made up a much smaller portion of the U.S. strategic force. This meant that a preemptive Soviet attack, even if it managed to wipe out most of the U.S. ICBMs, would still leave the Americans with an overall edge in deliverable nuclear warheads. It also meant, since land-based missiles were much more vulnerable than those launched by submarine or aircraft, that the Soviets were potentially far more susceptible to a first strike than were their U.S. adversaries. Still, to American hardliners, these arguments missed the point: it was the *perception* of U.S. vulnerability, rather than the reality, that might well embolden the Soviets and immobilize the Americans during a major crisis.

All of these concerns came to the fore in summer 1979, when Jimmy Carter returned from Vienna and submitted the freshly signed SALT II treaty to the U.S. Senate for ratification. Nobody expected an easy fight. Carter was an enigmatic president, disliked by many in his own party, with little popular support or personal loyalty to draw upon. His standing in the polls was low, thanks to a shaky economy and double-digit inflation. He had earlier offended military hawks by canceling plans to build the B-1, a sophisticated new U.S. bomber, without even trying to use it as a bargaining chip in the arms control talks. His "inaction" in the face of Soviet Third World gains, his conclusion of a treaty giving up control over the Panama Canal, and his "abandonment" of Taiwan in order to normalize relations with China had won him many enemies on the right. And on the eve of the Vienna summit, Senator Henry Jackson, the influential Democrat who had bedeviled Nixon's efforts at détente, had scorned the SALT II treaty and accused the administration of "appeasement."

Additional problems arose during the ratification process, which was destined to last six months. In September, there arose a major flap over the "discovery" of a Soviet "combat brigade" in Cuba, during which Senate hearings on SALT II were temporarily suspended. The "crisis" lasted until 1 October, when President Carter declared that he had received Soviet pledges not to enlarge the brigade, which it turned out had been there for years.

Meanwhile, developments in Europe were placing an added strain on U.S.–Soviet relations. NATO leaders, who had generally supported détente, were nonetheless concerned that the SALT treaties might undermine the security of Western Europe. German chancellor Helmut Schmidt in particular had expressed the fear that, by neutralizing the superpowers' strategic arsenals, SALT II would amplify the Warsaw Pact's military preeminence in Europe. In effect, the less danger there was of a global nuclear conflict, the more temptation there might be for the Soviet bloc to use its superior forces to attack Western Europe. To Schmidt, this meant that NATO must either upgrade and modernize its forces to provide a more credible deterrent or else convince the Soviets to downgrade and weaken theirs.

Since 1977, there had been growing concern in NATO about the ongoing Soviet deployment of an accurate new triple-warhead intermediate-range ballistic missile (IRBM) called the SS-20. Unlike its unreliable predecessors, the SS-20 was *mobile* and thus less vulnerable to a Western strike in the event of a European war. The Carter administration was not much worried at first, but with the signing of the SALT II treaty, it wanted to reassure both its NATO allies and domestic critics that it could be tough in dealing with Moscow. Therefore, in August of that year, it decided to modernize its NATO forces in Europe by replacing older weapons systems with 108 Pershing II IRBMs and 464 Tomahawk ground-launched cruise missiles.

The reaction in Moscow was swift and vehement. On 6 October, Brezhnev gave a major speech in which he vigorously denounced this decision as destabilizing and destructive, warning that it would undermine détente. From a Soviet perspective, the new weapons were potentially strategic in nature, since they carried nuclear warheads and were capable of reaching the USSR. In some respects, they were even more dangerous than ICBMs, since the Pershing IIs reportedly could reach their targets in less than ten minutes, and the slower cruise missiles flew too low to be detected by radar. Brezhnev, therefore, offered to reduce the number of Soviet IRBMs capable of reaching Western Europe if NATO would agree not to deploy the new U.S. weapons. NATO responded in December with a "dual-track" approach, resolving to proceed with negotiations to reduce intermediate-range nuclear forces (INF), while simultaneously preparing to install the new missiles in 1983. The deployment would be canceled, the Soviets were assured, if agreement could be reached by then in the INF talks. For Western politicians, this approach served two important purposes: it gave the Kremlin an incentive to bargain in good faith, and it helped allay the fears of the jittery populations in the nations where the new missiles were slated to be deployed. But it could hardly be expected to win them points in Moscow.

THE CRISIS IN IRAN

In November 1979, while the U.S. Senate was still considering the SALT II treaty, and while NATO leaders were pondering their response to Brezhnev's IRBM offer, the focus of world attention suddenly shifted to Iran. On 4 November, an Iranian mob stormed the U.S. embassy in Tehran and seized a large number of American hostages, setting in motion a crisis that was destined both to undermine détente and to destroy the Carter presidency.

The crisis in Iran was the culmination of a long series of developments that had transformed that nation from a friend to a foe of the United States. From 1953 until 1979, Shah Mohammed Reza Pahlavi had ruled Iran in accordance with Washington's interests, and the country had become a U.S. surrogate in the Persian Gulf. The exploitation of Iran's oil deposits had brought the nation vast wealth and equally vast problems. Oil revenues had grown from $34 million in 1953 to $20 *billion* in 1978. The government had spent huge sums on economic and social projects which the shah called the "White Revolution," but industrial advances and access to education and medical care had been offset by the strains and stresses of rapid modernization. By the late 1970s, Tehran and other cities were swollen with internal migrants seeking industrial employment. Health care and sanitation systems could not keep pace with this influx, and nearly half of urban families lived in a single room. Meanwhile, traditional Muslim values had eroded as materialism challenged religious beliefs. Drug abuse and premarital sex had ravaged a whole generation of young people. In response, a conservative religious opposition had emerged, headed by Muslim clerics like the Ayatollah Ruhollah Khomeini, who had been exiled to Iraq in 1963.

Several events had combined in 1978 to doom the shah's regime. In response to newspaper columns attacking Khomeini, widespread rioting erupted in the holy city of Qum, and the political and clerical oppositions joined forces. Simultaneously, the country was flooded with Khomeini's writings and taped cassettes of his sermons smuggled in from Iraq. When the shah protested, the Iraqis expelled Khomeini, who moved to Paris and issued directions to the revolution by radio via the British Broadcasting Corporation. He preached that Zionism, Christianity, and Marxism were all in league against Islam and that Muslims must adopt a theocratic state in order to defeat them. Carter's role in brokering the Egyptian-Israeli accords lent credibility to these words. In the context of the Cold War, this ironically placed Moscow and Washington on the same side, in opposition to a revolution which would benefit neither of them. It would, of course, hurt the United States more, since Iran was a U.S. satellite.

In a few months, everything fell apart in Iran. The suspicious destruction of a packed movie house, bloody riots in Tehran that killed hundreds, and a deadly earthquake that took nearly 20,000 lives all undermined the regime. Khomeini became the symbol of a united opposition, keeping the character of his movement vague and ill-defined, so that all antigovernment forces could support it. Unable to govern, the shah on 6 January 1979 appointed Shahpour Bakhtiar of the liberal opposition National Front as prime minister and then left the country for cancer treatment. On 1 February, Khomeini returned to Iran. A few days later, a temporary anti-shah coalition including air force technicians, Marxist guerrillas, and Islamic fundamentalists took power in Tehran. Khomeini quickly installed a theocratic state and continued his vehement denunciations of the United States. The stage was set for crisis.

On 22 October 1979, anti-American sentiments in Iran were inflamed when the former shah, by this time dying of cancer, was admitted to a U.S. hospital. This led to mass demonstrations, and eventually to the storming of the U.S. embassy in Tehran and the seizure of American hostages on 4 November. Some hostages were soon released, but the majority would be held captive for the next fifteen months, producing a drawn-out, debilitating crisis. From November 1979 until the liberation of the remaining hostages in January 1981, America would appear to the world as an impotent giant, unable to win the release of the hostages yet unwilling to ignore them and move on to other issues. This added to the impression of Carter's weakness and eroded his support still further. And the loss of U.S. intelligence facilities in Iran, by hampering American capacity for monitoring Soviet compliance with SALT II, further undermined the treaty's chances within the U.S. Senate. Not only had the shah's government served as an American surrogate in maintaining the flow of Persian Gulf oil; it had also provided the CIA with electronic listening posts from which Soviet troop movements, rocket launchings, and nuclear tests could be monitored. In the absence of such facilities, key senators proved unwilling to ratify the SALT II treaty. The crisis in Iran thus had an enormous impact upon East-West relations, weakening détente and providing the setting for a full-scale resumption of the Cold War.

The crisis also brought severe problems for Iran. Carter froze all Iranian assets in the United States, and, since Khomeini lacked the experience needed to create an effective government, the country careened toward chaos. Emboldened by such developments, neighboring Iraq would go to war against Iran in 1980, beginning a crippling conflict which would cost the lives of millions. Despite the fact that Khomeini's regime was as violently anticommunist as it was anti-American, Moscow sought to gain influence in Tehran by blaming the United States and selling arms to Iran. But by this time, the Kremlin, led by the aging and sickly Brezhnev, was seriously distracted by a major crisis of its own.

THE SOVIET INVASION OF AFGHANISTAN

By December 1979, it was already clear that East-West relations were in very serious trouble and that the SALT II treaty was floundering in the U.S. Senate. Détente had been bruised and battered, and its survival was much in doubt. Then, at the end of the month, came the final *coup de grâce:* the USSR launched a massive invasion of the neighboring state of Afghanistan.

The Soviet invasion of Afghanistan came in response to a series of events that had threatened Moscow's recently gained hegemony in that country. In April of 1978, a communist coup had overthrown the Western-oriented regime of Muhammad Daoud and brought to power a leftist dictatorship headed by Nur Muhammad Taraki. At first, the Kremlin was delighted to gain a new client in a neighboring country, but before long it was watching in dismay as an extremist faction led by Hafizullah Amin tried to force radical socialism down the throats of the fiercely independent and devoutly Muslim Afghan people, alienating almost everyone. The moderate Communists, led by Babrak Karmal, were quickly forced out of government. Before long, the whole country was in rebellion, and by August of 1979 the Soviets were quietly urging Taraki to slow the pace of reform and get rid of Amin. His attempt to do so backfired, however, and Amin wound up ousting Taraki and taking full power himself. This merely served to intensify the revolt as Afghanistan disintegrated into chaos.

Initially, Washington had shown little concern over events in Afghanistan, a barren, landlocked country with minute strategic significance. But by late 1979, as the Soviets increased their involvement and began to assemble troops near the Afghan border, the Carter administration became increasingly disturbed. It tried to warn the Kremlin not to get further involved, but this was to no avail.

On 24 December 1979, Soviet troops began crossing into Afghanistan; three days later Soviet paratroopers stormed the government headquarters and carried out a bloody coup. Amin was killed, and the moderate pro-Soviet Babrak Karmal was installed at the head of a new regime. By January of 1980, Moscow had sent some 85,000 troops to help stabilize the situation, bolster the new government, and crush the Afghan revolt.

The Kremlin's actions were mainly designed to salvage its recent gains in Afghanistan and make the best of a bad situation. Amin's brutal rule had done little more than discredit communism with the Afghans and ignite a massive rebellion. By replacing him with the more prudent Karmal, and by applying overwhelming force, Moscow hoped to be able to disarm the opposition and quickly defeat the rebels. The intervention might well bring an international outcry, as had the earlier Soviet invasions of Hungary and Czechoslovakia, but this seemed preferable to watching its Afghan clients be overthrown and replaced by hostile forces. Besides, experience had shown that the clamor would eventually die down.

Of all the miscalculations of the Brezhnev regime, this was the most calamitous. The Afghanistan invasion turned out to be a disaster of the first magnitude for the USSR. Karmal, though less radical, proved no more popular than Amin, and the vast influx of Soviet forces served only to unite the various rebel factions against him. The Kremlin's reputation for heavy-handed brutality was greatly enhanced, and its credibility in the Third World was seriously strained—especially when it clumsily tried to claim that it had been "invited" to intervene by the Afghans and that Amin had been conspiring with the Muslims and the CIA. As time went on, even its military prestige was diminished by its inability to bring the war to a successful conclusion. For the next decade, Soviet troops would be tied down in a bloody, dispiriting and unwinnable war against Afghan guerrillas armed with zealous Muslim faith and Western-supplied weapons. As the Soviet economy staggered, valuable resources were siphoned off by the long, debilitating conflict. And the USSR, which looked to be the essence of indomitable power and control, was destined to last only a dozen more years.

15

The Return of the Cold War, 1980–1985

The Cold War, which had thawed appreciably in the mid-1970s, returned with full frigidity at the start of the 1980s. For the next five years, international affairs would be dominated by a renewed arms race and a rekindled spirit of confrontation between the superpowers. In 1980, the United States responded to the Soviet invasion of Afghanistan by cutting off sales of technology and grain to the USSR, boycotting the Moscow Olympics, and substantially increasing its military spending. That same year the Americans elected a new president who was a committed Cold Warrior, vigorously opposed to détente and inherently distrustful of what he would call the "evil empire." Relations degenerated into name calling and recrimination, as both sides sought to enhance their military capabilities, discredit the other's reputation, and gain the upper hand in the Third World. Not until 1985, when a new generation of leaders came to power in Moscow, would significant progress in East-West relations once again be made.

THE DEMISE OF DÉTENTE

The Soviet invasion of Afghanistan cut the ground from under American supporters of U.S.–Soviet rapprochement and drove a final nail into the coffin of détente. President Jimmy Carter, reacting vehemently, told an interviewer that these developments had made "a more drastic change in my opinion of what the Soviets' ultimate goals are than anything they've done in the previous time

I've been in office." They also prompted a drastic change in his policies. On 3 January 1980, he asked the Senate to defer consideration of the SALT II treaty, effectively shelving the cornerstone of détente. The following day he declared that he was imposing sanctions against sales of grain and electronic technology to the USSR, restricting Soviet fishing rights in American waters, and taking a number of other punitive steps. Eventually, he would even go so far as to organize a sixty-nation boycott of the 1980 Olympic Summer Games in Moscow.

Carter's actions were governed not just by a personal sense of indignation and betrayal but also by concerns that the attack on Afghanistan was part of a larger Soviet strategy designed to gain access to the Indian Ocean and the Persian Gulf. This, he feared, would leave Moscow in a position to disrupt the Western world's crucial oil shipments. To preclude this, in his State of the Union message on 23 January 1980, he announced what came to be known as the Carter Doctrine. Henceforth, he declared, "an attempt by any outside force to gain control of the Persian Gulf will be regarded as an assault on the vital interests of the United States of America, and . . . will be repelled by any means necessary, including military force." He also initiated a number of measures designed to increase American military preparedness, including a reinstitution of draft registration and substantial increases in defense spending. He promised military and economic aid to Pakistan, Afghanistan's neighbor to the south, and the United States began secretly funneling aid through that country to the Afghan *mujaheddin* rebels. And in July, following a lengthy review of U.S. global strategy, he signed a presidential directive (PD-59) which seemed to shift the U.S. strategic emphasis from merely deterring nuclear war to actually planning to fight and win such a conflict. Although PD-59 was classified, its basic thrust was purposely leaked to the press as an indication to Moscow and others of Carter's tough new approach.

Meanwhile, the president was matching his anti-Soviet measures with renewed efforts to win the release of the American hostages in Tehran, including an attempted rescue mission in April which was aborted by the White House after eight U.S. soldiers were killed in a helicopter-airplane accident in the Iranian desert. That summer, Carter overcame a strong challenge from Senator Edward Kennedy and won renomination as the Democratic candidate for president, while Ronald Reagan emerged as his Republican opponent. Foreign policy concerns, including a growing perception of Soviet belligerence and U.S. impotence, promised to play a huge role in the upcoming fall campaign.

Then, as the election campaign was starting, Iran and Iraq went to war. Their conflict grew out of a longstanding Iraqi dream to unify the Arab world the way Prussia had united Germany in 1871. It was also conditioned by Baghdad's concern over Iran's Islamic fundamentalism, which threatened the secular regime of Iraqi president Saddam Hussein. In September, Hussein accused Iran of violating a 1975 treaty which guaranteed Iraq access to the

Persian Gulf through the Shatt al-Arab waterway. Using this as a pretext for war, he hoped for a quick victory over a nation at odds with its longtime American protector: with its U.S. assets frozen, he figured, Iran would be unable to obtain spare parts for its American-made jets and tanks. For his part, Iran's new leader, the Ayatollah Khomeini, hoped to weaken Iraq by appealing to Islamic fundamentalists therein. Both would be disappointed.

The war was destined to last eight years and to cost the lives of over a million Iraqis and perhaps two million Iranians, as each side wreaked havoc on the other's oil pipelines and refineries. Iraq was supported by Jordan, Saudi Arabia, Egypt, and Kuwait, while Iran was backed by Libya and Syria. Islamic fundamentalism, seen as a threat by those backing Iraq, would also be a factor in the assassination of Egypt's Sadat in 1981. Moscow opportunistically sold arms to both sides but eventually veered toward Iran. Israel weighed in by sending warplanes to destroy an Iraqi nuclear reactor in 1981. The United States supplied Iraq with intelligence data in an effort to balance the scales but otherwise played both ends against the middle throughout the long war, which would finally end in 1988 with a modest Iraqi victory.

The wars in Southwest Asia left East-West relations in shambles. Brezhnev's long search for international respect and economic stability, as well as his efforts to end the Cold War, had been sacrificed to the Kremlin's compulsion for solving its problems with force, especially in Afghanistan. By its failure to show restraint, either in its strategic buildup or in its Third World adventures, Moscow had persistently managed to embarrass its Western friends and play into the hands of its foes. Nowhere was this more true than in the case of Jimmy Carter, who had originally been willing and anxious to work with the Kremlin to create a more peaceful world.

Carter's forceful response to the Afghan affair was sufficient to dash any lingering hopes for détente, but it was not enough to save his presidency. Faced with a faltering economy and a leader who seemed powerless either to get the Soviets out of Afghanistan or to end the hostage crisis, Americans rejected Carter's bid for reelection in November 1980. Instead they elected an unabashed and unambiguous hardliner who believed that détente was a major mistake and who was determined to pursue a course of confrontation and competition with the Soviet regime.

THE REAGAN REVOLUTION

When he came to the White House in January of 1981, Ronald Wilson Reagan brought with him a sunny disposition, an abiding faith in the goodness of America, a visceral dislike of communism, and a lack of sophistication in world affairs. A former movie actor, he often tended to blur the lines between fiction and reality, to play loose with the facts, and to simplify complex issues into contests between right and wrong. At the same time, he possessed a remarkable knack for lifting people's spirits and projecting an image of optimism and confidence, qualities that would help make him one of the most popular and effective politicians of the entire Cold War era.

The Brezhnev regime, frustrated by the vacillations and inconsistencies of U.S. policy during the Carter years, was guardedly hopeful that Reagan would turn out to be a tough-minded yet pragmatic Republican in the Nixon mold. It was in for a big disappointment. Reagan did quickly jettison Carter's human rights approach, which the Kremlin had found so annoying, but he replaced it with a fervent and impassioned anticommunist crusade that tended to reduce superpower relations to a global struggle between good and evil. In his very first press conference, scarcely more than a week after taking office, he depicted the Soviet leaders as dangerous and dishonorable rogues who were bent on world domination and who would "reserve unto themselves the right to commit any crime, to lie, to cheat, in order to attain that." Two years later, in the most widely quoted speech of his presidency, he referred to the USSR as an "evil empire" and claimed that it was "the focus of evil in the modern world."

The new administration's approach to East-West relations was, thus, fundamentally different from those of the previous three. Rather than trying to control the arms race, the Reagan people wanted to intensify it. Many of them, like Secretary of Defense Caspar Weinberger and Assistant Secretary Richard Perle, believed that arms agreements with Moscow were inherently detrimental to American interests. Such treaties, they argued, tended to lull the West into complacency, legitimize Soviet behavior, and place more effective limits on the United States than the USSR, since the latter would invariably cheat. A renewed arms race, on the other hand, might further strain the Kremlin's resources, weaken the Soviet economy, and undermine the Soviet system itself. To these officials, whatever helped the USSR was bad for the United States, and whatever hurt it was good. Détente, to them, had bordered on unilateral disarmament, and the time had come to rearm.

So the first priority of Reagan's "foreign policy" was to build up the U.S. arsenal. The annual increase in defense spending, raised substantially during Carter's last year, was boosted again by Reagan, and Defense Secretary Weinberger vigorously resisted any effort to trim it. Weapons like the B-1 bomber, shelved by the Carter administration, were reintroduced, and existing arms programs were intensified. Over the next five years, the Pentagon would go on a spending spree, investing billions of dollars in programs like the "Stealth" aircraft (which were supposedly "invisible" to enemy radar), the Trident submarine and its D-5 missiles, the air- and ground-launched cruise missiles, the Pershing II intermediate-range missile, and the MX ICBM.

Among these weapons, the MX (or "Peacekeeper," as Reagan came to call it) raised some peculiar problems. A highly accurate and powerful ICBM which could carry ten nuclear warheads, it had been reluctantly approved by Carter in an effort to win military support for SALT II. But, since fixed land-based missiles were theoretically susceptible to a Soviet first strike, there was much debate about where and how to deploy it. A number of elaborate and expensive schemes were advanced to make the MX less vulnerable, but none of them proved practical. Finally, after several years of putting forth various alternatives, the Reagan administration decided simply to base the new missiles in converted Minuteman silos, after tacitly admitting that the "window of vulnerability" was not a serious concern.

The second priority, which arose out of the same mindset as the first, was to counteract the perceived Soviet threat in the Third World. This involved full-fledged support for authoritarian anticommunist regimes, whatever their record on human rights, and covert sponsorship of rebellions directed against Soviet client states. Abuses and atrocities committed by U.S. friends and patrons in Chile, El Salvador, Pakistan, South Africa, the Philippines, and elsewhere were generally overlooked, as long as the leaders remained rigidly anti-Soviet. Meanwhile, using indirect and sometimes direct means, the CIA helped provide arms and money to insurgent "freedom fighters" in places like Afghanistan, Angola, Ethiopia, and Nicaragua. Aid was even supplied to rebel forces in Cambodia, despite the fact that these forces included the murderous communist Khmer Rouge. Such policies did make some headway in countering the spread of Soviet influence, but they also undercut the U.S. image as a champion of democracy, legality, and human rights.

Nowhere was Reagan's new approach more apparent than in Central America, where a leftist insurgency in El Salvador and the victory of the Sandinista movement in Nicaragua in 1979 had raised fears of new Soviet inroads in the New World. President Carter had tried to save the Nicaraguan dictatorship of Anastasio Somoza but then continued U.S. aid to Managua after Somoza fell. When Reagan became president, he claimed that Central America had become the major target for Soviet Cold War expansionism. There was no definitive evidence to support this claim, but Moscow certainly did send military aid to leftists in both El Salvador and Nicaragua. The Reagan administration responded by organizing and equipping the Contra rebels, a Honduras-based military force bent on destroying the Sandinista regime. The resulting civil war ruined the Nicaraguan economy, but it would eventually lead to the ouster of the Sandinistas in a free election in 1990. Under Reagan, the United States also gave substantive aid to the democratic regime in El Salvador, despite an uncomfortable quantity of grave human rights abuses by that country's rulers and military.

Despite its confrontational attitude and its hard-line rhetoric, however, the Reagan administration was not entirely consistent in its anticommunist crusade. It lifted Carter's grain embargo against the USSR, largely in deference to domestic political and economic concerns. It adhered to the general terms of the unratified SALT II treaty, despite its disdain for that pact, since the Pentagon feared that renunciation might lead to an unrestrained Soviet arms buildup. And, although it toughened the U.S. stance significantly, it continued to negotiate with Moscow on issues of arms control. In the INF discussions, it put forth a "zero-option" plan calling for elimination of all Soviet intermediate-range missiles (especially the mobile SS-20s) and cancellation of NATO's planned deployment of cruise missiles and Pershing IIs. In the strategic weapons talks, it transformed SALT into START (Strategic Arms *Reduction* Talks) and then advocated sweeping cuts in the number of missile warheads allowed to either side. Critics charged, with some justification, that these were propaganda ploys rather than serious proposals, since they were heavily weighted against the USSR. And the Soviets indeed treated them as such. But Reagan, to the dismay of some of his advisors, had a genuine desire for real arms reduction. Several years later, in a much different climate, these proposals would serve as the basis for fruitful and productive negotiations.

There was, in fact, an interesting dichotomy in the Reagan approach to the USSR. On one hand, in order to justify its arms buildup and aggressive Third World policies, the administration liked to portray the USSR as a fearsome colossus with expanding power and influence, steadily increasing its military might and its dominion in the Third World. On the other hand, the Reagan people often displayed contempt for the Soviet potential to compete with the West and doubts about the viability of the Soviet system itself. The president himself, in March of 1983, prophetically dismissed communism as a "sad, bizarre chapter in history whose last pages are even now being written."

THE END OF THE BREZHNEV ERA

The latter depiction proved closer to the truth. By the early 1980s, the USSR had become a bumbling giant ruled by a gerontocracy of aging and infirm leaders who had increasingly lost confidence in themselves and their system. Brezhnev, who could barely stand up without support, continued to preside over a grossly inefficient economy and a vast bureaucracy rife with cronyism and corruption. Bogged down in Afghanistan and locked into a crippling new contest with the Americans, the Soviet Union drifted into the deadening "period of stagnation" that characterized the last few years of the Brezhnev era.

The Soviets did manage to maintain their hegemony over Eastern Europe but not without some difficulty. In the summer of 1980, in the midst of an economic crisis, there arose in Poland a genuine workers' movement which demanded and won the right to create a free and independent trade union known as Solidarity. Over the course of the next year, Solidarity grew increasingly popular and bold, organizing strikes and demonstrations and pressing for democratic reforms as well as economic concessions. As the situation deteriorated, and as the Polish government fell into disarray, Moscow grew increasingly alarmed. Fearful that the Polish Communists were losing their grip and that the unrest might spread throughout Eastern Europe, the Soviets began holding military exercises along the Polish border and hinting that they might intervene. NATO, in turn, warned Moscow to stay out, and by the fall of 1981 a potential crisis loomed. But the Kremlin, with uncharacteristic sophistication, succeeded in getting the Polish authorities to resolve the problem themselves. In December of 1981, the government of General Wojciech Jaruzelski declared martial law and swiftly cracked down on Solidarity, arresting many of its leading members and eventually outlawing the union. In the West, a frustrated Ronald Reagan could do little more than impose economic sanctions on both the USSR and Poland, while asking Americans to put candles in their windows as a sign of support for the Poles.

The imposition of martial law in Poland helped Moscow escape from an awkward situation, but it did not solve the underlying problem. Throughout 1982, the Polish economy continued to deteriorate, and U.S. sanctions only made matters worse. The USSR, already strapped by its own feeble economy and by its ongoing war in Afghanistan, was compelled to drain its own scarce resources to prop up the staggering Poles. Whatever its political and strategic benefits, the maintenance of Soviet influence in Poland and elsewhere was a serious economic liability.

Meanwhile, the Kremlin's "incursions" into the Third World were beginning to look more like defensive operations to prop up its sagging influence, or opportunistic attempts to capitalize on local rivalries, than elements of a coordinated quest for world domination. The USSR was able to realize few lasting gains from the Iran-Iraq War, despite its attempts to meddle, and it prudently passed up a chance to intervene in the short Falklands War between Britain and Argentina in 1982. In the latter conflict, the ruling Argentine military junta, having been led by American UN ambassador Jeane Kirkpatrick to believe that Washington would back its claims to the British-held Falkland Islands (which Argentina called the Malvinas), invaded those islands in April. When the Reagan administration instead supported the British counterattack with all aid short of war, the junta asked Moscow for assistance, holding out promises of favorable credit terms for the delivery of Argentine wheat to the USSR. But the concept of Soviet troops landing on remote islands in the south Atlantic to fight the British would have been ludicrous even had the Soviet army not been bogged down in the deepening Afghan quagmire. Britain won the war, the Argentine junta fell, and all the while the Kremlin remained aloof.

Moscow also suffered a serious loss of face in the Middle East that same year, when it failed to aid the PLO during an Israeli invasion of Lebanon designed to eradicate the Palestinian presence there. Worse still, perhaps, its reputation as a weapons provider was badly tarnished when Israeli pilots in American-made planes easily destroyed numerous aircraft, tanks, and weapons that had been supplied by the Kremlin to its Arab friends. Thus, although Israel was soon compelled to withdraw, and although 239 of the U.S. soldiers sent in to keep the peace would be killed by a terrorist bomb the following year, Moscow was able to draw little comfort from the Lebanese conflict.

Brezhnev's funeral, 1982, Pallbearers include his immediate successors, Andropov and Cherneko, on the right. (ITAR-TASS/Sovfoto/Eastfoto)

THE ANDROPOV OFFENSIVE

On 7 November 1982, the sixty-fifth anniversary of the Bolshevik Revolution, Leonid Brezhnev stood as usual atop the Lenin Mausoleum, reviewing the endless military parades in the cold, damp Moscow weather. Three days later he was dead. The last year of his life had been marred by a serious scandal affecting members of his own family, by a minor stroke that left him increasingly feeble, and by a behind-the-scenes power struggle among those who hoped to succeed him.

The winner of that struggle was Iurii V. Andropov. As the longtime head of the Committee on State Security (KGB), the Soviet police apparatus, Andropov had earned a reputation as an effective, innovative, and sophisticated administrator. Flexible, intelligent, and direct, he might have made a very effective general secretary had he come to power sooner. As it was, he was already sixty-eight years old and in poor health by the time he reached the top. In domestic affairs, he sought to instill more discipline and efficiency into the Soviet system, cracking down on the chronic corruption and absenteeism that had plagued the Brezhnev economy, and granting more autonomy to local industrial managers. He was blocked, however, by the inertia and stagnation of the immense Soviet bureaucracy and by his own kidney failure. He was destined to last only fifteen months in office.

On the international scene, Andropov at first sought to improve relations with both China and the West. In neither case did he achieve much success. He adopted a conciliatory tone toward China and, following through on an initiative that had begun under Brezhnev, reopened low-level discussions with Beijing early in 1983. Some progress was made in expanding trade, but there was little improvement of the political climate between the two countries. The Chinese made it clear that they could not normalize relations with Moscow as long as there were still Soviet troops in Afghanistan, Vietnamese forces in Cambodia, and a massive Soviet military presence along the Chinese border.

With respect to the West, Andropov launched a "peace offensive," hoping to revive the stalled arms talks and head off the scheduled deployment of U.S. missiles in Europe. Advised by his friend Georgii Arbatov, the top Soviet expert on U.S. affairs, he sought to take advantage of the growing peace movement in Western Europe and America. Here he was inadvertently aided by Ronald Reagan, whose aggressive rhetoric, along with the injudicious sabrerattling of some of his subordinates, had helped to create the impression that the United States was headed by a reckless band of trigger-happy cowboys.

In the early 1980s, as détente disappeared and the weapons buildup accelerated, fears of a nuclear holocaust had returned with full force. Books and films on atomic war contributed to public anxiety. Across America, there arose a grassroots "nuclear freeze" campaign, calling for an immediate end to the arms race. By 1983, polls showed widespread support for this movement, and in spring of that year a "freeze" resolution was adopted by the House of Representatives. Meanwhile, the U.S. Catholic bishops were publishing a sweeping pastoral letter challenging the morality of nuclear arms. In Western Europe, protests were directed against the proposed deployment of American Pershing II and cruise missiles, slated for the end of 1983. The "Greens," a left-wing political party which vehemently opposed this deployment, garnered impressive support in Germany, and antinuclear demonstrations were held in a number of places.

Andropov's peace initiative sought to build on these sentiments and use them to Soviet advantage. In December of 1982, he put forth a series of new arms control proposals, showing an apparent new flexibility in Moscow's position. In the START negotiations, he called on both sides to cut their strategic missiles by 25 percent, and to reduce significantly the number of nuclear warheads. In the INF talks, he evinced a willingness to scale back the number of Soviet intermediate-range missiles to equal the combined number of French and British missiles—as long as the pending U.S. deployment would be canceled. Like Reagan's "zero option," these offers were designed with an eye to public opinion in the West and worded so as to maintain the proposer's overall advantage. Still, they did show an increasing Soviet willingness to talk about *reductions* rather than limitations.

These proposals were followed by a public relations campaign, obviously designed to portray the Reagan crowd as warmongers and win sympathy for Moscow within the peace movement in the West. Speaking at Prague in January of 1983, the Soviet leader adroitly identified himself with the "forces of peace" and appealed for a new East-West nonaggression pact by which both sides would forswear first use of conventional or nuclear weapons. In February, letters to Andropov from concerned U.S. citizens began to appear in the Soviet press. In April, a young American girl named Samantha Smith, who had written one of those letters, was invited to visit the USSR, and in July she was warmly and publicly received by her Soviet hosts.

The Andropov peace offensive, however, eventually came to naught. One reason was that Western leaders were able to resist the pressures from the peace movement. In March, despite ill-concealed Soviet efforts to sway the election against him, conservative Christian Democrat Helmut Kohl was reaffirmed as West German chancellor. In May, the heads of the seven leading industrial democracies (Britain, France, Germany, Italy, Japan, Canada, and the United States) met at Williamsburg, Virginia, and endorsed the NATO decision to deploy U.S. Pershing II and cruise missiles. In June, Prime Minister Margaret Thatcher's Conservatives won a clear majority in the British House of Commons. To some extent, by raising the specter of outside influence, Soviet efforts to exploit the peace crusade may actually have helped the hardliners. At any rate, whatever their private misgivings about the Reagan administration, NATO leaders decided not to let internal and external pressures disrupt alliance solidarity.

THE STRATEGIC DEFENSE INITIATIVE

Another reason for the failure of the peace initiative was the fact that Ronald Reagan had his own agenda and his own unique dream. In March of 1983, he complicated the arms control process enormously by suddenly announcing, to the surprise of many of his advisors, a project to create and build an elaborate space-based weapons system designed to intercept enemy ICBMs. "What if free people," he asked in a televised address, "could rest secure in the knowledge . . . that we could intercept and destroy strategic ballistic missiles before they reached our own soil or that of our allies?" Keying in to the fears that had spawned the nuclear freeze movement, he challenged U.S. scientists to develop new technologies that would help make nuclear weapons "impotent and obsolete." Although Reagan would call this his "Strategic Defense Initiative," it soon became known as "Star Wars," after a popular American movie in which the forces of good used futuristic space technology to combat an evil empire.

The Strategic Defense Initiative, or SDI, raised several serious problems. For one thing, there was no guarantee that such a system would work, at least as the president envisioned it. Using advanced technologies, scientists might indeed be able to design weapons that could shoot down missiles, but there was no way to make them foolproof, and the few hostile missiles that did get through could still do incalculable damage. And, of course, there would be nothing to stop a sophisticated adversary from inventing weapons that could frustrate or destroy the SDI components. For these reasons, knowledgeable supporters of the project tended to see it not as an impenetrable shield for the entire country but rather as a more limited system capable of defending land-based missiles against a surprise attack.

Another problem with SDI was that it would violate the spirit, if not the letter, of the ABM treaty. For over a decade, the 1972 agreement had stood as a cornerstone of arms control and a bulwark of mutual deterrence. Now, by reopening the question of missile defense, Reagan called into question the whole basis of East-West discussions. And the president's offer to "share" this technology, even though it was apparently sincere, was so widely at variance with traditional U.S. behavior that it was not taken seriously in Moscow. For the next five years, Reagan's "shield" would hang like a dark cloud over the arms control process.

From the Soviets' perspective, the biggest concern about SDI was that it could negate their entire strategic deterrent. An American president, armed with such a system, might be tempted to launch a preemptive attack, knowing that Star Wars would be there to protect against surviving enemy missiles. But the United States would not actually need to attack in order to gain the edge: when two gunslingers face each other, even if neither intends to shoot, the one wearing armor has a distinct psychological advantage. Besides, although Soviet scientists discounted the possibility of a foolproof missile defense system, the very thought of SDI renewed Moscow's fears about the prowess of U.S. technology. Time and again, from the A-bomb to the MIRV to the cruise missile, the Soviets had seen their monumental efforts to achieve parity and security frustrated by Western technological advances. If Star Wars could be made to work, they would again be vulnerable.

From Reagan's perspective, however, the SDI provided several important benefits. To some extent, by promising to do away with the threat of nuclear war, it disarmed his critics in the peace movement. It helped him to answer Andropov's peace offensive without making major concessions on either strategic arms or INF deployment. It replaced his "reckless cowboy" image with that of a visionary, albeit one who would rely on technology to resolve human relations problems. And it provided him with a pathway to peace that the United States could pursue on its own, without having to rely on the cooperation of people that he instinctively distrusted.

The Kremlin's response to the SDI was as harsh as it was predictable. Andropov blasted the proposal as a U.S. attempt to "disarm the Soviet Union," then launched a new campaign to discredit Reagan's initiative. He enlisted the support of Soviet scientists, who published an appeal to their colleagues everywhere to oppose the Star Wars proposal. He publicly advocated intensified arms control efforts, hoping to preclude both SDI research and INF deployment. And finally, in a meeting with a U.S. delegation in August of 1983, he called for the total demilitarization of outer space, including a ban on all space-based weapons and antisatellite systems.

THE KAL INCIDENT AND THE GRENADA INVASION

The Soviet leader's initiative, however, was soon undercut by some portentous developments. One was his own illness: by fall 1983, he had disappeared from public view, a victim of the kidney disease that would eventually take his life. Another was a tragic incident that occurred in the skies near the Soviet island of Sakhalin, just to the north of Japan. A third was the U.S. invasion of a tiny Caribbean island.

On 1 September 1983, a South Korean airliner, KAL flight 007, veered off course during a scheduled flight between the United States and South Korea. It flew through Soviet airspace, passing over a sensitive missile and submarine base, until it was finally shot down by a Soviet pilot who evidently thought it was a U.S. spy plane. All 269 persons aboard were killed. The downing of the passenger aircraft and killing of innocent civilians brought a wave of international outrage against the USSR. Reagan accused the Kremlin of a deliberate act of "barbarism" and used the incident as a further justification for his weapons buildup. Moscow refused to accept the blame and, when it finally did admit responsibility, accused the United States of having precipitated the incident by using the civilian plane for an espionage mission. Vitriolic rhetoric emanated from both sides, and Andropov finally issued a statement saying that any illusions about an improvement in Reagan's policy had been dispelled "once and for all."

The KAL incident, and the bitter accusations that followed, contributed to a further poisoning of international relations, as did the U.S. invasion of the Caribbean island nation of Grenada in the fall of that year (see Map 7, p. 267). The Grenada expedition was undertaken in response to the overthrow of the Marxist New Jewel Movement by an even more radical Marxist group. Cuban engineers and construction workers were building an immense airfield on the island, and Washington distrusted their intentions. In October 1983, the Reagan administration sent a large contingent of U.S. Marines and Rangers to Grenada, overwhelming the small force of Cuban troops and installing a provisional government. The intervention was carried out quickly and destroyed the Marxist regime with nothing but verbal objections from Moscow, similar to the sort of protests with which Washington contented itself whenever the USSR moved against Eastern Europe.

As a result of these developments, any hopes for further progress in the INF talks were effectively destroyed, at least for the time being. In November, the planned deployment of U.S. cruise and Pershing II missiles began as scheduled in Britain and Germany. The Soviets responded, as promised, by breaking off the INF talks in Geneva, and shortly thereafter the START nego-

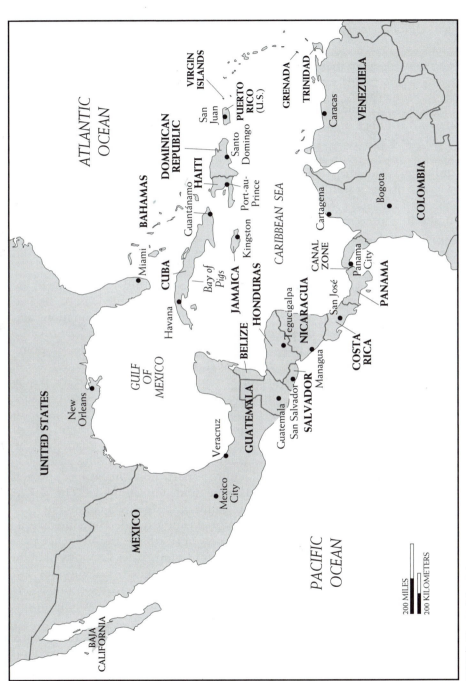

MAP 7 Central America

tiations were indefinitely recessed. By the end of 1983, superpower relations seemed to have reached a new low.

THE ENCORE OF THE SOVIET OLD GUARD

During the last several months of 1983, as his health deteriorated, Iurii Andropov began making a series of personnel changes designed to ensure his legacy. A number of younger, more energetic, reform-minded officials were promoted to positions of increased responsibility on both the national and the regional level. Growing prominence was given to Mikhail Gorbachev, Andropov's dynamic young protégé, as the dying party boss evidently sought to secure his succession. But Andropov did not live long enough to achieve his goal: on 9 February 1984, he finally succumbed to his illness. Four days later an old Brezhnev crony, Konstantin Chernenko, was named general secretary of the Soviet Communist party. In an apparent compromise between the old guard and the younger generation, Gorbachev was given the duties of "second secretary," effectively making him second in command.

Konstantin Ustinovich Chernenko was the oldest and least capable of the Soviet Cold War leaders. A man of modest ability and limited vision, he had risen through the party ranks by virtue of hard work, determination, and dogged loyalty to Leonid Brezhnev, his longtime patron and friend. During the last years of Brezhnev's regime, in fact, he had played a major role, propping up the infirm leader in public and conducting much of his business for him behind the scenes. Now, at the age of 72, Chernenko had reached the pinnacle of his career, but he had neither the energy nor the ambition to revitalize the Soviet system. Caution and prudence were the keywords of his watch. To some extent, then, his accession brought a return to the stagnation and drift of the last Brezhnev years and a short-lived resurgence of the old guard. Still, he did not seek to undo all of Andropov's reforms, merely to slow the pace.

For most of Chernenko's brief tenure as party boss, the Soviet approach toward world affairs remained rigid, static, and unimaginative. The war in Afghanistan continued with no end in sight, and Moscow's commitment to the Jaruzelski regime in Poland was reinforced and extended by a fifteen-year economic pact. Despite occasional glimmers of flexibility, intransigence generally reigned in dealings with the West. And Sino-Soviet relations likewise failed to improve. Unlike his predecessor, who had sought to enhance ties with the world's most populous communist country, Chernenko was noticeably cool toward China, especially as the climate warmed between Washington and Beijing.

Sino-American relations had suffered a temporary setback in the early Reagan years, thanks to the new president's sympathy for Taiwan and general antipathy toward all Communists. But as time went on, and as relations with the USSR worsened, Reagan and his advisors had begun to see some potential value in using Beijing as a counterpoise against Moscow. In 1982, they had taken a step toward accommodation by agreeing to gradually reduce their weapons sales to Taiwan, a major bone of contention between the United States and the PRC. During the course of 1983, a number of key American officials had traveled to China, and the atmosphere had begun to improve. The most dramatic developments, however, came in 1984. In January, Chinese premier Zhao Ziyang made a state visit to Washington, and in April President Reagan returned the favor with a high-profile trip to Beijing. No major accords were reached during these visits, but they did restore the momentum of U.S.–Chinese rapprochement. And, of course, they made great theater, giving Reagan a statesmanlike aura and enhancing his status in the upcoming presidential campaign.

Although Chinese officials politely but firmly rebuffed the president's efforts to enlist their support against Moscow, the Kremlin was clearly displeased by the Reagan visit. In May, shortly after the president had left Beijing, Moscow issued a statement denouncing the Chinese for their role in a border clash with Vietnam that had occurred while he was there. A few days later, the Soviets disclosed that an impending trip to China by First Deputy Prime Minister Ivan Arkhipov had been postponed.

Meanwhile, Soviet-American relations continued to deteriorate. Hoping that Ronald Reagan might somehow be defeated in the approaching U.S. elections, the Kremlin tried to avoid doing anything that might improve the international climate and thus boost his electoral standing. The START negotiations and INF talks remained suspended, as the Soviets resisted efforts by their unruly ally, Romania's Nicolae Ceausescu, to get them to moderate their stance. Unless the new U.S. missiles were removed from Western Europe, they continued to insist, no negotiations were possible. In May, the "deep freeze" between the United States and the USSR was intensified by the announcement that Soviet and Eastern European athletes would not attend the Olympic Summer Games in Los Angeles. Although the decision was officially attributed to concerns for the athletes' safety, few doubted that it was made in retaliation for Reagan's blatant anti-Soviet policies and Carter's boycott of the 1980 Moscow games.

In August, a bizarre incident added to the strain between Moscow and Washington. Playfully testing his sound equipment before a radio broadcast, Reagan announced that he had "just signed legislation which outlaws Russia forever," adding that "the bombing begins in five minutes." This peculiar attempt at humor was overheard by reporters and widely disseminated. Moscow responded by condemning the president's irresponsible conduct and blasting his blatant hostility toward the USSR. The episode had no lasting repercussions, but it did serve to highlight the "recklessness" of Reagan, the extreme sensitivity of the Kremlin, and the deplorable state of U.S.–Soviet relations.

If the Soviets believed that incidents like this, combined with heightened world tensions, would damage the president's reelection chances, their hopes were in vain. Reagan's standing in the polls remained high, and he recovered from a lackluster performance in his first televised debate by seeming strong and self-assured in his second. In November, he was returned to office by a wide margin. On the surface, at least, it looked as if the prospects for easing anxieties had once again been set back.

Behind the scenes, however, things were beginning to change. In the Kremlin, as the aging Soviet leaders grew increasingly feeble, the younger ones were becoming more assertive and more visible. In December of 1984, Mikhail Gorbachev made a highly publicized trip to Great Britain, where he handled himself with great confidence and spoke with apparent authority. It was he, rather than Chernenko, who announced to the world that month the death of Soviet defense minister Dmitri Ustinov, and it was he who led the mourners at the burial rites. A few months later, the young second secretary made another trip abroad, this time to West Germany. Meanwhile, Chernenko, whose health was rapidly failing, had largely disappeared from public view.

The growing visibility of Gorbachev was accompanied by a perceptible change in Moscow's foreign policy. Once it was clear that Reagan would be reelected, the Soviets began to moderate their tone and try to make the best of the situation. Late in 1984, they launched a new peace offensive, designed to mend their fences with both China and the West. In December, First Deputy Prime Minister Arkhipov finally made his long-delayed trip to Beijing, becoming the highest level Soviet official to visit China in over fifteen years. That same month, on his sojourn to Britain, Gorbachev cleverly reminded his listeners that he and they shared a "common European home" and suggested that their relations should not depend on what took place in Washington. This theme was expanded during his subsequent German trip.

In January of 1985, after a whole year of probing and posturing, the Soviets finally consented to resume the arms control talks. Bowing to reality, they dropped their insistence that Washington first remove its newly installed missiles from Europe. It was agreed, however, that space-based weapons should be added to the discussions, along with intermediate-range missiles and strategic arms. The new talks were set to begin on 12 March 1985. The day before they opened, word came from Moscow that Konstantin Chernenko had died the previous evening.

The death of Chernenko marked the passing of the generation of Soviet leaders who had risen in the ranks under Stalin and whose outlook had been shaped by the searing experiences of industrialization, collectivization, and World War II. Obsessed with concerns for security and control, they had built the USSR into a military colossus of awesome power and strength, while maintaining tight constraints over all aspects of domestic society. In so doing they had constructed a stultifying bureaucratic edifice that served both to secure their power and stifle creativity. Waiting in the wings was a new generation, unencumbered by the presentiments of their predecessors and fully prepared to make major changes in the way the USSR did business. A new age was dawning in the Kremlin.

16

The Thaw in the Cold War, 1985–1988

The selection of Mikhail Gorbachev as general secretary of the Communist party of the Soviet Union in March 1985 marked a major turning point in Soviet politics and East-West relations. As the representative of a new generation of Soviet leaders, Gorbachev had fewer qualms than any of his predecessors about overturning long-cherished policies and procedures. Over the next six years, he and his colleagues would introduce a breathtaking series of innovations in both the domestic and international arenas. These reforms, designed to transform the USSR into a more modern, open, and productive society, were eventually destined to fail. But before they did they would revolutionize Soviet and world affairs and bring the Cold War to an end.

THE DAWN OF THE GORBACHEV ERA

On 11 March 1985, only hours after the formal announcement that Konstantin Chernenko had died, the Soviet news agency officially reported that Mikhail Gorbachev had been chosen as the next general secretary. His selection was facilitated by longtime foreign minister Andrei Gromyko, who gave a strong nominating speech praising Gorbachev's intelligence, vigor, organizational skill, and strength. "This man has a nice smile," Gromyko allegedly remarked, "but he has iron teeth."

Mikhail Sergeevich Gorbachev was fifty-four years of age when he took over as general secretary, making him the youngest Soviet leader since

Malenkov. Born in a farming village in south central Russia, just north of the Caucasus Mountains, he had experienced as a youth both the rigors of physical labor and the trauma of the Nazi invasion. A gifted student, he attended law school at Moscow State University in the early 1950s and then returned to his native province, where he began working his way up through the ranks of the Communist Youth League and the Communist party. Talented, energetic, independent, and articulate, he possessed a supreme self-confidence and mental agility that made him a standout among local party officials. A devoted Leninist, he was nonetheless offended by the police state brutality of the Stalin years and thus much in sympathy with the reform-minded and humanizing policies of Nikita Khrushchev.

Although Gorbachev had less use for the Brezhnev regime, he was circumspect enough to play along with the system in order to advance his career. In the 1970s, he attracted the attention of several high officials, including future party boss Iurii Andropov, and in 1978 he was summoned to Moscow to serve as party secretary in charge of agriculture. Two years later he joined the Politburo, the party's main policy-making body, and in 1982 he supported Andropov's bid to become general secretary. Although he was groomed as Andropov's successor, his patron's early death delayed his succession, and he was obliged to bide his time during the thirteen months of Chernenko's ineffective rule. Now, at last, his turn had come, and he was ready to move.

The situation that Gorbachev inherited was nothing short of critical. Over the previous two decades, while military expenses had eaten up an enormous share of the Soviet budget, the rate of economic growth had declined. The nation's industrial equipment and transportation system had grown increasingly outmoded. Productivity was low, consumer goods were in short supply, their quality was shoddy, and living standards were closer to those of a Third World country than a modern superpower. In the workplace, drunkenness and absenteeism were epidemic, and the government bureaucracy was riddled with corruption and cynicism. Agricultural output was inadequate, and the USSR regularly had to import huge amounts of grain. Public health, too, was in sorry shape, with infant mortality rising and average lifespan shrinking. And, despite their awesome military might, the Soviets were falling so far behind in computer and electronics technology that they no longer could be sure of maintaining their superpower status in the foreseeable future.

A key element of Gorbachev's approach was the fresh spirit of openness, or *glasnost*, that he sought to impart to the political and cultural milieu. The USSR, he reasoned, could never hope to deal successfully with its problems if it continued to pretend they did not exist. What was needed, in his opinion, was a full and frank discussion of the Soviet situation, which would hopefully unlock the energy, originality, and creativity which had been stifled by the moribund system. Although *glasnost* did not amount to full freedom of speech, it did allow citizens a greater opportunity to speak their minds than ever before, and it enabled academics to begin to write the truth about Soviet society and the Soviet past. Eventually, it would also unleash a torrent of pent-up nationalist strivings and ethnic hostilities that would undermine the foundations of the USSR itself.

In domestic affairs, the new party boss launched a sustained effort at *perestroika*, or restructuring of the Soviet system. At first, it was fairly mild, largely mirroring the policies of previous reformers like Khrushchev and Andropov, and involving campaigns to combat alcoholism and absenteeism, to root out corruption, and to improve the productivity of Soviet workers. Eventually, however, Gorbachev would go far beyond his predecessors and introduce changes designed to decentralize the economy, grant more autonomy to farmers and factory managers, introduce profit incentives and a limited market economy, permit the establishment of privately owned businesses, and encourage foreign corporations to participate in enterprises within the USSR. To the end, however, he would resist the onset of full free market capitalism: his self-appointed mission was to save socialism, not to destroy or replace it.

To a certain extent, Gorbachev's approach was modeled after that of Franklin Roosevelt, the U.S. president who had likewise taken command of his country during an economic crisis. Aleksandr Yakovlev, one of Gorbachev's closest advisors, had done research on Roosevelt while at Columbia University and had been impressed with that president's pragmatic flexibility. Just as Roosevelt had "saved" capitalism by introducing elements of socialism into the U.S. economy, Gorbachev would seek to rescue socialism by fostering capitalist incentives in the USSR. Just as Roosevelt had initiated myriad new programs in an effort to find something that worked, Gorbachev would launch numerous initiatives with no clear pattern or scheme. Just as Roosevelt had launched a New Deal, Gorbachev would initiate New Thinking.

In Gorbachev's New Thinking, foreign policies and domestic goals were inextricably intertwined. If the USSR was going to maintain its superpower status, it would have to create an economy that was capable of fostering technological innovation and vastly increased production of goods and services. To do this, it would be necessary to stop the enormous drain caused by military expenses and support of foreign clients. The arms race had provided the USSR with enormous destructive power, but it had not brought security; if anything, it had given Moscow's foes the incentive to remain united and develop new weapons capable of destroying the Soviet homeland. The domination of Eastern Europe, and the sponsorship of socialist regimes in places like Cuba and Afghanistan, whatever the political benefits, had proven a massive burden for the weak Soviet economy to bear. Moscow needed to draw down its vast military forces, slash its defense budget, and make severe cutbacks in the amount expended to prop up the economies of client states. And it could not accomplish these things unless and until it achieved a more relaxed international climate and better relations with the West.

During his first few months in office, following through on the "common European home" theme that he had sounded during the waning months of the Chernenko regime, Gorbachev sought to improve relations with Western European nations in hopes of encouraging them to become more independent of their American allies. Just as Soviet belligerence had helped to forge the Atlantic alliance and keep it bound together, Soviet accommodation might, he hoped, erode the cohesion of that alliance by removing its raison d'être.

These efforts were unwittingly assisted by the U.S. president himself. In May 1985, Reagan's aides had arranged for him to visit a military cemetery at Bitburg, West Germany, as part of a trip to Europe to commemorate the fortieth anniversary of the end of World War II. Shortly after this visit was scheduled, however, it was discovered that a number of Nazi SS troops had been buried there, and Reagan was urged to cancel the engagement. But, under pressure from Bonn, the president went ahead with his cemetery speech, after a clumsy attempt to defend the SS members as "victims" of Nazism. He then sought to repair the damage with a hastily arranged visit to a Nazi concentration camp, in order to honor its victims, but the damage had been done. Reagan managed to offend veterans' groups, Jews, and other important constituencies on both sides of the Atlantic.

A more serious strain on U.S.–European relations was occasioned by the president's unreserved commitment to his Strategic Defense Initiative. The fact that SDI was designed to protect against the intercontinental missiles that endangered the United States and USSR, but not necessarily against the medium- and short-range weapons that threatened Western and Central Europe, was not lost on America's NATO allies. European leaders worried that the Star Wars system, combined with the probable Soviet development of a missile defense system in response, might increase the likelihood of war in Europe by lessening the dangers of such a conflict for the superpowers. Their worries were probably unfounded, since even with SDI in place, a war in Europe would still bring unacceptable risks and consequences for both Washington and Moscow. But Reagan's apparent obsession troubled the Europeans and conjured up old anxieties about the long-term reliability of their American ally.

Aided by Foreign Minister Gromyko, Gorbachev at first tried to play on these divisions and use them to Soviet advantage. He began publicly to criticize the SDI and to warn that, if the United States continued to pursue this venture, it would undermine the arms talks which had recently resumed in Geneva. He even implied that the Soviets might once again walk out of these talks if real progress was not made on the issue of space-based weapons. On a more positive note, in April 1985 he declared that the USSR would unilaterally halt its nuclear testing and cease deploying new intermediate-range nuclear missiles aimed at Western Europe. The following month, he announced that the USSR was anxious to improve relations with the European Economic Community, the so-called Common Market of Western

European nations. To this end, he added, Soviet bloc countries would be permitted for the first time to negotiate bilateral agreements with the EEC. This was an obvious attempt to encourage the growing independence of Western Europe and to treat it as a separate entity from the United States. But it also held out the prospect of a more subtle benefit for the Kremlin: if the nations of Eastern Europe could forge closer economic ties with the West, they might presumably become less of a drain on Moscow's inadequate resources.

For all of his focus on Europe, however, and despite some simultaneous efforts to improve relations with China, Gorbachev was enough of a realist to understand that no easing of world tensions was possible without direct negotiations between the USSR and the United States. He therefore began to move in this direction. A potential obstacle was removed on 2 July 1985 when Andrei Gromyko, long a symbol of negotiating intransigence, was removed as foreign minister and "promoted" to the largely ceremonial position of Soviet president. He was replaced as foreign minister by Eduard Shevardnadze, an urbane, articulate Georgian and a close friend of Gorbachev, who was soon to become a symbol of Moscow's new reasonableness and flexibility.

In their efforts to improve the international climate, Gorbachev and Shevardnadze would meet with a surprisingly ready response from Ronald Reagan, the very archetype of the hard-line anti-Soviet American Cold Warrior. For all of his bombast and belligerence, Reagan was something of a dreamer, and he had long harbored hopes of ending the nuclear threat and creating a more peaceful world. He abhorred the notions of nuclear deterrence and mutual assured destruction, and he was partial to schemes, like the SDI, that might end the balance of terror. During the course of 1984, with one eye on U.S. election-year politics and the other on European opinion, he had moderated his anti-Soviet rhetoric, talked of his plans to form a constructive relationship with the USSR, and bemoaned the fact that the aging Soviet leaders kept dying before he had a chance to meet them. In 1985, with his last campaign behind him and his place in history increasingly on his mind, he began to make good on this rhetoric. In March, when Vice-President George Bush went to Moscow for Chernenko's funeral, he brought with him a letter from Reagan inviting the new Soviet leader to visit the United States. Although Gorbachev was anxious to meet with the president, he was reluctant to have their first encounter take place on Reagan's turf, and several months of negotiations were needed to find an appropriate setting. Finally, in July, it was announced that the two leaders would meet in November at Geneva, the site of the ongoing arms control talks.

SUMMITRY, START, AND STAR WARS

The two world leaders prepared for their first meeting, and the first superpower summit conference in more than six years, in vastly different ways. Reagan, a simple and straightforward man who allowed his schedule to be determined in part by the advice of his wife's astrologer, was much more relaxed in his approach. Although his aides provided him with negotiating points, and even lined up a tutor to coach him on Russian affairs, the president was not the sort to immerse himself in details or to "bone up" for a historic encounter. His forte was person-to-person politics, and his main objective was to get to know the man with whom he shared the awesome responsibility of deciding the future of the planet.

Gorbachev, at his typical frenetic pace, moved forward simultaneously on several fronts, employing his considerable public relations skills to pressure the United States into a more accommodating position. In August, he gave an interview to *Time* magazine in which he noted with approval Reagan's expressed opinion that nuclear war was unwinnable and suggested that this might become the basis for future agreement between the two powers. In October, he flew to Paris, met with French president François Mitterrand, stressed the importance of Soviet relations with Western Europe, and declared that the USSR would pursue its agenda by "force of example" rather than "force of arms." He also offered to negotiate a 50 percent cut in strategic nuclear forces, provided that the United States drop its Star Wars program, and to work toward an agreement on medium-range missiles without waiting for progress on strategic and space-based weapons. That same month he consolidated his power in Moscow by securing the replacement of Nikolai Tikhonov, the elderly Soviet premier who had succeeded Aleksei Kosygin in 1980, with reformer Nikolai Ryzhkov.

The actual meeting in Geneva did not go according to script. Anxious for a "one-on-one" encounter with the Soviet leader with no advisors present, Reagan suggested that they spend their first scheduled break in a beach house, by a quiet fireplace, overlooking the beautiful lake. Much to the consternation of their aides, who didn't dare break up the private meeting, the planned twelve-minute interlude stretched on for well over an hour. With only their interpreters present, the two men talked about their hopes and dreams and responsibilities, expressed their mutual abhorrence of nuclear war, and even made tentative plans to meet again in Washington in 1986.

The formal meetings at Geneva produced little of substance. To be sure, a joint statement was issued calling for an interim agreement on intermediate-range nuclear forces (INF), and a decision was made to look into the feasibility of setting up "nuclear risk reduction centers" in Washington and Moscow. But, as Gorbachev quickly ascertained, Reagan was clearly captivated with SDI and not interested in making any concessions on it to facilitate arms control progress.

Still, the summit was far from inconsequential. The world's two most powerful leaders had met, taken each other's measure, and established a personal chemistry that would serve them well during the difficult years ahead. Although Gorbachev was frustrated by the president's Star Wars obsession, he was pleased to learn that Reagan was not afraid to discuss sweeping changes in the nuclear status quo. The president, for his part, was charmed by the Soviet leader, and this would have a profound impact on the thinking of Ronald Reagan. He had met with the leader of the evil empire—and found that he liked the guy! For a man who was more interested in personality than policy, this was a development of major significance indeed.

In the aftermath of the Geneva conference, Gorbachev moved quickly and boldly to maintain the momentum achieved and to give a boost to the Strategic Arms Reduction Talks (START) which had shown little progress since their resumption in March 1985. On 15 January 1986, in a highly touted speech, he put forth a stunning proposal for the abolition of all nuclear weapons, in three stages, by the year 2000. According to his plan, conventional weapons would likewise be reduced by then to a level that would preclude either side from launching a massive or sustained attack. In the INF arena, he announced that for the first time Moscow was ready to negotiate the removal of all U.S. and Soviet intermediate-range missiles from Europe, without reference to French and British nuclear missiles, thus effectively endorsing Reagan's "zero-option" proposal of 1981. And, in an aspect of his speech that received insufficient attention, he professed his willingness to accept comprehensive verification measures, including on-site inspections, to ensure that both sides complied. For four decades, Soviet resistance to such procedures had been a major obstacle to effective arms control.

These proposals were clearly designed partly to call Reagan's bluff and partly to steal a march on the Strategic Defense Initiative. Like his predecessors, Gorbachev was deeply impressed with the potential of U.S. technology, and he feared that a workable Star Wars system could upset the balance of terror and give the United States an overwhelming political and psychological advantage. Worse yet, from his perspective, U.S. progress on SDI would initiate a new arms race, forcing Moscow to follow suit with a costly missile defense of its own. This, in turn, would further strain Soviet resources and severely endanger his domestic economic agenda. In this context, Gorbachev's audacious proposal to eliminate all nuclear weapons provided a much cheaper and more secure way to accomplish what SDI was supposedly intended to achieve. If Reagan was serious about his oft-expressed desire to make serious cuts in both sides' nuclear arsenals, then perhaps he would agree to limits on SDI in return for real progress on arms reduction. If not, at least it would become clear to the world who was the real stumbling block to ending the nuclear threat.

In fact, the Soviet proposals did occasion some dissension in Western ranks. Certain of Reagan's advisors, including arms negotiator Paul Nitze, wanted to take up Gorbachev's challenge and work out a "grand compromise" whereby deep cuts in nuclear weaponry would be accompanied by U.S. agreement to confine Star Wars research to the laboratory. The president, however, was too deeply wedded to the SDI to go along with that. At the same time, many European leaders had serious reservations about reducing nuclear stockpiles too sharply. For one thing, having invested considerable political capital in getting their nations to accept the deployment of new U.S. medium-range missiles, they were in no hurry to see these missiles removed. For another thing, having depended for decades on nuclear deterrence to maintain the peace in Europe, they were a bit wary of the prospect that talk of a "nuclear-free world" might someday become a reality.

Events soon proved they had reason for concern. Throughout spring and summer of 1986, Gorbachev continued to press Reagan on the issue of SDI, and he persisted in putting forth creative arms control proposals. He called for a total ban on nuclear testing, including underground blasts, knowing that such a prohibition could hamper SDI research. He suggested that both sides pledge to abide by the ABM treaty, which expressly forbade the deployment of space-based missile defense systems, for at least fifteen years. In an obvious attempt to curry favor in Western Europe, he and his Warsaw Pact allies also proposed extensive reductions in conventional military forces.

The Reagan administration, acknowledging for the first time that Moscow seemed serious about arms reduction, scrambled to find a response and worked to arrange a second summit meeting. But Gorbachev, who had in Geneva accepted Reagan's invitation to visit the United States, now refused to come to Washington until progress was made in the arms reduction talks. Then in August a serious international incident brought a chilling reminder that the Cold War was not over. In New York, a Soviet UN official, Gennadi Zakharov, was arrested by U.S. officials on charges of spying. The USSR responded a week later by seizing an American reporter named Nicholas Daniloff and leveling similar accusations against him. The negotiating climate took a sudden turn for the worse. But both sides recognized that no summit could occur without a resolution of the Zakharov-Daniloff affair. After some negotiation, they agreed that both men would be released and that Reagan and Gorbachev would get together a few weeks later for preliminary talks in Reykjavik, the capital city of Iceland.

The Reykjavik meeting of 11–12 October 1986 turned out to be anything but preliminary. It was, in fact, the most astonishing and bizarre summit conference of the whole Cold War. In the barren and surrealistic atmosphere of Hofdi House, not far from the Icelandic capital, the two world leaders and their close advisors held an extraordinary series of discussions and came very close to working out a number of breathtaking agreements.

Somewhat to the surprise of the U.S. delegation, Gorbachev came prepared to talk about far more than INF concerns and preparations for a U.S. trip. Early on the first day of the two-day conference, the Soviet leader put forth a sweeping proposal calling upon both superpowers to implement a 50 percent reduction in all strategic weapons, eliminate their intermediate-range missiles in Europe, commit themselves to adhere to the ABM treaty for at least ten years, and recommence talks aimed at achieving a comprehensive nuclear test ban treaty. The Americans, caught off guard, labored to come up with an effective response. A long day and night of difficult negotiations ensued. Even Richard Perle, the assistant secretary of defense and the "dark prince" of U.S. hardliners, was caught up in the stunning scope of the discussions. With the concurrence of George Schultz, the taciturn secretary of state, he hammered together a U.S. counterproposal that would have eliminated all strategic missiles in ten years. After this, each side would have the right to deploy defensive systems against the remaining strategic weapons (long-range bombers and cruise missiles).

If the Americans, who had a substantial lead in both, expected the Soviets to reject this proposal, they were in for a surprise. On the second day of the conference, when Reagan revealed this plan to Gorbachev, the Soviet leader responded by dramatically upping the ante. Why not abolish *all* nuclear weapons, he suggested, and not just ballistic missiles, over the next ten years? Reagan, who suddenly found himself with a chance to fulfill his dreams of ending the nuclear threat, gave a rather positive response—somewhat to the chagrin of his subordinates. Amidst growing excitement, the two sides tentatively agreed to cut their nuclear arsenals in half by 1991 and to eliminate them entirely by 1996! But then it all came unraveled. Gorbachev insisted that SDI research be confined to the laboratory during the ten-year period, and Reagan refused. In the end, no accord was reached, the summit ended in failure, and the two leaders parted on unhappy terms.

In the aftermath of the Reykjavik debacle, it became apparent that efforts to improve East-West relations had suffered a serious setback. Washington and Moscow leveled charges against one another, each blaming the other for the unsatisfactory outcome. Western European leaders, meanwhile, reacted in horror to the news that the U.S. president had almost agreed to dismantle the NATO nuclear deterrent without consulting them. In Geneva, the arms control talks reverted to total deadlock, with each side retreating to earlier stances and resorting to disparaging comments and recriminations against one another. For the time being, the prospects for nuclear disarmament, and for a Gorbachev visit to Washington, seemed very dim indeed.

TRIALS AND TRIBULATIONS
IN MOSCOW AND WASHINGTON

The climate of gloom that followed the Reykjavik summit was reinforced by the declining fortunes of both Gorbachev and Reagan. In the USSR, a series of misfortunes and setbacks undermined expectations for *perestroika* and dampened the early enthusiasm of Soviet citizens for their dynamic leader. In the United States, a serious scandal shook the Reagan administration, eroding the president's public support and destroying the myth that he was a "teflon president," impervious to criticism and reproach.

Even before Reykjavik, Gorbachev's efforts to reform Soviet economics and politics had met with numerous frustrations. His ballyhooed antialcohol campaign, designed both to improve public health and to increase worker productivity, accomplished little save to create a sugar shortage, as resourceful Soviet drinkers bought huge amounts of that commodity to distill illicit spirits. His efforts at reform were hampered by sustained and systematic foot dragging by the army of bureaucrats who were being asked to change their ways. Even as he struggled to combat corruption and remove the Brezhnev holdovers from state and party leadership, his own supporters began to question in public the pace and tenor of his reforms. On one hand, impatient radicals like Boris Yeltsin, the new Moscow party boss, railed at the slow progress of *perestroika* and the continued existence of a privileged class of time-serving careerists who permeated the bloated bureaucracy. On the other hand, cautious moderates like Egor Ligachev voiced concern that reform might get out of hand and that the party might lose control of the Soviet system.

External and internal disasters, meanwhile, contributed to Gorbachev's woes. In Afghanistan, which the Soviet leader aptly depicted as a "bleeding wound," the death toll continued to mount, and the prospects of Soviet victory faded slowly out of sight. In 1986, armed with U.S.–supplied Stinger anti-aircraft missiles, the Afghan rebels began to turn the tide of battle by shooting down Soviet helicopters. In the USSR, a catastrophic accident occurred in April of that year at the Chernobyl nuclear power station located north of Kiev. A reactor exploded, killing dozens of people and sending forth into the atmosphere a huge cloud of radiation that would contaminate thousands of square miles in Belorussia and Ukraine and endanger the health of millions. Reverting to traditional behavior, Moscow first tried to cover up the disaster, but Gorbachev eventually decided to face the problem squarely and even ask for Western help. It was, nevertheless, a damaging blow to the Soviet nuclear industry, an embarrassment for Gorbachev, and a setback for his efforts to bolster his nation's prestige and improve its economic welfare.

Ronald Reagan had problems of a different sort. In the November 1986 elections, less than a month after Reykjavik, the president's Republican party lost control of the U.S. Senate, leaving both houses of Congress in the hands of his Democratic foes. At about the same time, reports began to emerge that members of the administration had taken part in an elaborate scheme to sell American weapons to Iran in return for Iranian assistance in freeing U.S. hostages being held in Lebanon. By the end of the month, it was publicly revealed that, in contravention of U.S. laws, profits from these sales had been used to support and equip the counterrevolutionary movement in Nicaragua. Thus began to unravel what would become known as the "Iran-Contra" affair, the most serious and damaging scandal of the Reagan years.

The Iran-Contra scandal had its roots in two separate sets of circumstances. One was the Reagan administration's determination to undermine the left-wing, Soviet-supported Sandinista regime in Nicaragua by backing the "Contras," an assortment of rebel "freedom fighters" and former military officers that was organized and assisted by the CIA. When Congress, alarmed by reports that the CIA was mining harbors and violating international law, voted in 1984 to forbid further aid to the Contras, the administration began seeking ways to circumvent this ban by funding the rebels through private aid from wealthy citizens and foreign governments. The other circumstance was the captivity of seven U.S. hostages, held in Lebanon by pro-Iranian elements, and Reagan's sympathy for them and their families. Despite his public commitment never to make concessions to hostage-takers, and over the strong objections of his secretaries of state and defense, the president in 1985 authorized the sale of U.S. antitank and antiaircraft missiles to Iran in return for Iranian efforts to get the hostages released.

These two unconnected situations were brought together by the activities of Lieutenant Colonel Oliver North, a Marine Corps officer attached to the staff of the president's National Security Council. North, a decorated Vietnam veteran and self-proclaimed superpatriot who had been tasked with raising money for the Contras, increasingly got involved also in the arms-for-hostages dealings. Enthralled by the prospect of having the anti-American regime of Ayatollah Khomeini in Iran inadvertently assist the "freedom fighters" in Nicaragua, North arranged to divert to the Contras some of the considerable profits from the Iranian arms purchases. Although he may not have realized it, this diversion was illegal, since the monies used were not private funds but direct proceeds from the sale of U.S. property.

The scandal broke in the fall of 1986. In October, a U.S. plane bringing weapons to the Contras was gunned down by Sandinistas, and captured crew member Eugene Hasenfus soon admitted publicly that he was part of a CIA operation. In early November, a Lebanese magazine blew the whistle on the arms-for-hostage deals. As the U.S. media began to piece together the story, administration officials scrambled to cover up the truth, and the president himself made deceptive and inaccurate statements. But on 25 November, following an in-house investigation, Attorney General Edwin Meese disclosed that arms sale proceeds had indeed been funneled to the Contras. Although Reagan immediately fired Oliver North and denied all knowledge of the diversion, his credibility was ruined, and his popularity plummeted precipitously. Americans concluded that their president either was lying about what he knew or was hopelessly out of touch with what went on in his administration. Even his ardent supporters, who could justify the Contra funding in the name of national security, were horrified that Reagan had let his minions sell weapons to Iran in an effort to free the hostages.

For the next year and beyond, the scandal slowly unfolded in full public view, with three separate investigations looking into the mess. The first, a Reagan-appointed commission led by former senator John Tower, absolved the president of direct illicit behavior in its February 1987 report but went on to disparage his lackadaisical management and poor control over subordinates. The second, a joint House-Senate probe, held televised hearings in the summer and fall of 1987, thus keeping the issue in the public eye. The third, an independent inquiry led by Special Prosecutor Lawrence Walsh, eventually brought charges against North and a number of others, but did not indict Reagan himself.

The scandal embarrassed Reagan and hurt his reputation, but it did not destroy his presidency. One reason for this was that, despite his aides' testimony that they had kept him informed, he continued to deny that he had fully understood what was going on. His confused and befuddled accounts of the affair made his denials plausible. Another reason was that, in spite of the wrongdoing in his administration, the public on the whole still liked him as a man and excused his failure to keep his charges in line. A third reason was that even his enemies in Congress were hesitant to put the country through another wrenching disruption only thirteen years after Watergate had forced President Nixon to resign.

The main reason that Reagan was able to rebound, however, was that world events intervened and captured center stage, allowing the old Cold Warrior to assume the role of peacemaker. And here he would get a major assist from his hard-pressed Soviet counterpart, who was likewise anxious to restore his flagging fortunes by working toward peace on the international scene.

THE REVIVAL OF DÉTENTE

Gorbachev's failure to achieve a breakthrough at Reykjavik, combined with the continuing poor performance of the Soviet economy, compelled him to reconsider his position early in 1987. Two things had become painfully obvious to the Soviet leader. One was that *perestroika* was not working and that economic progress was going to require more time, more radical reforms, and more serious cuts in defense spending than originally anticipated. The other was that Reagan had an obsessive attachment to his Strategic Defense Initiative and was unwilling to budge on this issue. Moscow could thus either bide its time until Reagan left office, assuming his successor would be less wedded to the Star Wars dream, or it could simply separate out the SDI and negotiate on other issues where there was a real chance to make headway.

In February 1987, abruptly abandoning the stand he had taken in Iceland, Gorbachev chose the latter approach. The economic news was so bad, and the domestic situation so desperate, that he did not have the luxury of waiting two years for progress on the international front. Besides, he already had a relationship with Reagan, and some idea of what he could expect, whereas a new U.S. president would be an unknown quantity with different aspirations and agenda. And the very fact that Reagan had been weakened by the Iran-Contra scandal, combined with the president's natural desire to score a diplomatic triumph before he left office, might make it easier to work with him than any potential successor.

At any rate, on 28 February 1987, the Soviet leader made the dramatic surprise announcement that Moscow was now prepared to negotiate an end to all intermediate-range missiles in Europe, irrespective of whether or not agreement could be reached on strategic or space-based weapons. The INF talks, this meant, could now be "de-coupled" from the SDI issue. This concession removed the primary obstacle to a comprehensive INF treaty based on the "zero option" that Reagan had put forth in 1981.

It nonetheless put the United States in a rather awkward spot. The zero option had originally been more of a propaganda ploy than a serious bargaining position, and there had been little concern in Washington that the Kremlin might actually go along. Now that the improbable had occurred, many in the West were having second thoughts: the elimination of all medium-range missiles from Europe would leave the USSR with a large conventional advantage, as well as with a number of intermediate-range missiles in Asia and shorter-range missiles in Europe. Still, the Americans could hardly abandon a proposal they had themselves initiated and advocated for six years. During the spring and summer of 1987, then, the United States found itself simultaneously pressing its allies to go along with an INF accord and urging the Kremlin to give up its remaining intermediate- and shorter-range missiles. The result, after concessions by both the Soviets and West Germans, was what came to be known as "global zero-zero." In September, the United States and USSR announced that they had agreed in principle to an arrangement whereby each nation would destroy *all* missiles that had ranges of 300 to 3,400 miles, with full on-site inspection and verification. For the first time in history, an agreement had been reached to abolish a whole category of weapons!

This preliminary understanding finally cleared the way for Gorbachev's oft-postponed visit to Washington. And what a visit it was! The mediagenic Soviet leader took the U.S. capital by storm, bantering with politicians, hosting a party for celebrities, and even getting out of his limousine to work the crowds like a U.S. politician, in front of the TV cameras. At the White House, on 8 December, he and Reagan signed the INF treaty, amidst self-congratulatory remarks about the unprecedented nature of what they were doing. In public, at least, the two leaders basked in the glow of their historic achievement and newly enhanced popularity.

Not all, of course, was sweetness and light. The INF treaty, even when fully implemented, would only eliminate about 4 percent of the superpowers' nuclear warheads. Serious discussions were needed if there was to be any real progress on reduction of strategic weapons or on resolving the Star Wars issue. Behind the scenes, Gorbachev chafed at Reagan's indifference to details and his propensity for providing unsolicited advice on democracy and human rights. Some progress was made on several START issues, but there was no breakthrough on SDI. In the end, the two sides papered over their discord by agreeing to instruct their Geneva delegates to work out an arrangement by which both sides would pledge to uphold the 1972 ABM treaty for "a specified period of time." Research and testing of space-based systems would be permitted, but only to the extent authorized by that treaty.

Ironically, by this time both the Soviets and Americans were coming to realize that SDI was a much more difficult proposition than Reagan had at first imagined and that even a scaled-down version of his original "shield" was unlikely to be deployed before the end of the century. Moreover, the growing U.S. deficit and Democratic control of Congress made it unlikely that funding would continue at the levels Reagan desired. As a result, SDI was losing its importance as an issue and, for the United States, its potential as a bargaining chip. As it faded into the background, other concerns and developments came to dominate East-West relations.

The most encouraging of these developments was the Kremlin's decision to pull out of the Afghan war. Unlike his predecessors, Gorbachev saw little value in investing scarce Soviet resources in Third World regional conflicts. Almost from the beginning he had been casting about for a face-saving way to disengage his nation's forces from Afghanistan. His first instinct had been to send more troops, hoping to overpower the resistance and quickly end the war. This, however, had achieved little more than to increase casualties on both sides and engender a massive flight of Afghans from their homeland. In 1986, therefore, the Soviet leader switched course and began seeking a negotiated settlement. Moscow engineered the ouster of Babrak Karmal, the despised Soviet-backed Afghan demagogue, and replaced him with the more pliable and accommodating security chief Najibullah. In June, Gorbachev called for "national reconciliation" of all Afghan forces, a signal that Moscow was ready to bargain seriously with the anti-Soviet insurgents. Shortly thereafter, however, the United States began supplying the rebels with Stinger anti-aircraft missiles, thus boosting their fortunes and relieving the pressure on them to work out a compromise with the Najibullah regime. The conflict thus continued, and for the next eighteen months the peace talks, which had been going on in Geneva since 1982, were stalled.

Finally, in February 1988, fresh from his triumphal trip to Washington, Gorbachev moved to cut the Gordian knot. In yet another of the stunning announcements that were fast becoming his trademark, he declared that the USSR was willing to withdraw its troops from Afghanistan over a ten-month period, beginning on 15 May. Difficult talks still remained, for the United States insisted on the right to provide continuing aid to the rebels, "symmetrical" to any assistance that Moscow gave Najibullah. Finally, the Kremlin accepted this arrangement, and the troop evacuation began on schedule in May. The following year, after it had been completed, Foreign Minister Shevardnadze would formally apologize to the international community for the Soviet role in Afghanistan.

Meanwhile, a few weeks after the withdrawal commenced, Ronald Reagan arrived in Moscow for his fourth summit conference with Gorbachev. Officially, the purpose of the meeting was to sign the instruments of the ratified INF accords, but this was largely a formality. Unofficially, it was designed to maintain the momentum of the new détente and to help Gorbachev shore up his sagging support at home. Although short on substance, it was rich in imagery, with the two leaders strolling together through Red Square and embracing at Lenin's tomb. In a trip laden with ironies, the most stridently anti-Soviet of all U.S. presidents found himself speaking in front of a statue of Lenin and standing at the Bolshoi Ballet while the U.S. national anthem was played.

The Moscow summit meeting of 1988 proved to be the climax and high point of the Gorbachev-Reagan relationship. The two men were destined to meet once again as leaders, in December of that year, when Gorbachev visited the United Nations to make another sensational speech. By that time, however, Reagan was a lame duck, and a new administration was preparing to take power in Washington. And skeptical U.S. hardliners, fearful that their hero had succumbed too readily to "Gorby-mania," were just as glad to see the old Cold War cowboy finally ride off into the sunset.

Still, improbable as it might have seemed only a few years earlier, the dynamic young Soviet leader had succeeded in winning over the aging anti-communist president to a new form of détente which was far more promising than the old. Brezhnev's version of "peaceful coexistence" had foreseen an end to the arms race, but with each side maintaining its vast nuclear forces, and with continued competition and conflict over regional issues. The USSR in those days was anxious to avoid nuclear confrontation, but it had no intention of abandoning either its hold on Eastern Europe or its support for "wars of national liberation." Gorbachev's vision, on the other hand, promised not just the termination of weapons-building programs but the actual elimination of existing weapons systems. And, for the first time, Moscow seemed ready to cut its losses and forgo its costly support for its immense network of client regimes and insurgencies. As the Reagan era neared its conclusion, there was better reason than ever before to hope that the Cold War, at long last, was coming to an end. Nevertheless, the dramatic events of the next few years would astonish even the most hopeful observers of 1988.

17

The End of the Cold War, 1988–1991

Between 1988 and 1991, a series of remarkable developments shattered the Soviet bloc, profoundly changed the structure of international relations, and brought the Cold War to an end. As Gorbachev's reforms floundered, their author pushed for further modifications in the Soviet system, which in turn released all sorts of centrifugal forces that pulled that system apart. The nations of Eastern Europe effectively separated themselves from Soviet control, ousted their communist leaders, and established themselves as fully independent states. Within the USSR, as *perestroika* failed and Gorbachev's popularity plummeted, many of the myriad nationalities began to assert claims to independence. In 1991, after a failed effort by communist stalwarts to seize control and restore the central power of the Marxist-Leninist regime, the USSR disintegrated and ultimately ceased to exist.

GORBACHEV AND BUSH

The last several months of 1988 brought changes within the leadership of both superpowers. On 1 October, Mikhail Gorbachev was selected as Soviet president after forcing the aged Andrei Gromyko into retirement. Although this position was largely an honorary one, it did make Gorbachev official head of state, and soon he would enhance its powers immensely. His selection marked the culmination of a series of bold political strokes that saw him remove or demote his main opponents and critics, win a resounding endorse-

Bush, Reagan, and Gorbachev in New York, December 1988. (Paul Hosefros/New York Times Pictures)

ment of *perestroika* by party and state officials, and gain a freer hand in pursuing his reforms. On 8 November, following a rather nasty campaign, Vice-President George Bush was elected to replace Ronald Reagan as president of the United States. Since Bush had broad experience in international affairs, and had participated in many of the policy decisions of the Reagan years, his election seemed to suggest a strong element of continuity in U.S. foreign policy. Still, although in public Bush had been loyal to Reagan, in private he was known to be much less enamored of Gorbachev, and much less enthralled by the SDI, than the outgoing president had been.

In some respects, the omens for continued improvement in East-West relations looked promising. In December 1988, Gorbachev made his second visit to America, this time to address the UN General Assembly in New York. In his speech, which turned out to be yet another blockbuster, he set the stage for a momentous shift in the conduct of Soviet foreign policy. Advocating "freedom of choice" for all nations, he declared that ideology had no place in international affairs and that strong nations must "renounce the use of force" in dealing with other countries. And, as if to demonstrate that these were not just empty words, he went on to pledge that his nation would unilaterally reduce its overall military forces by 500,000 troops and 10,000 tanks, and its presence in Eastern Europe by 50,000 troops and 5,000 tanks. While in New York he also took time to meet jointly with Reagan and Bush and to turn his patented charm on everybody in sight.

In other respects, however, the signs were less auspicious. Even as he was winning his battles within the Soviet leadership, Gorbachev had lost the support of the Soviet people, as their standard of living continued to decline and his reforms failed to take hold. A calamitous harvest in 1988 added to their discontent. Meanwhile, long-submerged ethnic rivalries and nationalist aspirations had begun to tear at the fabric of the enforced social discipline that held the USSR together. As if to underscore the gravity of the situation, and further complicate the Soviet leader's problems, a devastating earthquake hit Soviet Armenia while he was in New York. Government efforts to deal with the disaster proved inadequate and incompetent, forcing Gorbachev to cut short his U.S. visit, fly to the stricken region, and accept international aid in coping with the catastrophe.

Furthermore, when the new U.S. president took office in January 1989, it soon became evident that he and the Soviet president were operating on different wavelengths and at different speeds. Gorbachev was in a hurry: indeed, the very failure of his domestic policies seemed both to indicate he was running out of time and to encourage him to be ever bolder in his foreign policy initiatives. Bush, on the other hand, was determined to take his time and not to let himself be rushed into tumultuous new departures on the international scene. Thus, one leader sought to force the pace of change while the other tried to slow things down.

George Herbert Walker Bush, whose father had been a wealthy banker and U.S. Senator, was the closest thing to a blue-blooded aristocrat America can produce. Raised in comfort and privilege, he had become a model of *noblesse oblige*, performing heroically as a U.S. Navy pilot during World War II and later serving effectively in a wide range of government posts. Lacking strong political convictions, and admittedly deficient in what he called "the vision thing," Bush was the epitome of caution and prudence and the ultimate devotee of the politics of the status quo. Yet his presidency was destined to witness the most far-reaching changes in international affairs since the era of Harry Truman.

Like many seasoned Cold Warriors, who were automatically suspicious of anything emanating from Moscow, Bush worried that the dynamic

Gorbachev was potentially a far more formidable foe than his bumbling predecessors had been. Gorbachev, it was true, had pushed through many reforms, but he was still a devout Marxist whose ultimate goal was to strengthen his country by shedding its unprofitable enterprises with the help of the star-struck Western world. Even his promised force reductions, when seen from this perspective, seemed like little more than efforts to make the Soviet military more efficient while throwing the West off guard. Gorbachev might well be sincere, but he might also be a slick-talking salesman using charm and concessions to soften the NATO alliance and weaken Western vigilance. And George Bush would not be one to let his vigilance be weakened.

Consequently, with the help of his newly appointed secretary of state, James Baker III, Bush began his term with a lengthy review of U.S. foreign policy. For several months, all initiatives were placed on hold, as dozens of bureaucrats spent hundreds of hours appraising American strategies on numerous regions and issues. Determined to avoid the sort of early-administration pressures that had led Kennedy into the Bay of Pigs fiasco and the ill-starred Vienna summit (Chapter 10) and Carter into his poorly conceived arms control initiative (Chapter 14), Bush kept a relatively low profile on the international scene. He resisted efforts to arrange an early meeting with Gorbachev and responded only tepidly to the Soviet leader's force reduction proposals.

Gorbachev, however, was not to be denied. Taking advantage of the fact that Bush, at least for the time being, was conceding him the international limelight, the Soviet leader followed up on his UN speech with a series of actions and proposals making it clear that he was the one taking the initiative in trying to change the world. In January 1989, he revealed details of his force reduction plan, which would cut the size of the Soviet military by about one-eighth, and he assured Western skeptics that the tanks removed from Eastern Europe would be modern and not outdated ones. That same month most of his Warsaw Pact allies also announced cutbacks in their combat force levels. In February, the USSR reported that it had completed its withdrawal from Afghanistan on schedule. In March, new talks on Conventional Forces in Europe (CFE), replacing the long-stalled mutual and balanced force reduction (MBFR) talks (Chapter 13), began in Vienna with Foreign Minister Shevardnadze unveiling some conciliatory new Soviet proposals. In April, Gorbachev himself flew to London, met with Prime Minister Thatcher, complained about Bush's foot dragging, and solicited British help in getting the United States to be more responsive. In May, in the midst of a controversy in West Germany over U.S. plans to modernize its European-based tactical nuclear weapons (those with a range of less than 300 miles), he declared that Moscow would unilaterally eliminate 500 such weapons from its Eastern European stockpiles. He also offered to further reduce the number of tanks and artillery pieces deployed by the Warsaw Pact. And, in a private letter to the U.S. president, he disclosed that Moscow had stopped supplying weapons to its Central American clients.

All this activity, as intended, put George Bush on the spot. As the president was getting set to attend a fortieth anniversary NATO summit in late May, his allies and advisors pressed him to come up with an effective response to the Gorbachev challenge, in order to shore up both alliance solidarity and his own sagging public image. Bush responded by agreeing to negotiate with the Soviets on tactical nuclear weapons and then by using the NATO meeting in Brussels as a stage from which to put forth his own bold plan for sweeping military cuts. According to his proposal, both superpowers would reduce the number of troops they deployed in Europe (outside the USSR) to 275,000 and the number of combat aircraft to 15 percent below the current NATO level. The plan's image of equality was deceptive, since it would require the USSR to cut ten times more troops, and considerably more aircraft, than the United States. Nevertheless, it was welcomed by both the NATO allies and the Kremlin as a step in the right direction. Bush also played the propaganda game, challenging Moscow to relax its grip on Eastern Europe and noting that people who lived in a "common European home" should be "free to move from room to room."

Meanwhile, in mid-May, while the NATO leaders were getting ready for their Brussels summit, the peripatetic Soviet president once again went on the road. This time his travels took him to Beijing, for a "socialist summit" with Deng Xiaoping and other Chinese leaders. It was a tumultuous visit. Chinese students, emboldened in part by Gorbachev's reforms, were staging a massive prodemocracy protest when the Soviet leader arrived. Although his visit was designed to improve relations, Gorbachev did not hesitate to call openly for more democracy in China, while urging a peaceful resolution of the student demonstrations.

His words were of little help. On 4 June 1989, two weeks after Gorbachev left Beijing and shortly after Bush left Brussels, Chinese soldiers ruthlessly crushed the protests with appalling brutality and bloodshed. The Tienanmen Square Massacre, as it came to be known, provided ample and graphic evidence that the communist rulers of China were still willing to use wanton force to maintain their unfettered power. But that same weekend, elsewhere in the communist world, a far different picture was emerging. In Poland, peaceful and free elections were resulting in an overwhelming defeat for that country's communist rulers, and helping to set in motion a chain of events that was destined to bring down communist rulers throughout the Soviet bloc.

THE REVOLUTIONS OF EASTERN EUROPE

In his historic UN address of December 1988, Gorbachev seemed to indicate that the USSR was prepared to forsake the use of armed force in pursuing its foreign policy goals. To the peoples of Eastern Europe, the full implications of this new approach at first were not entirely clear. Was Moscow repudiating the Brezhnev Doctrine, by which it had long claimed the right to intervene as necessary in the affairs of socialist countries? In March of 1989, Gennadii Gerasimov, the Kremlin's most forthright spokesperson, seemed to answer this question in the affirmative when he announced that each Eastern European nation had the right to decide its own fate. In June, similar statements were made by other Soviet officials, and Gorbachev himself explicitly disowned the Brezhnev Doctrine during a visit to France.

These statements, of course, were just words. What mattered was not so much what the Soviet leaders *said* but how they would *react* to changes in Eastern Europe. As it turned out, the first true tests of the Kremlin's intent would be provided by Hungary and Poland, where major political changes were already under way.

In Hungary, the changes had begun in 1988 when János Kádár, who had ruled that nation since 1956, stepped down as general secretary. His successor, Károly Grósz, sought to emulate Gorbachev by launching his own version of *glasnost*. With the Kremlin's blessings, Grósz opened up Hungarian society, brought reformers into power, and instituted democratic procedures. In February of 1989, his regime announced constitutional changes designed to transform Hungary into a multiparty state and then scheduled free elections for the coming year. The leaders then scrambled to shed their communist image, hoping in vain to make a favorable impression on the voters. In May, they opened up their borders to the West by ripping down the barbed-wire fences that separated Hungary from Austria. The USSR did nothing to hinder this action, which tore a vast hole in the "iron curtain." Before long, thousands of East Germans entered Hungary, seeking to use that country as an escape route to the free and prosperous West.

In Poland, the road to reform was much more tortuous and contentious. Since 1981, the country had been led by Wojciech Jaruzelski, the general who had been responsible for declaring martial law and banning the Solidarity trade union movement. But Jaruzelski, one of the most enigmatic of all Cold War leaders, was both a pragmatist and a patriot, and he eventually came to realize that the outlawed labor union had far more authority than he did in the eyes of the Polish people. In 1987, he had initiated a *perestroika*-type reform of the anemic Polish economy but had failed to make any headway due to massive opposition from the proscribed Solidarity movement. Lech Walesa, a shipyard electrician who had risen from obscurity in 1980 to become the head of Solidarity and a Nobel Peace Prize winner, once again emerged as the effective leader of the Polish opposition. In 1988, during a televised debate viewed by millions of Poles, he scored a clear triumph over the party's selected spokesperson.

Early in 1989, as the deadlock continued and the economy deteriorated, Jaruzelski decided to seek accommodation with Walesa and his supporters. In February, roundtable discussions were initiated between government and union representatives. These talks led, in April, not only to the legalization of Solidarity but also to sweeping changes in the Polish political system. A new legislative body, the Senate, was created alongside the old *Sejm*, and elections were scheduled for the first weekend in June. All of the seats in the Senate, and 35 percent of those in the *Sejm*, were placed up for grabs, with the Polish people at long last given a chance to make a real choice. The result was a humiliating defeat for the government, which lost all the contested seats in the *Sejm* and all but one seat in the Senate, and an overwhelming victory for Solidarity. Under pressure from Gorbachev, the Polish Communists agreed to accept a coalition government, with Solidarity's Tadeusz Mazowiecki serving as prime minister and Jaruzelski as president.

The impact of the events in Hungary and Poland was profound. In two key Soviet satellites, under very different circumstances, the communist leaders had agreed to give up their monopoly of power and to share it with democratic forces. Moscow, far from blocking these developments, had actually encouraged them. In October, in an effort to illustrate this new approach, the irrepressible Gerasimov announced in Helsinki that the Brezhnev Doctrine was dead and that Kremlin policy was now in tune with a famous American singer. "You know the Frank Sinatra song *My Way*?" he asked his astonished listeners. "Hungary and Poland are doing it *their* way. We now have the *Sinatra* doctrine."

The developments in Hungary and Poland soon produced a chain reaction that would, by the end of 1989, lead to revolutionary changes throughout Eastern Europe. The glue that held the Soviet bloc together was provided by the Soviet army, which Moscow had used to suppress democratic reforms in Hungary in 1956 and Czechoslovakia in 1968. Once it was clear that Gorbachev did not intend to repeat these performances, the people of Eastern Europe began to challenge their communist rulers with growing audacity.

Events came to a head in the fall of 1989 in eastern Germany, the traditional focal point of Cold War confrontation. Despite a standard of living that was relatively high for a communist country, the people of East Germany were impoverished by comparison with those in the West. As Gorbachev's reforms brought a measure of democracy to the USSR, they had grown more and more resentful of the oppressive regime of party boss Erich Honecker.

Many decided that the time had come to leave. Throughout the summer, East Germans had continued to pour into Hungary, bent on traveling to the West through the recently opened border with Austria. At first, the Hungarian authorities refused to let them go, honoring an earlier agreement with the government of East Germany. But in September, as the numbers mounted, the Hungarians changed their mind and, with Gorbachev's approval, let thousands of these people make their way to the West. When East Germany responded by prohibiting travel to Hungary, those who wished to leave simply went to Czechoslovakia and jammed into the compound of the West German embassy in Prague. Finally, in early October, following awkward negotiations between Prague and East Berlin, they were allowed to travel to West Germany in special trains.

Others chose to stay and fight. In late September, a group called "New Forum" began sponsoring antigovernment rallies in Leipzig, calling for democratic reforms. Before long, similar protests were being held in other cities. In October, the Leipzig demonstrations became a weekly event, with the crowds increasing as the month progressed. With events spinning out of control, the East German government began to contemplate using massive force to quell the disturbances, much as the Chinese authorities had done at Tienanmen Square only four months earlier.

Into the midst of this dangerous situation strode Mikhail Sergeevich Gorbachev, who showed up in East Berlin in early October to help celebrate the fortieth anniversary of the German Democratic Republic. In a bizarre ceremony that seemed totally out of touch with reality, he joined Honecker and other officials in extolling the achievements of a state that was under siege. Large crowds gathered to greet the Soviet president, chanting "Gorby! Gorby!" and calling loudly for his help in bringing them their freedom. In public, Gorbachev referred to an earlier appeal made by Ronald Reagan to tear down the Berlin Wall and predicted that all walls separating Europeans must eventually fall. In private, he reportedly urged his hosts to consider reforms, noting that "life punishes those who come late," and warning them not to expect Soviet help in trying to quell the protests.

Soon after Gorbachev left, the regime was confronted with another massive demonstration scheduled for 9 October in Leipzig. To avoid bloodshed, local civic leaders convinced the police to let it proceed unhindered. The next week, over 100,000 persons took part in yet another protest. A few days later, the ailing Honecker was replaced as party leader by Egon Krenz, long his designated heir. But Krenz had assumed command of a ship that was rapidly taking on water, with thousands seeking to leave it on any lifeboat available. On 1 November, as the protests continued to grow, he went to Moscow to meet with Gorbachev, who urged him to move toward a more pluralistic society. Returning, the energetic Krenz tried to seize the moment by reforming the party and government, jettisoning unpopular officials, and calling for free elections. But the crowds in the streets kept growing, and the flood of refugees heading to the West became a virtual torrent.

Faced with an impossible situation, Krenz and his associates then took a desperate gamble. If East German citizens knew they could travel back and forth to the West at will, the reasoning went, perhaps they would be less anxious to permanently leave their homes. So on 9 November 1989, in a dramatic televised statement, the regime announced that it was lifting almost all restrictions on travel to the West. But the results of this declaration were far more sensational than anything the government intended. Within hours the Berlin Wall was opened, and hundreds of thousands of Berliners gathered to

Berliners celebrate the opening of the Berlin Wall. (AP/Wide World Photos).

celebrate in an atmosphere of unrestrained euphoria. Before long they had begun to dismantle the Cold War's most powerful symbol.

Although the opening of the Berlin Wall did help stem the flood of refugees, it did not save the regime. Instead it unleashed in both Germanies a tidal wave of support for the country's reunification. In December, Krenz and his associates were forced to step down, as the country began to prepare for democratic elections scheduled for March. Meanwhile, the historic events in Germany were followed in quick succession by sweeping revolutionary developments throughout Eastern Europe. One by one the remaining communist leaders, no longer protected by the threat of Soviet force, were toppled from their posts. In the last two months of 1989, events moved at a dizzying pace.

In Bulgaria, a revolution took place at the same time that East German authorities were opening up the wall. Todor Zhivkov, who had ruled his country as a dictator since 1954, had become a liability and embarrassment to his supporters, especially as he maneuvered to secure the advancement of his incompetent son. On 9 November, in a carefully conceived palace revolt, Foreign Minister Petur Mladenov replaced Zhivkov as general secretary. The next day, Gorbachev was among the first to congratulate the new Bulgarian leader. In the face of rising protests, Mladenov then moved quickly to reform his country and party, in preparation for free elections to be held the following June.

The revolution in Czechoslovakia followed hard on the heels of those in East Germany and Bulgaria. In late October, large demonstrations in Prague marking the seventy-first anniversary of the country's founding were broken up by police. On 17 November, another Prague demonstration turned into a vast rally in favor of democratic reforms. The communist regime, led by President Gustáv Husák and party boss Milos Jakes (who had succeeded Husák as general secretary in 1987), responded with brutal force, sending antiter-rorist troops and riot police to beat the assembled crowd. Far from intimidat-ing the protesters, however, this seemed to spur them on. A few days later they formed an opposition group called "*Civic Forum*" which took the lead in orga-nizing more and bigger protests. Each day, thousands would gather at Prague's Wenceslas Square to sing, chant for freedom, and listen to speeches by prominent figures like dissident playwright Václav Havel and former party boss Alexander Dubcek, the man who had led the reform efforts of 1968 (Chapter 12). As it had done elsewhere, Moscow made clear that it would not support the use of force to maintain the beleaguered regime. On 24 November, as the situation deteriorated, Jakes and other party leaders resigned; Husák followed them into involuntary retirement on 10 December. By year's end, a new government, made up mostly of non-Communists, had been formed, with Havel serving as president and Dubcek as head of the national assembly. With minimal violence and bloodshed, the people of Czechoslovakia had managed to end four decades of communist rule by stag-ing a "velvet revolution."

The people of Romania, however, were not so lucky. Their efforts to bring down the regime of Nicolae Ceausescu were met with harsh repression, and their revolution proved by far the bloodiest of all those in Eastern Europe. Ceausescu had ruled his nation ruthlessly since 1965, reserving the top posts for himself and his family and creating a Stalin-style cult of personality that portrayed him as a heroic and godlike figure. In a typical case of Cold War irony, this most brutal of all Eastern European tyrants had regularly been courted by U.S. leaders, since he had the temerity to pursue an independent course in foreign affairs. More recently, he had resisted Gorbachev's efforts to get him to institute reforms and had thus incurred the exasperation of the Soviet chief. Still, as his fellow communist dictators fell all about him in 1989, he stubbornly and fiercely clung to power.

It was not until mid-December, when riots broke out in the city of Timisoara over government attempts to evict a popular Hungarian pastor and human rights activist, that the regime began to crumble. Police efforts to crush the riots resulted in wanton bloodshed, and within a few days there were protest rallies in other Romanian cities. Ceausescu himself was shouted down when he tried to speak in Bucharest on 21 December. The following day, as rioters began storming government offices, a state of emergency was declared and troops were called out to disperse the crowds by force. But the soldiers refused to fire, defying the orders of their longtime leader, and instead joined the revolt. Ceausescu and his wife tried to flee, but they soon were captured, given a quick trial by officials who only days before had been their loyal underlings, and promptly sentenced to death. On 25 December, a firing squad pumped several hundred bullets into the bodies of Nicolae and Elena Ceausescu, putting a bloody end to the long Romanian nightmare. In the political maneuvers that followed, a "National Salvation Front" was established, and former Communist Ion Iliescu shortly emerged as the acting head of state.

GERMAN UNIFICATION
AND SUPERPOWER COLLABORATION

By late 1989, events in Eastern Europe had finally convinced George Bush, and most remaining skeptics, that the Gorbachev revolution was genuine. On 2–3 December, in the midst of the epic events that were shaking the Soviet bloc, the two leaders held their first summit conference, a relatively informal get-together aboard a Soviet ship in the surging seas off the Mediterranean island of Malta. Gorbachev, fresh from a visit to Rome where he had conferred with the pope about human rights and religious freedom in the USSR, was looking for help from America. He confided to Bush that his economic reforms were not going well and that his success hinged on his ability to improve the living standards of the Soviet peoples. The U.S. president responded by suggesting a host of specific proposals on arms control and initiatives designed to help the Soviet economy. The two men agreed to accelerate the pace of the START and CFE talks, and they expressed hope that the agreements would be completed and signed during the coming year. Both Gorbachev and Bush had reason to be pleased: superpower cooperation was the order of the day!

This did not mean, of course, that all problems had been solved. Only a few weeks later, superpower relations suffered a temporary setback due to the U.S. invasion of Panama, in which Bush used military action to topple the regime of Manuel Noriega, who had defied American efforts to halt the drug traffic through his country. Obviously, Washington had not bought Gorbachev's notion that great powers should renounce the use of force in dealing with other countries! Aside from this, difficult negotiations lay ahead on the questions of German unification and arms control.

During the course of 1990, the nations of Eastern Europe followed up on their revolutions by making the transition to democratic rule. In Hungary, when the long-awaited elections were finally held in March, voters rejected their former communist leaders in favor of candidates from "Democratic Forum" and other centrist groups. Arpád Goncz, a prominent writer and dissident, shortly emerged as the new head of state. In Romania, where elections in May were marred by charges of fraud, a "National Salvation Front" composed mostly of ex-Communists wound up as the overall winner, and Ion Iliescu was reaffirmed as president by a large majority vote. In Czechoslovakia, free elections were held in June, with "Civic Forum," and its candidates large-ly carrying the day and then reelecting Václav Havel as president. In Bulgaria that same month, the former Communists actually outpolled their democrat-ic opposition, but by October the democrats had gained control of both the presidency and legislature. Zhelyu Zhelev, detained for years under the Zhivkov regime, became the country's leader. In Poland, President Jaruzelski was induced to step down in September, and, in elections a few months later, Solidarity leader and national hero Lech Wa sa eventually emerged victori-ous. Moscow and Washington mostly stayed out of these events, content to sit back and watch history take its course.

In Germany, however, the situation was more complex. The future of that country depended not just on the voters of East and West Germany but also on its neighbors and the powers that kept it divided. These were by no means thrilled at the prospect of seeing the two Germanies unite into a single powerful state. Late in 1989, when West German chancellor Helmut Kohl put forth a plan for unification, the Soviets declared that the division of Germany was essential to European security. Soon Polish officials were voicing concerns that a united Germany might demand restoration of the territory ceded to Poland in 1945. Even Western politicians, who for years had paid lip service to the goal of German unity, secure in their belief that Moscow would never allow it, began to express misgivings. The ever-cautious Bush administration, con-cerned that events were moving the German Question back onto center stage, called for a prudent and gradual approach supervised by the four original occupying powers. This led to a "two plus four" framework (two Germanies plus four supervising powers), worked out at the Ottawa foreign ministers' meeting of February 1990.

The Germans, however, were not to be denied, and their long-sought unity was not to be delayed. In the East German elections of March 1990, the people voted overwhelmingly for candidates who favored a unified Germany, with a surprise victory going to the conservative coalition linked with West German chancellor Kohl. In May, the two Germanies agreed to integrate their economic and monetary systems, effective 1 July. For all intents and purposes, the East German economy was subsumed by the West, and the West German deutsche mark became the currency of both countries.

Despite the rapid progress, a major obstacle remained on the road to German unity. In order to allay the fears of his NATO partners, who had recur-rent nightmares about recreating an uncontrollable *Reich*, Kohl had promised that a united Germany would stay in the Western alliance. This, however, was initially opposed by Moscow, which still was allied with East Germany in the increasingly inconsequential Warsaw Pact and which clung to its traditional stance favoring a neutral, demilitarized Germany. The West Germans eventu-ally solved the problem simply by buying the Soviets off, making major eco-nomic concessions in return for Moscow's acquiescence. They agreed to ful-fill all of East Germany's financial obligations toward the USSR and to grant the Soviets an enormous bank credit of five billion deutsche marks. They also agreed to cut the size of their army and eventually to help pay the cost of removing Soviet troops from East Germany.

Finally, on a visit to the USSR in July, Kohl was able to gain Gorbachev's assurance that Moscow would not block unification and that the Germans could remain in NATO if they wished. This cleared away the last major hurdle. In September, the "two plus four" treaty was signed, ending the rights of the occupying powers and giving the Germans the green light to unite. On 3 October 1990, in a development that would have been almost unthinkable only a few years earlier, the German Democratic Republic ceased to exist, and East Germany was merged into the Federal Republic. The German Question, which lay at the heart of so many Cold War disputes, had at long last been resolved!

Meanwhile, with the Cold War winding down, the relationship between the superpower leaders continued to improve. In late May, Gorbachev flew to Washington for his second summit meeting with Bush. He arrived in a somber mood, acutely aware that the Soviet economy was getting worse and that nationalist pressures in the constituent republics were tearing the USSR asunder. But the Western air seemed to rejuvenate him: at home he had become a pariah, increasingly despised by his own people, but in America he was still a heroic figure with undiminished popularity. Huge, friendly crowds greeted him everywhere he went. President Bush, who by this time had become a full-blown Gorbachev booster, took him to Camp David, where the two men relaxed, played horseshoes, walked in the woods, and conducted wide-ranging talks on matters of global concern. The Soviet leader then traveled to Minneapolis and San Francisco, where he appealed to U.S. business leaders to launch new enterprises in the USSR. The symbolism could not have been more poignant: the head of the communist world was seeking aid from the titans of American capitalism!

Although the two leaders had hoped to sign a major arms control treaty during the Washington summit, slow progress in the START negotiations precluded this possibility. Still, they did sign statements outlining the framework for a comprehensive accord and advocating even greater cuts in the arsenals of both sides. They also signed a treaty calling for the cessation of chemical weapons production and reduction of existing stockpiles. Finally, in a testament to the growing emphasis on economic cooperation, they affixed their signatures to a new commercial agreement by which the United States would at last grant most-favored nation trading status to the USSR. Gorbachev returned to Moscow in early June, refreshed and reinvigorated for the challenges that lay ahead. A month later, on 6 July 1990, NATO issued the so-called London Declaration, proclaiming that Europe had entered a "new, promising era" and declaring that the Cold War was over.

Then, in August 1990, the spirit of superpower collaboration was put to the test by Iraq's sudden invasion of Kuwait (see Map 9, p. 230). Baghdad, saddled with an $80 billion debt from its 1980–1988 war with Iran, was unable to repay because a glut of oil on the world market had brought prices as low as $10 a barrel. Iraq owed much of this money to Kuwait, which opposed efforts in OPEC to set lower production levels and higher prices. In summer 1990, Iraqi leader Saddam Hussein pressed Kuwait to revise its position, and the tiny nation agreed to cut production, support higher prices, and make small territorial concessions to Iraq.

Saddam then miscalculated tragically. With the Cold War apparently over, with Moscow distracted by unrest among its ethnic minorities, and with the United States having taken an even hand in the recent war, he concluded that the time was ripe for an Iraqi initiative that would begin the process of unifying the Arab world. On 2 August 1990, he invaded Kuwait without warning and conquered the country in less than a day. That action gave Iraq control of 21 percent of the world's oil supply and shocked Washington. President Bush ordered a massive U.S. military buildup to defend Saudi Arabia against an Iraqi invasion, although there was no conclusive evidence that one was being considered. He quickly moved in the UN to isolate Iraq and impose economic sanctions to force it out of Kuwait. Moscow supported these measures, and the next month Gorbachev and Bush held a quick summit meeting in Helsinki to discuss the crisis, agreeing to work together to secure Iraqi withdrawal. For the first time since the Suez affair of 1956, the United States and USSR appeared to be on the same side during an international crisis. For a world accustomed to living with the fear that any local conflict might escalate into a full-blown superpower confrontation, this was heady stuff indeed!

Following the American congressional elections on 6 November, Bush moved in a more aggressive direction. He doubled the number of U.S. troops in the Persian Gulf to 500,000 and converted the force into an offensive one. Simultaneously, he obtained passage of UN resolution 660, calling for Iraqi withdrawal no later than 15 January 1991. Negotiations to achieve this proved fruitless. Moscow, fearing the destruction of its principal client in the region, tried to mediate the dispute, but decades of American efforts to exclude the USSR from a meaningful role in the Middle East now bore bitter fruit for Gorbachev. Even at the height of the Cold War, Moscow's intervention would have been resisted; now, with the Soviet economy crumbling and the Communist party losing its grip on power, Gorbachev simply lacked the political leverage to bring the parties together.

The Gulf War broke out on 16 January 1991. When it ended on 27 February, Kuwait was liberated and much of Iraq destroyed. The war altered significantly the power balance in the Middle East, and Washington at once moved toward implementation of peace negotiations between the Arab states and Israel, which had wisely remained out of the conflict despite Iraqi missile attacks on its territory. The Soviet presence in the Persian Gulf was virtually obliterated, due in part to Moscow's preoccupation with internal unrest, in part to the poor performance of its military hardware, and in part to its decision to cooperate with Washington.

Meanwhile, further progress in East-West rapprochement had come in November 1990, when an agreement to reduce conventional forces in Europe was signed by the members of NATO and the Warsaw Pact. The CFE treaty, which committed both sides to substantial reductions in the numbers of troops, tanks, and aircraft deployed on the European continent, marked the culmination of many months of difficult negotiations and the realization of a dream that had begun with the original MBFR talks back in 1973. Nonetheless, this historic accord would soon be overtaken by events. Its ratification was delayed in early 1991 by a dispute over the status of several Soviet divisions, which Moscow claimed to be naval forces rather than ground combat units. Even as this issue was resolved, the treaty itself was overshadowed by the ongoing Soviet withdrawal from Eastern Europe. On 1 July 1991, the Warsaw Pact, the very embodiment and symbol of communist military might, was formally dissolved.

By this time, at long last, a START accord had been reached. In summer 1991, the United States and USSR announced that they had finally achieved agreement on a comprehensive treaty to reduce strategic arms and reverse the nuclear arms race. Bush traveled to Moscow for yet another summit with Gorbachev, and, on 31 July, the two presidents signed the landmark treaty. In so doing, they committed themselves to take a major step toward the extensive weapons reductions envisioned at Reykjavik in 1986. Within seven years, the USSR would be required to cut its deliverable nuclear warheads by half, and the United States would reduce its by over a third.

In normal circumstances, the signing of the START treaty would have been widely regarded as an epic historic event. Indeed, after more than four decades of competing for strategic supremacy, and more than two decades of difficult negotiations, the two superpowers had finally agreed to end the arms race and make vast reductions in their enormous atomic inventories. Within months, both sides would put forth new proposals for still more drastic cuts. The nuclear arms race, the most frightening and debilitating aspect of the Cold War, had finally come to an end!

By summer 1991, in fact, there could be little doubt that the Cold War itself was over. All of its major components—the Soviet occupation of Eastern Europe, the German Question, the superpower contest for influence in the Third World, and the arms race—had been either eliminated or resolved. Still, as people tried to appreciate the enormity of these events and adjust to a new world order, the internal decay of the USSR was paving the way for even more startling developments.

THE COLLAPSE OF THE SOVIET STATE

Ironically, the disintegration of the USSR was facilitated by Gorbachev himself. In pursuing his reforms, he had managed to eliminate the pervasive fear that had governed the Soviet peoples since the time of Stalin. But that fear, it turned out, was part of the cement that held the Soviet Union together. Once it was gone, rather than working creatively to solve the nation's problems, many Soviet citizens would demonstrate that they had little loyalty to either the Communist party or the Soviet state.

This was especially true of the non-Russian nationalities, who comprised fully half of the country's population, and the various republics that made up the USSR. Since 1988, some had been acting with increasing defiance of the central government in Moscow. Early that year, a violent clash had erupted between Armenians and Azerbaijanis over Nagorno-Karabakh, a predominantly Armenian enclave in the midst of Azerbaijan. Gorbachev's efforts to resolve the dispute only made matters worse, and by 1989 the Kremlin was faced with two constituent nationalities effectively at war with one another. Meanwhile, the Baltic republics of Estonia, Latvia, and Lithuania, which had been annexed forcibly at the start of World War II, had begun consciously testing Moscow's resolve to keep them in the union. In summer 1988, nationalist demonstrations were conducted in Lithuania; later that year Estonia declared its right to repudiate Soviet laws.

The revolutions in Eastern Europe during 1989 gave a huge boost to nationalist aspirations within the USSR. As the nations of the Soviet bloc broke free of Moscow's control, the people in Soviet republics sought to follow suit. Lithuania took the lead by proclaiming its sovereignty, declaring invalid its 1940 annexation by the USSR, and ending the Communist party's monopoly of power in the republic. Estonia and Latvia followed closely behind. In Georgia, after a large nationalist rally in April was brutally suppressed by Soviet troops, separatist sentiments spread quickly. In Ukraine, nationalists founded an organization called "Rukh" ("the movement") to agitate for independence.

By 1990, it was clear that Moscow was losing control. In January, Gorbachev went to Lithuania to urge its rebellious people to behave with more restraint. His visit had little impact: on 11 March, the Lithuanian legislature issued a declaration of independence and elected the anti-Communist Vitautus Landsbergis as president. During the next few months, Moscow responded with shows of military force, seizing government buildings, sealing the republic's borders, and cutting off its oil and gas. In May, the crisis eased somewhat when the Lithuanians agreed to delay implementing their independence decree. By that time, however, both Estonia and Latvia had declared their intent to move toward independence. Armenia, still locked in intermittent conflict with Azerbaijan, followed suit in August. In June, Moldavia proclaimed its sovereignty and changed its name to Moldova. In October, elections in Georgia brought victory to a nationalist coalition, which soon announced its determination to pursue an independent course. By the end of the year, all the remaining republics had issued declarations of sovereignty, stopping short of asserting complete independence but moving toward greater autonomy.

Republics of the Former Soviet Union

It was in Russia, the largest and most populous republic, that the most serious challenge arose. In May, Boris Yeltsin, an outspoken reformer who had been dismissed from Party leadership after openly criticizing the slow pace of reform, was elected chairman of the Supreme Soviet of the Russian Republic. This made him, in effect, the president of Russia. Stubborn, flamboyant, confrontational and charismatic, Yeltsin had become a popular hero by virtue of his courageous denunciations of bureaucratic elitism and his populist democratic style. Under his leadership, the Russian republic quickly proclaimed its sovereignty, declared that its laws took precedence over those of the central government, and asserted greater control over its own territory and resources. This struck at the heart of the Soviet system: the USSR presumably could survive without the Baltic States and Armenia, but without Russia there could be no Soviet Union.

At first, Gorbachev responded to the challenges with creativity and flexibility, seeking always to stay one step ahead of his critics. Since 1988, he had moved to democratize Soviet politics, permitting contested elections, creating a popularly elected Congress of People's Deputies, instituting a revised and strengthened presidency, eliminating the Communist party's monopoly of power, and transferring much authority from the Party to the government. Ironically, however, the more freedom he gave his people, the more they used it to repudiate him and the system he represented. On 1 May 1990, at the annual May Day festivities in Moscow's Red Square, Gorbachev and his colleagues were loudly jeered by protesters. In October, when he was awarded the Nobel Peace Prize, even his supporters were quick to point out that he certainly did not merit the prize for economics.

And indeed it was the failure of his economic policies, in conjunction with the rise of national separatism, that spelled his ultimate doom. As the economy declined, the patience of the Soviet peoples wore thin, and their enthusiasm for *perestroika* was replaced by growing cynicism. Gorbachev's early confidence gave way to vacillation, as he wavered between a cautious, gradualist approach and a rapid transformation to a full free market economy. In the spring of 1990, Premier Nikolai Ryzhkov put forth a comprehensive plan calling for careful and deliberate reforms that would increase wages, prices, and market incentives within the context of continued central planning. Yeltsin soon countered by backing a bold and drastic 500-day plan to achieve a market economy by privatizing state properties and giving the republics control of natural resources, taxation, and economic policy. Not surprisingly, the republics liked Yeltsin's approach. Gorbachev temporized and hedged, at one point seeming to come to terms with Yeltsin, but later adopting a "compromise" plan that retained most economic power in the hands of the central state. He then pressed for and received special emergency powers to dictate economic policies and maintain internal control.

These moves seemed to indicate that Gorbachev was turning to the right, siding with conservatives in the Soviet leadership. On paper, at least, the changes enhanced his authority to deal with the growing crisis. But they also cost him the allegiance of reformers, who had been the main base of his support. Many of his own economic advisors went over to Boris Yeltsin, who defiantly announced his intention to push forward with the 500-day plan within the Russian Republic. In December, Foreign Minister Shevardnadze rocked the Soviet government by warning of a coming dictatorship and abruptly resigning his post. Throughout the republics, there was palpable dismay at the apparent reaffirmation of central political and economic control.

The dismay turned to anger in January 1991. Within the Kremlin, hardliners like Defense Minister Dmitrii Yazov and Interior Minister Boris Pugo pressed for strong action to keep the republics in line. On 2 January, the crackdown finally began, when the Ministry of Defense sent paratroopers to seven troublesome republics to root out military deserters and draft dodgers. On 11–13 January, with the world's attention focused on the looming Persian Gulf War, Soviet troops and tanks, aided by the Ministry of Interior's "Black Berets," seized control of Lithuanian press and broadcast facilities in a bloody show of force. A week later, a similar incident occurred in Latvia, with Soviet forces attacking the offices of the Latvian Ministry of Interior. Although Gorbachev denied that he had ordered these assaults, neither did he condemn them, and he tried to blame the nationalists for causing the disorders.

Meanwhile, however, in a desperate attempt to keep the USSR together, Gorbachev was promoting a new "union treaty," designed to provide the republics with a semblance of sovereignty while preserving central authority. According to this arrangement, the Soviet government would maintain dominion over finances, resources, transportation, communications, and the military, but the republics would be free to determine their own social and economic systems and exercise some internal autonomy. The USSR would become the "Union of Sovereign Soviet Republics," with "Sovereign" replacing "Socialist" in the official name.

In March, after several months of discussions on the proposed union treaty, Gorbachev held a national referendum on whether to preserve the Soviet Union "as a renewed federation of equal sovereign republics in which human rights and the freedoms of all nationalities will be fully guaranteed." The result was an apparent victory for Gorbachev, with 76 percent of the voters supporting the resolution. It was marred, however, by the fact that six of the fifteen republics (the Baltic States, Armenia, Georgia, and Moldova) refused to take part. Nevertheless, the Soviet leader went ahead with his plans, negotiating the final details of the agreement with the nine participating republics at a special conference in April. In June and July, the accord was ratified by the legislatures of eight of these republics, with only Ukraine electing to delay. It was then decided that the formal signing of the new union treaty would take place on 20 August 1991. Now, as the central government prepared to sign away some of its powers, it was the conservatives' turn to be dismayed.

Yeltsin waving to supporters, 1991. (Alexander Zemlianichenko/AP/Wide World Photos)

During all these maneuvers and crises, Washington maintained its attitude of caution and circumspection. Even as the Soviet people turned their backs on Gorbachev, the U.S. president refused to abandon his newfound partner and collaborator. Although he found the crackdown in the Baltics "disturbing," he avoided direct criticism of Gorbachev and continued his efforts to enhance cooperation between the United States and USSR. As he had shown a few years earlier, when he maintained his ties with Chinese leaders following the Tienanmen Square Massacre, George Bush preferred to deal with a known quantity rather than risk the consequences of international turmoil and leaps into the unknown. So he had little hesitancy about traveling to Moscow at the end of July to bolster the Soviet president and sign the START treaty.

Within three weeks of Bush's departure, the hardliners made their move. In the early morning hours of Monday, 19 August—the day before the union treaty was scheduled to be signed—the Soviet press agency announced that Gorbachev had been released from his presidential duties "for reasons of health." A state of emergency was declared, and a special eight-man emergency committee was formed to take control. Ostensibly led by Vice-President Gennadii Yanaev, it was dominated by conservatives like Yazov and Pugo. This was, in fact, a coup: tanks and troops were moved into Moscow and other major cities, the Baltic republics were blockaded, and attempts were made to seize control of the media. Gorbachev himself had been detained at his dacha in the Crimea, and cut off from contact with the outside world, since the previous day.

Almost from the beginning, however, the coup ran into problems. Russian president Yeltsin managed to avoid arrest and make his way to the Russian Parliament building in Moscow, where he proceeded to declare the attempted takeover unconstitutional and to call on all Russians to obey his government rather than the emergency committee. Then, in a dramatic gesture that captured popular imagination and galvanized public support, he climbed atop a nearby tank and issued an appeal for massive resistance to the coup. Before long, tens of thousands of people had surrounded the parliament building, where they spent the next few days erecting barricades, taunting soldiers, and listening to defiant speeches. Huge crowds assembled in Leningrad and other cities, as resisters everywhere responded to Yeltsin's plea.

By Tuesday, 20 August, the tide began to turn. Ensconced in his surrounded headquarters, Yeltsin managed to keep in touch with the outside world and even to take several supportive phone calls from George Bush. The U.S. president, whose first inclination had been to hedge his bets and prepare to work with the emergency committee, had been inspired by Yeltsin's courage to rally to the Russian leader's support. Besides, it was becoming increasingly apparent that the coup had been poorly conceived. As the emergency committee sent more troops into Moscow, soldiers who had gone over to Yeltsin's side prepared to defend the parliament building against the anticipated attack. But the onslaught never came: faced with overwhelming popular resistance, and not entirely sure of the loyalty of the troops under their command, military leaders called off their planned assault. The following day, as troops and tanks were withdrawn from Moscow and as several plotters hastily jetted to the Crimea to negotiate with Gorbachev, it was clear that the coup had failed.

Gorbachev was flown back to Moscow, where he resumed his official duties, but it soon became evident that the locus of power had shifted to Yeltsin and the other republic leaders. The Russian government moved quickly to take charge of most functions and offices hitherto controlled by the USSR. With nothing left to stop them, various republics renewed and made good their claims for independence. With some assistance from Yeltsin, Gorbachev tried to piece together a "Union of Sovereign States" that would preserve a modicum of central authority, but when Ukraine and other republics decided not to join this effort came to naught.

Finally, abandoning Gorbachev entirely, the presidents of Russia, Ukraine, and Belarus met at Minsk in early December and agreed to pursue a new course. Acknowledging that the USSR had effectively ceased to exist, they invited the former Soviet republics to join them in a loose confederation called the "Commonwealth of Independent States." More of a coordinating commit-tee than a government, the CIS had no central authority and placed no serious restraints on the sovereignty of its members. Within a few weeks, all former republics except the Baltic States and Georgia had agreed to participate.

Gorbachev was disconsolate, but there was little he could do. The man who only a few years earlier had been considered a giant, the most prominent and popular political figure in the world, now seemed pitifully dwarfed in stature. Bowing to the inevitable, on 25 December 1991 he formally relin-quished his duties and resigned his position as president of the USSR. His remarks on the occasion were short and subdued, but he did mention the momentous changes that had occurred in the years since he had assumed power. "We are now living in a new world," he reminded his audience. "An end has been put to the Cold War."

18

A Hard
and Bitter Peace

Gorbachev's resignation, and the subsequent hauling down of the Soviet flag from atop the Kremlin, marked the close of the final chapter of the Cold War. The division of the world into two armed camps, the terrifying and expensive nuclear arms race, the bloody conflicts in places like Korea and Vietnam, and the tensions and hatreds that had washed over the globe for nearly half a century had been relegated to the history books. Few were sorry to see the long twilight struggle end, but its demise, perhaps appropriately, occasioned little of the wild rejoicing that had followed the end of World War II. The sound heard 'round the world as the Cold War ended was a collective sigh of relief from a weary, somewhat cynical, but somewhat hopeful human race.

GENERAL CONCLUSIONS

For over four decades, the Cold War dominated international relations, profoundly influenced the global economy, and to some extent affected the life of almost everyone on the planet. Arising out of the ashes of wartime cooperation between the Soviet Union and the Western Allies, it had quickly degenerated into what John F. Kennedy called "a hard and bitter peace," full of confrontation, conflict, deception, and intrigue. As the superpowers and their allies strove mightily to gain the advantage, expending massive resources in the process, less powerful nations struggled merely to survive, or perhaps to derive some benefit from playing upon the global rivalry. The

Cold War was a long and complex process which defies easy explanations or facile judgments. Nevertheless, there are a number of general conclusions that we can draw about it.

First: Although the Cold War was not inevitable, given the relationship between the Soviet Union and the Western democracies between 1917 and 1941, conflict between them after Hitler's defeat was much more likely than friendship. For nearly twenty-five years, the Soviets had depicted the West as a society in the final, decadent stages of capitalist greed and exploitation, a rotten society fit only for consignment to the dustbin of history. They had denounced the democracies of Britain, France, and the United States in the same terminology they had used against the fascist dictatorships of Germany and Italy and had made repeated efforts to subvert all these political systems in order to establish communist rule. The West, for its part, had portrayed the USSR as a remorseless police state bent on the destruction not only of its political and economic rivals but also of organized religion, family values, and human decency itself. It had backed up these judgments with military intervention against the Bolsheviks in 1918 and consistent verbal hostility ever since.

Then Germany invaded Russia in June 1941, and Winston Churchill, in one of the most imaginative left-handed compliments ever recorded, declared his new-found friendship for Moscow by asserting that "If Hitler invaded Hell, I would at least make a favorable reference to the Devil in the House of Commons." For his part, Joseph Stalin treated his new-found allies with sarcasm, contempt, and suspicion whenever they differed with him on military judgments. The West suspected that he had ordered the massacre of tens of thousands of Polish military officers in the Katyn Forest in 1940 and knew that he had refused Allied planes permission to land on Soviet airstrips after flights to aid the anti-Nazi uprising in Warsaw in 1944. Franklin Roosevelt at first believed that he could do business with Stalin, whom he tried to flatter and treat as a confidant, but by the end of his life in 1945 he had come to believe that Stalin was more interested in Soviet aggrandizement than in friendship with the West. Once Hitler was gone, and the common threat of German domination was removed, there was little to hold the Soviets and the Western Allies together, and a great deal to push them apart.

Second: The Cold War began in Germany because Europe was the fulcrum of the global balance of power in 1945, and Germany was the fulcrum of Europe. No other region of the world was so valuable to the superpowers. Despite the terrible devastation caused by the war, Germany's tremendous industrial potential and its highly educated and ambitious population could not be overlooked. It was also, because of the territorial settlements reached at Tehran and ratified at Yalta, the one region in which Soviet and Western troops stood toe-to-toe. The border between West and East Germany, and particularly the divided city of Berlin, thus became the central focal points of the developing Cold War.

Additionally, Germany was the one area in which all-out war between the superpowers seemed not only possible but likely. Soviet fears of resurgent German militarism were profound: no one in the Kremlin, or in the country as a whole, wanted to live through (or die in) a third German invasion in the same century. The stakes in other areas of the world, including the oil fields of the Middle East, were simply not as high. After the construction of the Berlin Wall in 1961 and the energy crisis of the mid-1970s, this perception would change dramatically, but although history can be read backward, it must be lived forward. In the late 1940s, Germany was the great prize, and neither side was willing to let the other dominate this land.

Third: The availability of nuclear weapons was to a significant degree responsible for the unusual nature of the Cold War. The horrifying possibility of nuclear holocaust led the superpowers to be very circumspect in confronting one another directly, and this absence of direct confrontation may well have prevented a conventional third world war. Instead, the Soviets and Americans pursued each other by proxy, competing for the affections of newly emerging nations, threatening each other's surrogates, and occasionally (as in Korea, Vietnam, and Afghanistan) fighting conventional wars in regions where the other's vital interests were not directly threatened. From time to time, each side feared that its opponent might react to a crisis elsewhere by forcing a showdown in Europe, but this never occurred, in part because both sides feared that a European conflict might lead to nuclear war.

This "positive" influence of nuclear weapons was more than offset by negative ones. The nuclear arms race quickly took on a self-fulfilling aspect, prolonging the Cold War and giving military establishments on both sides a vested interest in that prolongation. As a result, each side ended up with the capacity to destroy the entire world dozens of times over, at a cost of colossal amounts of money, huge commitments of productive capacity, and devastating psychological consequences: hundreds of millions of people lived and died in fear that a nuclear war might break out either by design or by accident. The grinding frustration of money wasted and dreams deferred, juxtaposed with a permanent, subliminal balance of terror, help to account for the bitter edge so characteristic of the Cold War.

Fourth: The Cold War evolved through a number of phases, three of which were crucial to its development.

a. The Critical Period of 1948–1949, including the Berlin Blockade, the formation of NATO, and the Chinese revolution. The blockade convinced both sides that postwar crises could be contained and that the costs of war might well outweigh the prizes to be gained by winning. After the blockade, decision makers talked less about the inevitability of a third world war and more about the necessity of avoiding one. NATO provided a framework for the Cold War and the nuclear arms race. It led eventually to the creation of the Warsaw Pact and the redivision of Europe into heavily armed alliances, and it committed the West to vigorous efforts to maintain its atomic advantage, in order to offset the preponderance of Soviet conventional forces in that divided continent. The communist takeover in China intensified the burgeoning "Red Scare" in the United States and resulted in a massive U.S. global effort to counter the spread of communism. By the end of this period, the structures and beliefs that would dominate the Cold War were pretty much in place.

b. The Critical Period of 1961–1962, including the construction of the Berlin Wall and the Cuban Missile Crisis. The wall defused the chronic Berlin crises of 1948–1961 and reduced tensions in Germany considerably. The Soviets now had a way to staunch the hemorrhage of skilled workers fleeing from East to West, while Washington possessed a propaganda club with which to bludgeon Moscow. It was a situation that neither side especially liked, but it was one that both could live with. The missile crisis took the superpowers to the brink of nuclear war and convinced them not only that they must prevent such a catastrophe but also that each had an overriding interest in avoiding nuclear brinkmanship and lessening global tensions. At the same time, it helped persuade Soviet leaders to embark on a massive and sustained buildup of their naval and nuclear forces. The Cold War thus entered a new phase, as each side sought to minimize direct confrontation and maneuver for advantage through weapons buildup, arms negotiations, and struggles in the Third World.

c. The Critical Period of 1985–1986, including the passing of the World War II generation of Soviet leadership, the accession of Gorbachev, and the American decision to introduce advanced technological weaponry into the Afghanistan conflict. Ironically, many Western experts in the 1970s and 1980s had dreaded the inevitable demise of the older generation of Communists, fearing that younger Soviet leaders who had not experienced firsthand the terrible suffering of World War II would be more likely to risk war. Instead, the accession of Gorbachev brought to power a new group of leaders who were less shackled by fear of Germany and more willing to seek accommodation with the West. Finally, the devastating impact of sophisticated U.S. weapons on Soviet fortunes in Afghanistan helped to convince Gorbachev that the Soviet economy, in order to develop such technology itself, must take drastic steps to become more competitive with the West. These developments, as we have seen, broke the logjam that had existed for decades and set in motion the series of events which led to the end of the Cold War.

Fifth: Ironically, many of the things that the USSR did to strengthen itself during the Cold War provoked reactions in the West that actually weakened Soviet security. More often than not, whenever the Kremlin moved to upgrade its weaponry, redress the strategic balance (as in Cuba in 1962), or enhance its political leverage over a nonaligned nation, its actions provoked an American response that ensured Washington's relative supremacy. In the end, the economic and technological advantages enjoyed by the United States could not be overcome, no matter how diligently the Soviets worked to do so.

Sixth: The Soviet system proved to be more rigid than those of the Western democracies and, therefore, less adaptable to changing circumstances and technological progress. Gorbachev, recognizing this lack of adaptability, decided to seek both economic and political democratization simultaneously in order to reform the system from the roots to the branches. Unfortunately for him, his efforts at political democratization undercut his economic program, depriving the central authorities of the means to impose strict discipline and loosening the bonds of fear that held the whole system together. Gorbachev's attempt to do too much too quickly, coupled with his underestimation of the potency of the appeal of nationalism, split the Communist party and wrecked the Soviet Union.

THE LEGACY OF THE COLD WAR

The end of the Cold War and the collapse of the Soviet state brought on a worldwide surge of hopefulness and relief. Nations that had existed for years under occupation and oppression now found themselves independent and free. People who had lived most or all of their lives with the fear of a nuclear holocaust now could face the future with fresh confidence and security. In Russia and the United States, military budgets were slashed, force levels were cut, and nuclear arsenals were reduced. A new age of peace and freedom seemed to be dawning, as nations prepared to work toward what George Bush called a "new world order."

And yet, even as Eastern peoples celebrated their new-found freedom, and Western nations congratulated themselves on their "victory" in the Cold War, it was becoming painfully obvious that the new world order was not necessarily less perilous nor more stable than the old. In many of the successor states of the USSR, and among the newly independent nations of the former Soviet bloc, the heady flush of exultation soon gave way to the bitter realities of economic crisis and political chaos. The transition from central state planning to free market economy proved far more lengthy and painful than most had imagined, and economic reforms designed to facilitate this transition soon began to lose favor among the suffering peoples. Worse still, nationalist rivalries and antagonisms, long suppressed by the force of Soviet military might and a powerful communist police-state apparatus, quickly reemerged. The Cold War may have ended, but it had left behind a legacy of economic woes and political antagonisms, as well as hatreds, resentments, and fears, that would not soon disappear.

In retrospect, it seemed, there were some advantages to the Cold War. For over four decades, a large measure of international stability was maintained by the worldwide balance of terror. Ethnic hostilities in the USSR and Eastern Europe were held in check by the overwhelming reality of Soviet power, while civil and social strife in the socialist world was similarly suppressed. The military-industrial complexes on both sides of the iron curtain provided secure employment to many and impressive wealth to a few. Prosperity reigned in the capitalist world, fueled in part by the international tensions, and technological spinoffs from military research and space exploration helped to bring the "good life" to the masses. Even in the socialist world, where goods were scarce and life was comparatively drab, there was full employment, job security, and a broad panoply of state-supplied basic services ranging from health care to housing. And the international scene seemed simpler and more stable: in a bipolar world, alliances remained rather steady, and it was relatively easy to distinguish one's friends from one's foes.

Still, the Cold War was hardly a golden age of tranquility and stability. Although no new world war broke out, millions continued to perish in regional conflicts. Indeed, during most of the Cold War years, there was almost always a "hot" war going on somewhere, whether it be in China, Korea, Vietnam, Cambodia, Angola, Afghanistan, or elsewhere. At least fifteen million people died in such conflicts, as well as in the countless insurrections, civil wars, and persecutions that arose. The world lurched from crisis to crisis, any one of which could have led to a devastating local conflict or an all-out nuclear war. And, although there is no way to measure adequately the psychological impact of decades of life under the nuclear gun, there is no reason to suppose that it was beneficial to humanity.

The fact is, however, that the world survived the Cold War. Bitter adversaries, facing the possibility of mutual annihilation, somehow found ways to contain their conflict in the interest of self-preservation. Despite their rhetoric, leaders on both sides learned to live with the ambiguity inherent in a continual state of international confrontation and to adjust to a world in which nuclear weapons had radically altered the calculus of war and peace. At the end of the Cold War, as the nations of the world sailed into uncharted waters, they could take comfort in the fact that they had already made their way through very stormy seas and had managed to endure a hard and bitter peace.

For Further Reading

1. THE SEEDS OF CONFLICT

Beloff, Max. *The Foreign Policy of Soviet Russia, 1929–1941* (2 vols., 1947–49).

Bennett, Edward M. *Franklin D. Roosevelt and the Search for Security: American-Soviet Relations, 1933–1939* (1985).

Browder, Robert. *The Origins of Soviet-American Diplomacy* (1953).

Dulles, Foster Rhea. *The Road to Teheran: The Story of Russia and America, 1781–1943* (1944).

Fleming, D. F. *The Cold War and Its Origins, 1917–1960* (2 vols., 1961).

Gaddis, John Lewis. *Russia, the Soviet Union and the United States: An Interpretive History* (2nd ed., 1990).

Haslam, Jonathan. *The Soviet Union and the Struggle for Collective Security in Europe, 1933–1939* (1984).

Hochman, Jiri. *The Soviet Union and the Failure of Collective Security, 1934–1938* (1984).

Kennan, George F. *Russia and the West under Lenin and Stalin* (1960).

Langer, William L., and S. Everett Gleason. *The Challenge to Isolation: The World Crisis of 1937–1940 and American Foreign Policy* (1952).

Lenin, V. I. *Imperialism: The Highest Stage of Capitalism* (1916).

Litvinov, Maxim. *Against Aggression* (1939).

Maddux, Thomas R. *Years of Estrangement: American Relations with the Soviet Union, 1933–1941* (1980).

Marx, Karl, and Friedrich Engels. *The Communist Manifesto* (1848).

McKenzie, Kermit E. *Comintern and World Revolution, 1928–1943* (1964).

Medvedev, Roy A. *Let History Judge: The Origins and Consequences of Stalinism* (2nd ed., 1989).

Meyer, Alfred G. *Communism* (1960).

Meyer, Alfred G. *Leninism* (1957).

Pipes, Richard. *The Russian Revolution* (1990).

Ponomayov, B., A. Gromyko, and V. Khvostov. *History of Soviet Foreign Policy, 1917–1945* (1969).

Roberts, Geoffrey. *The Unholy Alliance: Stalin's Pact with Hitler* (1989).

Tucker, Robert C. *Stalin in Power* (1990).

Ulam, Adam. *Ideologies and Illusions: Revolutionary Thought from Herzen to Solzhenitsyn* (1976).

Ulam, Adam. *Stalin: The Man and His Era* (1973).

Uldricks, Teddy. *Diplomacy and Ideology: The Origins of Soviet Foreign Relations, 1917–1930* (1980).

Von Laue, Theodore H. *Why Lenin? Why Stalin?* (1971).

Watt, Donald Cameron. *How War Came: The Immediate Origins of the Second World War, 1938–1939* (1989).

Weinberg, Gerhard L. *Germany and the Soviet Union, 1939–1941* (1954).

Wilson, Edmund. *To the Finland Station: A Study in the Writing and Acting of History* (1972).

Wohlforth, William. *The Elusive Balance* (1993).

Wozniuk, Vladimir. *Understanding Soviet Foreign Policy: Readings and Documents* (1990).

Yakovlev, Nikolai N. *Russia and the United States* (1979).

2. ADVERSARIES AND ALLIES, 1939–1945

Alperovitz, Gar. *Atomic Diplomacy: Hiroshima and Potsdam* (2nd ed., 1987).

Bullock, Alan. *Hitler and Stalin: A Comparative Biography* (1992).

Burns, James MacGregor. *Roosevelt: The Soldier of Freedom* (1970).

Calvocoressi, Peter, Guy Wint, and James Pritchard. *Total War* (2nd ed., 1989).

Churchill, Winston. *The Second World War* (6 vols., 1948–54).

Clemens, Diane. *Yalta* (1970).

Dallek, Robert. *Franklin D. Roosevelt and American Foreign Policy 1932–1945* (1979).

Edmonds, Walter. *The Big Three* (1991).

Feis, Herbert. *The Atomic Bomb and the End of World War II* (1966).

Feis, Herbert. *Between War and Peace: The Potsdam Conference* (1960).

Feis, Herbert. *Churchill, Roosevelt, Stalin: The War They Waged and the Peace They Sought* (1957).

Gallichio, Mark S. *The Cold War Begins in Asia* (1988).

Gilbert, Martin. *Churchill* (1991).

Gilbert, Martin. *The Second World War* (2nd ed., 1991).

Herken, Gregg. *The Winning Weapon* (1982).

Keegan, John. *The Second World War* (1989).

Kitchen, Martin. *British Policy toward the Soviet Union during the Second World War* (1986).

Kolko, Gabriel. *The Politics of War* (1968).

Mastny, Vojtech. *Russia's Road to the Cold War* (1979).

McCagg, William O. *Stalin Embattled, 1943–1948* (1978).

McNeill, William H. *America, Britain, and Russia: Their Cooperation and Conflict, 1941–1946* (1953).

Rhodes, Richard. *The Making of the Atomic Bomb* (1987).

Sherwin, Martin. *A World Destroyed: The Atomic Bomb and the Grand Alliance* (1976).

Taubman, William. *Stalin's American Policy* (1982).

Ulam, Adam. *Expansion and Coexistence: The History of Soviet Foreign Policy, 1917–1967* (1968).

Weinberg, Gerhard. *A World at Arms* (1994).

Weinberg, Gerhard. *The Foreign Policy of Hitler's Germany: Starting World War II, 1937–1939* (1980).

Wheeler-Bennett, John W. *The Semblance of Peace* (1972).

Woodward, Llewellyn. *British Foreign Policy in the Second World War* (1962).

3. THE FORMATION OF THE COMMUNIST BLOC, 1944–1948

Coutouvidis, J., and J. Reynolds. *Poland, 1939–1947* (1986).

Crampton, R. J. *A Short History of Modern Bulgaria* (1987).

Dedijer, Vladimir. *The Battle Stalin Lost* (1971).

Djilas, Milovan. *Conversations with Stalin* (1962).

Fischer-Galati, Stephen. *The Socialist Republic of Romania.* (1969).

Gati, Charles. *Hungary and the Soviet Bloc* (1986).

Ionescu, Ghita. *Communism in Romania, 1944–1962* (1964).

Kaplan, Morton. *The Communist Coup in Czechoslovakia* (1960).

Kertesz, Stephen. *Between Russia and the West: Hungary and the Illusions of Peacemaking, 1945–1947* (1984).

Korbel, Josef. *The Communist Subversion of Czechoslovakia, 1938–1948* (1959).

Kovrig, Bennett. *The Hungarian People's Republic* (1970).

Kovrig, Bennett. *The Myth of Liberation* (1973).

Oren, N. *Bulgarian Communism: The Road to Power* (1971).

Roos, Hans. *A History of Modern Poland* (1966).

Rothschild, Joseph. *Return to Diversity: A Political History of East Central Europe Since World War II* (1989).

Seton-Watson, Hugh. *The East European Revolution* (1957).

Stokes, Gale, ed. *From Communism to Pluralism: A Documentary History of Eastern Europe since 1945* (1991).

Swain, Geoffrey, and Nigel Swain. *Eastern Europe since 1945* (1993).

Ulam, Adam. *Titoism and the Cominform* (1952).

Ullman, Walter. *The United States in Prague, 1945–1948* (1978).

Zinner, Paul. *Communist Strategy and Tactics in Czechoslovakia* (1963).

4. THE COLD WAR BEGINS, 1945–1948

Anderson, Terry. *The United States, Great Britain, and the Cold War, 1944–1947 (1981).*

Blackett, P. M. S. *Fear, War and the Bomb* (1948)

Bullock, Alan. *Ernest Bevin* (1983).

Davis, Lynn E. *The Cold War Begins* (1974).

Feis, Herbert. *From Trust to Terror* (1970).

Gaddis, John L. *The United States and the Origins of the Cold War, 1941–1947* (1972).

Gardner, Lloyd C. *Architects of Illusion* (1970).

Gimbel, John. *The Origins of the Marshall Plan* (1976).

Halle, Louis. *The Cold War as History* (1967).

Harbutt, Fraser. *The Iron Curtain* (1986).

Herring, George C. *Aid to Russia, 1941–1946* (1973).

Herz, Martin. *The Beginnings of the Cold War* (1966).

Hogan, Michael J. *The Marshall Plan: America, Britain, and the Reconstruction of Western Europe, 1947–1952* (1987).

Isaacson, Walter, and Evan Thomas. *The Wise Men* (1986).

Kennan, George F. *Memoirs: 1925–1950* (1967).

Lundestad, Geir. *America, Scandinavia and the Cold War* (1980).
Maddox, Robert. *The New Left and the Origins of the Cold War* (1973).
Mayers, David. *George Kennan and the Dilemmas of U.S. Foreign Policy* (1988).
Ninkovich, Frank. *Germany and the United States* (1988).
Pollard, Robert A. *Economic Security and the Origins of the Cold War, 1945–1950* (1985).
Rose, Lisle A. *After Yalta* (1973).
Rubin, Barry. *The Great Powers in the Middle East: The Road to the Cold War* (1980).
Sharp, Tony. *The Wartime Alliance and the Zonal Division of Germany* (1975).
Steel, Ronald. *Walter Lippmann and the American Century* (1980).
Thomas, Hugh. *Armed Truce: The Beginnings of the Cold War, 1945–1946* (1986).
Williams, William Appelman. *The Tragedy of American Diplomacy* (1959).
Yergin, Daniel. *Shattered Peace* (1977).

5. THE BATTLE FOR GERMANY, 1948–1952

Acheson, Dean. *Present at the Creation* (1969).
Backer, John H. *The Decision to Divide Germany* (1978).
Calleo, David. *The German Problem Reconsidered* (1978).
Clay, Lucius D. *Decision in Germany* (1950).
Cook, Don W. *Forging the Alliance: NATO 1945–1950* (1989).
Davison, W. Phillips. *The Blockade of Berlin* (1958).
Donovan, Robert J. *Tumultuous Years: The Presidency of Harry S. Truman, 1949–1953* (1982).
Gimbel, John. *The American Occupation of Germany* (1968).
Hiscocks, Richard. *The Adenauer Era* (1966).
Holloway, David. *Stalin and the Bomb* (1994).
Jonas, Manfred. *The U.S. and Germany* (1984).
Kaplan, Lawrence S. *The United States and NATO: The Formative Years* (1984).
Kuklick, Bruce. *American Policy and the Division of Germany* (1972).
Kuniholm, Bruce. *The Origins of the Cold War in the Near East* (1980).
Leffler, Melvyn P. *A Preponderance of Power: The Truman Administration, the Cold War, and American National Security* (1992).
Mayer, Herbert C. *German Recovery and the Marshall Plan, 1948–1952* (1969).
Merkl, Peter H. *The Origins of the West German Republic* (1963).
Milward, Alan. *The Reconstruction of Western Europe, 1945–1951* (1984).
Nettl, J. P. *The Eastern Zone and Soviet Policy in Germany, 1945–1950* (1951).
Peterson, Edward N. *The American Occupation of Germany: Retreat to Victory* (1978).
Prittie, Terence. *Konrad Adenauer, 1876–1967* (1972).
Richardson, James L. *Germany and the Atlantic Alliance* (1966).
Schwartz, Thomas A. *America's Germany* (1990).
Shlaim, Avi. *The U.S. and the Berlin Blockade* (1983).
Shulman, Marshall. *Stalin's Foreign Policy Reappraised* (1963).
Ulam, Adam. *Expansion and Coexistence: The History of Soviet Foreign Policy, 1917–1967* (1968).

6. THE COMMUNIST REVOLUTION IN CHINA, 1946–1950

Belden, Jack. *China Shakes the World* (1949).
Beloff, Max. *Soviet Policy in the Far East, 1944–1951* (1953).
Bianco, Lucien. *Origins of the Chinese Revolution, 1915–1949* (1971).
Bodde, Derk. *Peking Diary: A Year of Revolution* (1950).
Borisov, O. B., and B. T. Koloskov. *Soviet-Chinese Relations, 1945–1970* (1975).

Buhite, Russell D. *Soviet-American Relations in Asia, 1945–1954* (1981).

Chang Chia-ao. *The Inflationary Spiral: The Experience in China, 1939–1950* (1958).

Chang, Gordon H. *Friends and Enemies: The United States, China, and the Soviet Union, 1948–1972* (1990).

Chassin, Lionel Max. *The Communist Conquest of China: A History of the Civil War, 1945–1949* (1965).

Chiang Kai-shek. *Soviet Russia in China: A Summing-up at Seventy* (1957).

Fairbank, John King. *The United States and China* (2nd ed., 1958).

Feis, Herbert. *The China Tangle: The American Effort in China from Pearl Harbor to the Marshall Mission* (1953).

Fitzgerald, C. P. *The Birth of Communist China* (1964).

Fried, Richard M. *Nightmare in Red: The McCarthy Era in Perspective* (1990).

Griffith, Robert. *The Politics of Fear: Joseph R. McCarthy and the Senate* (1970).

Iriye, Akira. *The Origins of the Cold War in Asia* (1977).

Isaacs, Harold. *The Tragedy of the Chinese Revolution* (1961).

Johnson, Chalmers A. *Peasant Nationalism and Communist Power: The Emergence of Revolutionary China, 1937–1945* (1962).

Kuei, Ch'ung-chi. *The Kuomintang-Communist Struggle in China, 1922–1949* (1970).

Landis, Mark. *Joseph McCarthy: The Politics of Chaos* (1987).

Loh, Pichon Pei Yung. *The Kuomintang Debacle of 1949: Conquest or Collapse?* (1965).

Moore, Harriet. *Soviet Far Eastern Policy, 1939–1945* (1945).

North, Robert C. *Moscow and Chinese Communists* (1953).

Oshinsky, David M. *A Conspiracy So Immense: The World of Joe McCarthy* (1983).

Pavlovsky, Michel N. *Chinese-Russian Relations* (1949).

Pepper, Suzanne. *The Civil War in China, 1945–1949* (1978).

Quested, R. K. I. *Sino-Russian Relations: A Short History* (1984).

Rigg, Robert B. *Red China's Fighting Hordes* (1952).

Schaller, Michael. *The American Occupation of Japan: The Origins of the Cold War in Asia* (1985).

Schaller, Michael. *The U.S. Crusade in China, 1938–1945* (1979).

Schrecker, Ellen. *The Age of McCarthyism* (1994).

Schwartz, Benjamin. *Chinese Communism and the Rise of Mao* (1953).

Schwartz, Harry. *Tsars, Mandarins and Commissars: History of Chinese-Russian Relations* (1964).

Snow, Edgar. *Red Star over China* (1937).

Terrill, Ross. *Mao: A Biography* (1980).

U.S. State Department. *The China White Paper, 1949* (2 vols.,1967).

Westad, Odd Arne. *Cold War and Revolution: Soviet-American Rivalry and the Origins of the Chinese Civil War, 1944–1946* (1993).

Whiting, Alan S. *Soviet Policies in China, 1917-1924* (1954).

7. THE CONFLICT OVER KOREA, 1950–1953

Acheson, Dean. *The Korean War* (1971).

Ambrose, Stephen E. *Eisenhower: Soldier and President* (1994).

Baldwin, Frank, ed. *Without Parallel: The American-Korean Relationship since 1945* (1974).

Beloff, Max. *Soviet Policy in the Far East, 1944–1951* (1953).

Berger, Carl. *The Korea Knot: A Military-Political History* (1965).

Cumings, Bruce. *The Origins of the Korean War* (2 vols., 1981–90).

Ebon, Martin. *Malenkov: Stalin's Successor* (1953).

Foot, Rosemary. *The Wrong War: American Policy and the Dimensions of the Korean Conflict, 1950–1953* (1985).

George, Alexander L. *The Chinese Communist Army in Action: The Korean War and Its Aftermath* (1967).

Goodrich, Leland M. *Korea: A Study of U.S. Policy in the United Nations* (1956).

Gordenker, Leon. *The United Nations and the Peaceful Unification of Korea: The Politics of Field Operations, 1947–1950* (1959).

Guttman, Allen, ed. *Korea: Cold War and Limited War* (1972).

Higgins, Trumbull. *Korea and the Fall of MacArthur* (1960).

Hoyt, Edwin Palmer. *The Bloody Road to Panmunjom* (1985).

Hua, Ch'ing-chao. *From Yalta to Panmunjom: Truman's Diplomacy and the Four Powers, 1945–1953* (1993).

James, D. Clayton. *The Years of MacArthur: Triumph and Disaster, 1945–1964* (1985).

Kaufman, Burton I. *The Korean War: Challenges in Crisis, Credibility and Command* (1986).

Kim Chull Baum, and James I. Matray, eds. *Korea and the Cold War: Division, Destruction, and Disarmament* (1993).

Lee, Chong-sik. *The Politics of Korean Nationalism* (1963).

MacDonald, Callum A. *Korea: The War before Vietnam* (1986).

Manchester, William R. *American Caesar: Douglas McArthur, 1880–1964* (1978).

May, Ernest R. *American Cold War Strategy: Interpreting NSC 68* (1993).

Paek, Son-yop. *From Pusan to Panmunjom (1992).*

Pruessen, Ronald W. *John Foster Dulles: The Road to Power* (1982).

Rapoport, Iakov L. *The Doctors' Plot of 1953* (1990).

Rees, David. *Korea: The Limited War* (1964).

Scalapino, Robert A., and Chong-sik Lee. *Communism in Korea: Part I. The Movement* (1972).

Schaller, Michael. *Douglas MacArthur: The Far Eastern General* (1989).

Spanier, John W. *The Truman-MacArthur Controvery and the Korean War* (1959).

Suh, Dae-Sook. *The Korean Communist Movement, 1918–1948* (1967).

Vatcher, William Henry, Jr. *Panmunjom: The Story of the Korean Military Armistice Negotiations* (1958).

8. NEW LEADERS AND NEW REALITIES, 1953–1957

Alexander, Charles C. *Holding the Line: The Eisenhower Era, 1952–1961* (1975).

Ambrose, Stephen E., and Richard H. Immerman. *Ike's Spies: Eisenhower and the Espionage Establishment* (1981).

Barnet, Richard J. *The Alliance: America, Europe, Japan: Makers of the Postwar World* (1983).

Berding, Andrew H. *Dulles on Diplomacy* (1965).

Beschloss, Michael R. *Eisenhower: A Centennial Life* (1990).

Brands, H. W., Jr. *Cold Warriors: Eisenhower's Generation and American Foreign Policy* (1988).

Brant, Stefan. *The East German Rising* (1957).

Childers, Erskine B. *The Road to Suez* (1962).

Cook, Blanche Wiesen. *The Declassified Eisenhower: A Divided Legacy of Peace and Political Warfare* (1982).

Crankshaw, E. *Khrushchev: A Career* (1966).

Cronin, Audrey Keith. *Great Power Politics and the Struggle over Austria, 1945–1955* (1986).

Dallin, David J. *Soviet Foreign Policy after Stalin* (1961).

Divine, Robert A. *Eisenhower and the Cold War* (1981).

Eisenhower, Dwight D. *The White House Years: Mandate for Change, 1953–1956* (1963).

Ferrell, Robert H., ed. *The Eisenhower Diaries* (1981).

Frankland, Mark. *Khrushchev* (1967).

Gehlen, Michael. *The Politics of Coexistence: Soviet Methods and Motives* (1967).

Gerson, Louis L. *John Foster Dulles* (1968).

Graebner, Norman A. *Cold War Diplomacy, 1945–1960* (1972).

Greenstein, Fred I. *The Hidden-Hand Presidency: Eisenhower as Leader* (1982).

Grose, Peter. *Gentleman Spy: The Life of Allen Dulles* (1994).

Guhin, Michael A. *John Foster Dulles: A Statesman and His Time* *(1972).*

Hoopes, Townsend. *The Devil and John Foster Dulles* (1973).

Immerman, Richard H. *The CIA in Guatemala: The Foreign Policy of Intervention* (1982).

Immerman, Richard H., ed. *John Foster Dulles and the Diplomacy of the Cold War* (1989).

Kennan, George F. *Memoirs: 1950–1963* (1972).

Khrushchev, N. S. *The Crimes of the Stalin Era: A Special Report to the 20th Congress of the Communist Party of the Soviet Union* (1962).

Khrushchev, N. S. *Khrushchev Remembers* (1970).

Khrushchev, N. S. *Khrushchev Remembers: The Glasnost Tapes* (1990).

Khrushchev, N. S. *Khrushchev Remembers: The Last Testament* (1974).

Lacouture, Jean, and Simon Lacouture. *Egypt in Transition* (1958).

Louis, William Roger, and Roger Owen. *Suez 1956: The Crisis and Its Consequences* (1989).

McCauley, Martin, ed. *Khrushchev and Khrushchevism* (1987).

McCauley, Martin. *Nikita Sergeevich Khrushchev* (1991).

Medvedev, Roy. *Khrushchev* (1983).

Neff, Donald. *Warriors at Suez: Eisenhower Takes America into the Middle East* (1981).

Parmet, Herbert. *Eisenhower and the American Crusades* (1972).

Pistrak, Lazar. *The Grand Tactician: Khrushchev's Rise to Power* (1961).

Rostow, W. W. *Open Skies: Eisenhower's Proposal of July 21, 1955* (1982).

Sobel, L. A. *Russia's Rulers: The Khrushchev Period* (1971).

Syrop, K. *Spring in October: The Polish Revolution of 1956* (1958).

Toulouse, Mark G. *The Transformation of John Foster Dulles: From Prophet of Realism to Priest of Nationalism* (1985).

Wolfe, Bertram D. *Khrushchev and Stalin's Ghost* (1957).

Zinner, Paul, ed. *National Communism and Popular Revolt in Eastern Europe* (1956).

Zinner, Paul. *Revolution in Hungary* (1961).

9. THE PERPETUATION OF THE COLD WAR, 1957–1961

Aliano, Richard A. *American Defense Policy from Eisenhower to Kennedy* (1975).

Beschloss, Michael R. *Mayday: Eisenhower, Khrushchev, and the U-2 Affair* (1986).

Bloomfield, Lincoln, et. al. *Khrushchev and the Arms Race* (1966).

Boffa, Giuseppe. *Inside the Khrushchev Era* (1963).

Borstelman, Thomas. *Apartheid's Reluctant Uncle: The United States and Southern Africa in the Early Cold War* (1993).

Bundy, McGeorge. *Danger and Survival: Choices about the Bomb in the First Fifty Years* (1988).

De Gaulle, Charles. *Memoirs of Hope: Renewal, 1958–1962* (1971).

Divine, Robert A. *Blowing in the Wind: The Nuclear Test Ban Debate, 1954–1960* (1978).

Eisenhower, Dwight D. *The White House Years: Waging Peace, 1956–1961* (1965).

Horne, Alistair. *Macmillan: 1957–1986* (1989).

Jackson, Henry F. *From Congo to Soweto: U.S. Foreign Policy toward Africa since 1960* (1982).

Lacouture, Jean. *De Gaulle* (2 vols., 1990–91).

Lesch, David W. *Syria and the United States: Eisenhower's Cold War in the Middle East* (1992).

Linden, Carl. *Khrushchev and the Soviet Leadership, 1957–1964* (1966).

McDougall, Walter A. *The Heavens and the Earth* (1985).

McMahon, Robert J. *The Cold War on the Periphery: The United States, India, and Pakistan* (1994).

Medvedev, Roy and Zhores Medvedev. *Khrushchev: The Years in Power* (1978).

Melanson, Richard A., and David Meyers, eds. *Reevaluating Eisenhower: American Foreign Policy in the Fifties* (1987).

Noer, Thomas J. *Cold War and Black Liberation: The United States and White Rule in Africa, 1948–1968* (1985).

Powers, Francis Gary, defendant. *The Trial of the U-2: Exclusive Authorized Account of the Court Proceedings of the Case of Francis Gary Powers* (1960).

Ranelagh, John. *The Agency: The Rise and Decline of the CIA* (1986).

Schick, Jack M. *The Berlin Crisis, 1958–1962* (1971).

Smolansky, Oles M. *The Soviet Union and the Arab East under Khrushchev* (1974).

Tatu, Michel. *Power in the Kremlin* (1969).

Ulam, Adam B. *The Rivals: America and Russia since World War II* (1971).

Wise, David, and Thomas B. Ross. *The U-2 Affair* (1962).

Wyden, Peter. *Bay of Pigs: The Untold Story* (1979).

Zimmerman, William. *Soviet Perspectives on International Relations, 1956-1967* (1969).

10. CRISIS AND COEXISTENCE, 1961–1964

Abel, Elie. *The Missile Crisis* (1966).

Allison, Graham T. *Essence of Decision* (1971).

Allyn, Bruce, James Blight, and David Welch, eds. *Back to the Brink: Proceedings of the Moscow Conference on the Cuban Missile Crisis, January 27–28, 1989* (1992).

Beschloss, Michael. *The Crisis Years: Kennedy and Khrushchev, 1960–1963* (1991).

Blight, James, and David Welch, eds. *On the Brink: Americans and Soviets Reexamine the Cuban Missile Crisis* (2nd ed., 1990).

Brugioni, Dino A. *Eyeball to Eyeball* (1991).

Cate, Curtis. *The Ides of August: The Berlin Wall Crisis, 1961* (1978).

Catudal, Honoré Marc. *Kennedy and the Berlin Wall Crisis: A Case Study in U.S. Decision-Making (1980).*

Costigliola, Frank. *Cold Alliance* (1990).

Dinerstein, Herbert S. *The Making of a Missile Crisis: October, 1962* (1976).

Garthoff, Raymond L. *Reflections on the Cuban Missile Crisis* (1989).

Gelb, Norman. *The Berlin Wall: Kennedy, Khrushchev, and a Showdown in the Heart of Europe* (1986).

Gittings, John. *Survey of the Sino-Soviet Dispute, 1963–1967* (1968).

Hilsman, Roger. *To Move a Nation: The Politics of Foreign Policy in the Administration of John F. Kennedy* (1967).

Hyland, William, and Richard W. Shryock. *The Fall of Khrushchev* (1969).

Kennedy, Robert F. *Thirteen Days* (1969).

Larson, David L., ed. *The "Cuban Crisis" of 1962* (1963).

Mahoney, Richard D. *JFK: Ordeal in Africa* (1983).

Mehnert, Klaus. *Peking and Moscow* (1963).

Nathan, James A. ed. *The Cuban Missile Crisis Revisited* (1992).

Page, Martin. *The Day Khrushchev Fell* (1965).

Paterson, Thomas G. *Contesting Castro: The United States and the Triumph of the Cuban Revolution* (1994).

Paterson, Thomas G. *Kennedy's Quest for Victory: American Foreign Policy, 1961–1963* (1989).

Pope, Ronald R. *Soviet Views of the Cuban Missile Crisis: Myth and Reality* (1982).

Robin, Gabriel. *La Crise de Cuba (Octobre 1962)* (1984).

Rusk, Dean, with Richard Rusk. *As I Saw It* (1990).
Schlesinger, Arthur M. *A Thousand Days: John F. Kennedy in the White House* (1965).
Seaborg, Glenn T., and Benjamin S. Loeb. *Kennedy, Khrushchev and the Test Ban* (1981).
Slusser, Robert M. *The Berlin Crisis of 1961* (1973).
Sorenson, Theodore C. *Kennedy* (1965).
Wyden, Peter. *Wall: The Inside Story of Divided Berlin* (1989).
Zagoria, Donald. *The Sino-Soviet Conflict, 1956–1961* (1962).
Zimmerman, William. *Soviet Perspectives on International Relations, 1956-67* (1969).

11. VIETNAM WAR AND COLD WAR, 1964–1970

Arnett, Peter, and Michael Maclear. *The Ten Thousand Day War* (1981).
Berman, Larry. *Lyndon Johnson's War: The Road to Stalemate in Vietnam* (1989).
Blum, Robert M. *Drawing the Line: The Origin of the American Containment Policy in East Asia* (1982).
Buttinger, Joseph. *Vietnam: A Dragon Embattled* (2 vols., 1967).
Capps, Walter H. *The Unfinished War: Vietnam and the American Conscience (1982).*
Chandler, David P. *A History of Cambodia* (1983).
Chanoff, David, and Doan Van Thai. *Portrait of the Enemy: An Oral History* (1986).
Duiker, William J. *U.S. Containment Policy and the Conflict in Indochina* (1994).
Fall, Bernard B. *Street without Joy: Insurgency in Vietnam, 1946–1963* (1963).
Giap, Vo Nguyen. *Unforgettable Days* (1978).
Halberstam, David. *The Best and the Brightest* (1972).
Hammer, Ellen J. *A Death in November: America in Vietnam, 1963* (1987).
Henderson, William. *Why the Vietcong Fought* (1979).
Herring, George C. *America's Longest War* (1986).
Honey, P. J. *Communism in North Vietnam* (1963).
Johnson, Lyndon Baines. *The Vantage Point: Perspectives on the Presidency, 1963–1968* (1971).
Karnow, Stanley. *Vietnam: A History* (1983).
Lacouture, Jean. *Ho Chi Minh: A Political Biography* (1968).
Lewy, Günter. *America in Vietnam* (1978).
▸McNamara, Robert S. *In Retrospect: The Tragedy and Lessons of Vietnam* (1995).
Olson, James S. and Randy Roberts. *Where the Domino Fell: America and Vietnam, 1945 to 1990* (1991).
Pike, Douglas. *PAVN: People's Army of Vietnam* (1986).
Pike, Douglas. *Vietnam and the Soviet Union: Anatomy of an Alliance* (1987).
Powers, Thomas. *Vietnam, the War at Home: The Antiwar Movement, 1964–1968* (1984).
Sheehan, Neil. *A Bright Shining Lie: John Paul Vann and the American Experience in Vietnam* (1988).
Sheehan, Neil, et. al. *The Pentagon Papers* (1971).
Snepp, Frank. *Decent Interval: An Insider's Account of Saigon's Indecent End* (1977).
Sulzberger, C. L. *The World and Richard Nixon* (1987).
Summers, Harry G., Jr. *On Strategy: The Vietnam War in Context* (1981).
Turley, William S. *The Second Indochina War* (1986).

12. CHINA, SALT, AND THE SUPERPOWERS, 1967–1972

Aitken, Jonathan. *Nixon: A Life* (1993).
Ambrose, Stephen E. *Nixon* (3 vols., 1987–92).
Binder, David. *The Other German: Willy Brandt's Life and Times* (1975).

Burns, Richard Dean, ed. *Encyclopedia of Arms Control and Disarmament* (3 vols., 1993).

Burns, Richard Dean, and Susan Hoffman Hutson. *The SALT Era: A Selected Bibliography* (1979).

Catudal, Honoré M., Jr. *The Diplomacy of the Quadripartite Agreement on Berlin (1978).*

Chang, Gordon H. *Friends and Enemies: The United States, China, and the Soviet Union, 1948–1972* (1990).

Clubb, Oliver Edmund. *China and Russia: The Great Game* (1971).

Dawisha, Karen. *The Kremlin and the Prague Spring* (1984).

Deutscher, Isaac. *Russia, China, and the West* (1970).

Dornberg, John. *Brezhnev: The Masks of Power* (1974).

Dulles, Foster Rhea. *American Foreign Policy toward Communist China, 1949–1969* (1972).

Edmonds, Robin. *Soviet Foreign Policy, 1962–1973* (1975).

Ellison, Herbert, ed. *The Sino-Soviet Conflict: A Global Perspective* (1982).

Francisco, Ronald A., and Richard L. Merritt. *Berlin between Two Worlds* (1986).

Friedman, Leon, and William F. Levantrosser, eds. *Cold War Patriot and Statesman: Richard M. Nixon* (1993).

Golan, Galia. *The Czechoslovak Reform Movement: Communism in Crisis, 1962–1968* (1971).

Griffith, William E. *The Ostpolitik of the Federal Republic of Germany* (1978).

Haslam, Jonathan. *The Soviet Union and the Politics of Nuclear Weapons in Europe, 1969–1987* (1990).

Howard, Michael, and Robert Hunter. *Israel and the Arab World: The Crisis of 1967* (1967).

Hughes, Barry B. *The Domestic Context of American Foreign Policy* (1978).

Kissinger, Henry. *White House Years* (1979).

Kulski, W. W. *The Soviet Union in World Affairs: A Documented Analysis, 1964–1972* (1973).

Labedz, Leopold. *The Sino-Soviet Conflict: Eleven Radio Discussions (1965).*

Medvedev, Roy. *China and the Superpowers* (1986).

Merritt, Richard L., and Anna L. Merritt. *Living with the Wall: West Berlin, 1961–1985* (1985).

Newhouse, John. *Cold Dawn: The Story of SALT* (1973).

Nixon, Richard M. *RN: The Memoirs of Richard Nixon* (1978).

Oksenberg, Michel, and Robert B. Oxman, eds. *Dragon and Eagle: United States–China Relations Past and Future* (1978).

Remington, Robin A., ed. *Winter in Prague: Documents on Czechoslovak Communism in Crisis* (1969).

Ross, Robert S., ed. *China, the United States, and the Soviet Union: Tripolarity and Policy-Making in the Cold War* (1993).

Salisbury, Harrison. *War between Russia and China* (1969).

Schaller, Michael. *The United States and China in the Twentieth Century* (2nd ed., 1990).

Seaborg, Glenn T., and Benjamin S. Loeb. *Stemming the Tide: Arms Control and the Johnson Years* (1987).

Shawcross, William. *Dubcek* (2nd ed., 1990).

Smith, Gerald. *Doubletalk: The Story of the First Strategic Arms Limitation Talks* (1980).

Snow, Edgar. *The Long Revolution* (1971).

Sodaro, Michael J. *Moscow, Germany, and the West from Khrushchev to Gorbachev* (1990).

Sonnenfeld, Helmut, and William G. Hyland. *Soviet Perspectives on Security* (1979).

Stent, Angela. *From Embargo to Ostpolitik* (1980).

Sutter, Robert G. *China Watch: Sino-American Reconciliation* (1979).

Sutter, Robert G. *Chinese Foreign Policy after the Cultural Revolution, 1966–1977* (1978).

Valenta, Jiri. *Soviet Intervention in Czechoslovakia in 1968: Anatomy of a Decision* (2nd ed., 1991).

Volten, Peter M. E. *Brezhnev's Peace Program* (1982).

Waterbury, John. *The Egypt of Nasser and Sadat* (1983).
Wettig, Gerhard. *Community and Conflict in the Socialist Camp: The Soviet Union, East Germany, and the German Problem, 1965–1972* (1975).
Whetten, Lawrence A. *Germany's Ostpolitik* (1971).
Young, Kenneth T. *Negotiating with the Chinese Communists: The United States Experience, 1953–1967* (1968).
Zartman, William, ed. *Czechoslovakia: Intervention and Impact (1970).*

13. THE HEYDAY OF DÉTENTE, 1972–1975

Brezhnev, Leonid I. *Peace, Détente and Soviet-American Relations* (1979).
Chace, James, comp. *Conflict in the Middle East* (1969).
Davis, Nathaniel. *The Last Two Years of Salvador Allende* (1985).
Dawisha, Karen. *Soviet Foreign Policy towards Egypt* (1979).
Freedman, R. O. *Soviet Policy toward the Middle East since 1970* (3rd ed., 1982).
Garthoff, Raymond L. *Détente and Confrontation* (1985).
Goldman, Marshall. *Détente and Dollars* (1975).
Heikal, Mohammed. *The Road to Ramadan* (1975).
Hersh, Seymour. *The Price of Power* (1983).
Holloway, David. *The Soviet Union and the Arms Race* (1983).
Hyland, William G. *Mortal Rivals: Understanding the Pattern of Soviet-American Arms Conflict* (1987).
Kanet, Roger. *The Soviet Union and the Developing Nations* (1974).
Landis, Lincoln. *Politics and Oil: Moscow in the Middle East* (1973).
Litwak, Robert S. *Détente and the Nixon Doctrine: American Foreign Policy and the Pursuit of Stability, 1969–1976* (1984).
Luttwak, Edward. *The U.S.–USSR Nuclear Weapons Balance* (1974).
Mazlish, Bruce. *Kissinger* (1976).
Morton, Henry W., and Rudolf L. Tökes. *Soviet Politics and Society in the 1970s* (1974).
Newhouse, John. *Cold Dawn: The Story of SALT* (1973).
Olson, James S. and Randy Roberts. *Where the Domino Fell: America and Vietnam, 1945 to 1990 (1991).*
Petras, James, and Morris Morley. *The United States and Chile: Imperialism and the Overthrow of the Allende Government* (1975).
Pipes, Richard. *U.S.–Soviet Relations in the Era of Détente* (1981).
Primakov, Yevgeny M. *Anatomy of the Middle East Conflict* (1979).
Schulzinger, Robert. *Henry Kissinger: Doctor of Diplomacy* (1989).
Shawcross, William. *Sideshow: Kissinger, Nixon and the Destruction of Cambodia* (1979).
Smith, Hedrick. *The Russians* (1975).
Stevenson, Richard W. *The Rise and Fall of Détente: Relaxations of Tensions in U.S.Soviet Relations, 1953–1984 (1985).*
Stoessinger, John G. *Henry Kissinger: The Anguish of Power* (1976).
Ulam, Adam. *Dangerous Relations: The Soviet Union in World Politics, 1970–1982* (1983).
Willrich, Mason, and John B. Rhinelander, eds. *SALT: The Moscow Agreements and Beyond* (1975).
Yodfat, Aryeh. *The Soviet Union and the Arabian Peninsula* (1983).

14. THE DECLINE OF DÉTENTE, 1975–1979

Arnold, Anthony. *Afghanistan: The Soviet Invasion in Perspective* (1985).
Bradsher, H. S. *Afghanistan and the Soviet Union* (1983).

Brzezinski, Zbigniew. *Power and Principle: Memoirs of the National Security Advisor, 1977–1981* (1983).

Carter, Jimmy. *Keeping Faith: Memoirs of a President* (1982).

Collins, Joseph. *The Soviet Invasion of Afghanistan* (1986).

Ford, Gerald R. *A Time to Heal: The Autobiography of Gerald R. Ford* (1979).

Forsythe, David P. *Human Rights and U.S. Foreign Policy: Congress Reconsidered* (1988).

*Forsythe, David P. *Human Rights and World Politics* (1983).

Freedman, R. O. *Soviet Policy toward the Middle East since 1970* (3rd ed., 1982).

Gelman, Harry. *The Brezhnev Politburo and the Decline of Détente* (1984).

Hammond, Thomas T. *Red Flag over Afghanistan: The Communist Coup, the Soviet Invasion, and the Consequences* (1984).

Harding, Harry. *China's Second Revolution: Reform after Mao* (1987).

Holloway, David. *The Soviet Union and the Arms Race* (1983).

Kissinger, Henry. *Years of Upheaval* (1982).

Kusnitz, Leonard A. *Public Opinion and Foreign Policy: America's China Policy, 1949–1979* (1984).

Legum, Colin, and Bill Lee. *The Horn of Africa in Continuing Crisis* (1979).

Morley, Morris H. *Washington, Somoza, and the Sandinistas: State and Regime in U.S. Policy toward Nicaragua, 1969–1981* (1984).

*Mowers, Glenn, Jr. *Human Rights and American Foreign Policy: The Carter and Reagan Experiences* (1987).

Muravchik, Joshua. *The Uncertain Crusade: Jimmy Carter and the Dilemmas of Human Rights* (1986).

Pipes, Richard. *U.S.–Soviet Relations in the Era of Détente (1981).*

Sanders, Jerry W. *Peddlers of Crisis: The Committee on the Present Danger and Containment* (1983).

*Sick, Gary. *All Fall Down: America's Tragic Encounter with Iran* (1985).

Smith, Gaddis. *Morality, Reason and Power: American Diplomacy in the Carter Years* (1986).

Sutter, Robert G. *The China Quandary: Domestic Determinants of U.S. China Policy, 1972–1982* (1983).

Sutter, Robert G. *China Watch: Sino-American Reconciliation* (1979).

Talbott, Strobe. *Endgame: The Inside Story of SALT II* (1979).

Vance, Cyrus. *Hard Choices: Critical Years in America's Foreign Policy* (1983).

Vogelgesang, Sandy. *American Dream, Global Nightmare: The Dilemma of U.S. Human Rights Policy* (1980).

15. THE RETURN OF THE COLD WAR, 1980–1985

Arbatov, G. A. *The Soviet Viewpoint* (1983).

Byrnes, R. F., ed. *After Brezhnev: Sources of Soviet Conduct in the 1980s* (1983).

Cannon, Lou. *President Reagan: The Role of a Lifetime* (1991).

Chernenko. K. U. *Selected Speeches and Writings* (1982).

Dallek, Robert. *Ronald Reagan: The Politics of Symbolism* (1984).

Dallin, Alexander. *Black Box: KAL OO7 and the Superpowers* (1985).

DePorte, A. W. *Europe between the Superpowers: The Enduring Balance* (2nd ed., 1986).

Ebon, Martin. *The Andropov File: The Life and Ideas of Yuri V. Andropov* (1983).

Freedman, Lawrence. *Signals of War: The Falklands Conflict of 1982* (1990).

Garton Ash, Timothy. *The Polish Revolution: Solidarity (1984).*

Goldman, Marshall. *The USSR in Crisis: The Failure of an Economic System* (1983).

Gromyko, Andrei A. *Peace Now, Peace for the Future* (1984).

Haig, Alexander M. *Caveat: Realism, Reagan, and Foreign Policy* (1984).

Hazan, Baruch. *From Brezhnev to Gorbachev: Infighting in the Kremlin* (1987).

Hersh, Seymour. *"The Target Is Destroyed": What Really Happened to Flight 007 and What America Knew about It* (1987).

Hough, Jerry F. *The Struggle for the Third World: Soviet Debates and American Options* (1986).

Hutchings, R. L. *Soviet East European Relations: Consolidation and Conflict* (1987).

Johnson, R. W. *Shootdown: Flight 007 and the American Connection* (1987).

Kaplan, Fred. *The Wizards of Armageddon* (1983).

Kelley, Donald R. *Soviet Politics from Brezhnev to Gorbachev* (1987).

Krieger, Joel. *Reagan, Thatcher, and the Politics of Decline* (1986).

Kyvig, David, ed. *Reagan and the World* (1990).

Labedz, Leopold, ed. *Poland under Jaruzelski: A Comprehensive Sourcebook on Poland during and after Martial Law* (1984).

LaFeber, Walter. *Inevitable Revolutions* (2nd ed., 1992).

Laird, Robbin, and E. Hoffman, eds. *Soviet Policy in a Changing World* (1986).

McMichael, Scott R. *Stumbling Bear: Soviet Military Performance in Afghanistan* (1991).

Medvedev, Zhores A. *Andropov* (1983).

Morley, Morris H., ed. *Crisis and Confrontation in Ronald Reagan's Foreign Policy* (1988).

Mowers, Glenn, Jr. *Human Rights and American Foreign Policy: The Carter and Reagan Experiences* (1987).

National Conference of Catholic Bishops. *The Challenge of Peace: God's Promise and Our Response* (1983).

Nye, Joseph S., ed. *The Making of America's Soviet Policy* (1984).

Oye, Kenneth A., Robert J. Lieber, and Donald Rothchild, eds. *Eagle Resurgent? The Reagan Era in American Foreign Policy* (1987).

Polk, William K. *The Elusive Peace: The Middle East in the Twentieth Century* (1979).

Reagan, Ronald W. *An American Life* (1990).

Schaller, Michael. *Reckoning with Reagan: America and Its President in the 1980s* (1992).

Scheer, Robert. *With Enough Shovels: Reagan, Bush and Nuclear War* (1982).

Talbott, Strobe. *Deadly Gambits: The Reagan Administration and the Stalemate in Nuclear Arms Control* (1984).

Talbott, Strobe. *The Master of the Game: Paul Nitze and the Nuclear Peace* (1988).

Talbott, Strobe. *The Russians and Reagan* (1982).

Weinberg, Alvin M., and Jack N. Brakenbus, eds. *Strategic Defenses and Arms Control* (1988).

Weinberger, Caspar. *Fighting for Peace: Seven Critical Years in the Pentagon* (1990).

Wills, Garry. *Reagan's America: Innocents at Home* (1987).

Yanov, Alexander. *Détente after Brezhnev: The Domestic Roots of Soviet Foreign Policy* (1987).

Zemstov, Ilya. *Andropov: Policy Dilemmas and the Struggle for Power* (1983).

16. THE THAW IN THE COLD WAR, 1985–1988

Balzer, Harley, ed. *Five Years That Shook the World: Gorbachev's Unfinished Revolution* (1989).

Bell, Coral. *The Reagan Paradox: American Foreign Policy in the 1980s* (1989).

Bialer, Seweryn, and Michael Mandelbaum, eds. *The Global Rivals* (1989).

Bialer, Seweryn, and Michael Mandelbaum, eds. *Gorbachev's Russia and America's Foreign Policy* (1988).

Brune, Lester H., and Richard Dean Burns. *America and the Indochina Wars, 1945–1990: A Bibliographic Guide* (1992).

Callahan, David. *Dangerous Capabilities: Paul Nitze and the Cold War* (1990).

Cate, Curtis, ed. *Afghanistan: The Terrible Decade, 1978–1988* (1988).

Crozier, Brian. *The Gorbachev Phenomenon: Peace and the Secret War* (1990).

Dallin, Alexander, ed. *The Soviet System in Crisis: A Reader of Western and Soviet Views* (1991).

Daniloff, Nicholas. *Two Lives, One Russia* (1988).

Doder, Dusko, and Louise Branson. *Gorbachev: Heretic in the Kremlin* (1990).

Eklof, Ben. *Soviet Briefing: Gorbachev and the Reform Period* (1989).

Gorbachev, Mikhail. *At the Summit* (1988).

Gorbachev, Mikhail. *Perestroika: New Thinking for Our Country and the World* (1988).

Hanson, Philip. *From Stagnation to Catastroika: Commentaries on the Soviet Economy, 1983–1991* (1992).

Harlo, Vilho, ed. *Gorbachev and Europe* (1990).

Hough, Jerry. *Russia and the West: Gorbachev and the Politics of Reform* (1988).

Hudson, George E., ed. *Soviet National Security Policy under Perestroika* (1989).

Jacobsen, Carl G., ed. *Soviet Foreign Policy: New Dynamics, New Themes* (1989).

Kaiser, Robert G. *Why Gorbachev Happened: His Triumphs and His Failures* (1991).

Kerblay, Basil. *Gorbachev's Russia* (1989).

Ligachev, Egor. *Inside Gorbachev's Kremlin* (1993).

McCauley, Martin, ed. *The Soviet Union under Gorbachev* (1987).

⦁ Medvedev, Roy. *The Truth about Chernobyl* (1991).

Morley, Morris H., ed. *Crisis and Confrontation in Ronald Reagan's Foreign Policy* (1988).

Oberdorfer, Don. *The Turn: From the Cold War to a New Era. The U.S. and the Soviet Union, 1983–1990* (1991).

Reagan, Ronald W. *National Security Strategy of the United States* (1987).

Shansab, Nasir. *Soviet Expansion in the Third World* (1986).

Tatu, Michel. *Mikhail Gorbachev: The Origins of Perestroika* (1991).

Urban, Mark. *War in Afghanistan* (1988).

Wells, Samuel F., and Robert S. Litwak. *Strategic Defenses and Soviet-American Relations* (1987).

Wettig, Gerhard. *Changes in Soviet Foreign Policy toward the West* (1991).

Yakovlov, Alexander. *On the Edge of an Abyss* (1985).

Zacek, Jane S. *The Gorbachev Generation: Issues in Soviet Foreign Policy* (1988).

17. THE END OF THE COLD WAR, 1988–1991

Abel, Elie. *The Shattered Bloc: Behind the Upheaval in Eastern Europe* (1990).

⦁ Allison, Graham, and G. Yavlinsky. *Window of Opportunity: The Grand Bargain for Democracy in the Soviet Union* (1991).

Beschloss, Michael, and Strobe Talbott. *At the Highest Levels: The Inside Story of the End of the Cold War* (1993).

Bornstein, Jerry. *The Wall Came Tumbling Down: The Berlin Wall and the Fall of Communism* (1990).

Brown, J. F. *Eastern Europe and Communist Rule* (1988).

Brown, J. F. *Surge to Freedom: The End of Communist Rule in Eastern Europe* (1991).

Colton, Timothy J., and Robert Legvold, eds. *After the Soviet Union: From Empire to Nations* (1992).

Croft, Stuart, ed. *The Conventional Armed Forces in Europe Treaty: The Cold War Endgame* (1994).

Daniels, Robert V. *The End of the Communist Revolution* (1993).

Diller, Daniel C. *Russia and the Independent States* (1993).

Duffy, Michael, and Dan Goodgame. *Marching in Place: The Status Quo Presidency of George Bush* (1992).

Freedman, Lawrence. *Europe Transformed: Documents on the End of the Cold War* (1990).

Freedman, Lawrence. *The Gulf Conflict, 1990–1991: Diplomacy and War in the New World Order* (1993).

Gaddis, John Lewis. *The United States and the End of the Cold War* (1992).

Garthoff, Raymond L. *The Great Transition: American-Soviet Relations and the End of the Cold War* (1994).

Garton Ash, Timothy. *In Europe's Name: Germany and the Divided Continent* (1993).

Garton Ash, Timothy. *The Magic Lantern: The Revolution of '89 Witnessed in Warsaw, Budapest, Berlin, and Prague* (1990).

Gati, Charles. *The Bloc That Failed* (1990).

Glenny, Misha. *The Rebirth of History: Eastern Europe in the Age of Democracy* (1990).

Gorbachev, Mikhail. *The August Coup: The Truth and the Lessons* (1991).

Gwertzman, Bernard, and Michael Kaufman, eds. *The Collapse of Communism: By the Correspondents of the New York Times* (2nd ed., 1991).

Hämäläinen, Pekka Kalevi. *Uniting Germany: Actions and Reactions* (1994).

Hancock, M. Donald, and Helga A. Welsh. *German Unification: Process and Outcomes* (1993).

Hogan, Michael J. *The End of the Cold War: Its Meaning and Implications* (1992).

Hyland, William G. *The Cold War Is Over* (1991).

Jarausch, Konrad H. *The Rush to German Unity* (1993).

Jervis, Robert, and Seweryn Bialer, eds. *Soviet-American Relations after the Cold War* (1991).

Loory, S. H., and A. Imse. *Seven Days That Shook the World: The Collapse of Soviet Communism* (1991).

Mason, David S. *Revolution in East-Central Europe: The Rise and Fall of Communism and the Cold War* (1992).

Miller, Judith, and Laurie Mylorie. *Saddam Hussein and the Crisis in the Gulf* (1990).

Morrison, John. *Boris Yeltsin: From Bolshevik to Democrat* (1991).

Remnick, David. *Lenin's Tomb: The Last Days of the Soviet Empire* (1993).

Schwartau, Anke. *Berlin in November* (1990).

Shevardnadze, Eduard. *The Future Belongs to Freedom* (1991).

Stokes, Gale. *The Walls Came Tumbling Down: The Collapse of Communism in Eastern Europe* (1993).

Wheaton, Bernard, and Zdenek Kavan. *The Velvet Revolution: Czechoslovakia, 1988–1991* (1992)

White, Stephen. *Gorbachev and After* (1991).

Yeltsin, Boris N. *Against the Grain: An Autobiography* (1991).

GENERAL WORKS ON THE COLD WAR

Adomeit, Hannes. *Soviet Risk-Taking and Crisis Behavior* (1982).

Bialer, Seweryn. *The Soviet Paradox: External Expansion, Internal Decline* (1986).

Boll, Michael M. *National Security Planning: Roosevelt through Reagan* (1988).

Brands, H. W. *The Devil We Knew: Americans and the Cold War* (1993).

Brzezinski, Zbigniew. *The Grand Failure: The Birth and Death of Communism in the Twentieth Century* (1989).

Burns, Richard Dean, ed. *Guide to American Foreign Relations since 1700* (1983).

Burrows, William E. *Deep Black: Space Espionage and National Security* (1986).

Callahan, David. *Dangerous Capabilities: Paul Nitze and the Cold War* (1990).

Chace, James, and Caleb Carr. *America Invulnerable: The Quest for Absolute Security from 1812 to Star Wars* (1988).

Crockett, Richard. *The Fifty Year War* (1994).

DePorte, A. W. *Europe between the Superpowers: The Enduring Balance* (2nd ed., 1986).

Diller, Daniel C. *Russia and the Independent States* (1993).

Dudley, William, ed. *The Cold War: Opposing Viewpoints* (1992).

Dukes, Paul. *The Emergence of the Superpowers: A Short Comparative History of the USA and the USSR* (1970).

Dukes, Paul. *The Last Great Game: USA versus USSR* (1989).

Dunbabin, J. P. D. *The Cold War: The Great Powers and Their Allies* (1994).

Evangelista, Matthew. *Innovation and the Arms Race: How the United States and the Soviet Union Develop New Military Technologies* (1988).

Feste, Karen A. *Expanding the Frontiers: Superpower Intervention in the Cold War* (1992).

Fontaine, André. *History of the Cold War* (2 vols., 1968).

Frankel, Benjamin, ed. *The Cold War, 1945–1991* (3 vols., 1992).

Freedman, Lawrence. *The Evolution of Nuclear Strategy* (1989).

Freedman, Lawrence. *US Intelligence and the Soviet Strategic Threat* (2nd ed., 1986).

Funigiello, Philip J. *American-Soviet Trade in the Cold War* (1988).

Gaddis, John Lewis. *The Long Peace: Inquiries into the History of the Cold War* (1987).

Gaddis, John Lewis. *Strategies of Containment: A Critical Appraisal of Postwar American National Security Policy* (1982).

Garton Ash, Timothy. *The Uses of Adversity: Essays on the Fate of Central Europe* (1989).

George, Alexander L., Philip J. Farley, and Alexander Dallin, eds. *U.S.–Soviet Security Cooperation: Achievements, Failures, Lessons* (1988).

Gray, Colin S. *The Politics of Super Power* (1988).

Hamerow, Theodore S. *From the Finland Station: The Graying of Revolution in the Twentieth Century* (1990).

Hanson, Philip. *Trade and Technology in Soviet-Western Relations* (1981).

Hill, Kenneth L. *Cold War Chronology: Soviet-American Relations, 1945–1991* (1993).

Hyland, William G. *The Cold War: Fifty Years of Conflict* (1991).

Jervis, Robert. *The Meaning of the Nuclear Revolution: Statecraft and the Prospect of Armageddon* (1989).

Kaplan, Fred. *The Wizards of Armageddon* (1983).

Kaplan, Lawrence S. *NATO and the United States: The Enduring Alliance* (1994).

Kaplan, Lawrence S., and Robert W. Clawson, eds. *The Warsaw Pact: Political Purpose and Military Means* (1982).

Kegley, Charles W., Jr., ed. *The Long Postwar Peace: Contending Explanations and Projections* (1990).

Kennan, George F. *The Nuclear Delusion: Soviet-American Relations in the Atomic Age* (1982).

Kennedy, Paul. *The Rise and Fall of the Great Powers: Economic Change and Military Conflict from 1500 to 2000* (1987).

Kolko, Gabriel. *Confronting the Third World: United States Foreign Policy, 1945–1980* (1988).

LaFeber, Walter. *America, Russia and the Cold War, 1945–1992* (7th ed., 1993).

Lamphere, Robert J., and Tom Schachtman. *The FBI-KGB War: A Special Agent's Story* (1986).

Landau, Saul. *The Dangerous Doctrine: National Security and U.S. Foreign Policy* (1988).

Litwak, Robert, and Samuel F. Wells, Jr. *Superpower Competition and Security in the Third World* (1987).

Lukacs, John. *A New History of the Cold War* (1966).

MacKenzie, David. *From Messianism to Collapse: Soviet Foreign Policy, 1917–1991* (1994).

Maier, Charles S., ed. *The Cold War in Europe: Era of a Divided Continent* (1991).

Marantz, Paul. *From Lenin to Gorbachev* (1988).

May, Lary, ed. *Recasting America: Culture and Politics in the Age of Cold War* (1989).

McCalla, Robert B. *Uncertain Perceptions: U.S. Cold War Crisis Decision Making* (1992).

McCormick, Thomas J. *America's Half Century: United States Foreign Policy in the Cold War* (1989).

Mead, Walter Russell. *Mortal Splendor: The American Empire in Transition* (1987).

Melton, Keith. *CIA Special Weapons and Equipment: Spy Devices of the Cold War* (1993).

Morris, Charles R. *Iron Destinies, Lost Opportunities: The Arms Race between the USA and the USSR, 1945–1987* (1988).

Newhouse, John. *War and Peace in the Nuclear Age* (1989).

Nitze, Paul H. *From Hiroshima to Glasnost: At the Center of Decision* (1989).

Nogee, Joseph, and Robert Donaldson. *Soviet Foreign Policy since World War II* (4th ed., 1992).

Noti, Nissani. *Lives in the Balance: The Cold War in American Politics, 1945–1991* (1992).

Oudenaren, John Van. *Détente in Europe: The Soviet Union and the West since 1953* (1991).

Partos, Gabriel. *The World That Came In from the Cold: Perspectives from East and West on the Cold War* (1993).

Paterson, Thomas G. *Meeting the Communist Threat: Truman to Reagan* (1988).

Paterson, Thomas G. *On Every Front: The Making and Unmaking of the Cold War* (1992).

Powaski, Ronald E. *The Entangling Alliance: The United States and European Security, 1950–1993* (1994).

Powaski, Ronald E. *March to Armageddon: The United States and the Nuclear Arms Race, 1939 to the Present* (1987).

Prados, John. *Presidents' Secret Wars: CIA and Pentagon Covert Operations since World War II* (1986).

Sivachev, Nikolai V., and Nikolai N. Yakovlev. *Russia and the United States* (1979).

Sodaro, Michael J. *Moscow, Germany, and the West from Khrushchev to Gorbachev* (1990).

Stares, Paul B. *The Militarization of Space: U.S. Policy, 1945–1984* (1985).

Udall, Stewart L. *The Myths of August: A Personal Exploration of Our Tragic Cold War Affair with the Atom* (1994).

Walker, Martin. *The Cold War: A History* (1994).

White, Colin. *Russia and America: The Roots of Economic Divergence* (1987).

Whitfield, Stephen J. *The Culture of the Cold War* (1991).

Wohlforth, William C. *The Elusive Balance: Power and Perceptions during the Cold War* (1993).

Young, John W. *Cold War Europe, 1945–1989: A Political History* (1991).

Young, John W. *Longman Companion to Cold War and Détente, 1941–1991* (1993).

INDEX

and Korean War, 101, 102, 104, 106, 107, 116, 117
and Southeast Asia, 126, 181-83
U.S. relations with, 97, 116-17, 147, 156, 212, 220, 264
in World War II, 16-18, 28-29, 33-35, 73, 88, 90
Japanese-American Security Treaty, 156
Jaruzelski, Wojciech, 261, 268, 291, 292, 297
Jaurès, Jean, 4
Johnson, Lyndon B., 156, 179, 181, 191-200, 207, 208, 212
Jordan, 130, 132, 133, 229, 231, 232, 257
Jupiter-C missile, 171, 174-75

Kádár, János, 46, 128, 129, 291
KAL flight 007, 266
Karmal, Babrak, 253, 254, 284
Kasavubu, Joseph, 154, 155
Kassem, Abdel Karim, 133, 229
Katanga province, 154-56
Katyn Forest, 40, 310
Kaunda, Kenneth, 155
Keating, Kenneth B., 171
Keeler, Christine, 177
Kennan, George F., 56-58, 62-64, 66, 67, 111, 139
Kennedy, Edward M., 256
Kennedy, John F., 156-79, 195, 206, 233, 289, 309
and Africa, 151-52
American University speech, 178
and Indochina, 189-91
Kennedy, Robert F., 174, 175, 198, 199
Kent State killings, 201
Kenya, 155
Kenyatta, Jomo, 155
KGB. See Committee on State Security
Khmer Rouge, 236, 237, 246, 247, 259
Khomeini, Ayatollah Ruhollah, 252, 253, 257, 281
Khrushchev, Nikita S., 114, 133-36, 138, 145, 211, 272-73
and Berlin, 141-42
character and views, 121-23
and China, 204-206
and Eastern Europe, 122, 127-30, 133
and Indochina, 189-92
and Kennedy, 156, 158, 160, 164-68, 170-75, 178-80, 233
secret speech, 127, 138
and Third World, 123-27, 151
and U-2 Affair, 146-51
visit to America, 142-44, 157
Khrushchev, Nina P., 143
Kiesinger, Kurt G., 211, 215
Kim Il-song, 103-6, 108, 116
Kimbangu, Simon, 154
King, Martin Luther, Jr., 157, 199
Kirkpatrick, Jeane J., 261
Kishi, Nobosuke, 156
Kissinger, Henry A., 200, 201, 211-14, 219-26, 234, 237-40
Kitchen Debate, 143
KMT. See Kuomintang
Kohl, Helmut, 264, 297, 298
Korea, 55, 119, 186, 266, 309, 311, 314. See also Korean War
Korean War, 68, 79-82, 100-117, 192-95, 199, 203-4, 217
Kostov, Traicho, 81
Kosygin, Alexei N., 180, 202, 206, 210, 212, 229, 276
at Glassboro summit, 196, 207
Kozlov, Frol R., 142
Krenz, Egon, 293, 294
Krock, Arthur, 66
Kuomintang (KMT), 86-92, 94, 95, 97, 98
Kurchatov, Igor, 35, 76
Kurile Islands, 22, 28, 157
Kuwait, 229, 257, 298, 299
Iraqi invasion of, 229, 257, 298, 299
Kwantung Army, 28

Laird, Melvin R., 200
Landsbergis, Vitautus, 301
Lao Dong Party, 191-94, 196, 200, 225
Laos, 164, 179, 185-86, 201, 225, 236, 248
Laotian crisis (1961-62), 189-90
Latvia, 12, 13, 301, 304. See also Baltic States
League of Nations, 7, 9, 24, 58, 69

Leahy, William, 28
Lebanon, 32, 69, 133, 142, 261, 280, 281
Le Duc Tho, 200, 225, 226
Leipzig demonstrations, 293
Le May, Curtis E., 194
Lend-lease, 17, 32
Lenin, Vladimir I., 4-6, 98, 262, 285
Libya, 19, 54, 257
Lie, Trygve, 106
Ligachev, Egor, 280
Limited Test Ban Treaty (1963), 177, 178
Lin Biao, 92, 192, 218, 220
Linkage, 142, 213, 214, 223
Lippmann, Walter, 60, 67
Lithuania, 12, 301. See also Baltic States
Litvinov, Maxim, 12
Liu Shaoqi, 205
Lodge, Henry Cabot, 191
Lon Nol, 201
London Conference of Foreign Ministers (1947), 67, 70
London Declaration, 298
London government (Polish), 23, 25, 32, 40, 41
Long March, 87, 246
Long Telegram, 56-60, 63, 66, 67
Lublin government (Polish), 23, 25, 28, 40
Lumumba, Patrice, 154-56
Luxembourg, 67, 69, 73. See also Benelux nations

MacArthur, Douglas, 106-8, 110-12
Macmillan, Harold, 149, 151, 157, 176, 177
MAD. See Mutual assured destruction
Magsaysay, Ramón, 182
Maisky, Ivan, 17
Malaya, 18, 181, 182
Malaysia, 126
Malenkov, Georgi M., 114-15, 121, 123, 127, 134, 272
Malik, Jacob, 111
Malinovsky, Rodion, 150, 174
Malta summit conference (1989), 296
Manchuria, 22, 28, 87, 90-98, 101-2, 110, 204
Mansfield, Mike, 167, 191, 224
Mao Zedong, 85, 110, 203, 204-6, 246
and Sino-American rapprochement, 217-19
and Stalin, 97-98, 100, 203
and struggle for power in China, 87-90, 95
and Vietnam, 187, 191, 192
Mariam, Mengistu Haile, 243
Marshall, George C., 61-67, 72, 83, 91
Marshall Plan (European Recovery Program), 47, 63-67, 75, 185
impact of, 65-67, 70, 78, 79, 83, 85
Marx, Karl, 2, 3, 5, 98, 157
Marxism, 2-5, 67, 98, 130, 152, 164, 252
Masaryk, Jan, 47
Massive retaliation, 119, 120, 122, 135, 141, 169
Matsu, 156, 217
May, Alan Nunn, 34, 56
Mayaguez incident, 237
Mazowiecki, Tadeusz, 292
MBFR. See Mutual and balanced force reductions
McCarthy, Eugene, 198-199
McCarthy, Joseph R., 96, 112-13
McCarthyism, 66, 83, 96, 112-13
McCone, John, 131
McNamara, Robert S., 169-71, 195-96, 206-7, 225
Meese, Edwin L., III, 281
Meir, Golda, 232, 233
Mendès-France, Pierre, 185, 186, 190
Mexico, 34, 199
Michael, King of Romania, 42-43
Mikolajczyk, Stanislaw, 25, 41
Mindszenty, Joszef, 81
Minuteman missile, 169, 206, 249, 259
MIRVs. See Multiple independently targeted re-entry vehicles
Missile gap, 136, 157, 158, 169, 170, 175, 249
Mitterrand, François, 276
Mladenov, Petur, 294
Mobutu, Joseph-Désiré (Mobutu Sese Seko), 155, 156
Moldavia, 301. See also Bessarabia, Moldova